IS GOD AN AMERICAN?

An Anthropological Perspective on the Missionary Work of the Summer Institute of Linguistics

*Edited by Søren Hvalkof
and Peter Aaby*

IWGIA/SI

IS GOD AN AMERICAN?

This is a joint publication
by the following two organizations:

INTERNATIONAL WORK GROUP
FOR INDIGENOUS AFFAIRS (IWGIA)
Fiolstræde 10,
DK - 1171 Copenhagen K,
Denmark.

SURVIVAL INTERNATIONAL
36 Craven Street,
London WC2N 5NG,
England.

ISSN 0105-4503
ISBN 87-980717-2-6

First published 1981 by
IWGIA and Survival International.

Printed in Denmark by Vinderup Bogtrykkeri A/S.
Front cover by H. C. Poulsen.

IS GOD
AN AMERICAN?

*An Anthropological Perspective
on the Missionary Work
of the Summer Institute
of Linguistics*

EDITED BY
Søren Hvalkof and Peter Aaby

INTERNATIONAL WORK GROUP FOR INDIGENOUS AFFAIRS

Objectives

IWGIA is a politically independent, international organization concerned with the oppression of indigenous peoples in many countries.

IWGIA's objective is to secture the future of the indigenous peoples in concurrence with their own efforts and desires:

1. By examining their situation, and publishing information about it.

2. By furthering international understanding, knowledge and involvement in the indigenous peoples' situation.

3. By fighting racism and securing political, economic and social right, as well as establishing the indigenous peoples' right to self-determination.

4. By arranging humanitarian projects and other forms of support of indigenous peoples and ethnic groups with a view of strengthening their social, cultural and political situation.

Activities

By organizing the research and the collection of information, IWGIA endeavours to draw attention to the situation of the indigenous peoples throughout the world. Through the communications of the indigenous peoples themselves and through reports from investigators who have lived in the relevant territories, IWGIA tries to inform and exert influence on governments, international organization and on public opinion.

IWGIA's DOCUMENTS are an English written series published about 5 times per year. Each DOCUMENT deals with a subject related to the indigenous peoples' situation.

A NEWSLETTER is also published. This contains articles, notices and reviews of books about the situation around the world.

IWGIA also seeks to support the fight of indigenous peoples for decent living conditions by granting financial aid to humanitarian projects and other activities and additionally by supporting in practical and financial terms the preparation of congresses undertaken by the indigenous peoples' own organizations.

SURVIVAL INTERNATIONAL

SURVIVAL INTERNATIONAL is a non-political, non-denominational organisation existing to help aboriginal peoples to protect their rights. This is a problem of extreme urgency, for many societies face the prospect of irreparable destruction.

Procedure must vary with local circumstances, but there are two essential priorities. The first is to secure the rights of aboriginals to the land on which they live. The second is to provide knowledge and understanding of the outside world, so that they can take effective action themselves.

The danger to aboriginal populations has reached global proportions, SURVIVAL INTERNATIONAL's immediate aims are: to carry out specific programmes with threatened groups; to extend international responsibility and action; and to publicise the problems and aspirations of all aboriginal people.

The work has been increasingly based on the principle of establishing close co-operation with other bodies so that we present a unified and coherent front in all that is done.

SURVIVAL INTERNATIONAL supports a series of field Projects mainly in South America (Brazil, Chile, Colombia, Ecuador, Paraguay, Peru, Venezuela), but also in Indonesia and Australia.

There is also a quarterly REVIEW (annual subscription £8/$16) which carries in-depth articles on the subject; world news; book reviews and reports on films being planned or made.

The S. I. Document Series carries material which is too long and detailed to be included in the REVIEW, such as our Projects Director's Report on Colombia and his forthcoming one on Peru.

Joint publications demonstrate the above-mentioned principle of cooperation, and S. I. has already had the pleasure of one such previous joint publication with IWGIA (The Yanoama in Brazil 1979). Another publication is published jointly with the Royal Anthropological Institute, written by S. I.'s International Law Adviser, Gordon Bennett (Aboriginal Rights in International Law).

SURVIVAL INTERNATIONAL has a number of supporting groups throughout the world in America, Eire, France, Germany, Italy, Japan, Luxembourg and Spain.

Acknowledgements

This study would never have been completed were it not for the numerous encouragements and support received from individuals and organizations concerned with the plight of indigenous groups. Without the help of IWGIA, Survival International and the Anthropology Resource Center in locating potential authors, a book of this kind would not have been possible.

The contributing authors as well as many other colleagues and friends have offered valuable comments on earlier versions of our introduction and conclusion. Special thanks are due to David Stoll, who undertook the laborious task of compiling the index, and to Fiona Wilson, Stephen Sampson and John Bodley who helped with the translation and offered challenging comments.

Publication of the book was made possible administratively through the support of the staff of IWGIA and the Institute of Ethnology and Anthropology, University of Copenhagen, and it was financed by grants from Survival International and from the Danish Social Science Research Council and IWGIA.

The authors have decided that royalties on the book should go to IWGIA and Survival International.

Copenhagen, January 1981

Søren Hvalkof   *Peter Aaby*

Contents

Campa Indians (Asháninga), Gran Pajonal, **Peru.** *Copyright: Søren Hvalkof, 1975.*

Introducing God in the Devil's Paradise

by SØREN HVALKOF and PETER AABY

>*Don't believe the Eden stories some anthropologists are trying to push. The jungle Indians are not living in paradise*« *(SIL missionary in Hefley and Hefley 1972:60).*
>*Satan has had a free hand among the Macunas for hundreds of years. He is not the least bit pleased that we have come. Already we have had much opposition. Pray that we will not easily become discouraged and that we will show forth the Love of Christ to those Satan would use to disrupt the work. 'Prayer Changes Things'*« *(field-letter from SIL missionaries to supporters, SIL Doc. 1).*

This book is a collection of anthropological essays about Wycliffe Bible Translators (WBT)/Summer Institute of Linguistics (SIL), currently the world's largest Protestant missionary society in terms of members sent abroad (Dayton 1976:52). In contrast to other missionary societies, WBT/SIL considers its prime task to be that of translating the Bible into all the languages of the world. WBT is that branch of the organization responsible for raising funds in the US, while SIL carries out the actual mission work; this book focuses principally on SIL.

The vast majority of the world's unwritten languages are spoken by ethnic groups without long histories of integration into statelevel societies. WBT/SIL's expansion has thus meant that most of its work takes place among such tribal groups, though it works also with peasant populations. The goal of this book is to analyse some of the social and cultural implications of WBT/SIL's attempt to bring the Word to these tribal groups, or the »Bibleless tribes« as they are called by the organization (Townsend 1963:8).

Since tribal and peasant populations have been the study objects of anthropologists, and since many anthropologists and linguists had carried out fieldwork in the same areas as SIL missionaries, it seemed natural to ask some of them to describe and analyze the consequences of SIL's work.

★

While WBT/SIL's institutional and ideological development is well described by Stoll in his article »Words Can Be Used in So Many Ways«, it is still necessary to give a general overview of the WBT/SIL organization, its expansion, its ideology, and its methods of operation. The founder of WBT/SIL was William Cameron Townsend, or »Uncle Cam«. In 1917, Townsend joined the Central American Mission, working among the Cackchiquel Indians of Guatemala. He soon realized, however, that the Cackchiquel could not understand Spanish and thus had no interest in the Bibles he was trying to sell. Consequently, Townsend took it upon himself to translate the Bible into Cackchiquel, a task which took him 14 years. During this interval Townsend received a vision where he would bring the Word to all of the »Bibleless« tribes:

Søren Hvalkof, born 1951, is a graduate student at the University of Copenhagen, and did preliminary fieldwork in the Amazon in 1975. He has been working since 1972 with youth education, and has published on the situation of indigenous peoples of Latin America and Canada, epistemology and ecological anthropology, as well as educational material.

Peter Aaby, born 1944, graduated in anthropology (Mag. Scient.) from the University of Copenhagen in 1974. Co-editor of IWGIA Document Series 1971-75. Since 1978 employed on a health and nutrition project in Guinea-Bissau.

>*after having seen the transformation the Word brought to the Cackchiquels, I dreamed of reaching all other tribes*« (Townsend 1963:7).

Townsend was unable to realize his divine vision, however, because the Central American Mission was more interested in traditional missionizing and refused to support his plan. So, in 1932 Townsend left Guatemala to start his own project, later to become WBT/SIL. In 1934, Townsend established »Camp Wycliffe«, in an abandoned farmhouse near Sulphur Springs, Arkansas. With the intent of training translation teems for work in Mexico, he held the first summer course in linguistics – for two students.

Townsend was well aware that his new linguistics missionizing strategy would have to overcome some specific problems. Outside the U.S., missionary work in many Latin American countries was becoming a political liability. This was especially true in Mexico, where Townsend's group had intended to start work. Mexican social movements at that time were strongly anti-American and anti-ecclesiastic. Presenting their project to political authorities as an evangelical mission might have led to their being denied entrance into the country. Townsend and his collaborators adopted an alternative image – and represented themselves as a linguistic and cultural institution. Within the United States, the old-line Protestant organizations expected converts rather than Bible-translations. Townsend and his collaborators thus had to establish extensive contacts with various church organizations and individuals, explaining the true Christian character of their project and trying to secure the necessary spiritual and financial support. Thus, they learned to «play» missionaries at home and linguists abroad. This dual identity was finally institutionalized in 1942, when the Wycliffe Bible Translators and the Summer Institute of Linguistics were incorporated in the U.S. as two different entities, whereas before the group had only been incorporated in Mexico as one institution.*

The dual identity was a logical, if not ingenious, solution to the problems faced by the organization. SIL attended to the scientific and linguistic aspects, organized the summer courses, arranged the field work and dealt with foreign governments. The WBT emphasized the religious side of Bible translation, raised money and recruited personnel in the U.S. WBT also took charge of relations with those religious groups, churches, bible associations and individuals who provided financial backing. Of course, this separation of functions did not imply that the linguists of SIL were not missionaries. On the contrary, they were. The dual identity, however, made it possible to adjust to the requirements of the situation, as suggested by the following excerpt from one of WBT's own pamphlets:

> «The experience of the Wycliffe Bible Translators has shown that an anti-ecclesiastical government can, without losing face, accept a Bible translating organization if it has a positive, scientific and cultural contribution to make to the country» (SIL Doc. 2:3).

The organization carried the division between WBT and SIL to the point where any relation between the two was categorically denied. It was not until 1953, when the SIL came into serious conflict with the Catholic church in Peru, that Townsend was unmasked and forced to admit to the connection. Even then he maintained that the religious objectives were only secondary while the primary role of the organization was scientific and cultural.

Townsend once defined the battle cry of his crusade as »Two thousand tongues to go«. This goal has not been reached but the organization has expanded extremely rapidly since its humble beginnings in 1934. When incorporated in 1942, WBT/SIL has 37 translators working in 18 languages. By 1963, it had worked among 308 linguistic groups (Cowan 1963:9). In 1975, WBT/SIL reported its staff to be 3500 (Dayton 1976:367). The most recent census indicates that it has 3700 persons working on 675 languages in 29 countries, not counting those countries where it works on the languages from the outside (see appendix).

This truly remarkable expansion has inspired all kinds of guesswork concerning the financing of such a giant organization. In 1975, WBT/SIL had a reported income of US $ 16,900,000 and was rated the sixth richest U.S. Protestant missionary organization (Dayton 1976:53). The financing of SIL is based

---

* While SIL and WBT are the two main bodies of the organization the tremendous expansion into isolated, often inaccessible areas has necessitated the establishing of a special section for transportation and communication, called the Jungle Aviation and Radio Service (JAARS). JAARS recruits members on the basis of both technical and spiritual qualifications.

largely on donation - from wealthy individuals, churches, religious foundations and business organizations. It also receives money from the governments in some of the countries in which it works, and from U.S. and European aid organizations (cf. Hart 1973:16,22,24; Franklin 1975:33). The most probable reason for SIL's financial success is its decentralized funding: it is the individual members themselves who must secure support from their home community or church. With community support, the SIL members are usually able to cover most of their training and field expense and no expense to the organization.

The WBT/SIL's expansion and success is undoubtedly a result of its ability to play off its dual identity. The securing or recruits and the decentralized form of fund raising both depend on the ability of WBT to convince home constituencies of its *missionary* aspect. The SIL, meanwhile has cultivated a *scientific* image for itself, and several contributions to this book show how its leadership has pragmatically sought to merge its goals with those of national political elites.

Although SIL is interdenominational, its mandatory Statement of Doctrine (see p. xx) ensures that recruits come from the conservative wing of U.S. Protestantism; composition has been estimated roughly at two parts »evangelical« to one part »fundamentalist«, these terms denoting the conservative and ultra-conservative tendencies in North-American Protestantism. WBT/SIL's expansion has also led to its recruiting more and more members from other western countries. Nevertheless, members are overwhelmingly white Americans (see Appendix). Like Townsend most also have social backgrounds in conservative Evangelical circles in the Mid-west and South.

The prime motivation of SIL members is to bring the Word to the Bibleless before it is too late. Receiving the Word will prepare the way for their eternal salvation. This necessarily involves a struggle against Satan. For the SIL missionaries, Satan is not just an abstract concept embracing any evil human tendencies. He is, instead, a very real social incarnation whose clearest manifestation is Communism. Considering the social background of SIL members, this identification of Satan with Communism seems logical. Similarly, there is an equally natural tendency for God to be transformed into an American. As shown by one of the introductory quotes, this particular type of ideology has the benefit of allowing the categorizing of any opposition as the work of Satan. In this world-view, religious and political categories have become interchangeable:

> »*God uses military troops, but He has other methods also. God turned the tables in Indonesia on the eve of a Marxist revolution, and the spiritual response of thousands turning to Christ has been tremendous. Cambodia put all missionaries out of their country in 1965, and it seemed God's work there was finished. Suddenly – a coup d'etat and a new responsiveness to mission work*« (*Richard Watson, Translation, Oct.-Dec., 1971, p. 2*).

To prepare for their missionary work, SIL members attend three summer courses in linguistics and a survival training course before receiving their field assignments. Once in the field – usually working in teams of two – they build suitable housing and a landing strip for establishing air contact with the central SIL base. Initially, they should collect general ethnographic and ethnolinguistic data, so as to obtain knowledge of the culture as well as the language of the group. This work is usually done by selecting one or more informants, usually younger persons, who are paid for placing their knowledge as well as themselves at the disposal of the missionaries. The projects can be quite lengthy, often taking over 15 years to produce a translation of the New Testament.

During the field project, the missionaries try to establish a relationship of trust with the community and especially with their informants. At times, the missionaries will bring their informants to the SIL base, where better working facilities are available and the translation work is uninterrupted by outsiders or by problems of everyday village life.

The SIL bases serve a key function in SIL's mode of operation. At the base one finds language laboratories, hospitals, libraries, workshops, air base, radio station, schools for missionaries' children, modern American-style houses, well-trimmed gardens, and even Coca-cola vending machines. It is possible to live a comfortable, middle class American life-style at the base and be completely isolated from the surrounding Third World society.

For the native informants attached to SIL, this brand of Americanism often constitutes their first major introduction to industrial civilization. Obviously, such a display of wealth can sometimes contribute to the informants' losing faith in their own native identities and adopting the ideology and standards of the translators. In fact, the informants frequently become the first converts; where circumstances permit, they also become the first bilingual teachers. Regardless of whether the informants become only converts or also official teachers, the intention is always that they should return to their home communities and spread both the written word and the good Word. On returning to their home villages, the informants begin a campaign of alphabetization, literacy, and conversion, using SIL-prepared educational materials and aided by visiting SIL linguists. It should be stressed that this education takes place in the native language, and that SIL usually has complete control over the production of written materials. The first publications may be sections of the New Testament, but they could also be shorter works such as Christian hymns, the UN's Declaration on Human Rights, native myths, folktales or schoolbooks. Arcand's, Pereira's and Smith's articles provide illuminating examples of how these publications are sometimes slanted so as to steer the community in the direction desired by SIL. Several of the contributors emphasize another recurrent feature of SIL's methods of cultural manipulation: the distribution of cassette tape recorders having only play-back facility, together with tapes of American hymns in the native languages.

SIL missionaries also carry out other duties such as providing medical assistance; at times they attempt to promote community development via agricultural innovations, cattle breeding, forestry, trade and transport activities. However, as a WBT/SIL »Statement of Policy« makes clear, these activities should always remain secondary:

> »Finishing the New Testament shall have higher priority than socioeconomic and community development projects« (SIL Doc. 3:2).

When translations of the New Testament and selected parts of the Old Testament have been completed, and after having created a nucleus of believers capable of reading the Bible and continuing the project, the translators should leave for new tribes. SIL frequently emphasizes its non-sectarian and non-ecclesiastical character, stating that it has no intention of establishing its own church in the areas where it sends missionaries. The basic idea is to promote the creation of *indigenous* churches. Thus, the missionaries aim at rendering their presence superfluous:

> »The Word of God starts the action and soon a self propagating church spreads the message among its own people« (SIL Doc. 4).

For the SIL missionaries, this is a process of cultural advancement or even cultural evolution. According to Townsend:

> »Witchcraft, killings, superstition, ignorance, fear and sickness are giving way before the Light of the Word, literacy, medicine, and contact with the best in the outside world. Tribesmen formerly lost to the lifestream of their respective nations are being transformed by the Word« (1963:8).

★

Nevertheless, the Indians' social situation has many other aspects aside from missionaries' attempt to show them the way to paradise. The frequent descriptions of their situation as one marked by genocide and ethnocide indicates that it may be more proper to speak of »The Devil's Paradise«, as Hardenburg (1912) called the Putumayo area during the rubber boom at the beginning of this century. One of the clearest indications of this situation is Ribeiro's statistical analysis of genocide in Brasil during 1900-1957. Ribeiro shows that 87 out of 230 tribal groups were exterminated during this period, and that the remaining groups were greatly reduced (1967:92). The direct causes of this catastrophic situation were the epidemics and the violent clashes brought on by the hunt for new resources. Within the general expansion, Ribeiro differentiates three economic frontiers which have experienced varying rates of extermination. The »extractive frontier« has wiped out 45.7 % of the group with whom it came into contact; the »pastoral« has wiped out 30.2 % and the »agricultural frontier« 60 %. The extractive economy brought Indians into contact with mobile groups of men who searched for commercially valuable raw materials such as rubber, nuts, diamonds or gold. The contact was often violent, and when the situation demanded, the newcomers forced the Indians to work for them. The pastoral and agricultural economy came into contradiction with the Indian tribes because it was based on permanent proprietorship of the land. As a rule, the agricultural frontier involved higher population concentrations and greater investments in infrastructure and control institutions; it therefore led to the most drastic decline in Indian population.

During the period of Ribeiro's study (1900-1957), 27.3 % of the Brazilian Indian groups lived in »unexplored areas« whereas the proportion living in areas classified as »extractive«, »pastoral« and »agricultural« frontiers were 49 %, 21 % and 2.8 % respectively (1967:96). Thus the extractive frontier was undoubtedly the most important factor influencing the Indian situation, alone accounting for the extermination of 59 tribes. In spite of its having demographic declines just as drastic as the agricultural and pastoral forms of expansion, the extractive frontier can be said to have been less destructive to Indian culture because, unlike the others, it laid no permanent claim to Indian lands. Furthermore, being more dependent on the demands of the world market, the extractive frontier was less stable and its occasional breakdowns thus gave at least some Indian groups a chance to regain their strength and cohesion. In 1957, the more permanent colonization connected with the pastoral and agricultural expansion had affected »only« 23,8 % of the Brazil Indian groups.

Countless other works during the last two decades have clearly proved that the expansion has intensified and has led to establishing more permanent forms of colonization. A marked increase in agricultural settlement projects and live-stock farms has occurred, along with a drastic expansion of the internal road·network to facilitate transport of raw materials from the areas and colonization by peasant settlers (Bodley 1975, Davis 1977). Thus Doria and Ricardo's (1972:20) analysis of all the 63 groups in Brazil's Amazon region shows that the number of remaining isolated groups decreased from 21 in 1957 to 8 in 1971, i.e. a decrease from 33 % to 13 %. Today, the extractive frontier means more than just small, scattered groups of men gathering valuable natural resources. It is now characterized by large, well-organized, often multinational firms drilling for oil, opening mines, felling timber or building hydroelectric dams. Thus, the extractive industry is acquiring the same permanent features and the same irrevocable effects which characterize the agricultural and pastoral expansions.

With greather or lesser variations, this tendency has manifested itself in all those areas of Latin America which are the homes of marginal groups. The cause of this intensified expansion is, of course, the industrial worlds's growing need raw materials; this affects the entire globe, from the arctic regions to the most inaccessible jungle areas. An important contributing factor in the expansion has been the Latin American states' attempts to suppress social conflicts in the countryside by compelling the poor peasants to migrate to »uninhabited« Indian zones. Rather than carrying out genuine land reforms, the states have thus opted for internal colonization. Historic geopolitical conflicts over uncontrolled or unclear borders have led to increased expansion into border zones; this expansion encompasses both military presence and national settlement campaigns to prove that they are well-populated and effectively integrated into the respective national societies.

In combination with economic expansion, this has necessitated extending various social and ideological institutions which will control or serve the national society's own members, while »civilizing« the Indians. Consequently, the Indians now rub shoulders with doctors, teachers, researchers, »development experts«, police, and officials of the Indian protection service. Most importantly, they have also met Catholic and Protestant missionaries who are out after their souls, but who also work in various service functions such as schools, clinics, development projects, etc.

During the last two decades, the Indian groups have thus been exposed to a more far-flung and permanent encapsulation by the state. That these confrontations have probably been less violent and less costly in human lives than in the first part of this century can be attributed to the greater amount and higher sophistication of state control and the Indians' increasing resistance to »European« diseases. Such an »improvement« should not be exaggerated. In certain areas, epidemics, exploitation and repression still cause the extermination of Indian groups (Davis 1977, Arens 1976, Lewis 1978, Münzel 1973), while those governments which have taken an integrationist or protectionist stand in relation to »their« ethnic minorities can easily shift to more repressive methods. Even if the expansion in over-all terms has become less genocidal, the ultimate consequences must still be considered ethnocidal. The Indians' resource base is being destroyed by economic exploitation and land expropriation. Indian culture and identity are being broken down by various cultural and political pressures. The result of this »integration process« is often a marginal survival solely on the terms of the national society: as casual laborers, prostitutes, servants, and the like.

While this book takes a critical look at the missionaries, it must not be concluded that missionaries are the fundamental cause of the Indians' problems. In the spectrum of representatives from the national society who have a role in perpetuating the Indians' misery, the missionaries are probably the most ambiguous group. Missionaries have often served state interests in controlling and re-moulding the Indians, but they have simultaneously worked with the intention of saving them, both spiritually and physically; thus the missionaries' equivocal situation. The real source of »the Indian problem« is the socio-economic structure that brings about the expansion. The effects of foreign investments, resettlement schemes, national development projects and military consolidation are crucially important factors necessary for an understanding of the extent of the problem. Such analyses, however, easily end up depicting the Indians as passive objects of exploitation and destruction, as inevitably disappearing »species«.

Many Indians are dying as a consequence of the present development, but they are not fading away. Some decades ago, there was a fairly direct relation between the extent of the Indians' isolation and their chances for survival (Ribeiro 1967:115). This has provided grounds for many analyses and proposals which advocate maintaining or re-establishing isolation as a solution to the Indians' problem. Today, however, the expansion has become so far-flung and permanent that only a complete break-down of the western capitalist world could make a general strategy of isolationism realistic. Therefore, a critical analysis and search for alternatives must start with the assumption that the Indian societies to survive must confront the many kind of pressures emanating from the expansion. The missionaries' attempts to change Indian society *from within* cast light on those social preconditions needed in the Indians' struggle to find a suitable survival strategy against the persistent expansion. Therefore a book about the missionaries.

The fact that SIL is the world's largest Protestant mission society should by itself merit a deeper analysis of the organization, but there are additional reasons for a book particularly about SIL. SIL has become probably the largest single institution to concern itself with the plight of indigenous peoples. Furthermore, SIL's method of operation deserves anthropological scrutiny because through its use of the native language and creation of an indigenous elite it represents a modernized form of cultural imperialism. Analysis of SIL's origin, size and contacts also reveals some of the international aspects of the Indians' situation.

This book concentrates mainly on SIL's role in Latin America, since this is our major area of interest and contacts. Latin America is SIL's oldest and largest field of operation (see Appendix). SIL's work in Asia and Africa has received less attention, so it remains for future studies to determine whether its effects have been as dramatic in those areas as they have been in Latin America.

In its history of work in Latin America, SIL's dual identity – as missionaries and as linguists – worked to its advantage in obtaining both financial and spiritual support at home and political acceptance abroad. Nevertheless, with the general undisguised repression and annihilation of Indians and the ambiguous organization of SIL, it itself has now become an issue. In recent years, SIL has been criticized by everyone from Indian organizations to certain government agencies demanding their expulsion. Accusations against SIL have ranged from spying for the U.S. and CIA infiltration, to conspiracy with foreign firms and smuggling; there have even been allegations that the organization itself carried out forced sterilization, ethnocide, or impeded economic development of the indigenous peoples (cf. CEDE TIM 1976). In many ways, the organization has only itself to blame for the criticisms. SIL has avoided taking part in the debates about its activities, and it has sought to build a smokescreen preventing public knowledge of its operations. SIL's dual image has naturally given rise to speculation about the real interests behind the organization. Considering that SIL has worked mainly in areas which, though classified as »marginal«, possess rich resources and strategic military value, a suspicion that larger economic and military interests lay behind the organization would be hardly surprising.

The contributors to this book provide background for the SIL debate, and its ultimate source in the unequal relationship between the U.S.A. and the Latin American states.

In his first contribution Stoll describes SIL/WBT origins, traces the development of the dual identity and shows how a bearer of the Word of God has abused discourse to mystify its program. In »Higher Power: Wycliffe's Colombian Advance«, Stoll focuses on one of the major controversies over SIL. Robinson's contribution describes the social-historical background of American Evangelists and how millenarian expectations have led them into missonary work which tries to force Third World peoples to choose religious salvation instead of political struggle, as the SIL members' forefathers did at the turn of the century. Pereira makes plain how the mission organizations' work – including SIL's – in Bolivia is interwoven with national and international military and economic interests. The paper by d'Ans and by Rus and Wasserstrom show how SIL has ingratiated itself with the rulers in Peru and Mexico. The other contributors also shed light on these connections even though they focus exclusively on SIL within well-defined local areas.

In the current situation, SIL's dual identity might be said to have inadvertently aided it by misdirecting the critique; thus, much of the debate has focused on unveiling the scientific mask and demonstrating that SIL's cover is part of a larger »imperialist plot«. This is just part of the picture, however. A more important problem than the organization's foreign connections is the processes of social change which it has set in motion among the »Bibleless tribes« themselves. Hopefully, this book can contribute to an understanding of these processes. Vickers' article compares the Jesuits' strategy of 200-300 years ago with that used by the SIL today. Hahn also describes the Jesuits, but this time they are today's Jesuits who have pacified and administered the Rikbakca (Brazil) during the last 20 years. In this case SIL has functioned in a technical capacity – as linguists – while the Jesuits have the real responsibility for the area. In the other situations, however, it is the SIL which is the responsible institution. Arcand analyzes SIL's attempts to re-socialize the Cuiva Indians (Colombia), who are presently being forced to change their hunting-gathering way of life. Smith, using excerpts from his own diaries, gives a distressing picture of how the SIL's activities have divided the Amuesha of Peru. Disruption and fragmentation are persistent themes running through most of the papers. This is most graphically described by d'Ans in his account for how SIL controls a society through the school system it sets up. Moore portrays how a SIL missionary has administered affairs among Peru's Amarakaeri, a group which has only recently come into permanent contact with the national society. Rus and Wasserstrom analyze the SIL's work among various peasant groups in Mexico. While these studies examine highly variable historical and social backgrounds, it nevertheless becomes clear that there are significant uniformities in SIL's methods and its effects on subject populations.

The perspective of this book is »anthropological« in that it mostly concentrates on the effects of SIL's work in specific communities. The local level focus is important not just for its descriptive value, but also because it helps us understand the kind of relations SIL has with the Latin American governments under whom it works. The perspective is not »anthropological« in the sense that we believe that the Indians live(d) in paradise. Like all other societies, the Indians have their share of internal conflicts and externally caused problems. SIL's technique is to exploit these conflicts and problems in order to interject its own culture-imperialist message.

A prominent theme in the book is the Indians' attempt to find alternative survival strategies in the Devil's Paradise. One such strategy could be to accept SIL's message. Another could be a complete rejection of SIL, while a third could involve false acceptance in order to avail themselves of the organization's resources or to use it as a buffer against the incursion of national institutions.

Naturally, the Indian struggle cannot be *confined* to the local *plane* alone. The responsible parties or institutions are linked to national or even international institutions. For anthropologists, with our tradition of community studies in small scale societies, this supra-local dimension poses at least two problems: first, we may get an incomplete picture of the organizations' work; second, the organizations might exonerate themselves from critical attacks by protesting that the specific community is unrepresentative.

The only way to avoid these pitfalls is to synthesize our experiences from various communities, and incorporate into our analyses the effects of such non-local phenomena as multinational corporations, particular international development organizations, and the development policies of specific states. This should make it possible for anthropology to avoid the problem of trivialization, and make a substantial critique of those institutions which really control our lives. Hopefully, such critiques can also help the struggles at the local level.

We hope this book will help articulate this kind of anthropological perspective.

Bibliography

Arens, T. (ed.)
1976 *Genocide in Paraguay,* Temple University Press, Philadelphia.

Bodley, J.
1975 *Victims of Progress,* Cummings Publ. Comp., Menlo Park.

CEDETIM
1976 Equateur, CEDETIM, no. 38, Paris.

Cowan, G.
1963 Who? Where? and Why?, in Slocum and Holmes (eds.).

Davis, S.
1977 *Victims of the Miracle,* Cambridge University Press, Cambridge.

Dayton, E. (ed.)
1976 *Mission Handbook: North American Protestant Ministries Overseas,* Missions Advanced Research and Communication Center, Monrovia, California.

Dória, C. et Ricardo, C.
1972 Populations indigènes du Brésil: Perspectives de survie dans la région dite »Amazonie légale«, Bulletin de la Société Suisse des Américanistes, no. 36, pp 19-35.

Franklin, K.
1975 SIL Language Strategy in Papua New Guinea, Research in Melanesia, vol. 1, no. 2.

Hardenburg, W.
1912 *The Putumayo. The Devil's Paradise,* Fisher Unwin, London.

Hart, L.
1973 Pacifying the Last Frontiers, NACLA, no. 10, pp 15-31.

Hefley, J. and Hefley, M.
1972 *Dawn over Amazonia,* Word Books, Waco, Texas.

Lewis, N.
1978 *Eastern Bolivia: The White Promised Land,* IWGIA Document no. 31, Copenhagen.

Münzel, M.
1973 *The Aché Indians: Genocide in Paraguay,* IWGIA Document no. 11, Copenhagen.

Ribeiro, D.
1967 Indigenous Cultures and Languages of Brazil, in Hopper, J. (ed.) *Indians of Brazil in the Twentieth Century,* Institute for Cross-Cultural Research, Washington.

SIL Documents
no. 1 Field letter to supporters from Jeff and Jo Smothermon.
no. 2 Introduction to the Basic Policies, pamphlet.
no. 3 Corporation Conference Report 1967-1969, Translation Oct.-Dec., 1969.
no. 4 The Call of the Bibleless Tribes, pamphlet.

Slocum, M. and Holmes, S. (eds.)
1963 *Who Brought the Word,* Wycliffe Bible Translators, Santa Ana, California.

Townsend, W.
1963 Tribes, Tongues and Translators, in Slocum and Holmes (eds.).

Appendix

Summary of Summer Institute/Wycliffe Operations, advances and reverses.

Country	Year arrived	How entered	Groups entered 1978	Personnel 1978	Recent Situation
Mexico	1935	Based on work for Central American Mission in Guatemala, William Cameron Townsend invited to Mexico by the Presbyterian indigenist, Móises Saenz. First Camp Wycliffe, sponsored by Pioneer Mission Agency, held 1934. Townsend won support of Pres. Lázaro Cárdenas and incorporated SIL 1936. WBT incorporated 1942.	106	372	In 1977 *patronato* included President Jóse Lopez Portillo. In September 1979 Department of Public Education revoked SIL's contract but branch continues to operate.
Peru	1945	SIL invited to Peru by Prado government, signing contract with Ministry of Public Education. Jungle Aviation and Radio Service (JAARS) started here in 1948. SIL's first bilingual school system initiated by Odria government in 1953 during an oil rush. Base Yarinacocha, near Pucallpa.	43	234	In April 1976 Morales Bermudez govt. ordered SIL out of country by end of year; January 1977 granted SIL a new five year contract. Advance into highlands delayed by breakdown of 1964–70 bilingual project at Ayacucho, accusations 1975–6 that SIL failed to secure authorization for highland teams. Six teams now at work on Quechua dialects, branch plans to produce New Testaments in eighteen Quechua dialects and five Campa dialects. New ten year government contract signed late 1979.
Ecuador	1952	Signed contract with Ministry of Education under Galo Plaza, whose successor Velazco Ibarra welcomed first teams. As in Peru bilingual, health and occupational-training programs. Cooperated with govt. and oil companies in removal of Auca from oil lands to reservation, 1968–72. Base Limoncocha, JAARS program.	12	100	Plans for highland bilingual education program delayed by lack of government and foundation support.
Guatemala	1952	During Arbenz government SIL signed a contract with Ministry of Education through National Indigenist Institute. In 1960 SIL pledged Pres. Manuel Ydigoras to support his government against insurgency.	29	91	U.S. Agency for International Development has supported bilingual education program.
Honduras	1960	Administered by Central America branch headquartered in Guatemala.	3	4	
Bolivia	1955	Townsend met Pres. Paz Estenssoro at 1954 Inter-American Indigenist Conference in La Paz. Contracts with Ministries of Education, Health and Rural Affairs. Trains Indians in health, leadership, radio communications and business. Base Tumi Chucua, near Riberalta, Beni. JAARS program.	17	115	Cordial relation with Banzer government, plans to complete work by 1985. Aymara and Quechua teams work with Protestant and Catholic agencies. Donald Burns, who began highland Quechua work in Peru and Ecuador, on loan to USAID mission promoting bilingual education.
Brazil	1956	Contacts at 1954 La Paz conference led to agreements with National Museum (1959), U. Brasilia (1963) and National Indian Foundation (FUNAI) of the Ministry of Interior (1969). Bases at Porto Velho, Cuiabá, Belém and Manaus; JAARS program; cooperative programs with FUNAI and Catholic missions.	44	302	c. 1975 FUNAI asked SIL to expand in Rio Negro area, ahead of a new highway, but began revoking SIL's work permits elsewhere. December 1976 FUNAI contract expired. November 1977 Minister of Interior ordered all SIL personnel to retire from tribal areas. Work continues at bases.

Country	Year arrived	How entered	Groups entered 1978	Personnel 1978	Recent Situation
Colombia	1962	Overtures to govt. from early 1950s frustrated by Vatican Concordat until October 1961, when Lleras Camargo government allowed SIL to negotiate contract with Ministry of Government. Base Lomalinda, near Puerto Lleras, Meta. JAARS program.	39	217	Government's promised phased withdrawal of SIL never begun despite periodic controversies since 1970.
Panama	1970	1968 Inter-American Indigenist Congress led to invitation from Minister of Education in 1969. Administered as Colombia-Panama branch.	5	17	Government announced that contract, expiring in June 1979, would not be renewed and gave SIL seven months to terminate work.
Surinam	1967	Contact at an Inter-American Linguistic Conference led to agreement with the Ministry of Education.	5	20	Works with native American, Bush Negro and East Indian languages.
Chile	c. 1977	A translator couple assigned to the Peru branch are working in Pascuense, on Easter Island. Overtures to *Venezuela* since the late 1940s have failed to produce a contract. In 1972 a SIL couple were advising Mennonite missionaries in Paraguay on bilugual matters, with the hope of extending work to that country, apparently without further result. That same year SIL was also considering beginning work in *Argentina,* also apparently without result.			
Philippines	1953	Richard Pittman won support of Defense Secretary Ramon Magsaysay at height of Huk rebellion. When Magsaysay became president, SIL given contract and authorized to work in militarized zones. Contracts with U. Philippines and Dept. of Education, JAARS contract with Dept. of Defense. Bases in Manila and Nasuli, Mindanao.	57	251	Friends include Mr. and Mrs. Marcos, Carlos Romulo. 1976 translator kidnapped by Moslem rebels in Sulu Sea area, released with help of Philippine Constabulary. 1976 new contract with Dept. of Education and Culture. Training Filipinos in linguistics and Bible translation.
Papua New Guinea	1956	Arrangements made through Australian Protestant missionaries. Until independence in 1976, agreements with the Australian Territorial Government. JAARS program, bilingual education and occupational training programs, base at Ukarumpa near Lae, heavily staffed by Australians.	120	546	U.S. Agency for International Development (USAID) is giving branch $ 568.000 for "leadership training" of 300 indigenous persons in thirty language groups for 1977–80 (Grant No. AID/Asia-G-1250). Branch has also begun to train converts to translate the Bible for remaining six hundred languages. Proposal to organize national translators into a separate agency.
Republic of South Vietnam	1957 (1975)	Magsaysay recommended SIL to Pres. Ngo Dinh Diem. Contract with Dept. of Education. 1967–70 USAID supported bilingual programs for the Montagnards, chiefly in relocation centers near garrisons to which most SIL teams retired. Two translators and a child killed in fighting, another translator died as POW of the NLF.	21	(66)*	Retired at collapse of Saigon govt., two translators captured by NLF released after eight months. Branch regrouped in Philippines, finishing some translations, arranging broadcasts over Far Eastern Broadcasting Co. and working with Montagnard refugees in U.S. For initiatives of reconstituted Mainland S.E. Asia Branch, see below.
Cambodia	1971 (1975)	Invited to begin work by Lon Nol govt. following U.S. invasion. Supervised by Vietnam branch.	2		Two teams began work with Brao and Cham near Thai border, retired at collapse of Lon Nol govt.

*) Personnel last year of operation in country.

Country	Year arrived	How entered	Groups entered 1978	Personnel 1978	Recent Situation
Australia	1961	Subsidies from Australian govt. for linguistic work.	20	82	
British Solomon Islands	1977	Several teams began work on some seventy languages spoken by 150,000 people.			
India	1966	SIL secured sponsorship by Deccan College, Poona but never won confidence of federal govt. In 1969 govt. withdrew visas for non-Commonwealth personnel, crippling operation.			Here SIL has been trying for some time to recruit Indian Christians to become translators. In 1977 twelve Indian missionaries went to Britain for eight months of intensive training in linguistics and Bible translation.
Nepal	1966 (1976)	Contacts in India led to contract with Tribhuvan University, Kathmandu.	18	(83)*	In June 1976 govt. ordered all SIL personnel out of country by August, apparently for violation of national laws prohibiting propagation of faiths other than Hindu. Since then SIL has tried to maintain contact with its congregations.
Indonesia	1971	Official contacts initiated under Sukarno failed. Introduction by Philippines Foreign Secretary Carlos Remulo to his counterpart Adam Malik led to contract with University of Cenderawisih at Jayapura.	9	81	1974 govt. approved development of base at Danau Bira (Lake Holmes) in new Irian Jaya (former Dutch New Guinea). Next year Kenneth Pike signed new contract; permission for radios and airplanes also granted. Forty-one members assigned 1975 have had visa problems. Branch wants to integrate Indonesians into the program.
Mainland S.E. Asia Branch		1975–78 efforts to secure government permission to work in *Laos, Thailand, Malaysia* and *Bangladesh*. Also working with *Burmese* translating the Bible.			
Malaysia	1977	As of December 1977, members of the Mainland S.E. Asia Branch were waiting for visas to enter Sabah, on Borneo. In 1973 Townsend was invited to *Pakistan* by the Ali Bhutto government, but apparently without result. Unconfirmed reports of 1978 diplomatic initiatives in *Iran*.			
Ghana	1962	John Bendor-Samuel, Wycliffe Great Britain, negotiated contract with University of Ghana. Approved by University Council of Kwame Nkrumah.	13	46	Branch has recently formed Ghana Institute of Linguistics, composed of SIL members and Ghanaians, to which it hopes eventually to transfer responsibility for the work.
Nigeria	1962 (1976)	Agreements with University of Nigeria, Nsukka, and Ahmadu Bello University, Zaria. SIL became Institute of Linguistics (IL). Work began 1964 in E. region; when Biafra seceded (1967) work in sixteen of seventeen groups halted but IL allowed to expand in the north.	22	(71)*	After 1972 govt. blocked new allocations. 1975 branch began organizing Nigerian Bible Translation Trust (NBTT) comprised of Nigerians. June 1976 IL terminated by govt.; SIL-advised NBTT now occupies former IL center at Jos and works in fifteen to twenty languages.
Cameroun	1967	Contract with the University of the Cameroun. A few teams displaced by the Biafran war resumed work here across the border.	20	65	In 1975 Kenneth Pike signed a new contract with the government's Research Institute stipulating greater national involvement.

*) Personnel last year of operation in country.

Country	Year arrived	How entered	Groups entered 1978	Personnel 1978	Recent Situation
Togo	1967		4	16	Supervised by neighboring SIL-Ghana branch.
Ivory Coast	1970	Contract with University of Abidjan.	} 18	57	Translation center at Abidjan serves other missionaries and national translators.
Upper Volta	1974	Government invited SIL-Ivory Coast to do language surveys, administered through Ivory Coast.			
Ethiopia	c. 1973	First SIL couple arrived in Addis Ababa in 1973, next year taught thirteen Ethiopians linguistics at Debra Zeit evangelical college. By 1977 several other couples translating Scripture in cooperation with Protestant missions and local churches.			
Sudan	c. 1974	In 1974 SIL surveyed languages in S. Sudan under auspices of Education ministry, by 1977 assigning workers to this country and planning extensive literacy program in conjunction with Education ministry.			Africa Area Office, with headquarters in Accra, Ghana and staff of 82, currently administers work in Ethiopia, Sudan, Kenya and Nigeria.
Kenya	1977	Contract with University of Nairobi to permit SIL to establish a regional center for East Africa.			
Chad	1977	SIL's agreement with government stresses training of national translators.			SIL's agreement with N'Djamena government stressed training of national translators. Personnel evacuated in 1979 because of civil war.

SIL members have also surveyed languages in *Zaïre* and the *Central African Republic*, presumably preparatory to beginning work in these countries as well.

Country	Year arrived	How entered	Groups entered 1978	Personnel 1978	Recent Situation
North-America	1944	Operates without government contract in Canada and the United States.	33	100	Problems include refusal of tribal councils to permit translators to live on reservations, impossibility of hiring full-time language informants at Third World wage levels.
Soviet Union		Wycliffe displayed interest in working in the Soviet Union during WW II. After Lázaro Cárdenas visited U.S.S.R. and China in 1958-9, Townsend contacted Russian diplomats in Mexico, again in 1967, and made first of at least eight trips to the Soviet Union. In 1972 he published a book praising the well-developed Soviet bilingual program. For a time it was hoped that arrangements could be made through the Colombia-Panama branch; several senior translators moved to Moscow but continuing negotiations with the Academy of Sciences have apparently yet to produce a satisfactory agreement. In October 1977 the Academy of Sciences agreed to have its linguists produce translations of John's First Epistle in several languages.			
Displaced Languages Project	c. 1976	A translation program directed to expatriates: Basques and Kurds in the western United States, Circassians in West Germany, speakers of an Albanian dialect in Detroit, and perhaps other languages spoken in communist countries. Seven personnel assigned.			

Sources

Most personnel counts are based on the Wycliffe Bible Translators *Prayer Directory* for 1978. Numbers for Nepal, Nigeria and South Vietnam date to the Summer Institute's last year in these countries. According to the directory, members' country of origin is as follows: U.S.A. (2,668); Canada (287); Australia (279); Great Britain (214); Switzerland (76); West Germany (68); New Zealand (43); Sweden (14); Finland (14); Republic of South Africa (11); Japan (8); France (6); Peru (6); Norway (5); Belgium (3); Austria, Denmark, Mexico and Brazil (2 each); and Ghana, Hong Kong, India and Panama (1 each). Total membership at the beginning of 1978 was therefore 3,700; approximately 72% from the U.S.A.; and approximately 99.6% from North America, Europe, Japan, Australia an New Zealand.

Most figures for language-groups entered are also based on the 1978 Prayer Directory; they total approximately 675. SIL's estimates for groups-entered vary; this may reflect new assigments, temporary or permanent abandonment of uncompleted assignments, or official confusion as to what constitutes an assignment.

Most of the other information in this chart was compiled from the Wycliffe bulletins for home supporters, *Translation* (1943–1975) and *In Other Words* (1975–), and the following articles and books:

Hart, Laurie
1973 »Pacifying the Last Frontiers« in *Latin America & Empire Report*, December, North American Congress on Latin American Affairs, New York.

Hefley, James and Marti
1974 *Uncle Cam*, Waco, Texas: Word Books.

Thompson, Phyllis
1974 *Matched With His Hour*, London: Word Books.

Townsend, William C.
1972 *They Found A Common Tongue*, New York: Harper and Row.
1976 *Lázaro Cárdenas: Democrata Mexicano*, Mexico: Grijalbo.

Townsend, William C. and Pittman, Richard S.
1975 *Remember All The Way*, Huntington Beach, California: WBT.

SIL's Campa informant from Gran Pajonal, Peru. He was flown in to the Yarinacocha base camp together with his wife, for »linguistic« research. Copyright: Søren Hvalkof, 1975.

Words Can Be Used In So Many Ways

by DAVID STOLL

> *Brian Moser:* »*Your primary objective is to get the Word to the tribes, why wasn't this said in your contract?*«
>
> *Clarence Church:* »*We certainly, in the contract? (sic) of course we could not say this in the contract because the government, this would be hard for the government to defend after all the government is not a religious organization and SIL coming in – SIL is not a religious organization either.*
>
> »*We made it very clear that we have come to give the Indians the message of God's love. There has been nothing done in a corner, this has been perfectly known ever since the beginning. It is true that this is not in the contract as such but if you will read the contract carefully you will notice that all of the, excuse me, ninety percent of the emphasis is on linguistics, this is where we have put ninety percent of our efforts.*«
>
> – **War of the Gods,** »Disappearing Worlds Series,« Granada Television, London.

It used to be, sometimes still is and may forever be. If the wrong kind of person asked the Summer Institute of Linguistics about its religious activities, spokesmen downplayed them in favor of SIL's linguistic activities. If such persons pressed concerning the Wycliffe Bible Translators, spokesmen spun distinctions between SIL's »scientific« and WBT's »spiritual« purposes. The stature of these presentations emerges only when they are compared to a more audacious performance, which for SIL-South America passed out of fashion after 1953: to deny that SIL had any religious purpose at all.

The theme of this essay is how a bearer of the Word of God has abused words. Elsewhere in the collection Bernard Arcand and Richard Chase Smith address SIL/WBT's use of Cuiva and Amuesha language. Here I examine the dual identity, a system of presentation which has permitted a single, Janus-faced organization to explain itself as a faith mission to home supporters in the United States, and as anything but that on the mission field.

Wycliffe constructed the dual identity in response to political requirements in the field and at home. The guiding objective has been to win unlimited access to native people, the method to secure government contracts. As a supposedly non-sectarian linguistics institute, SIL (WBT) has offered governments technical service in return for sweeping operational rights under state charter. In passing the contracts may mention that SIL will promote the »moral improvement« of native people, or that it will translate books of »high moral value«. Into this loophole SIL directs all its energies. By the time SIL generates serious opposition it has proved its value to the government and secured implicit permission to evangelize the native population. Yet the methods necessary to win and maintain the contracts have offended mission supporters in the United States: the Wycliffe image has contained the backlash.

The dual identity is therefore a constituting principle of the Wycliffe operation, knitting together state and evangelical plans for native people. As a semantic device, the dual identity is an institutional plausible denial. It operates on a shifting presentation between a SIL and a WBT »context« or »emphasis«. Crucial omission and strategic ambiguity are used to avoid facts which might displease the audience.

David Stoll (1952-   ) comes from Grand Rapids, Michigan and graduated from the University of Michigan in 1974 with a bachelor's degree in anthropology. In 1975-77 he interviewed SIL members and their opponents in Colombia, Ecuador and Peru. He has been preparing a book on the Summer Institute in Latin America with the assistance of the Louis M. Rabinowitz Foundation of New York.

Because the performance violates the evangelical standard of honesty, Wycliffe has had to sanctify it as the Lord's leading. The ultimate justification is that Wycliffe is an agent of the Lord's will, that the most serious opposition to its plans can be attributed to the Devil, and that the end therefore justifies the means. Since this last point cannot be recognized, it may be projected onto Satanic Marxism. And so one of Wycliffe's achievements has been to sanctify semantic Machiavellianism as basic Christianity, permitting some members to present themselves in a dubious manner with hot sincerity and accuse sceptics of religious persecution.

Since Wycliffe's alliances with governments are usually predicated upon the dual identity, it cannot be abandoned even now that it lends credence to espionage charges. It is nevertheless a flexible instrument which Wycliffe has used to legitimate itself in diverse political situations and at unfolding stages of the work, as supposedly non-sectarian linguistic investigation issues in sectarian church-building. In the Latin American experience with SIL, three phases can be discerned.

During the first, the Summer Institute functions as a virtual front for the Wycliffe Bible Translators. Not only is SIL's relation with WBT never mentioned, it may be denied along with SIL's religious purpose. In South America this performance dates from 1945 to 1953, when the Catholic Church exposed it.

The second phase is the most well-known. As Richard Chase Smith reported from Peru in 1975, the two identities are still »kept very separate, each reserved for its own audience, each revealed according to the image needed for the situation.« Upon inquiry it emerges that SIL and WBT are »affiliated« or »sister« organizations which have different purposes. As a SIL-Colombia official was forced to explain to *El Tiempo* (June 28) in 1975: »The Institute and the Wycliffe Bible Translators are the same people, but it is a question of two corporations dedicated to different things. Ours is a scientific organization.«

Now that controversy has destroyed the credibility of this performance by turning it into a laughing matter or the most sinister of conspiracies, SIL is manipulating longstanding ambiguities in its work to wrest a new legitimacy from crisis. It has happened before, thanks less to SIL's arguments than to its state alliances. To defend SIL against hostile social scientists and Indians, spokespersons are emphasizing the compatibility of science and religion, the relativity of belief systems and SIL's respect for indigenous culture and self-determination.

The dual identity may seem to fade in favor of a unitary presentation. Yet the contradiction between SIL's sectarian basis in the U.S. and its non-sectarian pledge in the field remains, so that even this performance requires strategic ambiguity and crucial omission. With great sincerity and the best of intentions, SIL is trying to mystify the contradiction between its program of moral improvement, which expresses the plans of states and evangelicals for native people, and the indigenous self-defense movements.

The Origin of the Dual Identity

Until recently, the most glaring omission in the Wycliffe accounts was how the SIL/WBT arrangement came to be. Rather than address this sensitive question, the official Wycliffe history (Wallis and Bennett 1959) dwells upon the favor in which the Lord evidently held William Cameron Townsend (1896-   ), the architect of the dual identity and the founder of SIL/WBT. Uncle Cam to the membership, the rustic but canny Townsend began life as the son of a poor, devoutly Presbyterian tenant farmer in Orange County, California. His first missionary experience (1917-32) was with the Central American Mission of Dallas, Texas among Mayan peasants in Guatemala.

The Central American was a faith mission, one of a number organized in the late 19th Century for »the evangelization of the world in this generation.« Like other inter-denominational faith enterprises, it was a child of the millenarians, intellectual fathers of the 20th Century fundamentalist and evangelical movements. The millenarians saw through an age of robber barons and social protest to an impending Great Tribulation which would precede the Millennial Kingdom, the thousand year reign of Christ on earth. Although the gathering evil of this premillennial scheme could be identified as capitalism, the contrary association of Satan with protest against capitalism soon prevailed. Social redemption would have to wait until Christ himself returned to smite the wicked. As poor people like Townsend's family prospered, they found their promised land to love and defend this side of the Great Tribulation, and a Gospel of imminent doom issued in a Gospel of progress under capitalism. But in keeping with Matthew

24/14, it was not forgotten that the evangelization of the world might pave the way for the Second Coming of Jesus Christ.

In Guatemala, Mayan peasants were beginning to convert to Protestantism even before North American missionaries arrived in their towns. In the mission bulletins Townsend deplored what he called the »oppression« of the Maya and saw that it extended to the treatment meted out by *ladino* (non-Indian) to Indian converts. He therefore dedicated himself to building Mayan churches in the vernacular rather than Spanish, by working with Mayan evangelists, translating the New Testament into Cakchiquel Maya and experimenting with bilingual education.

Cameron Townsend with Mayan Evangelists at the »Robinson Bible Institute«, Panajachel, Guatemala. Copyright: 1922. Townsend is the fair-haired missionar at center-right (without Glasses, below the left-hand Door).

To some Maya, Protestantism offered freedom from debt peonage and a wider margin of survival. To plantation owners, who were trying to switch from forced to wage labor, Townsend (1924) offered better workers. Department governors and three presidents of the republic praised his work. In two important respects the future SIL founder was following in the path of earlier Catholic missionaries. One was the linguistic approach, which the Catholics had used among the Cakchiquel Maya as late as the mid-19th Century (Brinton 1884). The other was his close attention to state requirements. With SIL's government contracts he would try to match and undermine the agreements between South American governments and the Catholic Church.

By 1932 Townsend had achieved a measure of fame, was feeling trapped in the narrow confines of the Central American Mission and looking for new fields to conquer. He was encouraged by Leonard Livingston Legters (?-1940), an older missions entrepreneur. Backed by wealthy Philadelphia millenarians of the Victorious Life Testimony, in 1921 Legters had helped organize the Pioneer Mission Agency to reconnoiter and finance work in unreached fields. Unfortunately, the onset of the Great Depression made it impossible to finance Townsend's dream of an airborne advance in the Amazon.

Several circumstances seem to have turned their attention to the more economical Mexico. For one, the Pioneer Mission's James and Dr. Katherine Neel Dale were organizing the Mexican Indian Mission to liberate an estimated forty-five tribes from illiteracy, serfdom and the Catholic Church.

Townsend could also count upon the support of Moises Saenz, like most of the Pioneer brethren a Presbyterian, and also a leading Mexican indigenist whose brother General Aaron Saenz was crony to the *jefe maximo* of the Mexican Revolution, Elias Plutarcho Calles. Finally, by 1933-4 anti-clericalism had reached such a pitch in Mexico that Protestant missionaries, until this point supporters of the revolution, were afraid that it was going Red.

In February 1933, the month after Moises Saenz (1936:295) resigned from the Department of Education because of his disagreements with Marxist colleagues, Townsend and Legters reportedly agreed to train Bible translators for Mexico's Indian languages (Hefleys 1974:75). Support for the Dales' envisioned Mexican Indian Mission was apparently the plan.

Townsend's first expedition to Mexico in late 1933 was so discouraging that he commited himself to several stratagems of formative importance to Wycliffe. As detailed recently by Townsend's biographers James and Marti Hefley (1974:82-9), these included to: 1) »enter Mexico as linguists rather than missionaries« 2) explain that »individuals« in the U.S. were financing him (rather than mention the Pioneer Mission conduit) and 3) advertise himself as a supporter of the Mexican Revolution.

During his second expedition to Mexico in late 1934 Townsend began composing an undeservedly neglected novel. For the most part, *Tolo the Volcano's Son* (1936) is a thinly disguised account of his years with the Central American Mission in Guatemala. However, it closes with an, apparently quite fictional, Mayan revolt led by a Russian Bolshevik in the plantations south of Townsend's mission stations. The bloodthirsty plot is foiled by an infiltrator, the missionary's (Townsend's) Mayan Bible translation assistant. The Russian flees across the border into Mexico: figuratively speaking, author Townsend was preparing to engage in hot pursuit. The novel times the (again, apparently fictional) Guatemalan revolt with an historical one, that of Pipil Indians in neighboring El Salvador in January 1932, which has a claim to be the first communist-led revolution in Latin America. In reaction to this event, and anticipating the Bolshevik threat in Mexico, Townsend therefore composed an apology for counter-revolutionary conspiracy as he was laying the foundation of SIL/WBT.

In mid-1934, shortly before he started his novel in the Saenz home town of Monterrey, Townsend held the first training camp for Bible translators in an abandoned farmhouse at Sulphur Springs, Arkansas. The session was named Camp Wycliffe, after the first translator of the Bible into English. It was also called the Pioneer Missionary Camp (*Camp Wycliffe Chronicle* January 1936) after its sponsor the Pioneer Mission, a point neglected in the Wycliffe accounts. To avoid confusion, this event would later become the conventional origin of the Summer Institute of Linguistics.

By the end of the second Camp Wycliffe in 1935, Townsend had secured permits to bring half a dozen students to Mexico for linguistic research. A new persident, General Lazaro Cardenas, had deposed the Calles clique in which Aaron Saenz figured and was about to discourage anti-clericalism in favor of serious reform. According to the Hefleys, to »some« Mexican officials Townsend explained that he wanted to translate the Bible. Friendly indigenists like Moises Saenz, as well as Townsend's flattering report on the Mexican Revolution to U.S. Ambassador Josephus Daniels, soon brought his work to the attention of President Cardenas, who apparently knew that Townsend was a missionary and cemented the welcome.

The conspiratorial air of these early years emerges in a 1942 pamphlet on evangelical prospects in Mexico. Cameron Townsend appears under the pseudonym of »James Warren,« a missionary linguist from California and intimate of the President. »You know, Mr. Warren,« a leftist Bureau of Indian Affairs director tells him:

> *you are not deceiving me. In so far as I am concerned, I know the utlimate meaning of your activity. Your interest is not scientific per se... You are a Protestant propagandist, are you not? But have no fear, I like the Protestants.*

In one of his heart to heart talks with the President, Warren argues for a new »philosophy of motives« as opposed to the old-fashioned »philosophy of rules.« »The spiritual content of a message is the real thing,« Warren proposes, and »the point is that when you have a good motive, rules become secondary.« (Rembao 1942:16,19)

The Pioneer Mission's distaste for Townsend's methods triggered the first of two reformations which created the SIL/WBT arrangement as we know it today. After only a few months in Mexico he was talking about organizing his own mission, which was not in the original training camp scheme and trespassed on the Mexican Indian Mission plan of James Dale. The unfortunate Dale had thrown in his lot with the even more unfortunate General Saturnino Cedillo, who would die in an abortive rebellion against Cardenas in 1938. The unnamed missionary who denounced Townsend to Pioneer for making dishonest presentations (Hefleys 1974:99, Townsend and Pittman 1975:15) was almost certainly Dale.

The Pioneer board of directors demanded that the Camp Wycliffe alumni in Mexico organize a committee, a group of elders in the United States who would supervise Townsend's field proceedings and relieve Pioneer of responsibility. According to the Hefleys (1974:95-6), Townsend felt that such a home board might not »understand« all procedures and events which came to its attention. In keeping with an element of the faith mission tradition, he therefore persuaded his followers to »run our own affairs from the field under the Lord's leading.« To incorporate in Mexico they would have to be a scientific agency rather than a mission. And so we arrive at the birth of the Summer Institute of Linguistics (late 1936), a name which Townsend already was using to place Camp Wycliffe in an appropriate light to the Mexican audience.

The metamorphosis from faith mission to linguistic institute required constraint on Townsend's recruits, whose ruling ambition was to save souls. Since the 1935 welcome by Mexican indigenists, Townsend had been claiming to be non-sectarian. When his followers attacked the alliance with Cardenas, whom they considered a Bolshevik, Townsend called for political neutrality. And in Townsend's response to the problem of practice – how to be non-sectarian sectarians – we see the beginning of SIL's claim to be »non-ecclesiastical.« Since Mexican law barred foreigners from clerical functions, Townsend advised members to obey the law and confine themselves to Bible translation. They were to refrain from distributing tracts, keep their distance from religious controversy and »witness (evangelize) only on a personal level to friends.« (Hefleys 1974:113–15) As we might expect, it was difficult for some members to respect such rules, a discrepancy which SIL tolerates to the present. Moreover, from the beginning SIL defined »non-ecclesiastical« to include working closely with other evangelical missions and organizing native churches. As David Legters quoted his father, the principle was »have native teach natives wherever possible.« (Dame 1968:72) Since this was becoming standard evangelical procedure, the non-ecclesiastical claim has never really distinguished Wycliffe from other missions.

Two events in 1941 led to the second reformation, the break with the Pioneer Mission and the organization of Camp Wycliffe/SIL along today's lines. The first was another ultimatum from the Pioneer board, which never really reconciled itself to Townsend's policies even though it had continued to channel funds from supporters in the United States. Now that Townsend was doubling his missionary force to one hundred, Pioneer wanted him to organize his own home office. The second event was an invitation to move Camp Wycliffe to the University of Oklahoma at Norman.

While Townsend's alliance with Cardenas had opened the door to Mexican Indians, the reaction at home had damaged group finance. Here too an appropriate facade was mandatory. In late 1941 Townsend's conferees – Camp Wycliffe linguists Kenneth Pike and Eugene Nida, as well as the group's fundraiser William Nyman – therefore accepted his suggestion to form »two organizations« whose membership and board of directors would be the same. While the Summer Institute of Linguistics in Mexico would continue to be non-sectarian, the Wycliffe Bible Translators would have a statement of doctrine like every other faith mission (Hefleys 1974:117-19).* Nyman incorporated the two entities in California in 1942, and the same year Camp Wycliffe moved to the University of Oklahoma as SIL. Judging from Wycliffe publications, home supporters were not informed that their missionaries were operating in the field under the auspices of the Summer Institute until 1956–7.

Peru 1953

The dual identity proved itself spectacularly in Peru. Here Cameron Townsend signed SIL's first state contract, in 1945 with the Ministry of Public Education. Since a Catholic monopoly barred advance in

---

* Every six years, or upon returning to the field from furlough, each member must reaffirm his/her belief in the Wycliffe Statement of Doctrine. Applicants are informed that should their views on these points change, they »must be prepared to resign.« The statement includes»1) The doctrine of the Trinity 2) The fall of man, his consequent moral depravity and his need of regeneration 3) The atonement through the substitutionary death of Christ 4) The doctrine of justification by faith 5) The resurrection of the body, both in the case of the just and of the unjust 6) The eternal life of the saved and the eternal punishment of the lost 7) The divine inspiration and consequent authority of the whole canonical Scriptures – the last of which is interpreted to imply Scriptural inerrancy.« (WBT c).

the Amazon, SIL identified itself as a dependency of the »University of the State of Oklahoma, of the United States of America.« This claim confused it with the U.S. government's technical »services« or »missions« which were soon incorporated into the Point Four program. As for WBT and even Bible translation, they were never mentioned. The U.S. embassy assisted by bringing the University of Oklahoma linguists into its diplomatic aura.

SIL-Peru became a laboratory for future advances, to develop a program which would serve governments opening up jungle as well as SIL's evangelical aim. The Jungle Aviation and Radio Service (JAARS), incorporated in 1948, ran supplies to military garrisons and relied upon commercial traffic, especially oil company traffic, to subsidize flights for Bible translators. To further strengthen SIL's alliance with the state against Catholic challenge, Townsend (1955) promoted colonization and promised that under SIL's influence Indians would cooperate. In May 1953 he introduced the Texan industrialist and »partner of God« Robert Le Tourneau to President Manuel Odria. Le Tourneau's party included SIL treasurer William Nyman: the *Peruvian Times* (May 22) reported that Le Tourneau was one of SIL's »principal backers.« From President Odria Le Tourneau secured 400,000 hectares of jungle for experiments in mechanical jungle-clearing and roadbuilding, colonization and evangelization.

The previous year, in October 1952, the Odria government had opened Peruvian oil lands to foreign, chiefly U.S. capital, setting off an oil rush in the Amazon. A month later the minister of education approved Townsend's plans for a government-subsidized, SIL-administered bilingual school system. The Catholic bishops lodged a protest which the government ignored, and Townsend brought Le Tourneau to Peru as if to strengthen his hand. On August 8, 1953 Monsignor Buenaventura Leon de Uriarte rose to meet the enemy in *La Prensa* of Lima.

The bishop accused SIL of »making an active and tendentious campaign to convert the Indians of our Amazon to evangelical Protestantism.« He charged that SIL »realizes a vast proselyting action, hiding its true itentions behind a series of disguises.« He even accused the Summer Institute of being an arm of the »Wicleffe Bible Translators.«

La Prensa printed Townsend's reply beside Uriarte's charges. »How could a scientist,« he began, »who believes in our loving Jesus Christ live among human beings who adore the boa, and keep their mouths closed to avoid telling them anything about Christianity?« »We do not perform evangelical work,« Townsend continued, »because the Institute has a mission of scientific character and not a religious end.« On the other hand, reported the interviewer, »Dr. Townsend admitted that personally he is a member of 'Wicleffe Bible' but made clear that the Institute had nothing to do with it.«

Four days later Uriarte produced a University of Oklahoma bulletin mentioning SIL's relation to Wycliffe. He also raised the Le Tourneau issue. According to *La Prensa* (August 12), Townsend was now declining comment and asking where he could find Uriarte, »to make a detailed exposition of the Linguistic Institute.« The Hefleys (1974:179–181) omit reference to Townsend's first published statement. Instead, they describe him preparing his »one reply.« In his second reply Townsend made no reference to his first, either to suggest that he had been misquoted or admit that he was retracting his earlier statements:

> We have, then, a double aspect. Our work of dual nature brings us contacts of dual nature and for this reason I founded a second institution which is also non-sectarian, called *Wycliffe Bible Translators.*
>
> It consists of a small office in Glendale, California and another, even smaller, in Chicago, Illinois. It has absolutely no life apart from the Summer Institute of Linguistics and exists solely to obtain funds and recruits for our work. The two institutions are analogous in many respects.

Townsend also explained that his group was »non-sectarian« because »no sect contributes donations to our work. They are individuals and independent groups which sustain us.« As for the »principal backer,« Townsend explained that SIL was cooperating with everyone, even Mr. Le Tourneau, »with whom we have no other connection than a recent friendship.« (*El Comercio* August 19). The week before a Le Tourneau spokesman explained that SIL had been »included once in the contributions made by the Le Tourneau Foundation to various organizations, but we do not have connections with (it).« (*La Prensa* August 13).

The Peruvian archbishops were not impressed and issued a declaration backing Uriarte (*La Prensa* August 23). President Odria increased SIL's subsidy and decorated Townsend, who had legitimated a new way of presenting conventional missionary activity. According to a Catholic missionary who long ago became a friend of SIL-Peru, is quoted as such in the Wycliffe literature and thoroughly approves of their work, the first SIL linguists often acted as pastors, not only gathering data but leading religious services as well.

Wycliffe tried to spare home supporters Townsend's statements of August 1953, but in the *New York Times* (August 30, 1953) some must have read that, according to general director Townsend, SIL-Peru supplied primers to and even trained teachers for Catholic schools, made its planes equally available to Catholic and Protestant missionaries, and did not make Protestant converts.

Soon less money was arriving from the homeland. The reaction to Townsend's Peruvian policies peaked in 1958-9 with an inquest by the Interdenominational Foreign Missions Association (IFMA), which comprised much of the faith mission industry (Hefleys 1974:200-06). One issue was Townsend's frequent claim that SIL's primary purpose was scientific rather than spiritual. * Another was Townsend's policy of conceding Catholic missionaries occasional flight service in return for good behavior. Judging from Wycliffe publications, this policy was not mentioned to home supporters until 1958-9, after denunciations had flushed it into the open.

Wycliffe withdrew from the IFMA in late 1959, after soliciting an endorsement from leading evangelicals like Billy Graham, at that time a Wycliffe board member. Eight years later *Christianity Today* (October 27, 1967) thought that Wycliffe's success was second only to Graham's. This evangelical herald was most impressed by Townsend's penetration of Catholic states, calling the ministry contracts »the backbone of Wycliffe strategy.« While other evangelical missionaries accused Wycliffe of »implicit duplicity« and violating the American principle of church-state separation, *Christianity Today* suggested that they were jealous because Wycliffe often produced four times as many converts. Entering communits countries was Wycliffe's next challenge.

The Dual Identity Is Alive and Well

To keep a deliberate muddle in perspective, Wycliffe has always been careful – but only when addressing the right audience, composed of those who appreciate the blessings of the Gospel – to explain its goal in the plainest of terms. »The Camp's one purpose,« Wycliffe noted at an early date, »is to aid in the accomplishment of our great commission, world-wide evangelization.« (*Camp Wycliffe Chronicle* 1939) As much is obvious from the Wycliffe home literature to the present. As it fell to the U.S. journalist Malcolm Burke to confirm for the Lima press in 1953, »the linguists are missionaries.« (*La Prensa* August 10)

Yet the linguists were not missionaries, or so the Summer Institute would have preferred Peruvians to believe. In his second reply to the Catholic charges Townsend admitted that SIL was motivated by a profund love of God; he confessed that it was connected to Wycliffe Bible Translators; he declared that it intended to translate the Bible; but he scarcely admitted that he and his people were missionaries. All to the contrary, SIL was such a non-sectarian, non-ecclesiastical outfit that it would have to leave the teaching of all but a few simple truths to an altogether different class of human beings, the »missionaries be they Catholic or Protestant.«

Once SIL's secret was exposed or divulged, it still usually had to distinguish itself from other evangelical missions to protect the state contract. The first line of defense remained the linguistic identity itself: while the connection with Wycliffe would be admitted, it would not be advertised. The second line of defense has included various claims – non-sectarian, non-ecclesiastical, non-denominational – as well as the three-fold program of science, social and spiritual service, symbolized by a triangle. These devices have established that SIL is different from or only partly an evangelical mission.

To ensure the peace of mind of its members, Wycliffe has even found a theological basis for confusing them over their identity. This is a deduction from Biblical literalism which has become Wycliffe's institutional credo: the Word of God translated to the vernacular is sufficient to bring people to Christ, totally apart from any corrupting human influence. In keeping with this proposition, members often explain that it is the Word of God, not the translator, which effects conversions. »We only bring

---

* By 1940 in Mexico Townsend was expounding SIL's »threefold« program (Wallis and Bennett 1959:14). According to a 1956 Townsendian presentation in California, SIL's »primary function« was linguistic investigation; second, social service; and »third,« to »try to leave behind something for the spiritual welfare of the groups contacted.« (*The Register*, Santa Ana, August 6)

the Word of God,« a JAARS-Colombia man told the Matallana Commission. »If there is deculturization, it is the work of God, we do not transform anyone; the only one who can transform men is God.« (University of Antioquia 1976:36)

From this belief is derived another which often figures in presentations: that Wycliffe's only role is to offer native people an alternative, which they may accept or reject as they will. »We don't go around telling Indians not to chew coca or drink chicha, (not to commit) the naughty nine or dirty seven (sins),« another SIL-Colombia member told me. »We just tell them they have a choice. We might say, we've got this book here. When Indians read the Bible and take it to heart, they know for themselves what the Lord commands: they stop chewing the coca of their own free will... Cathcart and Lowers (a translation team) don't give the Cacua any easy answers. When someone goes to drink chicha, they don't say 'no,' but they do say 'ask God, should I do this?'«

On such grounds, in 1975–6 in Colombia and Peru, I found a number of SIL members wavering on the question of whether or not they were missionaries. Yet other evangelical missionaries, with the same beliefs, identify themselves as missionaries and realize that they rather than their Scripture will have to take responsibility for making converts. And the home Wycliffe literature constantly refers to SIL members as missionaries. It turns out that, while SIL has carefully defined the term »Bible translation« to mean something less than evangelization for the world at large, for home supporters it has done everything it can to make this term into a synonym for church-building.

In host countries SIL usually cannot afford to acknowledge one simple fact which starkly contradicts the non-sectarian claim and associated baggage. This is the fact that the Summer Institute of Linguistics is a faith mission. A faith enterprise is based on a home public which wants the world evangelized with the one, true religion in defiance of Satan, therefore a consciousness which anyone but a believer recognizes as sectarian. Not only are most SIL recruits imbued with this sectarian ambition; their finances are predicated on pursuing it and, should they change their minds about its wisdom, witch-hunting colleagues within and without SIL may hold an early Judgement Day.

Because the first faith entrepreneurs were breaking from denominational boards, they sanctified their departure with the watchword »reliance on the Lord.« In keeping with this direct line to the Almighty, Wycliffe regards prayer and its promotion as the motor of the operation. The vehicle of communication from the mission field to the home front is the prayer notice, a request for petition (concerning a problem) or praise (for the solution to a problem) linked to »need,« for further effort to help and redeem the lost. Supporters respond not only with prayer but money. Following Wycliffe's imagery, its far-flung translation teams are backed by an army of »prayer warriors« in the United States. On their prayers depend the outcome of Wycliffe's struggle against darkness.

Since each new member tends to draw money from his/her social network and the pool of potential recruits cuts across denominational boundaries, this highly sanctified tap to the grass roots has created rapid growth. Yet faith entrepreneurs have encouraged and exploited unrealistic expectations: if supporters decide their faith has been abused, as it often has, their hearts and purses snap shut. And as faith enterprise has grown up into industry as represented by the associations, supreme caution reigns. »Support« and »losing support« preoccupy the Wycliffe administration, determining what information does and does not reach home supporters.

In fear of God and financial insolvency, it has therefore come to pass that one organization has two different purposes. Various contradictory rationales have been proposed to support this position. Eunice Pike (1956:7) described herself as a member of Wycliffe when she translated the Bible, a member of the Summer Institute when she studied a language, and a member of both when she taught people how to read. John Beekman explained that he and his colleagues were officially in Mexico as scientific investigators, but that as individuals each was committed to indigenous church-building principles and translation of the Word (Hefley and Beekman 1968:151). More recently Bill Merrifield (1976:5–6), charged with the difficult task of representing SIL at scientific congresses, posited »two organizations« to distinguish the »purely scientific ends of SIL« from »WBT goals« and suggested that, in the sense that WBT activities are directed to home supporters, »it can safely be said that WBT never leaves the homeland.« SIL, on the other hand, provides »a congenial context for reaching both its own goals and those of WBT.«

The Dual Identity as Divine Privilege

Never have missionaries become scientists in greater numbers. The Camp Wycliffe/Summer Institute schools were their port of entry to the linguistic profession, its techniques and prerogatives. But Wycliffe went a step further. Judging from the way it has used linguistic credentials, young missionaries have been marched into the summer schools to emerge as something else. Not only could missionaries be scientists: they could present themselves as scientists to disguise the fact that they were also missionaries.

To justify their presentations Wycliffe spokesmen have appealed to expediency: governments would not have accepted us as missionaries, but they did accept us as linguists. This does not satisfy many evangelicals: it does not sound Scriptural. To make it Scriptural Townsend himself has addressed the question. In *Remember All The Way,* a collection of talks to the membership published in 1975, he argues that 1) God led us into the policy 2) businessmen do the same 3) SIL's host governments think it is fine, and 4) there is Biblical precedent for it. Namely, just as Jesus came out of Nazareth »disguised very effectively« as a carpenter, Wycliffe missionaries go to the field as linguists. Asks Townsend: »Was it honest for the Son of God to come down to earth and live among men without revealing who He was?« (Townsend and Pittman 1975:58–63)

Based upon this principle, in order to harness state power to an evangelical plan for Indians, Townsend taught his people to become a new kind of missionary, to some degree in practice but more in presentation. It used to be said of mission builders that they were men greatly used of God: Cameron Townsend used God, faith became his handmaiden. By self-definition recruits were servants of the Lord's will, Townsend derived his authority from the Lord, and those who did not like his methods could leave. Many more flooded into Wycliffe in obedience to God's call.

For the membership Townsend constructed a new and sanctified semantic universe, a cult of divine expediency derived from evangelical meanings but essentially privy to Wycliffe itself. Within this privileged world, members could be non-sectarian, non-ecclesiastical Christians whose task was building sectarian congregations. Crucial omission and strategic ambiguity became »waiting for the Lord's time in witnessing.« (Townsend and Pittman 1975:82) The business of moving from a SIL contract to Wycliffe church-building became an »outworking« of God's unfolding plan for salvation. Reflecting the discrepancy between the requirements of honesty and empire, Wycliffe institutionalized the plausible denial as Holy Writ.

The plausible denial has operated in the form of a shifting presentation, which in turn hinges upon the widely exploited claim to a value-free, objective science. Wycliffe learned from supposedly value-free scientists who mocked the evangelical faith: alternatively it could present itself as value-free and value-laden, stressing this or that »side« of the work according to the requiremments of the audience. »Oh,« a spokesman might declare when confronted with a discrepancy, »when I said *that* I was speaking in the *context* of the Summer Institute.«

Over the years SIL legitimated its use of words among evangelicals, and a linguistics institute became an acceptable synonym for evangelization even beyond the evangelical perimeter. But now that many social scientists are abandoning the value-free claim and challenging SIL's use of it, SIL's presentation is changing accordingly. Since everyone has values, the argument goes, cultural relativists cannot distinguish themselves from missionaries and therefore have no right to challenge SIL's use of scientific credentials. Since the SIL operation is relative like everything else, SIL is the victim of religious persecution. Cultural relativists must try to resist their prejudices against missionaries and honor their principles by suspending judgement when dealing with SIL's intervention in native societies. Contrary to the long-standing separation into scientific and spiritual roles, it may now be argued that »you have to understand us as a whole.«

Understanding Wycliffe as a whole necessarily begins with the Lord's leading. As Wycliffe was earning its linguistic credentials, it was also sanctifying itself to perform a highly sectarian operation in native communities. Convinced that the Lord's business was its own in any and every indigenous society, Wycliffe was also sure that the resistance it generated was Satanic in origin: a divine end and a Satanic opposition justified the means, misrepresentation to secure state contracts. Acceptance of the dual identity became a necessary test for recruits and from this act of faith, originally performed in Mexico, the Lord's blessing permeated the operation and its use of words.

After forty-five years it remains Wycliffe's pride and scandal that its fundamental commitments have not changed. Wycliffe continues to believe that opposition to its plans is Satanically inspired, a belief which locates Satan in and around human beings and can be used to justify anything. In particular the Satanizing practice continues to justify the genius of the Wycliffe operation, the articulation of its divine mission to the requirements of host states. The juncture of state and evangelical plans for Indians, coupled by a still vital dual identity, has been summarized in the »moral improvement« proviso of some SIL contracts: native people are to be improved to the satisfaction of both evangelicals and the host government. In the next two sections I look at moral improvement in terms of SIL's political conformism and conversion strategy.

Obey the Government

Some Wycliffe members have deep misgivings about their contracting governments and Townsend has always stressed the importance of obedience to them. As he has explained the expedient:

> *The one property which all officials have is power. Power, in its simplest form, can either be used for you or against you. The best way to keep it from being used against you is to get an official to start using it for you (Townsend and Pittman 1975:118).*

But undiscriminating submission to the state is also vulgar evangelical doctrine which he drummed into the membership, abusing Paul to the Romans 13, as »Obey the government, for God is the one who has put it there.« (Townsend and Pittman 1975:103)

In my New Testament translation, provided by an SIL-Ecuador official whose integrity I admire, the key qualifier is that »legitimate« authority is derived from God. In any case, most evangelicals and SIL members will agree that directives contrary to God's may be disobeyed. The Christian position toward government is therefore not unqualified obedience, as Townsend's statements would suggest, but a willingnes to disobey when God's laws have been transgressed. All hangs on one's opinion of what is and is not contrary to God's law, and therefore on one's political opinions. So it comes as no surprise that, where laws have barred evangelization, Wycliffe has considered its duty to evade them. But that where popular resistance to bad government has emerged, SIL members have often counselled converts that it is their duty to obey the government.

Townsend was not blind to exploitation: in 1940 he published a ringing indictment of the U.S. oil companies in Mexico. But that was an expedient gesture for the Cardenas government and now Wycliffe tends to work for rightwing dictatorships. It appears that Wycliffe judges the legitimacy of government according to a single criterion: its willingness to give Wycliffe license to evangelize the native population. If the opposition is »communist« and opposed to Christianity as represented by missions like Wycliffe, it is Godless. But so long as a regime grants Wycliffe licence to evangelize, it is in step with the divine plan and what it does to its population is of secondary importance. Neddless to say, this unconditional attitude has ingratiated SIL to governments and helped to insure that its licence will be extended. In exchange for long-term access to native people, as reinforced by a selective interpretation of Scripture, Wycliffe therefore has preached submission to regimes which not only encourage the Gospel but guarantee that many children will get to heaven sooner.

Partly because Christianity for hire is so un-Christian and basic to Townsendian wisdom, SIL claims that it has no political mission and tries to be apolitical. Spokesmen have also begun to claim that, although expatriate status (the state contract) precludes political activity (opposition to government plans), SIL sympathizes with Indian political movements. Some SIL members do. But to SIL in general it therefore must be possible to sympathize with Indian militants, typically forced to confront the state to defend their land, by Satanizing their traditionalist unity and teaching converts that it is their Christian duty to obey the state.

Conversion Strategy

The Summer Institute's defense of its non-sectarian, non-ecclesiastical Christian work among Indians is based on the doctrine of free will. According to SIL's view, it presents Indians with an alternative belief system and the Holy Spirit moves them to believe it. The individual has a choice; coercion is proscribed.

Another way of looking at SIL's work is in terms of the *patrón*-client relationship. Divorced from the connotation of debt-peonage, this relation describes most dealings between native people and outsiders. Generally speaking, missionaries try to offer Indians better terms of exchange – cheaper trade goods, western medicine, schooling – than rival *patrones*. Missionaries may succeed in setting up alliances with Indians against other colonizers and communicating with Indian religiosity, leading to evangelical movements. But here I am concerned with the claim to free choice in a *patron*-client milieu: it is a problematical claim since, while native people may be able to switch *patrones,* they face an endless series of tight double binds, one example of which is to be found in Wycliffe's stated goals.

According to a 1969 policy statement, work in a language group is completed when 1) the whole New Testament and portions of the Old have been translated and published 2) some people are capable of reading and 3) »there is a nucleus of believers to carry on by themselves or another evangelical group which will take the responsibility for establishing such a nucleus.« (WBT 1969). While SIL concedes individuals the right to accept or reject salvation, it therefore does not concede the language group's right to reject this presentation of alternatives. And while SIL says that it only establishes itself in communities with permission of the inhabitants, the Wycliffe literature indicates that, once serious resistance develops, translators often dig in and attribute the opposition to Satan.

On arrival in a community the standard two-person team typically dispenses medicine, gifts and explains that it has come to learn the language, translate and teach people to read. Bible translation may or may not be mentioned. Language informants, usually young men, are hired by the hour or day, and soon the translators ask them to come to the base.

The usually rustic but well-appointed translation bases are the hub of the operation wherever SIL has been able to set them up. Through the bases flow people recruited at the field outposts, either to work as informants or attend courses in bilingual education, occupational training and medicine. While these transients do part-time labor like gardening, the bases also depend upon permanent wage laborers drawn from the local population. Since the proprietors are white foreigners, the bases reproduce prevailing class relations from the hinterland to the U.S. metropolis.

For informants the bases are a concentrated acculturation experience, a lesson in class society (usually not the first) which emphasizes their low position and offers upward mobility. At least a few have complained of mistreatment; many want to come back. Some find the bases so exciting that, after a visit or two, they demand to learn English and be taken to the United States. Many more surrender to Christ. Judging from the Wycliffe accounts, informants usually convert in the Christian atmosphere of the base rather than at home in their own community.

While some translators would like to keep their informants clear of the bases, SIL has consciously made the non-sectarian, purely technical labor of linguistics and Bible translation at these centers a device for recruiting first converts (Wycliffe b). Once the work sessions turn from linguistics to Bible translation, which is as fast as possible, the translator is likely to »witness« to the informant. Since the relation is one to one, the translator is not breaking SIL's frequently broken regulation against preaching.* Translators may even deny that they are evangelizing, on grounds that it is the Word of God at work in the heart of the informant, not any influence on their part, wich leads to conversion.

Wycliffe calls its informant-converts the »seed« of indigenous churches. To meet native demands and promote church-building SIL has organized educational programs wherever it can. SIL-Peru's government bilingual schools, which Townsend defended against the Catholics in 1953 and on later occasions, are a model in this respect. But I discovered that SIL-Peru officials were reluctant to discuss how their branch has used the program to salary church-building cadre on government money. While the schools have always been under the nominal authority of the education ministry, SIL translators have always selected the candidates and until recently supervised the teachers at their posts.

The widely acclaimed SIL-Peru bilingual schools turned hired informant/converts into ministry-

---

* As part of the ban on ecclesiastical functions (marrying, burying, pastoring congregations) in the field, all or most SIL branches prohibit members from preaching in a language other than their own. Interpretation hinges on definition of the term »preach.« In Peru, for example, a number of translators have regularly preached to Indians at worship services or in bilingual schools. Other members told me that these translators must have been only »witnessing« or »sharing their faith,« which is allowed, or only »assisting« at a service actually led by a convert. One official admitted the rule is broken, said he wished it were observed and asked me how he could possibly enforce it. Another of SIL's non-ecclesiastical activities has been essential to church-building. This is the training of native evangelists by the group, or »Bible teaching« as opposed to preaching, or whatever difference can be construed between religious instruction in a class and in a sermon.

salaried teacher/pastors. The Wycliffe home literature described bilingual education and evangelization, the role of teacher and pastor, as insparable (Wallis and Bennett 1959:198). In 1969 an SIL-Peru linguist was making the same equation, along with a token disclaimer. The Hefleys are visiting the branch's highland Quechua teacher-training program in Ayacucho. Asks James Hefley, clearly in line with expectations: »Are all the teachers believers – real Christians?« SIL-Peru's Donald Burns replies:

> *Remember this is a government program and teachers cannot be judged on their religion. I can tell you this: all those who weren't believers when they entered have since accepted Christ. A few were evangelicals when they started. Fernando, the supervisor, was and still is a lay minister. We attend his church. Another lay preacher who came into the program had been stoned when he tried to preach in a certain village. He went back to this same place and won thirty-five people to the Lord. The program is only three years old and already we know of believers in over ten villages (Hefleys 1972:170).*

Former Ayacucho bilingual teachers remember Burns as a man who meant well, but they also say that he and his wife expected all forty or so of them to surrender to Christ and went to great lengths to encourage them, so that many did so with the conviction that their careers depended upon it.

Into jungle communities SIL's far larger lowland bilingual program channelled a massive flow of trade goods and cash, chiefly in the form of teacher salaries. The operation gave translators and their assistants a great deal of power. With the encouragement of some translators and despite the wishes of others, the informant-convert-teacher-pastor chain lengthened another link, to entrepreneur, so that SIL-Peru often rolled school, church and store into one.

Native elites are a predictable result of integration programs; for understandable reasons many Peruvian Indians have regarded SIL translators as useful friends, and they change their ways of doing things like everyone else. The issue is how and to what end SIL has been channelling their simultaneous adjustment and resistance to highway, colonization and oil projects. In 1972 SIL-Peru claimed converts in thirty-three of the thirty-six groups in which it has operated. Strings of bilingual school congregations extend along the rivers through the larger groups like the Campa and Aguaruna, among whom SIL claims thousands of converts.

As SIL was promising Peruvian governments that it would reconcile Indians to colonization, more often than not translators were fostering new relations of exchange and systems of authority with less regard for social cohesion than for the Kingdom of God. The resulting divisions will probably outlast patience with evangelical religion. The many services performed by SIL and Le Tourneau – JAARS, experiments in road-building, jungle-clearing and cattle-raising, to say nothing of the native integration programs – demonstrate that, perhaps out of the ordinary for Wycliffe, SIL-Peru has functioned as a wet-nurse of capital penetration. A limited, philanthropic and sanctified investment – as a support committee in the U.S. explains, »the dividends are eternal« (Board of Trustees 1977) – has performed preliminary tasks for profit-extracting investment, the destructiveness of which in the Amazon is now legendary and unfortunately true.

The Wycliffe literature itself shows that, far from respecting indigenous self-determination as it now claims or even individual freedom of choice, SIL-Peru has often orchestrated state power and evangelical zeal to impose its religion, foreclosing other possibilities and in particular united self-defence against corrupt government officials and colonizers. As Wycliffe quoted a Campa bilingual teacher under the eye of translator Will Kindberg:

> **»I learned to read and write through working with Mr. Kindberg. If this had not happened, none of you would be learning. You would not be able to read the Bible and to be Christians.«** (emphasis added).
> *Then Will, adding his word of instruction, said: »Jesus is in heaven, and we accept Christ's resurrection as proof that there is resurrection and He will raise us up...« After Will spoke, the students sang »Onward Christian Soldiers« in the Campa language (WBT 1963:55).*

The anecdote indicates that the problem posed by Wycliffe transcends a single model operation. Wycliffe was able to educate home supporters to this effect with a clear conscience thanks to its fundamental conviction that native people are in need of moral improvement.

Wycliffe's Response to Crisis

Until 1975 the Summer Institute had never lost a state contract. This was the year its host government in Saigon collapsed. The next year SIL was forced to leave Nigeria and Nepal, the focus of its investments in these regions. The Nepal expulsion suggests that, in a Himalayan monarchy where the only legal religion is Hinduism, SIL may have used the dual identity as it did in Peru from 1945 to 1953.*

In Latin America SIL seemed invulnerable until very recently. The Colombian government's promised phase withdrawal of SIL has never materialized. And in Peru, where SIL lost its contract in 1976, the branch won an extension and three years later a new, ten year state charter. Left-nationalist spying charges in the Andean countries nevertheless found a ready ear among right-nationalists in Brazil. Apparently in retaliation for the U.S. government's nuclear and human rights policies, in late 1977 President Geisel of Brazil and his Interior Minister Mauricio Rangel Reis decided not to renew their SIL contract and banned the branch from native communities. A year and a half later the Panamanian government announced that its SIL contract would not be renewed. The crowning blow (so far) has been the loss of the Mexican contract in September 1979. SIL's field training program in Chiapas, Mexico, the famous Jungle Camp, has been repatriated to the unjungled and Indianless hills of central Texas.

While the loss of state contracts is the most obvious sign of Wycliffe's crisis, in themselves such events only mean that a government feels it has something to gain, perhaps a useful scapegoat. The most significant development in the Colombian, Peruvian and Mexican controversies is Indian political resistance to SIL. This is a striking departure from past SIL-Latin America crises, in which Indians figured only as the spoils in patronage battles with the Catholic Church and other interested parties. While the patronage fight is ever present, the tradition-based Indian political movements strike directly against moral improvement and other forms of paternalism.

Despite many members' belief that Satan is responsible for the antagonism they generate, SIL has always tried to improve communication with native people, its response to indigenous demands and ability to overcome resistance to moral improvement. As state contracts are lost and Indians get angry, a dramatic but perhaps futile expression of the technifying, managerial tradition is SIL's new International Linguistics Center in Dallas, Texas, a virtual linguistics college affiliated to the University of Texas at Arlington. Here new translators are to be equipped with masters degrees early in their career and older members refitted.

In keeping with the logic of the linguistic approach and the wider trend in Indian management, SIL has tried to develop a more culture-sensitive approach to native resistance. To please prevailing opinion, Townsend (1936, 1955) used to claim that the linguistic approach would speed the extinction of native languages. However, he was far more interested in using the languages than destroying them. By the late 1950s SIL was discovering that ethnic disintegration did not favor indigenous church-building, and the ethnocidal zeal of some translators was appalling others. Some SIL members began to argue that Christianity should reinforce the culture rather than undermine it.

Such differences reflect an easily overlooked diversity within a regimented institution. Following the SIL courses or other training, recruits go through a rigorous screening procedure and indoctrination in Wycliffe policy at the Jungle Camps. On the mission field SIL has tried to contain the influence of native communities on translators in a variety of ways. At the bases, where social mood may fluctuate a great deal in reaction to events in the tribes or the capital, serious dissent is likely to be interpreted as a spiritual crisis, in which case appropriate supportive measures are applied. However, the machine-like, super-religious atmosphere does not necessarily preclude hot internal politics. And as a number of

---

* SIL-Nepal enjoyed the favor of officials and even King Birendra for a decade, despite the regularly enforced laws against propagating and converting to anything but Hinduism. Then in June 1976 Tribhuvan University terminated its SIL contract and members were given until the end of August to get out of the country. According to United Press International (August 14, 1976), SIL's Bible translations as well as »four specific cases of conversion« influenced the decision. The U.S. Embassy in Kathmandu cabled that SIL's religious program had been an »open secret« and the subject of long debate, having irritated conservatives in the king's palace and government (U.S. State Department 1976). During the same period the government was deciding against education in minority languages, in favor of universal Nepali education. The decision against the minority languages may have been influenced by SIL's use of them: »... since it is illegal... to evangelize or for a Nepali to change his religious beliefs,« Wycliffe later reported home, »the burden of bringing people to Christ lay entirely with the translation and distribution of the Word of God. And God used the testimony of His Word. Today there are believers in fifteen different language groups and flourishing congregations in three.« (*In Other Words* March 1977)

35

people who have spent time with Wycliffe members have learned, one or another degree of disagreement, dismay or disillusion with the program is common.

Such »protestantism« often emerges in response to rotting harvests of the Lord. While Satanic opposition will explain any reverse to some members, to others it does not. As members have to deal with the results of their own work or that of others, branch administration may give them leeway to criticize and salvage what had once been advertised at home as a Gospel triumph. Once a certain number of mistakes have been commited, some members – and perhaps an entire branch if it is small, older and no longer expanding – may be able to forgo church-building in favor of something approaching SIL's avowed non-sectarian program.

Non-conformers may stay with Wycliffe for a number or reasons. Perhaps they are still commited to linguistics and Bible translation, strictly defined as opposed to church-building. Or they feel too old to start a new career, or hope to help colleagues sensitize their practice, or believe that the only way they can help Indians defend themselves against damage inflicted by Wycliffe and others is by staying with Wycliffe. But despite possible achievements in localities, as institutional reformers they run into the wall of moral improvement, the highly sanctified commitment representing the home and state interests upon which Wycliffe depends. And while dissenters have often been forced to leave, they have been essential to Wycliffe's adaptive repertoire, as people ahead of their time whose insights are eventually adopted or coopted into the service of moral improvement.

It is not strange, therefore, that many members are responding to Wycliffe's crisis in a manner which mystifies its source. The vehicle of this reaffirmation of the founding purpose is Charismatic Renewal or Neo-Pentecostalism, an ecumenical-minded, middle class descendant of the poor people's religion which swept depressed areas of the United States around 1900 and now accounts for a large majority of Latin American Protestants. Like other fundamentalists and evangelicals, Wycliffe used to reject Pentecostalism: what poor blacks and whites regarded as baptism in the Holy Spirit could be possession by evil spirits.

By the 1960s careful Pentecostalism was becoming respectable in U.S. evangelical and Catholic churches. I am told that in 1965-6 SIL-Colombia had a Pentecostal revival, with the result that U.S. headquarters dispatched someone to restore order. But as Neo-Pentecostalism became acceptable in the United States, worry over repercussions in the support base slackened. By 1972 most of SIL-Peru was turning Charismatic (Buckingham 1974: 138–61). More recently Wycliffe's Hugh Steven (1974,1978) has described SIL Pentecostal experiences in the Philippines and Brazil.

It may be possible for Charismatic Renewal to coexist with a critical spirit toward a sanctified institution like Wycliffe. However, it usually does not. Especially during crisis, increased consciousness of the Spirit leads to increased consciousness of Satan. In Wycliffe's most recent Charismatic account (Steven 1978), Satan is constantly attacking the translators and their state of faith seems more at issue than redemption of the Indians. Thanks to Wycliffe's sanctification of itself, renewed faith in Christ is very difficult to separate from renewed faith in Wycliffe. And where Wycliffe is under assault, increased consciousness of spiritual warfare is making it easier to blame everything on anthropologists and communists.

Basic Concepts

In a necessary readjustment between moral improvement, Wycliffe expansion and changing political conditions, the ongoing controversies have forced SIL to try to relegitimate itself as it did with the 1953 crisis in Peru. Although the distinction between SIL's scientific and Wycliffe's spiritual purposes may be fading in favor of »holism,« the dual identity remains in the foundation because in most countries SIL cannot afford to give it up. The credibility of the new presentation – stress on culture relativism, indigenous self-determination, the alternative, political neutrality – matters less than SIL's entrenched position with host governments and the advantages which inevitably accrue.

Like the claim to apolitical philanthropy, SIL's culture enhancing arguments have served for inhouse consumption by troubled translators as well as perimeter defense. Reflecting SIL's response to indigenous resistance, what was originally presented as a program to destroy native language and culture now appears to Wycliffe as a program which strengthens them. This contention, that Wycliffe both transforms and fortifies language and culture through the Word, is based upon an evangelical version of cultural relativism. Ex-SIL President Kenneth Pike may have been the first to make the argument in print, in 1962:

> The missionary must learn that a moral system, present in every culture, cannot be smashed without breaking a control system blessed of God to preserve tribes from chaos. Christianity as a moral system should operate like a yeast, entering a culture quietly, transforming its institutions, changing their forms to contribute more effectively to the culture. Christianity was not designed to destroy the individuality of individuals or of cultures. Just as a person unified with and transformed by Christ still lives, so should a culture be infused with the fruits of the Spirit to change by the power of God harshness to kindness, and dirtiness to cleanliness.

Many SIL translators did not take the hint. By 1976 spokespersons were making startling claims which did not reflect the practice of many of their colleagues.

An example of this confusion, between SIL's record and projects for reforming SIL, is the paper presented by three SIL-Peru representatives at Paris in 1976. According to the linguists, SIL-Peru members bring what might appear to be relativist criteria to their work, analyzing culture traits in terms of positive and negative values for the culture and its component individuals. When confronted by a negative culture trait, SIL members present alternatives and permit the people to make their own decision. In any case, SIL-Peru maintains »careful impartiality in regard to religious doctrines« and »does not lend assistance to any economic system.« (Loos et al 1976:25,39).

Given the impossibility that Amazonian Indians be left alone, the authors believe that:

> it is necessary to find an alternative to help (indigenous people) retain their identity inside a viable culture... whose values can survive the culture contact (Loos et al 1976:7).

This alternative is of course Christianity. Unfortunately, the authors are rather vague about what they mean by Christianity, to the point that their »basic concepts« which SIL members bring to the field do not include the Wycliffe Statement of Doctrine. This particular set of concepts is binding on all members and, with its implications, would seem highly relevant to their goals for indigenous peoples, at least as these have been explained to home supporters. So long as SIL remains true to this prior commitment, it must be prepared to argue that it is desirable to convert members of all indigenous societies to evangelical Christianity. Since Christianity as understood by most SIL members implies cross-cultural constants, such as a definitive end to belief in the traditional spirit world, SIL must be prepared to argue that these traits can be demonstrated to be negative in all indigenous societies. And since most evangelicals believe that all human beings must be reached by the Gospel but that not all will be saved, SIL must also be prepared to argue that it is desirable to introduce an ideological division into each indigenous society.

This is quite a program. It is only defensible in terms of two highly sectarian, ethnocentric assumptions: 1) that unlike all other belief systems, Wycliffe's version of Christianity is a divine essence or yeast above culture, and 2) that society can be reduced to component individuals, to the point that society and culture become ephemeral categories.

Let us look at the second point in more detail. While Wycliffe's respect for native people abstracted from their society (»individuals«) may be high, officially sanctioned respect for their culture is quite limited, extending only to those features deemed compatible with Christianity. The model translator poses »alternatives« not to collectivities but to individuals, so that Wycliffe has been using a parochial (but in the U.S. easily defended) definition of freedom and dignity to justify itself. In effect, Wycliffe has been subverting the range of choices available within every culture with its own, highly individualist and divisive option: saved or damned. SIL has offered native communities a choice between ideological dissension and fighting SIL.

Because this scheme is irreconcilable with respect for indigenous cultures, Wycliffe is occasionally tempted to »kill« culture as a category so that it cannot be accused of degrading or destroying it. SIL's only business is »liberation.« As SIL's anthropological coordinator explained recently:

> We are interested in the temporal liberation of indigenous peoples. The emphasis here is on people rather than upon cultures. Our study of Scripture leads us to accept life as better... than death, and our ontology leads us to believe that such states can only have metaphorical reference to other than biological objects. We thus reject genocide as wrong and ethnocide as a myth. People die, but cultures do not; they change (Merrifield 1976:7).

Following the same logic, a Wycliffe friend has dismissed the »death of a culture« as an analogy applied to an abstraction. In all fairness it must be pointed out that, since »individual« is a recent construction of which the Apostles themselves must have been ignorant, a »reborn individual« may be regarded as an abstraction qualified by an analogy. Needless to say, Wycliffe's ontology – what »really is« – shows no sign of admitting that a recent and dominant mode of property and exchange, whose social expression is the »individual« as we presently know it, is something less than the divine plan.

Conclusion

To Wycliffe, indigenous self-determination and apolitical philanthropy are saturated by moral improvement, a program reflecting the plans of states and evangelicals for native people. Indeed, Wycliffe's three pillars of wisdom may be considered the dual identity, the state contract and the divine mission, the last of which bears an uncertain relation to God's Word. The dual identity has dissembled the divine mission; the divine mission has sanctified the dual identity; and the two are now inseparable thanks to the state contracts.

The compatibility of Christianity and science, the relativity of belief systems, scarcely explain Wycliffe's performance. Were SIL an introversionist sect, dedicated to its own salvation, it would have the right to perform any religious exercise it cared, to itself. But Wycliffe has definite religious and political goals for other people. It has used linguistic credentials to mystify these objectives, exploiting the relativity of language to harness state power to the imposition of its, once again absolute, truth on native people.

SIL continues to make misleading claims, defend its program with an irrefutable faith and Satanize opponents. Far from a lapse of good behavior, to many members this is an expression of the highest morality because SIL is a faith mission. As a faith mission, SIL necessarily considers itself infallible concerning central matters; despite an unprecedented experience with native peoples, it cannot permit the unregenerate to endanger its founding postulates. In conjunction with the University of Texas at Arlington, therefore, SIL's International Linguistics Center is producing the translators for that push into hundreds more native languages around the world. New vistas are opening in Africa.

Bibliography

Board of Trustees, International Linguistics Center, Inc.
1977 »What One Cause of International Importance Has Brought Us Together,« pamphlet, Dallas, Texas.

Brinton, Daniel G.
1884 *A Grammar of the Cakchiquel Language of Guatemala,* Philadelphia: American Philosophical Society.

Buckingham, Jamie
1974 *Into the Glory,* Plainfield, New Jersey: Logos International.

Dame, Lawrence
1968 *Maya Mission,* New York: Doubleday

Hefley, James C.
1970 *Aaron Saenz, Mexico's Revolutionary Capitalist,* Waco, Texas: Word Books.

Hefley, James C. and Beekman, John
1968 *Peril By Choice,* Grand Rapids: Zondervan.

Hefley, James and Hefley, Marti
1972 *Dawn Over Amazonia,* Waco, Texas: Word Books
1974 *Uncle Cam,* Waco, Texas: Word Books

Le Tourneau, Robert Gilmour
1960 *Mover of Men and Mountains,* Chicago: Moody Press

Loos, Eugene E. and Davis, Patricia and Wise, Mary Ruth
1976 »El cambio cultural y el desarollo integral de la persona: Exposición de la filosofía y los metodos del Instituto Lingüistico de Verano en el Peru,« mimeo, Yarinacocha: SIL

Merrifield, William R.
1976 »Anthropology, Ethnocide and Bible Translation,« mimeo, paper read at the Anthropological Symposium of the American Scientific Affiliation, August 23, Wheaton, Illinois
1977 »On the Ethics of Christian Mission,« mimeo, paper read at the annual meeting of the American Anthropological Association, November 29–December 3, Houston, Texas
1978 »Education for Minority Language Groups,« mimeo, paper read at the symposium »Amazonia: Extinction or Survival,« April 18–22, Madison, Wisconsin

Miller, Carolyn Paine
1977 *Captured!* Chappaqua, New York: Christian Herald Books

Moser, Brian
1971 »War of the Gods,« Disappearing Worlds Series, London: Granada Television

Pike, Eunice V.
1956 *Not Alone,* Chicago: Moody Press

Pike, Kenneth
1962 *With Heart and Mind,* Grand Rapids, Michigan: Eerdmans

Pioneer Mission Agency
1926–1950 Pioneer News, Philadelphia
1936–1940 Camp Wycliffe Chronicle,
Philadelphia Rembao, Alberto
1942 Outlook in Mexico, New York: Friendship Press

Saenz, Moises
1936 *Carapan,* Lima: Libreria y Imprenta Gil

Steven, Hugh
1974 *It Takes Time to Love,* Huntington Beach, California: WBT
1978 *To the Ends of the Earth,* Chappaqua, New York: Christian Herald Books

Townsend, William Cameron
1920 »The Guatemalan Indian and the San Antonio Mission Station,« September 15, Paris and Dallas, Texas, Central American Mission: Central American Bulletin
1924 »A Great Cakchiquel Evangelist,« serial, July 15–January 15, 1925, Central American Mission: Central American Bulletin
1936 »Tolo, the Volcano's Son,« serial, April–October, Philadelphia: Revelation magazine
1940 The Truth About Mexico's Oil as observed by W. Cameron Townsend, Los Angeles: Inter-American Fellowship
1950 »Barriers Shattered by Linguistic Approach,« June, WBT: Translation
1955 »Discurso del Senor Doctor Guillermo Townsend,« *Dos Lustros Entre Los Selvicolas,* Lima: SIL

Townsend, William Cameron and Pittman, Richard S.
1975 *Remember All The Way,* Huntington Beach, California: WBT

U.S. State Department
1976 cable, U.S. Embassy-Kathmandu to State Department, June 8, released to author under Freedom of Information Act, May 1979

University of Antioquia
1976 *»El Instituto Lingüístico de Verano«* (in Colombia), anthology, Department of Anthropology, Boletin 15, Vol. 4, Medellín: Antropologia

Wallis, Ethel.E. and Bennett, Mary A.
1959 *Two Thousand Tongues To Go,* New York: Harper and Row

Wycliffe Bible Translators (Glendale, Santa Ana and Huntington Beach, California)
1943–1975 Translation, irregular, then bimonthly
1975– In Other Words, monthly
1963 Who Brought The Word
1969 »1967–69 Corporation Conference Report,« October-December, Translation
1972 Language and Faith
a »Introduction to the Policies and Practicies of WBT,« no date but distributed 1977
b »The Wycliffe File: Inside Information About WBT, Inc.,« no date but distributed 1977
c »Statement of Doctrine, WBT, Inc.,« no date but distributed 1977.

*The HCJB radiostation
in Quito, Ecuador.
Copyright: René Böll.*

*Kayapa house, Pacific Ecuador.
Copyright: René Böll.*

Fulfilling The Mission:
North American Evangelism in Ecuador

by SCOTT S. ROBINSON

Three generations of America's finest stock have been preaching a peculiarly anachronistic Christian gospel to Latin America and the Third World at large. This is a mitigating and revelatory brand of faith, born of nineteenth century social frustrations, and bent upon changing the world through mass religious conversion. This evangelical message is curiously American in the moral issues it embraces as well as the social system it represents. It is ideologically opposed to confronting the issues of social injustice and capitalist exploitation. And recently, during the Nixon-Ford hegemony in United States politics, evangelical Christianity began to collaborate more openly with strategic aspects of the »Pax Americana« throughout the world.

Darcy Ribeiro once remarked: »United States exude a very special messianism« (personal comunication, Barbados Symposium, 1971), quite apparent in the history of evangelical endeavors throughout Latin America. For example, over the years thousands of families have made their »commitment to God's work« and left the United States for their foreign »mission«. In fact, the numbers multiplied significantly during the heady climax years of the American empire, until defeat in Vietnam (See Table I). Elaborate institutional apparata have been erected to provide logistical support for these families, a few unmarried women, and increasingly nowadays, the children of the former who are not able to adjust to a continental American society they no longer understand nor enjoy. Three generations' work has made a profound impact upon those societies where missionaries have been busy building their churches, tending school, and counselling converts in the midst of the evolving class conflicts that shape their lives.

Table I

Number of North American Missionaries (Canadian and U.S.) working abroad	Year
29,380	1959
35,800	1967
34,460	1969
35,070	1973

Source: **Mission Handbook; North American Protestant Ministries Overseas,** 10th ed., Monrovia, California, MARC, 1973, p.81.

In this essay I focus on the sociology of evangelical missionary groups, historically recruited on the basis of faith and kinship, moving abroad, settling down and administering native societies' access to the market system and the emerging national polity. The case in point is Ecuador. Here, as elsewhere, this process unfolded as another expression of imperial strategies born of western capitalism's increasingly sophisticated instruments of resource management and political influence. On balance, evangelism and capitalism have evolved together throughout the Third World. But this has taken place more because of profound changes inside American society, rather than due to any aggressive, overarching imperial design.

An ideology – a set of blinders on social reality – is present in any social expression of organized religious commitment. Within the organized churches these canons of judgments along with a corpus of doctrine, constitute a theology. Inside American evangelical Protestantism since the turn of the century there evolved a theology justifying the organization of resources and evangelical effervescence by missio-

Scott S. Robinson was born 1941 at Walla Walla, Washington, USA. Educated at Occidental College, B.A. in Political Science; Ph.D. in Social Anthropology, Cornell University and Co-signer of the Declaration of Barbados, 1971; currently member of the Board, CADAL, Mexico; and partner in Grupo Cine Labor, documentary filmmakers.

nary exporting churches. What is consistently absent, however, from these doctrinal discussions is any reference to the political and social implications of missions and missionary work. Evangelical Protestantism traditionally has denied any link between social change and the needs of its faithful. Instead, a diluted millenarianism has provided the rationale for the missionary activities sketched in this essay.

There is an undeniable, synchronous link between evangelical missionary efforts and United States strategic interests. The Cold War years of the 1950's firmly associated the devil's work with the »communists and fellow travellers that ferry evil to the innocent«. When the Republican Party returned to power under Richard Nixon's authoritarian leadership, it was only natural that the simplistic rhetoric of a prior decade would be instrumental in convincing the religious groups to perform covert intelligence tasks, particulary in areas where strategic petroleum and mineral resources abound. The far right of Nixon's Republican Party had impressive strength in Southern California and rural areas where many missionary organizations have their home offices and recruit their staffs (e.g. The Wycliffe Bible Society is headquartered in Santa Ana, California). Nixon and the Republican elders understood, as did members of the American missionary elite, that the Pax Americana has always been blessed by an anticommunist God.

A market system links the society that produces missionaries with those regions and communities where they work. What is too often overlooked, however, are the set of social relations and economic transactions born of industrialism that evoked changes in rural America as significant as those occurring presently in the strategic, back-country portions of nations such as Ecuador. American missionaries themselves are products of a class struggle and political process which the evangelical mission abroad is now bent upon denying. The frustrated millenia of American evangelicals have been projected upon tribal and native peasant societies whose political liberation has been jeopardized in the doing. The defensively »nonpolitical« posturing of evangelicals at home effectively disguises their quest for power and influence abroad.

From whence came the majority of American evangelical missionaries is an historical situation ironically akin to that of their Ecuadorean converts. Of course, these separate conditions existed at two very distinct moments on the spectra of social evolution. Nevertheless, in both societies – the rural United States and Ecuador – a peasant economy has been transformed rapidly by the rationalization of the market and a corresponding concentration of wealth and resources in fewer hands. This process unfailingly generates a propensity for a collective religious response to the unsatisfactory old order; and the pace of change itself redefines a people's perception of their situation and destiny.

In rural America, the small, white and religious communities of farmers and petty merchants suffered dearly at the hands of aggressive railroads, usurious eastern bankers, and »plutocrats«, in fact, all manner of scoundrels. The Populist movement of 1890–92 was a legitimate and widespread revolt that floundered for lack of enduring alliances with urban working class groups. And presently, the grandchildren of some of those who participated in this profound expression of social protest (perhaps unknowingly) labor to prevent Ecuadorean *campesinos* from uniting with the progressive labor movement. Such an alliance would undoubtedly overturn the Ecuadorean ruling class' monopoly on politics and for that reason has been combated strenuously by the United States and local interests since the possibility emerged.

In the United States, the economic upswing after the severe »slump« of 1893 was fed in some measure by the buoyant prosperity of the avowedly imperialist Spanish American War and the period thereafter. At this time, the first missionary ventures in Ecuador took place (See Table II). Mid-American peasant family farms were abruptly integrated into the expanding market system. Suddenly, supply and demand for agricultural commodities affected the fortunes of entire families, formerly self-reliant. This loss of autarky certainly found some expression in the religious idiom. Certainly, too, the railroad boom, and later the automobile, provoked many changes in the rhythm of social life and patterns of morality in the frontier rural America of that day. The stresses and anxieties born of shifting family ties and work habits contributed to a religious movement theologically and emotionally committed to redemption and a simplified millenarian solution to secular *angst*. The revivalist churches preached a ready and simplistic answer to people's problems (as they do today) and the fervor of their appeal matched the heady *communitas* of belonging. With legendary charisma, a few preachers mounted campaigns to redeem the morally dispossessed; and their nation, America, once saved, could save the world in turn.

One major determinant of the impetus for »devoting one's life to mission« was the failure of the fervent but politically naive populist surge of the 1890's and thereafter. As is often the case in American populism, the rhetoric outdistanced the results. Neither the Progressive Movement nor the National Farmer's Union, both twentieth century phenomena, encapsulated such fervor again. Unrequited hopes were soothed and reinforced by faith in a New Day whose achievement could be accelerated by »spreading the word of God« abroad where the devil's advance was an immediate challenge to all. This was tactically easier, of course, than denouncing the railroads and plutocrats at home. After all, faith led to material progress, as the missionary photographs evinced. Everyone could appreciate the flourishing missions and a steady growth in the newly converted flocks. It is significant that the first major export of missionaries occurred in 1896 and 1897 (see Table II), immediately after the frustrated populist movement. With exemplary sacrifice many small rural churches financed foreign missions employing their few resources and available theological justifications fully capable of converting a political defeat into a socially redeeming act.

Table II

| Organization name | Year Began Work | Personnel | | Institutions | | | | | | |
		Total Now	New 71/72	Hos-pital	Clinic	Msn. Sch.	Natl. Sch.	Sem-inary	Radio /TV	Other
ECUADOR Population 6,500,000										
Assemblies of God – Division of Foreign Missions	NR	10						1		
Berean Mission, Inc.	1959	4								
Campus Crusade for Christ International – Overseas Department	1965	NR								
Child Evangelism Fellowship, Inc.	1953	3	2							
Christian and Missionary Alliance Foreign Department	1897	60	10		7	1		1		
Church of The Brethren – Worl Ministries Commission	1942	2								
Church of The Nazarene, General Board – Department of World Missions	1972	2								
Churches of Christ	1966	15							1	
Evangelical Covenant Church of America – Board of World Mission	1947	12	6							
Fellowship of Independent Missions	1967	3	2		1					
General Conf. of The Mennonite Brethren Chs., Board of Msns. and Services	1953	3								
General Conf. of Seventh Day Adventists	NR	8								
Gospel Missionary Union	1896	69	9		2				3	
International Church of The Foursquare Gospel – Foreign Department	1956	4								
International Students, Inc.	1968	0			1					
Jungle Aviation and Radio Serv., Inc., Div. of Wycliffe Bible Translators	1954	NR								
Mennonite Church – Mennonite Board of Missions	1969	2								
Mission Aviation Fellowship	1948	4								
Mission Church – Missionary Church, Overseas Missions Department	1945	10	3		1		1			
OMS International, Inc.	1952	19	7		1					
Presbyterian Church in The United States – Board of World Missions	1946	2	2							
Protestant Episcopal Chruch in The U.S.A., Sec. for Jurisdctnl. Relations	1963	2	1							
Slavic Gospel Association	NR	6								
Southern Baptist Convention – Foreign Mission Board	1950	33			1		6	2		
United Methodist Church – World Division of Bd. of Global Ministries	NR	2								
United Pentecostal Church International – Foreign Missions Division	NR	4					1			
United Presbyterian Church in The U.S.A. – Program Agency	1945	2	4					1		
World Mission Prayer League, Inc.	1951	20	7				1	1		
World Radio Missionary Fellowship, Inc. (HJCB)	1931	166	20	2		1			2	
Wycliffe Bible Translators, Inc.	1953	83								
Totals		554	73	2	14	2	9	6	6	
U.S. Roman Catholic Personnel		26								

Mission Handbook: North American Protestant Ministries Overseas (10th ed.) (Monrovia, California: MARC, 1973).

Evangelicals multiplied by conversion as well as the steady growth of families through the years. Working class urban communities shared some of this religious ecstasy, but on balance, the source of this faith, this style of religious rhetoric and organization, remained in small, agricultural towns and villages all over the United States and Canada.

During and after the First World War many of these families as well as individuals were obliged to migrate to the cities. Urban evangelical churches grew around individual pastors' capacity to relate their preaching to their flocks' adjustment to urban life and a perceptible longing for an abandoned yet simpler past. The sinful urban experience provoked a new phase of reflection among theologically conservative protestants. Their writings focus on justifications of faith in trying moments of Christian witness, rather than the underlying social causes of urbanization and industrialization. It should come as no surprise, then, that Rural America lives and longs for a variety of religious and social experiences at odds with Urban America.

The urban experience of working people at the century's turn, on the other hand, was more often grim and downright oppressive. Women and child labor laws had yet to be enacted in the United States. In these working conditions, Eugene Debs wrenched forth a Socialist Party that became a genuine threat to capital interests in the America prior to World War I. This movement in alliance with rural populist groups took some electoral victories – in Oklahoma and North Dakota, for example – and enshrined an idiom of progressive politics peculiarly American. Except for the oft-cited successes, the American socialist movement languished for lack of firm alliances and the repressive power of a State at war.

As might be expected, the Protestant churches and the Catholics in the wake of the astonishingly radical papal encyclical, *Rerum Novarum* (1891), developed a theological commitment to social justice generally in accord with the principles of the formative labor movement. That these attempts at ideological vanguardism were part of a strategy to co-opt the cutting edge of the movement hardly needs mention. Nevertheless, after the war, Raushenburch's *Social Gospel* and Catholic financed socialist tracts sustained a movement beleaguered and shrunken by the godless prosperity of the 1920's.

Evangelicals, whose institutions took no active part in the labor movement, directed their energies toward expansion of their churches, at home and abroad. Their growth in numbers became a joyous index of their faith's strength. The »social question«, however, went unexamined and unattended. The liberal social justice theologians of the day, many teaching in the prominent urban seminaries (e.g. Union, Princeton, Pacific) played an exegetical role in the progressive movement of the epoch. Although justice was the watchword of this well-meaning rhetoric, it was, ironically enough, the evangelist churches that succoured the weary Wobblies on the dock, in the California fields and packing plants; and later, beleaguered CIO strikers elsewhere. The evangelical churches were of the people, whereas the liberal mainline protestant denominations postured for the people. Neither group, however, gave attention to the long range consequences of their missionary endeavors already well underway by the 1930's.

In retrospect we can appreciate how the mainstream and evangelical churches gradually assumed a strategic role in the Third World as their missions grew in size, budgets and converts. They were the respectable, white foreigners; those with »know-how« from abroad. Perhaps their power and apparent wealth derived from their god? Missionaries capitalized upon this new, ascribed status and expanded their missions with heroic stamina and the consequent testimony to faith's reward. Most importantly, however, these religious congregations became the only permanent organizations among a severely oppressed peasantry or in the remotest regions of a continent or country. In many vast regions they built the infrastructure for the post World War II era of national integration.

This historic process has been poorly documented, lengthy and expensive. Nowhere is its impact on society more open to analysis than in Ecuador. And why? Because this small nation contains a microcosm of social conflicts in different habitats – coastal plain, Andean Sierra and tropical rain forest, where the foreign missionary apparatus has invested heavily since early in the century. Also, the link between the missionary establishment's growth and United States strategic interests has taken on added significance in the light of Ecuador's substantial petroleum resources.

Since the moral demise and demystification of the United States Peace Corps in the nationalist South American states during the late 1960's, the need for local level information about social conflicts and the efficacy of government programs has been reported by the reliable and patriotic missionaries whose knowledge of the terrain is extensive and whose local alliances are varied. Missionaries have become essential informants to the American intelligence community.

Evangelical churches were established under the aegis of missionaries from the United States and

44

Canada at a time when North American capital was beginning to trickle into agricultural and mineral extraction ventures in several tropical and Andean nations. In Ecuador, for example, the liberal and anticlerical regime of Eloy Alfaro held the Church of Rome in check so that Protestant missionaries could freely settle and proselytize, beginning at the century's turn. Indeed liberal anticlericalism went so far as to imply the culturally redeeming qualities associated with evangelical missionaries' presence and travail. At the same time, however, the initial capitalist monoculture investments began reshaping land tenure patterns and peasant work habits throughout the coastal plain, and much later in the Sierra, provoking social conditions propitious for religious conversion.

»White missionaries« sharing a respected, forthright and industrious ethic were allowed to enter the country through the aid of anticlerical sentiments at large among the ruling coastal liberals. In rural highland provinces, the neo-feudal order, managed by propertied and racist »gente decente« was unable to prevent the settling of gringo missionaries along the rail link to Quito. In a measure, the racism and rigid social stratification of the Sierra facilitated the entrance of white foreigners. However, to have arrived and thrived in Ecuador is not necessarily a tribute to the shrewdness of a few evangelicals; rather, the matter rests in the context of a long-standing dispute between the Catholic Church, its clergy and faithful, and a political movement, Liberal in a word, anchored by its opposition to clerical privilege, ecclesiastical property and meddling in affairs of state. This liberalism endorsed the importation of missionaries as well as a laissez faire economic doctrine in harmony with a need for raw materials and markets in the burgeoning capital centers of fin de siecle imperialist expansion. Without recognizing it nor understanding why, the missionaries became the vanguard of the imperial order.

From Guayaquil, up the rivers of the tropical Guayas basin and along the railway corridor through the Sierra to Quito and Ibarra, there ventured forth evangelical missionaries bent on founding missions. There members grew, as did the size and comfort of their »compounds«. Many denominations were represented (see Table II), and they were united in their zeal, if not their methods and brands of faith. Disenchanted with the rapid pace of change in their rural villages and small cities of the industrializing North American prairie these religious pioneers staked a claim in accord with their inherited logic of manifest destiny and New Testament admonitions. As the expanding market system changed their lives, so they settled into and initiated a social process destined to alter the lives of their potential converts.

Small villages of Quichua campesions, huasipungueros, yanaperos, and small holders subsisted next to medium and large tracts of the best lands, owned by »blancos« and the established Church. Their mode of production was (and remains) precapitalist; their ritual life focused on assuaging the unpredictability of a harsh mother nature whose fortuitous whims guide the fertility of the human farming effort. The »cristos católicos« of the blancos were clearly a recent importation, whose alleged potency was diminished by the demeaning slavery imposed by their apologists, tonsured and secular. How was the justicia of the Christians to be reconciled with the stratified social order they had erected and violently administered? There were intelligent and sensitive Runakuna who perceived these contradictions; undoubtedly, some were receptive to an alternative gospel for redemption via organization and pious work, preached by tenacious and messianic gringos. These self-deported souls established their beachhead, learned Quichua and labored in the Lord's fields, garnering new believers. Slowly, congregations grew.

By the 1940's, there were several thriving Mission stations scattered throughout the coastal towns and in all the highland provinces. But no institution covered the vast tribal territories. Many evangelical churches established missions in the Sierra. I assume the Wycliffe organization decided to respect their colleagues' territoriality, their secular space so to speak, and not concentrate efforts in the Sierra. As a general policy, the SIL decided, for reasons yet unknown, to concentrate their investment and efforts in Ecuador among the tribal peoples of the tropical lowlands. On balance, this was true of SIL policy throughout South America.

SIL linguists did maintain, however, one translation team in a highland Quichua community, although there were other evangelical translators working simultaneously. There seems, in hindsight, something compelling about the possibility of being the first to bring an obscure tribal language into the purview of western sapience. Perhaps, though, there is another reason for this choice of audience, one which is commendably shrewd: the similarities of tribal precapitalist modes of production understandably generate similarities in cosmology and religious ideology that would facilitate a common evangelical strategy. This could also mean that team work could be mutually supportive because all SIL missionary families faced a similar challenge. Certainly, it was culturally shocking to be radically displaced from industrial society to the tribal. This was, perhaps, faith's major test.

Table III

Natural Resources and Extractive Corporations Common to SIL Tribes in Ecuador.

Tribe	Resources	Corporations
Kayapa (Pacific)	Timber	Boise Cascade (USA) Georgia Pacific (USA)
Colorado (Pacific)	Coffee Cacao	no data
Kofan	Petroleum	Texaco-Gulf (USA)
Siona	Petroleum	Texaco-Gulf (USA)
Secoya	Petroleum	no data
Huarani (Auca)	Petroleum	Texaco-Gulf (USA) Others
Shuara	Petroleum	no data
Quichua	Cattle Tea	no data

Did SIL.s founder, William Camaron Townsend, a crafty Yankee conservative, and his staff »know about« the bountiful natural ressources of Aamazonia, and Ecuador in paticular? (See Table III). Of course they did. Officers of the Office of Strategic Services (OSS), the predecessor of the Central Intelligence Agency (CIA) in the United States government, had reconnoitered the Amazon basin during the early part of the Second World War (1941-1943). They estimated and projected the existence of rubber, timber, minerals and petroleum. In Ecuador, of course, the Royal Dutch Shell Petroleum Co. already had drilled three test wells in 1939, before the outbreak of the war, and geologists had scouted the *oriente* in the 1920's (Ferndon 1947). As might be expected, no Ecuadorean institution, public or private, had invested in exploiting the region's economic worth. Capital scarce Ecuador faithfully reflects, then and now, the imperial condition: foreign capital interests exploiting resources and consumers. But the missionaries, not understanding these terms nor voicing a critique of this social process, settled in »sync« with same. The growth of the missionary apparatus coincides with Ecuador's insertion into orbit within the international capitalist system.

This process accelerated during the Second World War. The war transformed American society in a fashion only hindsight can perceive. For the first time in the United States significant numbers of men, rarely women, had learned to fly. The Army Air Corps trained thousands of pilots. They practised »shooting landings« at small strips scraped off the desert of Arizona, Texas and California. Some of these pilots were evangelical Christians. Light, single engine reconnaisance aircraft, reliable and easy to maintain, were developed for the Pacific theatre, where the war against Japan waged on atolls and across highland New Guinea. Jungle airstrips were part of one's training program, in theory if not in fact. Missionaries and investors began to fly.

After the war, the urgency of retaining hegemony over tropical regions, especially Amazonia, disappeared. But those government agencies entrusted with responsibility for global resource monitoring continued and in fact, grew as the Cold War evolved. SIL founder Townsend unquestionably consulted with the State Department and the intelligence network of »old boys« which reigned supreme at the time. It does not require too much imagination to appreciate the long range strategic value of having listening posts and political monitoring instruments in remote resource-rich areas of the Free World. This was when SIL leadership, under Townsend, designed today's infrastructure and cornerstones were blessed. In Ecuador, there was a shrewd consolidation of an earlier generation's toil. Many war veterans and their families strengthened skeleton mission staffs and more resources were available from a United States backing in post-war prosperity and ambivalently contemplating its new found global responsibilities. More precisely, this was when the battle with godless communism began.

Slowly, beginning in 1948, the SIL built modest missions, one by one, as means permitted and personnel recruited, throughout Amazonia, including by 1953 lowland Ecuador. Quite expectably, SIL an organization with considerable capital and technology at its disposition, constructed Little American villages whenever a country base was located. From Limoncocha, nestled on a lakeside bluff with its DC-3 airstrip paralleling the equatorial sun, SIL families fanned out to the Ecuadorean tribes. New Testament translations began, missionary children were born at the HCJB hospitals, families were raised in the forest; one could observe blond boys of thirteen racing down forest hunting trails, clad in *cushmas*, babling to their Kofan or Secoya age mates. A form of adolescent tribalism that evaporated with maturity and boarding school in Quito; a way of life so removed from »home« it was acceptable.

Children's schooling at »Limon« or in Quito meant leaving the village and the tribe only to return on religious holidays like Christmas and Easter. In their absence, believers, a sizeable group in most cases after fifteen years of work, led the Sunday prayer meetings, dispensed medicines and kept in weekly radio contact with the missionary family. Medical emergencies were reported by radio and Heliocouriers were dispatched for patients destined for the Limoncocha clinic or the Vozandes hospitals. Fixed band transistorized receivers were sold at »cost« to believers who then became part of the HCJB captive listening audience. Deep friendships grew and the missionaries' base villages were well tended in their medical, but not material needs. SIL social and economic »development« programs always had a low priority and still lower budgets.

The frontier economy of advancing industrial capitalism grew slowly and then, with the completion of trunk roads, suddenly evolved into a society where money and favors bought things, people and significant policy changes. In this scenario tribespeople did not count, they were non-people »Aucas« in a word, beyond civilization and official concern; what happened to them didn't matter. In similar frontier conditions, the American missionaries' grandfathers had pacified the American West and placed the »Indians« on reservations. Now their grandchildren in the service of the same 19th century God proposed *reservas* for the Shuara and Aucas. Imagine Ecuadorean native *»reservas«,* a legal entity, administered in effect by SIL missionaries; one hundred years later, things remained the same.

Two brief cases exemplify the clever and complex dimensions of contemporary American evangelical missionary strategies in Ecuador. These combine education, media and medicine. The Summer Institute of Linguistics' teaching of the »savage Aucas« and the Vozandes media and medical empire are sufficient testimonies to the penetration of the missionary apparatus in Ecuadorean society and politics. Unquestionably, in both cases, »taking Christ's mission to the heathen« has been a task suitably full of heroism, shrewd planning, sub-rosa diplomatic support and just plain good public relations. For example, in the *oriente* tropical lowlands, by attenuating the Ecuadorean military's paranoia with regards to territorial security (remember the Peruvian's successful flash invasion of 1940–41?) and by investing in a lengthy tribal pacification program, the SIL fulfilled the strategic task of penetrating and controlling formerly remote and valuable portions of the national trust (See Table III). Such has been the case throughout Ecuador where the Colorado, Kayapa, Shuara, Auca, Quichua, Kofan, Siona and Secoya peoples are being acculturated via bilingual education system established by contract with the SIL and the Ecuadorean Ministry of Education. This pattern of activities can be observed in neighboring countries as well, as other papers in this volume testify.

Huarani (Auca is Quichua for savage) aggression directed against their neighbors, *mestizos* and natives, has earned them a special place in the annals of the Civilization Process. In many ways, Auca evangelization exhibits the model behavior of the Christian missionary: undaunted faith; perserverance against formidable odds (the SIL missionary, Rachel Saint, learned to speak and write their language using an informant who had been taken prisoner in a retaliatory raid on an Auca frontier settlement years before); a devoted preparation of linguistic materials; and well-plotted efforts to overcome the work of the devil by sabotaging his barriers and that of the competition.

The Capuchin friars have been entrusted with Auca souls, in accord with the ecclesiastical domains of tropical South America. They are today elderly Spanish Basque priests and brothers who have settled in their mission base at Coca, Napo Province. They maintain four smaller mission schools along the lower Napo River near the Peruvian broder. This missionary enterprise has fostered the expansion of the incipient capitalist market throughout the region in a fashion remarkably similar to the American Protestants, although without such a dazzling display of technology and resources. Capuchinos obliged their Quichua faithful to help build a small sawmill at Coca which generated a profit from lumber gleaned from chopping down the rainforest. This clearing took place so that cattle pastures could be expanded and fenced. The mission was obliged to pay its way, so to speak, not having recourse to a large endowment »back home« or generous subsidies from Rome. But the use of mission native labor made it profitable to exploit people's work for the growth and sustenance of God's Will, and the friars as well.

No Capuchin has established systematic contact with the Aucas to date, and of course, no friar speaks their language. For years, the missionaries fantasized about their first contacts with the tribe. After a small aircraft was purchased and a friar trained to pilot it, the Capuchinos overflew the larger Auca villages (when located) and dropped candy to the people, as well as pictures of the Pope and St. Francis. But to no avail. The Aucas did not respond to these benevolent symbols with friendly gestures from the ground. Rather, circa 1965, they attacked the town of Coca, its Quichua inhabitants and mission workers, injuring some. A young Auca woman was captured in the fracas and taken to the mission. The Colombian Laurita Sisters nursed her wounds, bathed and dressed her in western clothes. And the incident was duly reported to Puyo and the *oriente* military garrison command at Shell Mera.

The following day, I was told, an Ecuadorean Air Force plane landed with orders to take the injured Auca girl to the Vozandes missionary hospital at Shell Mera. Rachel Saint accompanied the Ecuadorean officer in command and personally demanded the girl be taken from the Sisters and removed to the evangelical hospital. The Capuchinos and Lauritas refused vociferously, but the evangelist's influence held sway. After receiving treatment at the missionary hospital, the girl returned to her band of kin by SIL aircraft.

This minor incident is illustrative of the major elements in the current SIL alliance with the remaining dominant institutions in the Ecuadorean *oriente*. Indeed the Summer Institute plays a major part in a unique scenario of the lowland political system. Networks of trade-offs exist whereby friendships, gifts and outside pressures assure the military's prestige and control, native defensive postures are repressed, evangelical missionaries work unmolested, and the vast stretches of tropical forest become available for colonization and exploitation, thereby relieving agrarian tension in the Sierra. The concessions granted to United States oil companies in the late 1960's were easier to explore and exploit due to the evangelical hegemony and infrastructure. The oil companies courted the missionaries; *gringos* met with *gringos*. The situation was defined. The moral choices were clear – the oil was needed by America; and the evangelicals, under the strategic leadership of the more politically sophisticated SIL, supported the oil companies and an ethnocidal Ecuadorean government policy of encouraging highland homesteaders to stake out parcels along oil company access roads. After consultation with the Ecuadorean military, Auca converts flying above the remaining band of uncontacted kin in SIL heliocouriers operating on Texaco fuel, were urged to put down their arms and join their evangelized kin at Rachel Saint's *reserva* village. This is when the strategic interest of SIL and international capital coincide.

Of greater long run political significance for Ecuador, however, is the World Radio Missionary Fellowship, Inc. electronic media and medical empire. With offices and studios in Quito, *La Voz de los Andes* (HCJB call letters) radio service covers not only all of Ecuador, with a powerful AM signal, but adjacent regions of Peru and Colombia as well. There is, in addition, programming on the standard shortwave bands (25m 31 and 49 meters) in more than 30 languages. These evangelical messages are beamed around the world (to the USSR, Rumania and the Caucasus, for example) from a transmitter east of Quito fed by a hydroelectric plant built and maintained expressly for this purpose by the Fellowship.

Quito, Guayaquil and Cuenca, Ecuador's major cities, receive television programming from a central HCJB studio in Quito. Here, a staff of foreign missionaries and Ecuadoreans design and produce televised entertainment for virtually all of urban Ecuador. Daily programming also includes an array of canned American television westerns and situation comedies at odds with Ecuadorean reality and culture. Technically, the quality of the HCJB signal is superior to that of »commercial« Ecuadorean television, a fact that further enhances its ratings and viewer appeal.

Radio and television newscasts constitute the scenario for evangelical protestantism's interpretation of the world and its conflicts, particularly the domestic Ecuadorean drama. How the news is slanted, what is commented upon, and what is ignored provides insight into the World Radio Missionary Fellowship alliance with the ruling Ecuadorean elites. Because the HCJB news staff never openly opposes government policy nor engages in substantive and critical investigative journalism, it must be called to judgment for sins of omission. In fact, the listener/viewer becomes mesmerized by the alleged »balance« in news commentary – a production technique that puts the lie to imperial media. HCJB sounds and looks like most American television affiliates. And it really is one.

The Vozandes hospital in Quito is well-equipped, staffed by Ecuadorean physicians and American doctors who have returned to medical school for an Ecuadorean degree. This institution competently treats patients of all income levels and ethnic origins. As if a large corporation, the medical complex is vertically integrated. Laboratory, pharmacy, x-ray, physiotherapy and other medical services are all available at one place. The same is true on a reduced scale at the small branch hospital in Shell Mera, at the edge of the *oriente* missionary domain. Hospital and doctors' fees vary in accord with one's class status and, hence ability to pay. Believers are given special consideration. This policy enhances the attractiveness of an evangelical health service for a rural and urban population virtually without access to quality public health systems of any kind.

The Vozandes media and medical enterprise dovetails nicely with the programs of the Summer Institute of Linguistics and other missionary educational efforts throughout Ecuador (see Table II). Logistical support provided by the Jungle Aviation and Radio Fellowship (JAARS) for the Wycliffe Translators and, similarly, the Missionary Aviation Fellowship for other evangelical groups rounds out the missionary infrastructure. A covert design in the current overall evangelical strategy and the remarkable ideological solidarity displayed in its execution, point to a central question: just why all this? So that

God's work may be done? Is it farfetched to imagine a direct link with United States foreign policy and imperial strategy? Could the U.S. intelligence community be directly involved? Certainly, we can anticipate such a situation when nationalist and revolutionary movements and rhetoric threaten American military and missionary security, and accelerate the arrival of an unpredictable Judgment Day when Red devils may prevail.

Evangelicals ignore Old Testament admonitions about justice; their gospel, is devoid of social content. They rely instead on the creation and sustenance of a passive, yet passionate faith – in God and America – nurtured by the anxieties of domestic social changes few bother to analyze and fewer still are committed to act upon. Mindless but astute American evangelical anticommunism is today one of the Third World's and native groups' most potent enemies in the evolving struggle for liberation.

Bibliography

Davis, S.H. and R.O. Mathews,
1976. *The Geological Imperative,* Anthropology Research Center, Cambridge, Mass.

Ferndon, Edwin N., Jr.,
1947. »Notes to Accompany a Present Day Ethnic Map of Ecuador«, El Palacio, 54:155–168.

Missions Advanced Research and Communication Center,
1973. *Mission Handbook: North American Protestant Ministries Overseas,* 10th ed., Monrovia, California,

Robinson, Scott S.,
1972. *El Etnocidio Ecuatoriano,* Mexico, D.F. 1972. (reprint of Ecuador chapter in *The Present Situation of the South American Indians,* World Council of Churches, Geneva, 1972).

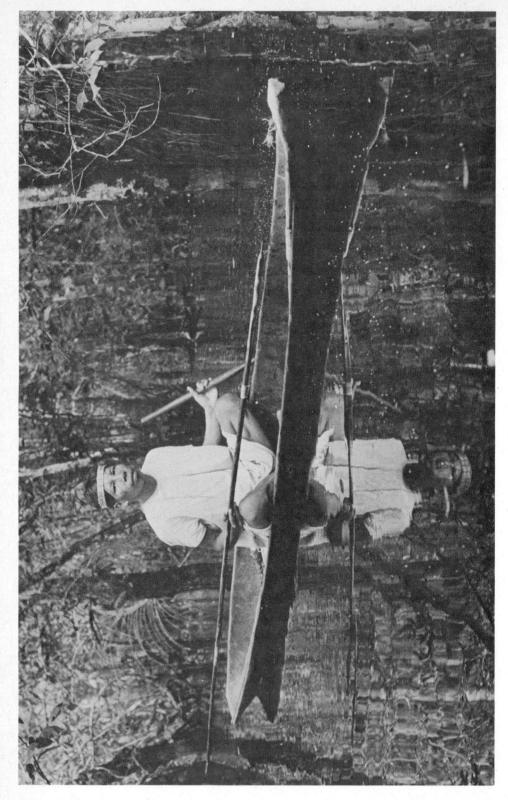

Siona youth spearfishing on upper Cuyabeno River, Ecuador. Copyright: William T. Vickers 1975.

The Jesuits and the SIL: External policies for Ecuador's Tucanoans through three centuries*

by WILLIAM T. VICKERS

Introduction

The Siona-Secoya Indians are slash-and-burn horticulturalists and hunters and gatherers of the Upper Amazon, and inhabit a territory near the confluence of the Aguarico and Napo Rivers in Ecuador and Peru. They are members of the Western Tucanoan linguistic group.[1] The traditional settlement pattern of the Siona-Secoya and their Western Tucanoan ancestors consisted of dispersed communal dwellings housing extended patrilocal, patrilineal households, each under a local headman-shaman. Relations between these communities were tenuous as accusations of sorcery and occasional raids fueled mutual antagonisms and fears. Settlements were separated by considerable distances and were periodically moved; the concomitant population density was low, about 20 people per 100 km² (Steward 1949:663). This pattern of dispersion and movement mitigated the depletion of the environmental resources that the Siona-Secoya exploited for their subsistence.

There have been two periods in Siona-Secoya history during which the imposition of external models on the native system has been attempted. The first occurred during the 18th century when the Jesuits labored to establish reductions along the Aguarico and Napo Rivers. The second began in the mid-1950s and continues to the present as modern missionaries under contract to the Ecuadorian Ministry of Education strive to establish nucleated settlements in order to facilitate mission activities and services. The attempts of the Jesuits failed; those of the modern mission appear more likely to succeed, although this »success« will be the harbinger of the loss of a way of life. The aim of this paper is to analyze the conditions of these two contact periods in an attempt to identify the similarities and significant differences of each, particularly with regard to the development of Ecuador as a nation.

Aboriginal Society

The Siona-Secoya are members of the western branch of the Tucanoan linguistic family living on the Aguarico River and its tributaries. For as long as myth and recorded history can recall, the land along the middle and lower Aguarico has been the home of Western Tucanoan speakers. Many terms have been applied to these peoples by the outsiders who came into contact with them. The early Franciscans and Jesuits called them *Encabellado* because of their long hair, which was sometimes worn in elaborate braided coiffures. In the 19th century they were known as the *Piojé*. Today, members of the Aguarico communities refer to themselves as *Siona* or *Secoya* depending upon the particular locations to which they trace their ancestral roots (cf. Vickers 1976:22-25).

The Encabellado were slash-and-burn cultivators who preferred to locate their settlements away from the banks of the main rivers. The typical settlement pattern consisted of dispersed residence groups

William T. Vickers is Assistant Professor of Anthropology at Florida International University in Miami. His major research interests are human ecology and South American ethnology. Since 1972 he has lived and conducted research among the Siona-Secoya Indians of Ecuador on three occasions. He has published a number of articles on his Amazonian research and is currently preparing reports for Ecuadorian government agencies in support of native land claims. Dr. Vickers is also contributing editor to the journal *Caribbean Review*.

* A preliminary version of this paper was presented at the 76th Annual Meeting of the American Anthropological Association, Houston, Texas (December 1, 1977) in a symposium entitled, »Local-Level Response to National Policies and Regional Development in Ecuador: Insights into the Workings of Complex Systems.«

located on small rivers and streams that fed into the Aguarico, Napo and Putumayo Rivers. The basic settlement was a patrilocal, patrilineal extended family residing in a communal dwelling. It was not unusual for this group to be expanded by the addition of nuclear households whose members did not form an integral part of another extended group. The leader of this community was the headman, who was the most respected elder shaman. The greater the charisma of the headman-shaman the larger the residential group tended to be as unattached households were attracted to his curative and protective powers.

The traditional religion of the Siona-Secoya encompasses a complex cosmological system of supernatural spirits, forest demons, anthropomorphic animals and explanations of physical phenomena. The key to understanding Siona-Secoya religion, and, indeed, the central focus of the culture is the class of hallucinogenic vines they call *yagé*, which consists of several species of the genus *Banisteriopsis*. (The stems of these plants contain the psychoactive alkaloids harmine, harmaline and d-tetrahydroharmine, Pinkley 1969). The use of *Banisteriopsis* is common among the tribes of the Upper Amazon, but it is doubtful that there are many cultures to which it is more significant than the Siona-Secoya. To them it represents the medium through which all knowledge is learned, the assurance of a good hunt, the power of healing, and the gateway to the afterworld.

The use of *yagé* is normally under the supervision of a shaman who is knowledgeable in its use, and who is believed to have attained a higher level of supernatural awareness and power by the repeated use of *yagé*, as well as a number of other plants with psychotropic or medicinal properties. The native term for shaman *(yahé unkukt)* literally means »drinker of *yagé*.« The prestige of an experienced shaman is great and a knowledge of shamanism is a requisite for the position of headman. Headmanship is bestowed upon the man whom the people recognize as having the greatest wisdom and knowledge in the community. The headman-shaman does not give orders to his fellow tribesmen, but influences them by his charismatic personality, the example of his behavior, his generosity and his counsel and advice.

A young man who aspires to be a shaman enters into an apprenticeship under the guidance of an experienced shaman. During this period his social contacts are limited and formalized, and his diet is restricted to the meat of a few animals, plantains and a little toasted maize. He must »become thin« and drink a great deal of *yagé* at frequent intervals so that he can experience contact with the spirit world. The way is not easy and many aspirants fail in their quest for knowledge. Apprentices may also be dismissed by the shaman if he sees that they lack the motivation to follow the strict regimen.

The experienced shaman »sees well« the visions of *yagé*. His soul flies to the heavenly realms to visit the spirit beings and may even approach the culture hero-creator *Baina*. He can descend to the underworld to ask *Weapo*, the keeper of peccaries, to send game to the village for the men to hunt. He can cure the ailments caused by the magical darts of a sorcerer by sucking or massaging them from the body of the victim, or, if he is evil himself, can send darts to harm his enemies. The headman-shaman is considered the wisest of men, yet his manner is modest. His prestige lies in the recognition of his great knowledge and experience with *yagé*, and his devotion to matters of the spirit. He is not a man like other men. His physical needs are few. He is a man with a vision of other worlds.

The use of *yagé* in Siona-Secoya culture takes place in a highly ritualized and religious context. It is not used as a means of rebelling against the norms of the society, but represents the highest and most sacred values of the culture. The drinking of *yagé* is a communal act and whole households join with the shaman at a ceremonial hut in the forest for the ceremony. There is no regular schedule of *yagé* ceremonies corresponding to specific dates; they are frequently held at intervals of about a month, but may be performed more frequently if the shaman has specific purposes in mind (e.g., to perform a healing ritual, to »call« game, or to appeal to the spirits for a cessation of the rains so that recently slashed garden plots may be burned).

The complex of beliefs and rituals surrounding the use of *yagé* in traditional Siona-Secoya life is the intellectual essence of their culture. It is the central aspect of all religion, the development of leaders, healing, good fortune in subsistence activities, and native theories of causality in the universe. The *yagé* ceremony is also an important rite of intensification that promotes ingroup solidarity through a shared personal experience (cf. Siskind 1973). This complex also serves important ecological functions. Its use reinforces the belief in the power of shamans and in witchcraft. One's local shaman is generally perceived as the healer of illnesses inflicted by a malevolent sorcerer residing in a distant village. The fear of sorcerers is a prevalent theme in Siona-Secoya life, and serves to rationalize the dispersed settlement-pattern characteristic of the culture. This places less pressure on the environmental resources that the

Siona-Secoya depend upon for their subsistence via a technology of hunting, fishing, collecting and shifting cultivation.

The Initial Mission Period

Although the first Jesuits arrived in South America in 1550 (Caraman 1976:27), they did not begin explorations in the Upper Amazon until 1615 (Phelan 1967:28). The first two Jesuit missionaries arrived in San Francisco de Borja on the Maranon in 1638, and in 1640 the order sent representatives to Philip IV to claim the entire Amazon Basin as their mission preserve. The members of the Jesuit Order in South America were carefully recruited men of education and their mission was to catechize the native populations and to maintain them in settlements independent of Spanish and Portuguese colonizers and under the jurisdiction of a semi-autonomous Jesuit state whose primary allegiance was to Rome rather than to the Crown. The Amazon mission of the Jesuits was extensive – it extended from the Pongo de Manseriche in the west to the Rio Negro in the east, a distance of over 1300 miles (Phelan 1967:32). A *cedula real* was issued in July 1683 that gave the Compania de Jesús exclusive rights to missionize the Indians of the Aguarico and Napo Rivers and allocated the Putumayo region to the north to the Franciscans (Chantre y Herrera 1901:316). The period between 1709 to 1769 was the heyday of Jesuit activity among the Encabellado; no fewer than 17 missions were founded during this time.

The Jesuits found the Encabellado scattered in small settlements off the main rivers. Since the number of missionaries was always very small and the territory large, they spent much of their time travelling. Their history is a record of comings and goings between the various mission sites, and journeys into the forest to search for newly-reported groups of Encabellado. The strategy was to take the Indians from thir small, dispersed settlements in the forest and concentrate them in reductions along the banks of the Napo and Aguarico to facilitate their catechization.

The Jesuit fathers were tenacious men who endured great hardships to contact the Encabellado and motivate them to relocate their settlements. They frequently travelled many days inland through forests and swamps searching for groups that had been reported by previously-contacted Encabellado. The Jesuits were largely successful in accomplishing this, but failed in the long term because they were unable to overcome the centrifugal forces that tended to pull the reductions apart.

Each individual Encabellado settlement under its headman feared the sorcery of other Encabellado. When the Jesuits attempted to get two groups to settle in one reduction some headmen refused outright. The Jesuit fathers were rigid in their adherence to doctrine, but pragmatic in dealing with problems they could not control. They allowed the recalcitrant groups to make individual settlements by the rivers in the hope that they could eventually be persuaded to unite in larger villages.

The Encabellado missions were notable for their instability. People fled them at the slightest difficulty or provocation. A major problem was the increased susceptibility to disease in the reductions, and the fact that the Encabellado believed that most illness was the result of sorcery. The discipline imposed by the Jesuits and their assistants also caused difficulties. The most significant episode of this type occurred when the headman Curazaba attempted to escape from the mission of San Miguel but was detained by Padre Francisco Real after a child spy revealed his intentions (Chantre y Herrera 1901:392). His escape attempt foiled, Curazaba began to use his influence against the priest, charging that the Indians were being taught Quichua in the mission school so that they could be sold into slavery. On January 4, 1744 Curazaba and his followers speared Padre Real and his two assistants, desecrated the chapel, burned the settlement and returned to the forest.

Having heard of the death of Padre Real and fearing punishment, the Encabellado of the missions of Nombre de Jesús, San Pedro, Soledad de María, Santa Teresa, Corazón de María, Mártires del Japón and San Estanislao fled also (Chantre y Herrera 1901:396). Only the people of San José, San Luis Gonzaga, San Bartolomé de Necoya, San Juan de Paratoas and Santa María de Guayoya stayed, largely due to the intercessions of Padre Joaquín Pietragrasa. The tenacity of the Jesuits is apparent in the fact that the experienced, but ailing, Padre Martín Iriarte returned from a convalesence and assumed the task of attempting to reestablish the lost missions. He was the only fluent speaker of the Encabellado language among the Jesuit missionaries (Chantre y Herrera 1901:398). Iriarte met with a degree of success, but the missions never attained their former prominence.

From 1746 to 1750 there were no priests active in the missions, their responsibility having been left

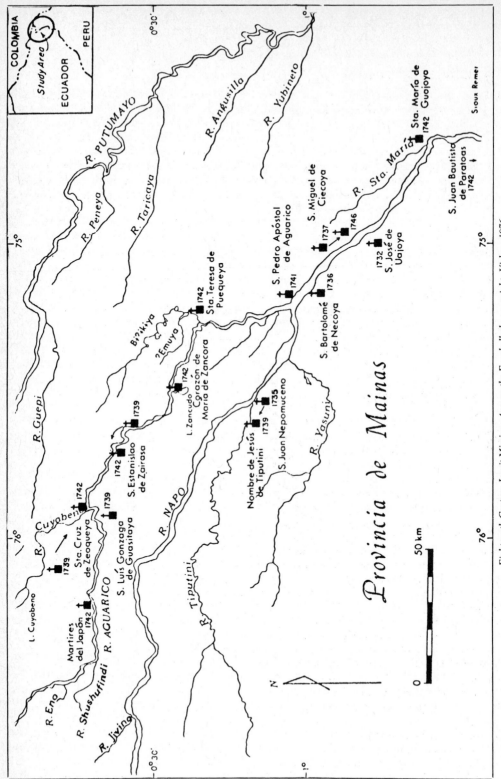

Eighteenth Century Jesuit Missions Among the Encabellado. copyright: Vickers 1976.

to one Hermano Sanchez, who attempted to force the Indians of San Bartolomé to resettle at San José, and sent Encabellado children to established Spanish towns such as Archidona for schooling. The Encabellado resisted these policies and the missions declined; by the late 1760s only two remained.

The Jesuit attempt to nucleate the Encabellado population met partial success, then failure. They succeeded in digging the local groups out of their forest enclaves and in settling them on the main rivers, but they could not make the various bands unite in stable communities. The few fathers with their limited resources could not overcome the epidemics and traditional centrifugal forces of Encabellado culture. Political events external to the Western Tucanoan territory eventually domed the mission program. The relative autonomy of the Jesuits irked the representatives of the Crown, who viewed the Jesuit estates in Latin America as potential sources of taxation. Furthermore, the Jesuit policy of protecting the Indians from white exploitation created enemies among the Spanish and Portuguese colonizers. These resentments led to jurisdictional battles and other conflicts that eventually resulted in Charles III's 1767 order expelling the Jesuits from South America.

The Second Mission Period

During the 19th century Encabellado contacts with the outside world shifted from the missionization efforts of the Jesuits to sporadic bartering with river traders, and the exchange of forest products and hammocks for iron tools, cloth and other manufactured items. The territory they occupied was essentially the same as before, but outsiders now referred to them as the Piojé. They were still considered to be savages, still fought occasional battles with the Awishira Indians from the south bank of the Napo River, and continued to be plagued by diseases introduced by whites (Simson 1886:193-197).

The events of the 20th century have drawn the Western Tucanoans of the Aguarico and Napo into ever-increasing contact with the outside world. There have been three somewhat overlapping phases of contact. The first was the rubber boom which began around the turn of the century and petered out by the 1920s, but which left a system of debt peonage that affected some of the Secoya on the Santa María River until the 1940s. The Siona of the Aguarico River appear to have been less drawn into the rubber collecting system, but epidemics introduced during this period ravaged the various local groups of Indians. The second phase was the renewal of missionary activity among the Siona-Secoya in the mid-1950s.

The most recent phase of contact stems from the oil boom beginning in the late 1960s, and the subsequent road construction into the Aguarico Basin and the colonization that has accompanied it. In 1967 a consortium of the Texaco and Gulf oil companies discovered large petroleum reserves in northeastern Ecuador. Following the location of the Lago Agrio and Shushufindi fields, Texaco-Gulf began the construction of a 318 mile pipeline from the Pacific port of Esmeraldas, over the Andes and down into the tropical rainforest. This line began operation in June 1972 with a capacity of 250,000 barrels per day. A road paralleling the pipeline was constructed from Quito-Lago Agrio-Coca, and the area became a hotbed of activity as oil crews, entrepreneurs and colonists moved into the region.

Virtually all of the Oriente has been divided into oil exploration concessions at one time or another. In general, the occupancy of the land by Indians has been ignored. The oil companies have no offical policies toward the aboriginal groups. In one case the Ecuadorian government did arrange to set aside 160,000 hectares as a temporary reserve for the hostile Waorani (»Auca«) Indians in 1969 (El Comercio March 31, 1972:1). The SIL was directly involved in the formulation of this policy which was intended to relocate the widely-scattered Waorani bands into a »secure« area so that oil exploration could be carried out in former Waorani lands.

Most adult Siona-Secoya men have been employed by oil exploration teams, although only for a month or two at a time. They usually worked clearing sites for camps, building shelters, and clearing trails through the forest. After a month or so they tired of the monotonous labor and separation from their families and returned to their homes with modest savings which they used to purchase clothing, aluminum pots, fishline and hunting ammunition.

Without a doubt, the primary impetus in the opening of the Oriente has come from the oil companies and not the Ecuadorian government. The activities of the companies are focused on exploration, drilling, and the pumping of crude oil from the ground. The oil industry is an extractive enterprise which does not consciously promulgate the general economic development of Ecuador's eastern regions. The road construction activities of the companies, however, have served as the catalyst for far-reaching changes in the Oriente. Spontaneous colonization along the routes of penetration has been so rapid that large areas of land have been settled or claimed by migrants, land speculators and agribusiness concerns (cf. Bromley 1972).

During the initial phases of colonization in the Aguarico region in the early 1970s there was little articulation between the Siona-Secoya and the newly-arrived settlers. The Indian settlement pattern is determined by the existence of lands suitable for cultivation in association with rivers that provide fish, domestic water, and routes of transportation. The initial wave of colonists settled along the roads which linked them to the markets of the Sierra. Since 1975, however, a 9850 hectare concession for a palm oil plantation has been granted on lands immediately adjacent to the largest Siona-Secoya settlement of San Pablo[2] on the Aguarico River, and the clearing for this plantation is resulting in the destruction of an important native hunting ground. Furthermore, colonists have now begun to penetrate the traditional lands of the Siona-Secoya from several directions.

In the mid-1950s members of the Summer Institute of Linguistics (SIL) made contact with Siona-Secoya Indians living on the Cuyabeno River (a northern tributary of the Aguarico). A missionary-linguist and his family established a residence in the native community and with Indian assistance constructed a small jungle airstrip, and later developed a school, health-care services, and a program of religious instruction. A number of additional innovations were introduced, including firearms and modern tools, and a variety of agricultural projects were attempted. In 1968 Western Tucanoan groups on the Santa María, Yubineto and Angusilla Rivers were visited by SIL personnel and from 1973 on efforts were made to encourage these Indians to join the mission station. The presence of educational, health-care and religious services were offered as incentives in the attempt to unify the dispersed native communities. As a consequence, a number of households (approximately 67 people) from the Angusilla River migrated to the mission station at San Pablo during the period of October 1973 to March 1975, and the population of the settlement grew to almost 200.

The missionary-instituted educational program is the central locus of the nationalization effort among the Siona-Secoya. The Summer Institute of Linguistics operates in Ecuador through a contract with the Ministry of Public Education and is charged with the mission to »study the aboriginal languages, compile the respective data and develop a program of practical, patriotic and moral services in each native tribe« (Instituto Lingüístico de Verano 1969:1, author's translation from the Spanish). As of 1975 SIL had established 37 bilingual-education schools among five ethnic groups in Ecuador.

Today, San Pablo has a school program staffed by three native teachers and offers four years of bilingual education plus two years of »fiscal« education. Teachers are generally recruited as boys by the SIL missionary-linguist on the basis of their intelligence, aptitude, and receptivity to Christian dogma. Candidates for these positions receive annual teacher training at the SIL basecamp at Limoncocha for six weeks under the tutelage of Ecuadorian instructors. The student-teachers also receive four weeks of pedagogical instruction from SIL staff members.

The curriculum of the village school includes literacy training, mathematics, and Ecuadorian history and geography. The teachers use both bilingual primers prepared by SIL linguists and Ecuadorian texts. The presentation of national ideology is manifested in the daily singing of the national anthem, the presence of national symbols such as the shield and flag in the classroom, text and lesson content, and the observation of national holidays. From time to time there are inspections by Ministry of Education officials during which students drill, perform the national anthem, and recite lesson materials to demonstrate their proficiency.

The teachers are paid a monthly salary the Ecuadorian government, and receive additional incentives such as enhanced travel opportunities (to attend conferences and the annual training sessions) and prestige. The senior teacher at San Pablo, with his superior command of Spanish and literacy, serves as a cultural broker for the community by mediating in the relations between the Indians, the missionaries, and the larger national society. He also serves as a gatekeeper for the goods and services made available to the Siona-Secoya through the missionary-Indian interface.

It is no coincidence that the senior teacher also serves as a Christian leader of the community, for an acceptance of Christian belief is a consideration in the selection of teacher candidates. However, religious instruction does not take place in the school setting; this is forbidden under the terms of the SIL-Ministry of Education contract. The primary environment for this activity is the protestant religious service, or *culto*, which is held in a thatch church near the center of the village.

Secoya teacher (right) translates religions message of Ecuadorian lay preacher (left) to Siona-Secoya during baptism cere-mony by the Aguarico River. Although the lay preacher is not a member of the Summer Institute of Linguistics, his visit was arranged by the organization. Copyright: William T. Wickers 1975.

A variety of additional projects and services are made available to the native community as a result of the SIL presence. The population receives vaccinations against the diseases that have been scourges since the conquest, including smallpox, measles and influenza. Two SIL-trained nurse's aides dispense medication and treat routine illnesses or injuries, and air evacuation to the Limoncocha infirmary or Quito hospitals is available in more serious cases. The mission attempts to maintain a system of service for fees, but it is doubtful that full expenses are recouped. The rationale for the fee policy is that it is intended to instruct the Indians in the value and management of money. However, many individuals avoid or delay treatment because of hesitancy to spend their scarce cash resources. Another difficulty is that the nurse's aides are placed in a bind when kin request medicines, for they must choose between their instructions to charge for services rendered and the traditional ties of reciprocity governing kin relations. During my field research in 1973-75 the medicine chest *(botiquín)* operated at a consistent loss.

Agricultural projects are another phase of missionary activity. At Shushufindi a number of new plant varieties have been introduced (e.g., rice, maize hybrids, grasses, citrus, and ornamentals) along with small-scale projects with cattle, pigs, goats and chickens. The success of these innovations has been mixed, and to date none have made significant contributions to the traditional subsistence system. The eventual goal of these projects is to allow intensification of food production so that a permanent, nucleated settlement can be maintained. This is felt to be of importance because the traditional territory of the Siona-Secoya is being circumscribed by agricultural colonists and hunting and fishing are expected to decline significantly within a few years.

The missionary aviation and radio network (Jungle Aviation and Radio Service or JAARS) provides transportation and communication facilities which are used by missionary-linguists, visitors, itinerant merchants, anthropologists and Indians alike on a fee for service basis. In fact, SIL missionaries sometimes encourage Indians to locate new villages closer to the SIL basecamp in order to save on the costs of air transport. This was one of the factors considered when many of the Siona-Secoya moved from a site on the Cuyabeno River to San Pablo on the Aguarico River in 1973-74. Because San Pablo is one of the closest villages to the SIL basecamp at Limoncocha, it is frequently a destination of supporters of Wycliffe Bible Translators (Wycliffe, SIL and JAARS represent divisions of the same organization) from the United States who are taken on a tour of an »Indian village«. The enthusiasm of many Siona-Secoya for these visits appeared to decline perceptibly during 1973-5 as on many occasions few Indians were observed going to the grass airstrip to welcome the JAARS aircraft, and the people frequently remained in their houses as the tour groups passed through the village.

The air service has also provided an avenue for acquiring desired goods from national markets, including such items as machetes, axes, ammunition, fishing hooks and line, radios and sewing machines. The missionary-linguist frequently serves as a purchasing agent in these transactions. The cash income of the Siona-Secoya is small, deriving primarily from the sale of ocelot and jaguar skins, hammocks and other artifacts, some agricultural products, and occasional wage labor for oil exploration parties, Quichuas, or the mission station. Individuals are frequently in debt to the mission, and although the mission probably absorbs a »loss« on these transactions, the accounting bears some similarities to the traditional patronage system of the Amazon. During the rubber period and on agricultural plantations the debt-peonage system was a means for the ruthless exploitation of native labor; today the patron-client relationship of the missionary and Indian is less insidious, and frequently arises as an Indian attempts to place the missionary in the patron's role through requests for credit for the purchase of desired objects. Although the missionaries tend to view this paternalistic largesse as something of a burden, it is the Indian client population that provides the *raison d'etre* of the missionary profession. Furthermore, the not inconsiderable income of the SIL is at least partly stimulated by their contributor's wishes to further projects which attempt to improve the living conditions of the Indians.

Missionary-Induced Transformations in Siona-Secoya Culture

In traditional Western Tucanoan culture the population was divided into groups according to membership in patriclans and geographical location. Since the religious ideology of the groups was essentially identical, there were no schisms based on differences in religious orientation. But the religious system supported a belief in sorcery, so there were schisms between local communities deriving from past and present accusations of witchcraft. As discussed previously, this was one of the mechanisms that served to maintain a dispersed settlement pattern and to regulate pressures on natural resources.

The presentation of a new religious ideology by modern missionaries has created a new cleavage in Siona-Secoya society. This cleavage is based on the distinction between *creyentes* (believers) and *no creyentes* (nonbelievers), or those who have been receptive to Christian teachings and those who have not. This distinction did not exist in the past because everyone believed in the traditional cosmological and religious system (Vickers 1975, 1976). Today, that which was formerly most sacred in Siona-Secoya belief is portrayed as false, and participation in the traditional *yagé* ceremonies is discouraged. Shamanism and participation in the old manioc beer drinking parties has likewise been associated with the newly-introduced concept of »sin.«

A conscious effort has been made to erode the constituencies of the remaining headmen-shamans in the Aguarico Basin and to promote the teacher-Christian leader as the *de facto* headman of the native community. Since the modern-day Siona-Secoya are enmeshed in an ever-intensifying culture-contact situation the teacher enjoys concrete advantages over the shamans as a cultural broker due to his Spanish fluency, literacy and educational experience in the non-Indian world. This fact is not lost on the Siona-Secoya, who look to the articulate teacher to represent them in dealings with outsiders.

Christian conversion does give the Siona-Secoya a »legitimate« religion in the eyes of Ecuadorian nationals who tend to view marginally-acculturated jungle Indians as *aucas,* or savages, who may be dealt with with impunity. The presence of a school in the community provides the native population with an additional claim to »civilized« status. Since the most flagrant cases of exploitation of Indians has been at the hands of petty officials, the military, river traders, and Mestizo neighbors (involving such abuses as forced labor, sales fraud, property theft, nonpayment of wages, forced conscription, kidnapping of children, rape and homicide) the »elevation« of Indians to »civilized« status may be of some value in correcting some of the more gross forms of injustice deriving from the traditional pattern of interethnic relations.

At the level of intracommunal relations, however, the missionization effort has given rise to some difficulties. The traditional religious practitioners have become a modern-day outgroup within the Aguarico community. The missionaries have established the doctrine that believers should not marry non-Christians. In effect, those who follow traditional beliefs have been stigmatized as an unmarriageable class. Apparently, this is a form of coercion designed to promote religious conversion. The effects of this policy have not been beneficial to the maintenance of a Western Tucanoan ethnic identity. The number of youths is not great, and many individuals are ineligible to be partners with one another because of marriage-rule restrictions deriving from the native kinship system. Therefore, the division of the community into believer and nonbeliever factions has made it increasingly difficult for individuals to secure marriage partners of the same cultural background. As a consequence a number of Siona-Secoya youths have been forced to forestall marriage or seek partners outside the community. Unions with outsiders are beset with greater than average difficulties as linguistic barriers, residence considerations, differences in food preferences, and cultural values must be dealt with. Several such marriages have led to violent encounters between kindreds, abrupt separations, or the frank exploitation of the labor of Siona-Secoya youths. The division of the Siona-Secoya into traditional and Christian factions has tended to weaken the communal solidarity of a people whose territory and culture are beset by a number of external pressures and assimilative influences.

The missionary attempt to establish a large permanent settlement at San Pablo also runs counter to the traditional system of slash-and-burn horticulture and hunting and gathering. Centrifugal forces still exist in Siona-Secoya society, and they derive from the basic subsistence ecology of the people. However, the traditional system faces a severe test as the traditional territory is now crisscrossed by highways of penetration and invaded by colonists from other regions of Ecuador. This development of the Oriente is having a significant impact on the ecological system upon which Indian life is based. The native subsistence pattern is predicated on the free use of extensive areas of land and associated flora and fauna. The intrusion of colonists and corporate enterprises into Indian territories is upsetting the balance of the native subsistence system. The construction of roads and the settlement along them have reduced animal populations and created barriers that limit Indian access to areas they used in the past. The missionaries have approached this problem primarily by attempting to intensify horticultural production and make stock raisers of hunters.

The most fundamental question, however, is that of land. As in most hunting and gathering and simple horticultural societies, there was no concept of individual land ownership in traditional Siona-Secoya culture; the people hunted and made their gardens wherever they wished. Today the former free-land situation is changing rapidly and drastically. As settlement increases and more roads are built outsiders will enter into direct competition with the Indians for their riverine sites. When such competition develops the Indians usually lose because they are greatly outnumbered and are unable to mobilize the agencies of the national government to intercede on their behalf.

The legalization of Indian land claims is not easily accomplished. The Ecuadorian government gives legal recognition to oil company concessions, commercial agricultural operations, and colonists along the highways of penetration, but comparatively little has been done to recognize the land rights of jungle Indians. Since the missionary presence in Ecuador is relatively ongoing, long-term, and well financed, they stand in a unique position to exert influence for the recognition of Indian lands. Although the SIL does not view the land issue as its first priority, SIL personnel have worked with the Instituto Ecuatoriano de Reforma Agraria y Colonización (IERAC) to achieve a limited land »grant« for the Siona-Secoya. In 1977 IERAC presented the Siona-Secoya with a title to 7043 hectares of land between the Eno, Aguarico and Shushufindi Rivers. Although this was a positive development in that it marked the first official recognition of Siona-Secoya land claims, the deeded land covers less than ten per cent of the territory currently exploited by the Siona-Secoya in their hunting, fishing, and gardening activities. The present grant provides a little more than 100 hectares per Siona-Secoya household, and some white colonists who have settled on the western boundary of the community have expressed the opinion that this is an adequate parcel. The fact remains, however, that a native group such as the Siona-Secoya, which is seminomadic and heavily dependent on wild animal and plant resources, and is experiencing a rapid growth in population (about four per cent per annum), requires a far larger territory in which to operate if it is to maintain its long-term viability. If Siona-Secoya culture is to survive the Ecuadorian government must recognize the legitimate claims of the native community for an expansion of their legal boundaries to include their traditional hunting and fishing grounds along the Aguarico and Cuyabeno Rivers. The native leaders are aware of the long-term significance of the land question and in August of 1979 began an attempt to organize the Siona-Secoya community to mark the boundaries of their territory and to make an appeal to the recently-established Instituto Nacional de Colonización de la Región Amazonica Ecuatoriana (INCRAE) for the recognition of these lands. The land issue is the most critical problem facing the native peoples of the Oriente today; it would be tragic indeed if the missionaries succeed in winning the souls of the native population just as they are disenfranchised of their traditional lands in the context of an expanding national frontier. Yet this is the scenario that presents itself today unless increased efforts are enjoined to protect Indian lands and civil rights.

Conclusion

The Jesuit attempt to incorporate the Encabellado into their religious empire failed. They strived to consolidate the dispersed Indian settlements, but were plagued by a lack of personnel to attend to the large native population, inadequate supplies, primitive transportation facilities, the inability to deal with the ravaging epidemics of the period, and the centrifugal forces inherent in Encabellado culture. The position of the Jesuits was further eroded by political difficulties with the crown, and this situation eventually led to their expulsion from the South American continent in the late 1700s.

The modern missionary attempt to nucleate the Siona-Secoya has many parallels to the activities of the Jesuits, but there are significant differences in the external conditions of the two periods. Although the native culture has remained viable into the 20th century, the current Indian population is very small, making the mission task far less difficult. Furthermore, modern technology has provided the SIL missionary-linguists with rapid transportation, secure supply lines, medical expertise, and a cornucopia of material goods with which to tempt native imaginations. Additional outside pressures have also begun to bear on the native population; Quichua-speaking peoples of the Napo River have expanded rapidly into the Aguarico Basin from the southeast, and from the west the traditional territory has been penetrated by oil company highways that have become avenues of colonization. Today the Siona-Secoya are a miniscule minority in a region where once they were the sole inhabitants. They are exposed increasingly to a national ideology that declares them to be ignorant and uncivilized, and which urges them to embrace strange new beliefs and practices in order to prove their worthiness as Ecuadorians. It is in this climate that segments of the community have opted to follow the new ways, and schisms with those who have not have become exacerbated.

The inexorable fact of the present situation is that the Siona-Secoya will continue to experience increasing contact with the national society as the Oriente is incorporated into the mainstream of Ecuadorian life after centuries of relative isolation. A remaining question, however, is whether missionaries and national planners can be influenced to recognize the inestimable value of maintaining a degree of ethnic diversity within Ecuador's broders, and be motivated to implement tangible programs to protect indigenous land and civil rights.

Notes

[1] During 1973-75 I conducted field research among the Siona-Secoya of Ecuador with grants from the Henry L. and Grace Doherty Foundation and the National Institute of Mental Health (1Fol MH 58552-01). The Instituto Nacional de Antropología e Historia under the directorship of Arq. Hernán Crespo Toral provided the Ecuadorian affiliation for the research. Follow-up fieldwork during June-August 1979 was made possible by a grant from the Florida International University Foundation, Inc.

[2] The settlement referred to as San Pablo was initially called »Shushufindi« by the Siona-Secoya when they established a fresh village site on the Aguarico River near the mouth of the Shushufindi River in 1973. In 1974 the senior teacher of the village had suggested »San Pablo« as a new name for the settlement, and by 1979 this designation was in general use. Some of my previous publications refer to the settlement as »Shushufindi« (cf. Vickers 1975, 1976).

Bibliography

Bromley, R.J.
1972 Agricultural Colonization in the Upper Amazon Basin: The Impact of the Oil Discoveries. Tijdschrift voor Economische en Sociale Geografie 63:278-294.

Caraman, Philip
1976 The Lost Paradise: The Jesuit Republic in South America. New York: The Seabury Press.

Chantre y Herrera, José
1901 Historia de las misiones de la Compania de Jesús en el Maranón espanol. Madrid: Imprenta de A. Avrial.

El Comercio
1972 Opónense a concesión para explotar madera en zona de protección de »Aucas.« Friday, March 31, 1972:1,3. Quito.

Instituto Lingüístico de Verano
1969 Entre los Aucas. Quito.

Phelan, John Leddy
1967 The Kingdom of Quito in the Seventeenth Century. Madison: The University of Wisconsin Press.

Pinkley, Homer V.
1969 Plant Admixtures to Ayahuasca, the South American Hallucinogenic Drink. Lloydia 32(3):305-314.

Simson, Alfred
1879 Notes on the Piojes of the Putumayo. Journal of the Anthropological Institute of Great Britain and Ireland 7:210-222.

Siskind, Janet
1973 To Hunt in the Morning. New York: Oxford University Press.

Steward, Julian H.
1949 South American Cultures: An Interpretative Summary. In Handbook of South American Indians, Vol. 5. Pp. 669-772. Washington, D.C.: U.S. Government Printing Office.

Vickers, William T.
1975 El mundo espiritual de los Sionas. Periplo 1(4):12-23. Madrid.
1976 Cultural Adaptation to Amazonian Habitats: The Siona-Secoya of Eastern Ecuador. Ph.D. dissertation, Department of Anthropology, University of Florida.

Whitten, Norman E., Jr.
1976 Sacha Runa: Ethnicity and Adaptation of Ecuadorian Quichua. Urbana: University of Illinois Press.

Cuiva woman and baby, Colombia. Copyright: Bernard Arcand.

Higher Power: Wycliffe's Colombian Advance

by DAVID STOLL

> *Some of us don't understand that far from being away from the center of attention, it is the down-and-outer who is the focus of today's world. It is wrong to assume that these people are forgotten... There are millions who care, and who put these down-and-outers* first—*to make them Communists. It is we in the Church who say that they don't matter. Neither God nor the devil says that.*
>
> **The peasant is the focus of Communist attack in many areas They want him and they get him.**
>
> – *Kenneth Pike, chapel talk at SIL-Norman, June 1962.*

It is no surprise that Satan chose to launch a stiff counterattack in a country where, with an eye to unsettled social conditions, the Summer Institute has tried to complete its mission with special haste. From Colombia come SIL-CIA charges which SIL's Clarence Church has called »probably one of the cleverest tricks to come out of the bag of the Evil One...«

Of the many mysteries SIL has posed Colombians, one remains outstanding. Through crisis after crisis, how has it managed to stay in the country? As the press was shocked to report after Jonestown, SIL is only one of a hundred or so foreign, mostly North American »sects« operating within the national frontiers. To hear Wycliffe tell it, SIL-Colombia is victim to one of the most appalling sequences of treachery and betrayal in history. The conviction is growing: Wycliffe is the victim of Satan and his children. As Clarence Church reminded us after the SIL-Jim Jones charges, in pointed reference to the Colombian opposition: »this is Satan's world, and we who know the Lord have been snatched out of (Satan's) Kingdom... those who have not yet been rescued can be devilishly clever in their attacks upon God's family...«

SIL's Political Mission: the Red Canard

The spiritual exchanges between North Americans and Colombians are paralleled by other exchanges like the cocaine and marijuana trade. U.S.-banned drugs probably have surpassed coffee as Colombia's leading source of foreign earnings. The battle against the U.S. drug habit which the U.S. government has taken to Colombian soil is one of many ways the United States exports its contradictions to Colombia.

As the United States exports capital to Colombia, it also provides institutions to stabilize the country for its own purposes. Somehow cross purposes work toward the larger purpose of subservience to the United States. Example: evangelical churches afraid illegal drugs are corrupting their youth send missionaries to Colombia. As the missionaries teach a Gospel of political conformity, a drug-dealing *clase emergente* turns Colombia into a gangster state.

U.S. purposes are shared by those comparatively few Colombians enriching themselves under the Pax Americana at the expense of the rest. While many prosperous Colombians are tired of this state of affairs, stirrings of independence in their government are usually stamped out.

Four hundred thousand Indians are part of the larger struggle. In the south Andes, for example,

U.S. money financing and suppressing the drug trade is disrupting native production and marketing of the coca leaf. Traditional users bear the brunt of the suppression campaign, mafias controlled by influential persons despoil producing communities, and consuming communities lose their supply.

On native land, capital dumps surplus population – a stabilizing, control or »safety valve« function. Capital also goes about multiplying itself – an extractive function which produces further instabilities. The struggle between Indians and encroaching settlers is always part of a wider struggle between peasants and land barons. In some regions there are now three-way contests between the drug mafias, guerillas and armed forces, in proximity to legal U.S. investments like oil fields, the growing properties of Colombian *latifundistas,* rebellious frontiersmen, Indians and missionaries. As a stabilizer of frontiers for host states, usually clients of Washington, Wycliffe fashions its usefulness according to such demands, the frontier politics.

Wycliffe understands the frontier politics in its own special way. Those who seriously oppose Wycliffe's plans for Indians are under the same baneful influence as those who oppose U.S. plans for Colombia. Defined rather broadly, Wycliffe's battle with Godless, Satanic Communism goes back to the foundation. As Cameron Townsend faced the Mexican Revolution in the 1930s, he wrote a novel in which a Bible translation helper – a native language informant like SIL teams use today – quells a revolt of Mayan plantation workers led by a Russian Bolshevik determined to destroy churches. No matter that no Russians were in the banana republics. Nor that, in the revolt upon which the novel is based, the 1932 El Salvador *Matanza* or massacre, mostly of Indians, Protestant converts were among the communists, who were deeply religious peasants fighting for land. The missionary of the novel, Townsend himself, explains »his most trusted weapon« against Bolshevism is the Bible (1936:350). Compared to SIL's first ambiguous years in Mexico, the Cold War must have seemed like coming home.

As the Cuban example seemed to threaten U.S. interests in Latin America, Wycliffe offered itself to the local and U.S. governments for the grand cause. General Juan Mendoza, the Peruvian education minister who authorized SIL's first bilingual school system, has described SIL's value in striking terms. While serving in the highlands, he learned his officers needed interpreters to communicate with their own Quechua troops (Hefleys 1972:21).

To bridge the gulf between defenders of the public order and those to be kept in order, a SIL team won friends with teacher salaries and schools. In the insurgent zone east of Ayacucho, SIL-Peru reported in 1966, Quechua children who a year before had been »terrified« simply to go to school were »out greeting and bringing food to soldiers, who came through to search out 'guerrilleros,' even showing off their ability to read... the bilingual primers.« (Orlandini 1966)

The SIL-Peru team probably considered the primers and Christianity more important than the fact that they were helping the army. While Wycliffe occasionally has served in the war of hearts and minds complementing military force, its humanitarian, salvationist mission poses a more diffuse problem than a Green Beret troop. Wycliffe is likely to turn against any popular movement which seems to threaten the plans of Wycliffe's backers. The problem is particularly evident in Colombia, where guerillas are not a serious contender for the state power and have not been attractive allies to Indians. If the politicians to which SIL reports feel threatened by native self-defense movements, if those movements have left-of-center alliance and ill words for the United States, then to SIL they may well be communist fronts.

SIL came to Colombia about the time Kenneth Pike alerted young missionaries to the danger of peasant guerillas in their future fields. SIL-Colombia's contracting government, the National Front, was quite familiar with peasant war. Fifteen years before, the Conservative Party set off the *Violencia* against the Liberal Party. As party war showed signs of turning into social war, the Liberals and Conservatives came together in the National Front.

But many peasants refused to surrender their arms and maintained self-defense zones beyond state control. After the Cuban Revolution these »red spots« became a matter of pressing concern to the North American government. The last were occupied in 1964-5 by U.S.-supported counter-insurgency operations.

Wycliffe says it took nearly ten years to win a state contract in Colombia. Cameron Townsend has summarized the results of at least six overtures as »No.« Then, in October 1961 as the United States strained every resource to nail down the hemisphere, Townsend made another attempt and rapidly secured a contract.

SIL Diplomacy in the Colombian Advance

By reason of religion, Wycliffe was not a likely candidate to help contain Colombian insurgencies. During the *Violencia,* back-country Conservative priests incited mobs against Protestants; the outcry in the United States made the Catholic hierarchy unhappy. Worse, based on the Vatican Concordat, the Catholic Church enjoyed total authority over education in the Indian territories. Liberals considered the Concordat Roman imperialism, but under the National Front they were bound to respect Conservative interests. Even worse, SIL no longer had the advantage of surprise. The performance in Peru had established it as a Protestant conspiracy and the Colombian bishops were not about to let it pull the same trick again.

As Townsend has reiterated, only a higher power can explain SIL's welcome. His own theory is that God did it, which Colombian Protestants found hard to accept because SIL was pledging love and cooperation to their persecutors. Others suspect the U.S. government was responsible. The Colombian bishops were sure it was another Liberal conspiracy. More recently it has been suggested that SIL tricked the National Front, by failing to explain it was an evangelical mission.

Wycliffe dates the Colombian campaign to 1952, the year Townsend met future National Front architect Alberto Lleras Camargo in Chicago. President of the Organization of American States, Lleras was addressing a business association called the Latin American Council. While the founder believed he had impressed this influential Liberal, his election to the Colombian presidency in 1958 did not open the door.

Townsend's charms and problems are suggested by his 1959 meeting with another sympathetic Liberal, the indigenist Gregorio Hernandez de Alba, who was organizing Colombia's first Department of Indian Affairs. If the founder wanted permission to evangelize Colombia's Indians, Hernandez de Alba was badly in need of linguists to deal with their languages. SIL could also provide flight service, start an indigenist-oriented, government-controlled integration program and train national linguists, all at little or no cost to Hernandez de Alba's tiny budgets. It must have been a tantalizing offer; in return SIL would enter Colombia's new Indian management bureaucracy on the ground floor. Two years later Hernandez de Alba drew up the contract, but in 1959 he told the founder the Vatican Concordat was insuperable.

As alarm over communist designs on Latin America mounted, Townsend kept »hoping and praying.« By late 1961, after the United States launched the Alliance for Progress, Townsend was so certain of a breakthrough that he turned down an invitation to visit England with the words: »the Lord has been speaking to me about Colombia. I want to be on standby when the opportunity comes there.«

Higher power came to the rescue in October 1961, when the Colombian ambassador to Washington spent a weekend with wealthy JAARS backers, the Henderson Belks, in North Carolina. According to Wycliffe, Ambassador Sanz Sanz de Santa Maria had been invited to the state fair. Townsend conferred with him in North Carolina, on the plane back to Washington and in Washington, then winged southward to meet Lleras Camargo, who assured him he would get a contract.

My guess is that when Townsend made an important, questionable deal with the men of high virtue who run this world, he stepped up the God-talk so that his members would go along with it. In this case he wanted them to believe the Belk-ambassador-Washington weekend was pure divine planning (WBT/SIL 1964:67-72). But early that month, in the same town from which the ambassador proceeded to North Carolina, Townsend was praying to another higher power: Assistant Secretary of State for Inter-American Affairs Robert Woodward. A week later SIL's Inter-American Coordinator in Washington, Robert Schneider, sent Woodward a project:

> to secure the goodwill of the peoples of Latin America while aiding them culturally. These groups, often living in isolated areas, are special targets of Communism. The project, then, would discourage Communism by equipping the people to read and write and by supplying literature of the free world (FOIA-State).*

The next year the Liberals were to hand the presidency to the Conservatives. The bargaining may have helped the Liberals slip the SIL contract past their counterparts, but the Catholic bishops remained a

---

* What was the project? Jacqueline Kennedy could chair a committee of president's wives from all over the hemisphere, to meet in Washington »to improve the lot of the poor of the Americas.« The committee's first step could be literacy: »Dr. and Mrs. Townsend would be available as international literacy consultants« and SIL »would be happy to lend (its) experience.« I suspect the State Department was more amenable to the Colombian project.

problem. While Wycliffe has Townsend winning over the bishops, the accounts suggest they understood his language too well for it to be very effective on its own.

To keep the bishops calm, Townsend agreed not to do missionary work. According to the February 1962 Ministry of Government contract, SIL would perform technical functions; promote the »social, economic, civic, moral and hygienic improvement« of Indians; and »respect the prerogatives of the Catholic Church, according to the terms of the Concordat...«

A year later all fifteen missionary bishops were sure their prerogatives were going to be violated anyway. Townsend rushed back to Colombia. In a meeting Wycliffe describes as Daniel meeting the lions, he explained the Summer Institute of Linguistics to the bishops. However, his director for the Colombian advance, ex-Inter-American Coordinator Robert Schneider, seems to have doubted God had sealed the victory. He worried that »our rapid growth may bother the bishops« and asked the founder to keep the truce, which he did by making Colombia his residence until 1965 (Hefleys 1974:172, 209, 221-9; Townsend and Pittman 1975:15-6, 121-2).

The now famous SIL base Lomalinda (beautiful hill) went up in the eastern plains or *llanos,* outside the poor river town of Puerto Lleras, Meta, on land donated by retired Air Force General Armando Urrego Bernal. The *llanos* have been contested by poor frontiersmen and cattle barons for a long time; the Liberal guerilla chieftan Dumar Aljure still did what he pleased in SIL's district. Fifty kilometers to the southeast is the Sierra Macarena, rich in exotic flora, fauna and probably minerals. Colonists protest plans to make it a park, saying they will be excluded in favor of transnational corporations. The nocturnal aviation (mostly drugs) through the region is heavy.

In 1962 all signs suggested SIL had better build fast, which it did: twenty language groups by 1966, seventeen more by 1970. In the next two years SIL hoped to field nine more teams. The major concern remained unstated to Colombians because it involved taking certain liberties with the contract. Victor Daniel Bonilla (1972) could only »risk the statement« that SIL's fundamental purpose was »spiritual.«

As elsewhere, legitimation by state contract made it imperative to cultivate influential men, most obviously the politicians passing through the top posts in the Ministry of Government. Catholic bishops and missionaries were also important. With JAARS and a careful performance, SIL cemented relations with some but, due perhaps to Catholic distrust, failed to win state subsidy for bilingual schools. Colombian linguists and anthropologists seemed less important. The new indigenist bureaucracy was so understaffed and powerless that both parties neglected the liaison. SIL became a circumspect, autonomous arm of the state, responding chiefly to pressure from the sub-ministerial and ministerial levels.

Soon SIL's understandings with church and state were not containing the resistance generated by its plans for Indians. By the time Camilo Torres died fighting the National Front in 1966, some Catholic clergy were realizing that sanctification of the received order was undermining their position. As the state undermined the Vatican Concordat, the anti-Concordat rationale behind SIL's alliances unravelled. The universities were producing more linguists and anthropologists, who owed SIL nothing, and it no longer could be argued that SIL was filling a technical vacuum. A state contract with less-than-candid U.S. missionaries looked strange.

These developments made it likely that SIL would be replaced as intermediary between state and Indians. But more was at issue than foreign versus national patronage. In the south Andes the Indian political movements, an attempt to defend land, date to about 1910. Until the *Violencia* there were others, in alliance with the left and an agrarian movement reacting to the dislocations created by the 1900-29 wave of capital into the countryside. Like most agrarian movements, the Indian self-defense movements seek and test alliances, often depending upon them for survival in the face of severe repression. After 1970 these movements reappeared and spread rapidly; in increasing numbers Colombian indigenists and Catholic missionaries are supporting them. By reason of faith and politics SIL did not; that was the threat SIL posed Indians and its attraction to the men controlling the state.

SIL-Colombia and the Indian Movements

Wycliffe expects to be contested by Satan in every community it enters, but by 1975 he was getting too well organized to handle in the usual manner. Accustomed to isolated resistance by a stubborn village, a witchdoctor or an old-fashioned priest, translators were being levered out of communities or in clear danger of the same all around the country. In each of the contests SIL detected the influence of other outsiders, so it was not hard to blame them.

The destruction of peaceful Indian cooperative at Planas was a turning point in the Indian/indigenist politics. Planas is in the *llanos,* an hour's flight from Lomalinda. An ex-civil servant named Rafael Jaramillo helped the Guahibo set up the cooperative but, as they said later told the Senate, it belonged to them. Some of the cattle ranchers did not like the venture; they said Jaramillo was a communist and whenever anything went wrong, he and the Guahibo were to blame.

Sometime between February and June 1970, JAARS flew a SIL man and Alejandro Reyes Posada, coordinator of the Indian Affairs office, around the terror zone. After more inspections, Reyes Posada decided that a settler had started the trouble. The man went around armed, threatened people and claimed 70,000 hectares. Next door lived a Guahibo family, the Arteaga. In February the settler told the police the Arteaga were robbing his cattle and squatting on his property. The police caught an old Arteaga and beat him up with their rifle butts.

Jaramillo took the old man to Villavicencio and went around to the governor, the police and the army, none of whom paid any attention. Some of the authorities had land interests around Planas. On his way back Jaramillo got into a fight with a settler, wounded him and fled firing shots into the air. That, said Reyes Posada in his report, was the beginning of Jaramillo's »guerilla.« (Bonilla 1970).

An evangelical settler named Hernandez was friendly to Guahibo, like some others. When he and his family were killed, then others far from Planas, Jaramillo was blamed. When the army arrived, the Guahibo fled, then began filtering back. As antagonistic settlers did their best to create a guerilla scare, the army began torturing Guahibo to find out where Jaramillo was and hunting them down in the bush. At some point the Indians may have fought back with hunting pieces and arrows.

Planas became a national scandal due to Catholic priests and anthropologists. Despite many demonstrations of concern, the official response confirmed that Indians could expect no justice from the state. The next year, over in the south Andes, Paez and Guambiano organized the *Consejo Regional Indigena del Cauca* (CRIC). Building on the pre-*Violencia* movement, CRIC has led unarmed invasions of land robbed by hacienda owners and joined the National Peasants Association (ANUC). CRIC leaders are still being murdered regularly and across the mountains in Tolima Paez are also being tortured and assassinated. Due to the work of several missions including SIL, some Paez and Guambiano are now Protestant. When I visited Silvia in 1975, teachers at the Christian and Missionary Alliance compound said they refused to support CRIC because it denies God (apparently the evangelical one) and does not respect the government. »The government treats us badly but God has ordered that we obey,« one told me, citing Romans 13:1-2. The SIL translators argue that CRIC's political struggle will lead to disaster; better that Indians buy land as individuals outside the constricted reserves than fight together to expand the reserves.

Back in the *llanos* some of the priests who made Planas an issue stayed on to help the Guahibo. In this respect evangelical missionaries were ahead of the Catholics. To the east in Vichada the massacres of Cuiva Indians were checked only after the New Tribes Mission insisted that authorities press charges. Their colleagues, a SIL linguist and nurse, have lived annually with one of the Cuiva bands. Anthropologists say the SIL women have performed important medical services and helped the Cuiva protect themselves.

But evangelical missionaries and the new wave in Catholic mission differed over how to help Indians. The priests with the Guahibo were encouraging them to maintain their traditions, for example. The Guahibo had been evangelized by the famous Sophia Muller, a fundamentalist from New York City credited with her own empire: thousands of converts in six tribes scattered across four departments of *llanos* and jungle, to say nothing of sweeping accomplishments in Brazil.

I talked to Muller in 1975, in Bogota. An old woman, she was no longer with the New Tribes Mission because she kept getting it into unmanageable scrapes with the authorities. Like SIL, she has been maligned but there is, as always, a basis for the legend. »Destroying the culture?« she exclaimed that Sunday morning: »I should hope so – drunkenness and wild dancing, you know dancing leads to immorality. The idiots had all this witchcraft, the men would drink and dance all night, then go off in the woods and (pause) do their immorality.« Muller says she was forever having to set Indians straight about who she was, because they usually thought she was from heaven.

By the 1970s her empire was crumbling at the periphery and dismaying younger evangelical missionaries at the core. »Influence?« Muller responded. »Not any more. That's a thing of the past when I could tell them what to do and they'd follow me. (Other outsiders) are coming in from all sides now, whole bands are going back to their old ways.« She was especially disgusted with the Cuiva and Guahibo, who destroyed their minds with a hallucinogenic powder. When she returned to a Guahibo village near Planas in 1974, she said only three families were still faithful. The rest had painted themselves up, were dancing, and snorting the powder. They would not let her stay in the village and someone told her she had deceived them.

Like the post-Planas priests she blames for such reverses, Muller was no friend of greedy cattle ranchers. In 1967 a man claiming 8,000 hectares in Vichada told a court she had arrived on his property with two hundred Indians armed with shotguns and arrows. Under her orders the Indians worked day and night to erect a barbed wire fence five hundred meters long; the rancher said he had been deprived of most of his claim (Perez Ramirez 1971:79).

But Muller was no friend of Jaramillo's cooperative either. She said her rivals the priests were communists. As she explained to me, in Revelation there are two beasts, one red and one white. One is going to rule the world and the other is the false church. »The first must be the communists,« she said, »they're the only ones who want to dominate the whole world, and the other must be ecumenism.«

»They want to get the gringos out first,« she explained, »and then the (Colombian evangelicals) so that they can get control over everyone. A cooperative is just the thing for them to get started. They tell everyone to buy and sell there, they get all that under their control and then they have it. That's what this Jaramillo did, he got the Indians into the cooperative and then told them to attack the white ranches. I told them not to join, I warned there would be trouble because the *junta* is directed by this non-believer who has other purposes. Join a cooperative with other believers, I told them. This is where the revolutions always start.«

SIL should not be lumped together with Sophia Muller. In theology if not in crisis most SIL translators are more liberal, their methods are rather different and, although there are more than a thousand of them, to my knowledge not one has ever led a land invasion. If SIL's Guahibo team and the Planas priests ever had a showdown, I did not hear about it. The SIL couple live far downriver and seem to be doing what they can to help the Guahibo defend themselves.

Following SIL's first successes in fighting off reform, it was accused of complicity in the Planas atrocities. According to what may be the only reference to SIL in the considerable Planas press, it »entered into collaboration with the government's civic action program« to pacify presumed Guahibo guerillas. Several SIL »professors« were working as liaison/translators and SIL had »provided the radio equipment to establish direct communications« between Planas and Villavicencio. Concluded Laurie Hart for the North American Congress on Latin American Affairs (NACLA) in New York:

> WBT/SIL did in fact »provide air and radio support, as well as interpreters, for national police and military units engaged in suppressing armed insurrection by the Guahibo Indians.«

Cited sources are a previous NACLA article and the newspaper story quoted above. While the newspaper report is plausible and SIL did not deny it at the time, I know of no corroborating evidence. SIL says its only service was flying Reyes Posada around. The implication of the SIL-Planas and similar charges was clear: Indians had to be liberated from SIL. But if we take the Guahibo as a hypothetical example, the people around the SIL team might well regard them as allies against the grosser abuses.

Planas summarized a great deal of Colombian experience which the Wycliffe translators had not assimilated. During the years immediately afterward, translators and left-of-center priests had some long talks. They could not reach common ground. From the priests, I gathered that translators could not appreciate the implications of Colombia-U.S. relations and their own aspirations for Indians. From translators, I gathered the priests were embarked on dangerous course, stirring up Indians for political ends which would only recoil to the Indians' harm.

The differences Planas implied between Colombian indigenists and SIL were soon reverberating through the Indian movements. Usually SIL had the backing of a village or faction enjoying its benefits and Indians were divided over its presence. The new battle was first joined in Vaupes Department, where the Indian movement was weak and SIL-Colombia had assigned more teams than in any other Catholic jurisdiction.

In the Eastern Tukanoans of Vaupes, bordering on Brazil, SIL saw more than a dozen languages requiring Bible translation. United by marriage exchange and a highly developed multi-lingualism, the Vaupes Indians have been fortunate compared to some. While the National Front brought thousands of settlers into the western edge of the department, it has not pushed the road through to the Tukanoans.

Except for the missionaries they have the eastern Vaupes more or less to themselves, in the form of a modified garden and hunting economy permitting a limited access to trade goods. But probably not for long. When Brazil extends its highway to the border, Colombia may feel obligated to bring its highway into the same region. In 1978 the Colombian Institute of Nuclear Affairs and the National Uranium Company of Spain signed a $ 500 million contract for uranium reserves in Guainia and Vaupes.

The Catholics were here first arriving about 1914 with a brutal performance by Dutch Monfortians. About the time Colombian Javerianos de Yarumal replaced them in 1949, Sophia Muller reached the northernmost Tukanoans, the Cubeo, and ran into a stiff Catholic blockade. By and large the Cubeo have sorted themselves into »evangelical« and »Catholic« villages, the relations between which are still strained even as the evangelicals lapse in their new religion. The many Tukanoans to the south remained under Catholic patronage.

The first SIL team arrived in 1963, was cordially received by the Javerianos and began working from their Acaricuara station. But when three more teams came into the same area, SIL says the Javerianos stymied their attempts to settle in outlying villages, apparently because Concordat violations were anticipated. SIL was persistent switching location when resistance developed for this or other reasons, and by 1970 there were ten translation teams in the Vaupes.

To the Javerianos it must have seemed that everything was weighted in SIL's favor. SIL commanded enough state backing to countermand Catholic protest, it had an impressive logistics system and a more sophisticated method. Thanks to the Catholic record, Javeriano command of Tukanoan loyalty was uncertain. From the SIL outposts evangelical movements might emerge like Sophia Muller's.

After 1967 some fresh blood including a new bishop, Monsignor Belarmino Correa, decided to remedy the situation. While the reforms responded to more than SIL, here relevance to SIL will be stressed. To fortify their position, the Javerianos had to rally diffident Tukanoans to the mission. One way was to plead no contest to the Tukanoan defensive dualism: Catholic to the outside world, Tukanoan among Tukanoan. In 1970 the Javerianos denounced the rubber *patrones* to the government, which ruled that any rubber bought from Indians would have to be paid for in cash. The Javerianos enforced the decree, suppressed debt peonage and helped various communities set up cooperatives. They also hired their *internado* graduates to set up primary schools in outlying communities. The teachers used their own languages as a means to Spanish language instruction.

In 1973 the teachers and *internado* students formed the Regional Indian Council of the Vaupes (CRIVA). Their program was education, organization and unity based, not on the Catholic faith, but on tradition and cultural continuity. Some of their concerns were government highway plans, SIL and *internado* education, the last of which led to disputes with the Javerianos. Still, the Catholics decided to support CRIVA and are supposed to exercise power within it. In regard to SIL, the agreement underpinning the CRIVA-Javeriano alliance is that Tukanoans will not be pressured into changing their religion again.

In 1970, the same year Clarence Church explained to a movie camera that SIL was not a religious organization, Mons. Correa says Church approached him with a plan for training bilingual teachers; Correa would have nothing to do with it. The same year, three more SIL teams were posted along the Papuri River in the heart of the Catholic domain. And in October, during the protest over Planas, Correa denounced the government's failure to defend Indians and their culture. SIL he called a neo-colonial force in the service of the United States. It may have been the first such declaration in all SIL's South American fields.

Soon airstrips at Catholic stations were being blockaded against JAARS planes. From c. 1970 to 1974 SIL's Jupda, Guanano, Piratapuyo, Tuyuca and Tucano teams were forced to leave the communities where they were working. As best I could determine, in two cases the villagers were responsible; in three Catholic staff or their Tukanoan students and teachers took the initiative; and in the latter three cases the SIL teams were soon back at work in the same place and probably more appreciated than before.*

---

* At Acaricuara in 1973 the Tucano translators were turned back at the airstrip by boarding school students, the Tukanoan teachers and a priest. When I visited in Janurary 1976, the *corregidor* held a meeting for my benefit. The sense of the meeting was that the 1973 blockade had been the *internado's* affair. Since the students and teachers came from other communities, they did not represent the village. No village meeting had been held prior to the action and once they reached the airstrip it was too late to bring the SIL women into the village.

When CRIVA demanded SIL withdraw from the Vaupes in June 1974, it was set off by events in a Carapana village. Once the SIL-Carapana translator had been jailed for confronting an abusive rubber *patrón*. Now, when two of the Catholic mission's Carapana teachers spoke against the SIL man in his absence, they came up against a food blockade. According to *internado* students, the blockade was organized by the headman's son, the SIL man's friend and assistant. According to the SIL translator, the headman's wife was responsible, by insisting the teachers work in the gardens for their food like other women. After the headman's son ordered the teachers to leave, the elders had a serious quarrel over the matter.

In August 1975, a few months before I visited the Vaupes, a Desano village asked their SIL couple to leave. According to the SIL translator, a community leader explained that »they« – the Catholic mission – had made it known the village could not have a school unless he left; he says the Javerianos blocked his own attempts to set up a school.

When I visited the village, a Catholic teacher home on furlough explained;

> *It's always a bother to have someone like this around. The people always divide among them-selves, as the linguist does favors, brings gifts and pays wages, so that people on one side of the village are friends with the linguist, while on the other side they're friends with the teacher.*

About 1971, the translator explained to a Lomalinda assembly, he was surprised when the village held a *yaje* dance, which he supposed they had given up. »Even though the village is tranquil and they say they are Catholics,« commented the translator:

> *this is what is deep in their souls, and we can see it in their reaction to medicine, to the primers, to any new thing that will better their lives.*

A village leader, the man who asked the translator to leave, had a different perspective:

> *The Catholics, the mission was here first and now we are with them, we do not want to change our religion again... We do not want the Bible in Desano because it is the same as the Catholics have, we do not need it.*

He seems to understand the purpose of the proposed Desano New Testament – to torpedo the Catholic to outsiders/Tukanoan to Tukanoan dualism – and be against the idea. What does SIL's alternative belief system mean to this man? Judging from the Wycliffe Statement of Doctrine and previous Gospel victories:

1) he has the opportunity to become a genuine Christian with a personal relationship to Jesus Christ;

2) he has no proper alternative except to watch his people divided into two ideological camps, his own tradition debilitated or destroyed.

Obviously Tukanoans are deciding not only their eternal destiny but their collective future. But it is not so easy to choose between here and eternity as might appear. In 1972 the Indian Policy Council anthropologists found leaders of seven communities, four in the Vaupes, very much in favor of their SIL translators, for reasons reading like a catalog of SIL's good works.

The translators learned the languages, gave sick people medicine, produced primers and taught how to read and write in their own languages, provided small livestock and new seeds, taught how to extract teeth, sometimes flew seriously ill people to hospitals and in some places sold tools and clothes and flew community products to market in airplanes.

In contrast, the anthropologists reported that Tukanoans around the Catholic stations said they opposed SIL for reasons like »we're Catholics« or »they come to impose dollar politics,« arguments which probably seem rather abstract in the lucky villages enjoying SIL's presence, if not to some of the people making them (Correal et al 1972).

But most of the people in the chosen, willing communities have not decided for Christ, a common situation in SIL-Colombia's communities to date. Except for the Cubeo, in 1974 the branch reported only one or several believers in each of the Vaupes languages, for the most part informants back from Lomalinda.

Wycliffe feels native alliance with other outsiders against its plans is foul play, but it recognizes the fact of native resistance. From a book about SIL-Brazil:

> *When a tribe first hears that the true God of the universe has communicated his desires and will in a Book, they are hesitant to accept an alternate spiritual lifestyle. There is first the struggle against Satan. This undisputed territory has been his since the beginning of time. And then there is the natural struggle common to all humanity – the resistance to change and to taking risks. Most find it a difficult struggle to grow out of the past and deal objectively with the present (Steven 1978:125).*

Face to face with the true God of the universe, it is no surprise that Tukanoan resistance to SIL's plan has surfaced in an alliance with the Javerianos. Thanks to SIL's ability to win native loyalty and the inevitable contradictions between the Javerianos and the Tukanoans, the struggle takes the form of a patronage battle.

The apple of discord between SIL and the Javerianos is the right to act as broker between the Tukanoans and the state, insofar as possible defining the terms of their encounter with the encroaching capitalist economy. Unlike the Javerianos, SIL is utterly dependent on the state for its future. Not coincidentally, SIL believes eternal salvation the Tukanoans' most important need and the movement it hopes to develop will have this as its focus. If the evangelical movement starts expanding again, more Tukanoans probably will sort themselves into evangelical and traditionalist villages like the Cubeo. If previous SIL behavior is any guide, believers will be instructed that it is contrary to God's law to disobey the government. Conceivably uranium mines could become God's will.

Like the Javerianos and CRIVA, SIL believes in organization, but primarily in terms of churches composed of redeemed sinners. One of SIL's Vaupes veterans told me movements like CRIC and CRIVA will destroy native culture faster than anything else and that mutual »blackmail« between rival intermediaries (permitting each to go about its plans for Indians as checked by the other) is a superior alternative.

At the Third ANUC Congress in 1974 Indians, probably for the most part CRIC, came to the following conclusions concerning SIL:

> *2. We study the ways in which the evangelical missions and the Summer Institute of Linguistics work. They claim to be interested only in the Bible and come to study our languages. In this way they can penetrate easier into communities which are already forewarned against the traditional methods of the (Catholic) Church.*
>
> *But in many areas we have removed the Summer Institute of Linguistics from our lands because we have realized that it is they, also, who are destroying our culture, traditions and customs. As well as this they exploit their knowledge of ourselves, of our lands and the riches of our earth in order to help the 'gringos' who follow them to open oil wells, to extract timber and gold, etc.*
>
> *3. The divisions which have been established within our communities, between Indians who adhere to the (Catholic) missions and to the evangelists, are used to keep us distracted, to keep our eyes covered so that we do not see how our real enemies are depriving us and destroying us.*
>
> *In many areas we have observed that what we need is unity amongst the Indians whether they be Catholic or evangelists; and so we have begun to fight in unity to defend our land and our culture. In other communities, as we begin to organize ourselves, we must understand this issue clearly.*
>
> *4. Our experience has shown us that we should not attack one another because we profess one or another religion. On the contrary we must reinforce our unity and strengthen the organization in order to win our struggles. And in the struggle we shall rediscover the roots of our own beliefs and traditions (Corry 1976:41).*

One can imagine the neat formulas, taking into account local needs and minimizing disruption, by which some SIL teams could have stayed on while others left and Colombians assumed the burden of essential services. But as reformers learned in the early 1970s, SIL-Colombia was not an operation readily cur-tailed or reformed to meet their own criteria or those of the Indian movements. It comes as a sweeping plan for Indians' future backed by the state power. Even when part of a community is opposed to SIL's presence, another faction usually continues to defend it and SIL carries on in defiance of evil powers not of this world. This chronic tension is at the root of the strenuous, so far unsuccessful attempts to per-suade the government to expel SIL across the board.

The Appeal to the State

To pose a mystery in simple terms, what exactly was a group of rightwing citizens of the major imperial power doing with an office in the Ministry of Government, a commodious base in the *llanos,* a flight and radio service, and teams in most of Colombia's minority groups? The technical facade had worked so well that the unveiling of SIL linguists as Protestant missionaries amounted to a scandal in itself. Basic issues in Colombian politics – the oppression of peasants and Indians, the cocaine and marijuana trade, guerillas, the domination of the national media by North American interests, control over production by transnational, preeminently North American capital, the compromise of the government by North Ame-rican interests – could resonate in a group of Bible translators.

In December 1970 the Bogota press published Mons. Correa's attack on SIL and on state Indian policy as exposed by Planas. SIL took generals, ministry officials, congressmen, indigenists and journa-lists out to Lomalinda. In February 1971 friends produced a series of seven articles explaining how wonderful the SIL program really was. »Unfortunately« – the word is Clarence Church's – SIL's friends were planning to turn Mons. Correa's denunciation into a review of the Concordat.

About the same time a commission – perhaps the National Council on Indian Policy – decided to investigate SIL. »Interestingly enough,« Church reported, while certain commissioners wanted to estab-lish their body as »some sort of permanent control over the work of SIL, our friends on the Commission, as well as the Minister of Interior himself, made sure that this did not happen.«

Church was addressing the May 1971 Wycliffe biennial conference. He had reason to be pleased but something was bothering him. True, there were »no crowds in the street yelling 'Yankee go home!'« But nationalism, »with its several implications,« was »very much the mode« and experience in other Latin American fields suggested »the time is potentially short.« (WBT 1971:71-4).

In October 1971 a Movement for the Defense of National Culture called for SIL's expulsion. Friends counter-proposed a new, reformed contract and SIL was conciliatory. »The new agreement must be more nationalist....« the new branch director Forrest Zander told *Tiempo.* »More training for the country's professionals must be included...« The national Council on Indian Policy commissioned a team of anthropologists and linguists to inspect SIL in the field.

Their calm and measured report of March 1972 praised SIL's linguistic and humanitarian work but recommended greater participation by Colombian professionals. That, rather than simply training, was one warning flag. But for SIL the most ominous recommendation was that it be prohibited from evange-lizing. The commission's reasoning was simple: deducing that »moral improvement« was the ultimate goal of the entity behind SIL, Wycliffe Bible Translators, it suggested that, since the constitution guaran-tees religious liberty, the state had no business contracting for religious education with any entity (Cor-real et al. 1972). It would have been a telling point in the United States.

Based on its commission's report, the Indian Policy Council recommended SIL be allowed a maxi-mum of four more years; that its personnel be replaced by Colombians; and that if it continued to evangelize its contract be revoked immediately. These suggestions were personally presented to the Minister of Government; they got lost. The ministry also lost interest in the council and apparently this was its last accomplishment (Friedemann 1975).

SIL had protected the near-total autonomy it required for business as usual, but at a cost. Now it was obvious the government's review process was bankrupt and there was no way to reform SIL. In the Ministry of Government North American missionaries counted more than Colombian indigenists. Based on the victories in Bogota, soon Lomalinda was known as »an independent republic in the middle of the *llanos.«*

In December 1973 then – Army Chief of Staff General Abraham Varon Valencia wrote a confiden-tial memo to the Minister of Defense. Frontier citizens are always reporting to Bogota mysterious activities, often perpetrated by North Americans or their business partners. Based on such reports, Varon Valencia stated the SIL, financed by an »Instituto Wyckliff« in the United States, was suspected of a variety of clandestine activities, centering chiefly around mineral exploitation, throughout the national territory. Five months later the defense ministry authorized a full-scale investigation by General José Joaquin Matallana Bermudez, Inspector General of the Army. A helicopter landed troops on the Lomalinda airstrip, they sealed the base and frogmen scoured the lake out back for evidence of suspected uranium mining. The commission also visited the sites of SIL's other alleged clandestine activities.

When the Matallana report leaked to the press a year later, it contained a number of surprises. One was that the commission had found neither »proof nor sufficient indications« that SIL personnel were engaged in covert activities. The commission even mentioned its »excellent opinion« of SIL members' integrity. But because it found some suspicious excavations in the vicinity of a translator and he seemed to be double-talking, it left this question dangling.

A second surprise was the report's reliance on Laurie Hart's anti-imperialist analysis for NACLA. Based on Hart, Matallana assailed SIL's dual identity and its manner of entering the country. SIL had deceived the government in 1962; there had been no national participation in the program and SIL had failed to honor its contract. It created »ideological confusion« among Indians, divided communities and destroyed cultural values. For these and other reasons, like national security, the commission recommended SIL's contract be terminated (University of Antioquia 1976).

A third surprise was that, a year after a senior army general reached these conclusions, SIL was still in the Ministry of Government, at its base in the *llanos,* working in most of the languages as if nothing had changed. Clearly there was more here than even a special military commission had been able to uncover.

In April 1975, two months before the Matallana report became available, the new director of the Indian Affairs office, Dr. José Gutierrez, resigned his post on grounds his superiors had prevented him from exercising any authority over SIL, his official responsibility. From what he could see, SIL had no business occupying an office in the Ministry of Government anyway. Between mid-1975 and early 1976 virtually all the linguists and anthropologists demanded SIL's expulsion.

Back in the *llanos* SIL was having problems in its labor pool, Puerto Lleras. In November 1974 a young politican named Oscar Beltran began denouncing SIL, prompting the town council to conduct its own investigation. They found little or nothing amiss, declared their sleuth *persona non grata* and, during the congressional denunciations, issued a statement praising SIL's many services for the community.

After the Matallana report appeared, Beltran claimed to have elicited dramatic revelations from SIL's livestock expert. Allegedly SIL not only had tracked down Che Guevarra in Bolivia but supplied the aerial photos necessary to localize the *llanos'* own Dumar Aljure. It was not a likely story – Aljure was killed in the vicinity of his house, a known locale – but it went into the pressure cooker.

The U.S. embassy minimized its interest in the SIL issue, but it was worth some diplomatic traffic. U.S. Ambassador Viron Vaky is supposed to have talked with Matallana. In early July Vaky reported to Washington that:

> SIL has a formidable critic in the person of General Matallana, (now) head of the national security police... (while the general) evidently found nothing incriminating, (he) remains nonetheless convinced that the SIL camp is involved in smuggling activities. Queried by the embassy, Matallana confirmed (the report which soon was published)...

In November France Presse and United Press International reported SIL was about to be expelled. At least in part, the error stemmed from the hemming and hawing of SIL's Government Ministry friend, Secretary General Hernan Villamarin, in reaction to two events. One was President Lopez Michelsen's vague declaration October 12 that he would »nationalize« linguistic affairs. The other was four nights of SIL denunciation in the congress by a failing opposition party, the *Alianza Nacional Popular.* Based on a copious, uneven documentation, ANAPO's Napoleon Peralta accused SIL of every offense known to imperialism, plus some which probably have not been invented yet. He even linked it to a secret U.S. rocket base in the Sierra Macarena, the existence of which was never verified. Defending SIL, largely by refuting the rocket base, were Defense Minister Varon Valencia and Government Minister Cornelio Reyes. Reyes is associated with the Cauca landowners assassinating CRIC leaders.

U.S. Ambassador Vaky hoped the October 12 Lopez statement would »take... the issue away« from SIL's opposition in congress. His language suggests a two – or three-party understanding:

SIL spokesman Will found nothing to object to in the Lopez statement... Coment: The Lopez approach gives the appearance of a unilateral government decision, while in effect implementing the basic terms of the long-standing proposal for a new government agreement with the SIL. The president's action will, we believe, eventually prove an effective way of removing the trouble-somme SIL question from the public eye.

... (The Lopez »Colombianization«) is essentially what the SIL has proposed for its new contract. The Lopez move may, accordingly, provide an arrangement satisfactory to both parties while providing an appearance of (government) action that should placate most SIL critics here.

Townsend made two visits to Bogota during the crisis, the first during the denunciation in congress. On the second, in February 1976, he tried to laugh away the CIA charges in a friendly radio interview and secured a letter of support from Education Minister Hernando Duran Dussan, a large landowner in the *llanos.*

SIL's critics were not as stupid as Ambassador Vaky hoped. They already had four years of experience with such stalling tactics. Since then SIL has hung on thanks to the support of a few powerful politicians and I would guess the U.S. embassy. Despite disappointments – the new contract always failed to materialize – SIL seemed to be recovering until mid-1977, when the Foreign Ministry stopped issuing visas for SIL and other missions. Many branch members left the country, on furlough or forever.

By early 1978 the branch again was hopeful it would get a new contract, but now there was an impeccable competing project. For some time a caucus from the Ministries of Government and Education, the National Department of Planning and the Anthropology Institute had been discussing the proper administrative solution. Their argument against SIL was two-fold:

1) the Colombian state and universities are capable of attending to the needs of native communities;

2) SIL proselytism is contrary to the official policy of respect of Indian tradition.

Proposing to give SIL its contractual one year notice, they stressed their *Plan Nacional Indigena* could be implemented with existing budgets given coordination between the various agencies.

According to a former MinGobierno official, President Lopez likes the proposal and in July 1978 asked Government Minister Alfredo Araujo to give SIL one year notice. Not a man interested in fulfilling the Lopez phase-out commitment, Araujo was indignant the proposal had come to Lopez through Education Minister Rafael Rivas.

That same month, in keeping with the ever-pending draft contract stipulating gradual withdrawal, the Government Ministry's Garcia Diaz Granados ordered SIL to withdraw from the Sierra Nevada and gave notice it could expect the same in Vaupes and Amazonas departments (about twenty SIL teams in all). Araujo nearly kicked Garcia Diaz out of the ministry and the order was revoked; Araujo also sat on the Lopez order until the Lopez administration ended a few weeks later.

Earlier that year the branch had praised the Lord for »meaningful relationships with local employees.« A few weeks after the Turbay Ayala inauguration seemed to restore branch prospects, SIL's assistant-to-the-director, hired c. 1975, published his letter of resignation in *El Tiempo*. Bernardo Camacho Arboleda accused SIL of mistreating its employees and concealing many of its activities from them. In the U.S. the branch asked for prayer, no details supplied.

Unlike his predecessors, the new Government Minister German Zea Hernandez is supposed to have been willing to study the SIL issue. On November 7, 1978 Foreign Minister Diego Uribe Vargas said SIL would be terminated by the end of the year. After Jonestown the armed forces announced that within two months they would present a proposal to expel SIL. Defense Minister Camacho Leyva and Government Minister Zea Hernandez said they would draft a protocol of expulsion in two weeks.

At this climactic moment, Satan having arrayed most of the Colombian government against SIL, who should ride to the rescue but the new mayor of Bogota? Hernando Duran Dussan is supposed to have gone to President Turbay and pleaded for SIL. Townsend dropped by, was received by Turbay Ayala and Zea Hernandez, and the ministerial trumpets fell silent. Soon visas were supposed to be moving again nicely.

Conclusion

Even the most improbable charges against SIL manifest the larger problem, SIL's articulation to the machinery of development and domination on the indigenous frontiers. Only one consideration could have overruled General Matallana in 1975, contravened the ministers in 1978 and justified the high political cost of retaining SIL: an essentially U.S. definition of Colombian national security. Wherever the balance of decision lies, SIL's persistence can be traced to its perceived value in obstaculizing the native self-defense movements. While SIL-Colombia translators are not exploiters, for their branch survival they can thank their attraction as a security measure, a tool in exploiting native domain. Judging from the experience of their Wycliffe colleagues in Peru, they have a tragic future in store.

The basic equation – originating in local exploiters, appealing to backward politicians and missionaries – is that native self-defense movements are communist fronts threatening nation, empire, Christendom. In Cameron Townsend's 1936 novel this kind of reasoning launched Wycliffe; it killed many Guahibo at Planas and will kill many Indians in the future. Only the empire and misappropriated wealth are at stake: to concede the self-defense movements anything of substance would inconvenience capital investment, which according to the U.S. formula is tantamount to national suicide. It is argued that the only way to deal with Colombia's social problems is to give capital maximum freedom to multiply itself, with the now-predictable result that Colombia's social crisis deepens.

SIL is still in Colombia full strength because hopefully it is obstaculizing elementary reforms. SIL is going along with the scheme in return for the extraordinary privileges it requires to perform its conception of the divine mission. Meanwhile it is poisoning relations between indigenists and the state, and Indians and the state, and among Indians themselves.

Not all Wycliffe translators are antagonistic to self-defense movements; some of them probably could provide important services to Colombian Indians for some time to come. But their institution will not compromise, however much it pretends to. SIL's questionable position can be seen in its recent claims to support indigenous self-determination. Where translators have brought their program to fruition, it often has led to highly sectarian movements pitting Indians against Satan in the guise of tradition and fellow Indians. There are ways to support indigenous self-determination; this is not one of them.

It must be hard for men like Cornelio Reyes and Duran Dussan to give up a North American troop which regards the rule of Cornelio Reyes and Duran Dussan as divinely ordained. We can only guess at that mysterious juncture when the men who rule Colombia decide that SIL is destabilizing more Colombians than it is stabilizing.

While purging SIL from the state apparatus will remove a specific threat to the self-defense movements, native support for SIL indicates that in some communities its departure will create a vacuum, a vulnerability to (or need for) patronage. These gaps in the state apparatus and local patronage will be filled. The change may lead to some improvements, but the results necessarily will be mixed. Victories for Indians will continue to depend largely upon the success of the self-defense movements.

Bibliography

Arcand, Bernard
1972 *The Urgent Situation of the Cuiva Indians of Colombia,* Copenhagen: IWGIA.

Bonilla, Victor Daniel
1970 »Disección de un etnocidio,« October 16, Bogota: Flash.

1972 »The Destruction of the Colombian Indian Groups,« *The Situation of the Indian in South America,* ed. W. Dostal, Geneva: World Council of Churches.

Church Clarence
1976 »Only One Master,« October, In Other Words, Huntington Beach, California: Wycliffe
1979 »The Real Battleground,« April, In Other Words.

Congress of Colombia
1975 Anales del Congreso, October 9, 14-5, 21; November 14, 20.

Correal, Gonzalo et al
1972 »El Instituto Lingüístico de Verano en Colombia,« March 10, Bogota: Consejo Nacional de Politica Indigenista.

Corry, Stephen
1976 *Towards Indian Self-Determination in Colombia,* London: Survival International.

FOIA-State
(documents released to author by U.S. State Department under the Freedom of Information Act, May 1979).

1961 letter and proposal from Robert Schneider to Robert Woodward, October 10.

1975 telegrams Bogota to Washington, July 2, October 14, November 20, signed Vaky.

Friedemann, Nina S. de
1975 »Niveles Contemporaneos de Indigenismo en Colombia,« *Indigenismo y Aniquilamiento de Indigenas en Colombia,* Juan Friede et al, Bogota: Universidad Nacional

Hart, Laurie
1973 »Pacifying the Last Frontiers,« December, *Latin America and Empire Report,* New York: North American Congress on Latin American Affairs.

Hefley, James and Marti
1972 *Dawn over Amazonia,* Waco, Texas: Word Books

1974 *Uncle Cam,* Waco, Texas: Word Books.

Hobsbawm, Eric
1977 »Ideology and Social Change in Colombia,« *Ideology and Social Change in Latin America,* ed. June Nash, New York: Gordon and Breach.

Maullin, Richard
1968 *The Fall of Dumar Aljure,* RM-5750-ISA, Santa Monica, California: RAND Corporation.

Orlandini, Pamela
1966 »Bilingual Quechua Schools Bring New Hope to Sierra Indians,« September 30, Lima: Peruvian Times.

Perez Ramirez, Gustavo
1971 *Planas: Un Ano Despues,* Bogota: Editorial America Latina.

Pike, Kenneth
1962 »Focus,« Summer, Translation, Santa Ana, California: Wycliffe.

Sorenson, Arthur
1974 »Multilingualism in the Northwest Amazon,« *Native South Americans,* ed. Patricia Lyon, Boston: Little, Brown.

Steven, Hugh
1978 *To the Ends of the Earth,* Chappaqua, New York: Christian Herald Books.

SIL-Colombia
1974 Communique, August.

Townsend, William Cameron
1936 »Tolo, the Volcano's Son,« April through October, Revelation magazine.

Townsend, William and Pittman, Richard
1975 *Remember All The Way, Huntington Beach, California:* Wycliffe.

University of Antioquia Anthropology Departement
1976 *»El Instituto Lingüístico de Verano,«* anthology, Boletin 15, Vol. 4, Medellin: Antropologia.

Varon Valencia, Abraham
1973 »Un Documento Secreto,« Sunday supplement, October 26, 1975, Cali: El Pueblo.

Wycliffe Bible Translators
1964 Biennial Conferende Reports.

1971 Biennial Reports

God is an American

by BERNARD ARCAND

Religious beliefs are not very interesting. I could never work up much enthusiasm for the idea that some people consider the sun a deity, while others wait for a messiah and my neighbours believe in the greatness of Allah or accept the notion of virgin birth. So, when the Summer Institute of Linguistics (SIL) claims that all the organization does is to offer Christian mythology as an alternative to indigenous mythologies, that statement, in itself, does not strike me as being especially disturbing. What bothers me though is the stupidity of the pretence that a mythology is something which can be offered as a simple alternative. Such a suggestion may apply within the context of a university graduate seminar in theology, but to claim that the same end can also be achieved through mission work in South America is not only ludicrous but criminal. From what I have witnessed of missionary work among the Cuiva Indians of Colombia, the efforts of the SIL may be said to have little to do with religious beliefs or mythology, and an awful lot to do with economics and politics.

The SIL became interested in the Cuiva during the mid-sixties. Following a rapid survey which showed that Cuiva language was significantly different from that of the neighbouring Guahibo (where the SIL already had a team at work), two missionaries were given the customary task of translating into Cuiva some if not all, of the New Testament with the usual goal of completing their work within a decade. Of course, it wasn't that simple and twelve years later much of the work remains to be done.

The missionaries sent to the Cuiva were two women in their thirties, one from Minnesota, the other from Ontario. These places of origin seem fairly typical of SIL recruitment in general. We often hear that the SIL is an organization of »American« missionaries, but they are not just any kind of Americans. They usually come from rural America and often from the mid-west, an area sometimes called »the heartland« of the US. I have never heard of a SIL missionary coming from Harlem or Cambridge, Massachusetts. They are most often recruited in smaller communities within the rural areas of the country, »the heartland of America«, »the silent majority«. This normally means that they look healthy, are physically large, tend to vote conservative and are totally dedicated to the Protestant ethics of hard work and individualism. These people have been brought up with the ideal of the American melting pot, the coming together of all cultures under God and the flag. It is not known how many of these missionaries are considered backward, ugly farmers by other Americans. How many carry abroad with them the feelings and the frustation of inferiority, or at least marginality, developed at home? How much a part of their upbringing were the stereotypes of the Indian conveyed by American culture?

The two missionaries sent to the Cuiva have had a difficult task. They began establishing contact with one particular band around 1965, at a time when the Cuiva were still living as nomadic hunters and gatherers. The two women trying to reach them would set up camp on the bank of the main river within the band's territory and then simply wait for visitors. The Cuiva would come, stay with the missionaries for a few days, accept all presents offered, and leave. With their awkward equipment of outboard motor, tent, cooking tools, clothing, tape recorders, etc., the two women could never hope to follow. The Cuiva, who carry very little are able to leave any camp within a few minutes and usually change site every few days. Under these circumstances, the best the missionaries could hope for was to establish preliminary contact and become known to the Cuiva, while learning perhaps some of the basic elements of the language.

Bernard Arcand graduated from Cambridge University. He later taught anthropology at the universities of Copenhagen and McGill. Presently he is teaching at Université Laval in Québec.

These short visits and very limited contacts could have gone on for years, but a tragic incident was to change profoundly the direction of Cuiva history. Faced with mounting pressures from Colombian settlers, who for the last twenty years had been slowly invading their territory, members of the band with which the SIL had established contact decided to build permanent houses and create a small village which would be used as a base camp for migrations and where the group would cultivate the soil to supplement hunting and gathering. »The site chosen for this village was minutes away from the ranch of a settler who had maintained friendly relations with the band and for whom quite a few Cuiva had worked in the past... The village experiment did not last long. As soon as a few houses were completed (others were in construction) and after the soil had been cleared and sown, Mario Gonzales, the neighbouring settler, whom the Cuiva thought friendly, together with five of his friends, came to the Cuiva village at midday on the 20th of July 1966. At the very moment when they were welcomed as friends, these settlers began shooting in all directions. Most of the Cuiva escaped into the forest, but one man (a cripple who could not run as fast as the others) was killed and six others were wounded. The settlers even took pains to cut up the body of the dead man and throw the parts into the river; some parts of the body remained hanging from branches overlooking the river«. (Arcand 1972:13).

The creation of the village had been encouraged by newly arrived American missionaries, unrelated to the SIL, whose mission was mostly to work with the local inhabitants of the neighbouring Colombian village of Cravo Norte, but who also occasionally travelled by boat to visit the Cuiva for a few hours. It was they who provided the tools and seeds for cultivation, who made sure all those injured in the massacre received proper medical treatment and who insisted with the local police authorities that charges be pressed against the settlers.

In the days following the attack on their village, the Cuiva regrouped, moved and pitched camp next to the ranch of a Swiss settler who had lived in Colombia for the last thirty years and who had always seemed to have a marked sympathy for the Indians. The Cuiva felt protected by this man's presence and, in any case, at this particular moment anything was better than massacre. Much of their traditional territory was now occupied by settlers and agriculture appeared to be the only possible way to survive. On a small plot of land next to the ranch, they began to build houses, create a village and cultivate the soil. Within a few months, the Cuiva lost an economy based on hunting and gathering for an economy which would soon become dependent on agriculture.

This radical change perfectly suited the aims of the SIL missionaries. They would no longer need to chase the Cuiva over their vast hunting territory. They encouraged the Swiss settler and the other American missionaries in Cravo Norte to supply the needed seeds, tools and advice. They paid some Cuiva to build a thatchroofed house for themselves, five times larger than any Cuiva shelter. They paid for the construction of a short air-strip in the nearby savanna. These constructions meant easy access by air to a field-camp with a population of roughly 200 Cuiva and a relatively comfortable house from which to operate. Nevertheless, the missionaries came only rarely. When I first met the Cuiva in 1968, the missionaries were back in the US on sabbatical leave. They returned to Colombia in 1969 and during all of the following year they visited the Cuiva village only twice, for a total of 11 weeks. When I returned to the same village in 1973, the missionaries were again absent. The main reason for this apparent lack of dedication seems to be that the missionaries prefer to do most of their work at the SIL Colombian headquarters at Lomalinda. There, they can find all the material comfort of North America in a camp inhabited only by SIL missionaries living in complete isolation from Colombian society. Since they must work on learning the language, they bring with them to this base two, three, or four Cuiva, to whom they offer room and board, in return for language instruction and domestic services.

From the missionaries' point of view, the result of this policy of bringing the Cuiva to onself rather than going to them is reasonable progress in learning the language, with the added and not so negligible advantages of comfort and tranquility. The price they must pay is ignorance of much of Cuiva culture. Not even the wildest theoretician of linguistic determinism, or the strongest proponent of formal analysis of language, would seriously claim that one can understand a culture by simply talking with a native speaker of a language in a closed room totally removed from the language's physical, social and intellectual contexts. What the missionaries learn this way is an elementary command of the syntax and grammar of the language. But their knowledge of semantics often seems minimal. One trivial example: the Cuiva use the word »Ako« to salute and welcome anyone coming to visit them or even just passing by their hammock; the visitor answers with »Hé«, an acknowledgement for the greeting; but the missionaries walk around the village shouting »Ako« at everyone, and this is answered with either »Hé« or »Ako«

by puzzled Cuiva who usually giggle at the confusion, a reaction which the missionaries no doubt understand as a sign of great friendship; one man even asked me if I would teach the missionaries to salute properly. The example may seem trivial but is symptomatic: the words »Ako« and »Hé« must be heard hundreds of times every day in camp and are literally the first two words any foreigner learns. But missionaries do not come to learn the meaning of things. They merely strive to acquire the means of transmitting their own message.

This message becomes very clear when we look at the tools by which they hope to teach literacy. Teaching the Cuiva to read is part of the SIL contractual engagement with the Colombian government and is the obvious prerequisite to giving them a translation of the New Testament. Besides the missionaries' direct interventions with Cuiva society which we shall consider later, the teaching of reading represents the SIL's strongest effort at influencing and modifying Cuiva culture. Their strategy uses two separate methods, one public and the other quite secret. The latter consists of giving the Cuiva written versions of their own myths which have been transformed to incorporate a Christian content. These texts are prepared on the SIL's private mimeographing machine and are almost certainly distributed without the knowledge of the government, since they are proof of a flagrant violation of the SIL contract with Colombia: the spreading of evangelical propaganda. Let me give you an example of this method. The Cuiva have a number of myths dealing with the character of »Namoun« (called »Nacom« by the missionaries, no doubt a difference in phonetic hearing), a cultural hero said to be responsible for the creation of people, the growth of trees, the menstrual cycle, and a few other things. In the hands of the missionaries, the story printed and distributed to the Cuiva becomes:

> »Nacom in the language of the non-Indians is called 'Dios!. He, Nacom, made the earth. He made all the earth and all the savanna. He made the animals and the birds. He made all Indians and all non-Indians. He blew on them. He made the sky, the stars and the moon. He made it all good«.

Then, in the following story, the missionaries introduce a mythical character totally alien to Cuiva culture:

> »Satan created all bad things, illness, death. He does not like Nacom, nor his son Jesus-Christ«.

And the stories go on and on. Having seen these mimeographed texts and being one of the few outsiders who can understand them, I consider myself in a privileged position to call a liar any SIL missionary claiming to respect indigenous cultures or claiming, as the SIL does in front of the Colombian government, that the organization is not involved in forcing Christianity onto other people.

Far less secret, the other method for teaching reading is directly supervised by the »Indian Affairs« department of the Colombian government. It involves printing and distributing short stories written in »basic Cuiva« and quite similar to primary school textbooks stories anywhere. But even these short stories carry a powerful message and seem aimed at teaching far more than literacy. Here is an example of one such story:

> »A man cleans the land surrounding his house with a rake. He decides to leave and go plant corn in his field. Soon he returns home because he has forgotten his hat. That night, he hears a woolly opossum that has come to eat his chickens. He gets up from his hammock and throws a stick at the animal to chase it away. One chicken is dead and the man proposes to eat it in the morning.«

This trivial little story appears innocent enough, but it is in fact yet another effort by the missionaries to transform the Cuiva way of life. Bringing them to a permanent village, where they will abandon their nomadic habits and depend mostly on agriculture, is the common goal of both the settlers who want the Cuiva land and the missionaries who want their souls. And each side blames the other for forcing the Cuiva to change their old ways.

This short story seems straightforward enough when it mentions the house, the field, the planting of corn and the ownership of chickens. Yet it is remarkable: every single detail of the story corresponds to the state of affairs which the missionaries are hoping for and which contrasts sharply with traditional Cuiva culture. »Cleaning the land surrounding a house« was rarely done by the Cuiva: only after remaining at the same site for a long period of time will the surroundings become dirty, and then it is much easier to change camping site than clean the surroundings. *»Soon he returns home because he has forgotten his hat«:* in over two years I had never seen a Cuiva forget anything when leaving on a trip (one does not go hunting forgetting one's arrows!); the hat of course is also new, but the very idea of needing a hat is interesting: hunters and gatherers typically leave the cool shade of the forest either early in the morning or late in the afternoon, when a hat is quite unnecessary; only an agriculturalist would be silly enough to cut down the trees for cultivation and to work under the burning sun. *»... he hears a woolly opossum ... gets up from his hammock and throws a stick at the animal to chase it away«:* the woolly opossum is considered a funny animal by the Cuiva, one that stinks badly and has a funny scream, but it is not in any way a dangerous animal and a man would never leave the comfort of his hammock in the middle of the night to chase it away; except, of course, if he had chickens to worry about. Finally, *»the man proposes to eat it* (the chicken) *in the morning«:* the Cuiva do not eat chicken and this is somewhat of a puzzle for settlers and missionaries; some Cuiva have had chickens for years (in 1973 I counted 14 chickens for 180 Cuiva in one band) and eat nothing but their eggs, refusing to kill the animals even in periods of hunger and always preferring to sell them to settlers.

This text is illustrated by rather poor drawings depicting a man wearing a hat and standing next to a woman in western dress. The two characters are situated in a clearing, not the forest, and in the background hangs a hammock with mosquito-net.

The missionaries would probably find these comments petty and unfair. I have heard them say this is obviously what the future will bring the Cuiva, that agriculture is their only hope for survival, that hats and mosquito-nets can be very practical and are in fact much appreciated by the Cuiva. Perhaps, but the point I am trying to make is that the SIL has no intention of »respecting cultures« as the official propaganda would have the world believe. It is involved in the imposition of a new culture and in the brutal destruction of the traditional Cuiva way of life. The missionaries play an active and essential role in a process which can only be to the advantage of settlers and other foreign invaders. Their intervention is deliberate effort to limit the Cuiva to a minimum space and get them to accept this as the irreversible outcome of history. Christian missionaries have been performing this colonial task for centuries and the SIL is certainly no different. What are perhaps different are the incredible public statements to the effect that the Cuiva were forced into this unfortunate situation by settlers and that all the missionaries are trying to do is to bring some relief into their lives, before God brings them final relief in heaven.

Any Cuiva would tell you what matters now is not so much the thought of heaven but the problem of securing land rights over their territory. The missionaries do not seem to be listening. After almost ten years of work with the Cuiva, the SIL has never lifted a finger to help these people to secure their rights over their traditional lands. They have done nothing, although their often privileged relationship with the Colombian government would have allowed them to intercede in a powerful way the Cuiva. The only occasion the two missionaries became involved in the issue of land rights was when they tried to obtain official papers confirming that the Swiss settler had indeed granted a small portion of his ranch for the village. This is a small piece of land, a few hectares for roughly 200 people, and certainly not the 13.000 km² of hunting territory traditionally occupied by the 600 Cuiva in the area. But then, the small village is where the missionaries want to see the Cuiva.

By transforming myths and imposing new stories, by remaining passive in face of the pressing land issue, the missionaries must have an impact on Cuiva culture. But they also interfere directly with society in a number of other domains which would seem to have little to do with religion and be rather remote from their stated goal of learning the language and translating the Bible.

Their very life-style is an influence. The missionaries have always owned the largest, best-built and, whenever they are in camp, cleanest house in the village. Between 1970 and 1973, they paid for the building of a new, larger and even more elaborate house and suggested the Cuiva build their houses in a semi-circle around it. Half the band did and the impression is that of a small medieval kingdom. Furthermore, the material wealth of the missionaries is awesome. They usually reach the village by means of a small plane filled to the brim with petrol tanks, cooking equipment, stove, plates, books, tape recorder, cloth hammocks, mosquito nets, etc. Life in their house is a pale effort to model middle-America, with hair-curlers and Jello pudding. It is not always easy for two women to live in a remote Indian village and they are tough enough to get by on what must seem to them the bare minimum. To anyone else the contrast is shattering: two tall women, adult but not married, using radio to keep in daily contact with Lomalinda and sometimes even with the US, while a few metres away Cuiva houses are little more than simple lean-to shelters, protecting a family of 6 or 7 in a crowded space littered with pieces of old cloth, oil cans and broken knives.

The missionaries hope to influence more than by simple example. They also very much want to encourage private ownership and the private use af gardens. When the Cuiva began cultivation, not everyone participated and even then not all with the same enthusiasm; the result has been that some families now own fairly large gardens, whereas their neighbours may never have bothered to plant anything. Nevertheless, at the same time, the Cuiva have maintained their traditional system of distributing all available food among all those present in camp. This is the customary egalitarian system adopted by most societies with an economy based on hunting and gathering; however, here it means that whether one cultivates or not will not really determine the amount of vegetables one will be able to eat; those who cultivate give to those who have no gardens. This seems to infuriate the missionaries. It conflicts with their beliefs on how society should be organized and with the principle that reward should come only to those who toil. It conflicts with what others would call the Protestant ethic and the spirit of capitalism. From their point of view, the Cuiva system of food distribution is an aberration and I have seen them blame people for scavenging from their neighbours and suggest that if they wanted vegetables they should themselves plant and harvest. The missionaries will be happy only when both production and consumption are fully individualized. Private ownership of the means of production, the possibility of creating surpluses, the birth of capital and profits... the rest of the story is well known. This is the way of God, and it seems as equally important to impose all this on the Cuiva as it is to translate the Bible.

These economic principles also regulate how the missionaries themselves relate to the Cuiva. Although they bring food as part of their own equipment, they remain partly dependent on hunters for their meat supply and always pay in money or goods whenever they obtain meat from anyone. To them, the anthropologist's habit of accepting food freely and reciprocating, often much later, with gifts was doubly scandalous: on one hand, I was exploiting the generosity of the Cuiva and on the other, I was perpetuating the Cuiva tendency to accept gifts for nothing. My behaviour was seen as unethical, if not clearly immoral. Yet, it followed closely the rules of Cuiva economy.

In 1973, those who worked gardens gave away their vegetables quite freely, but hunted less and gave far less meat than they received. If the missionaries have it their way, the gardeners could experience a rapid decline in the protein content of their diet, while the hunters, now limited to exploiting the relatively small area close to the village, could risk short term shortages if they can no longer rely on the more constant supply of vegetables produced by the gardeners. The longer term risk is the complete destruction of the Cuiva economy, with all this implies for the foundation of social relations, and its replacement by a privatized economy based on individualism and leading very likely to exploitation.

For the missionaries, it is the traditional Cuiva economy which is exploitative: some worked and produced more than others, yet in the end all were equal. Hard work was not recognized for its true worth and laziness could escape without penalty. This notion of fairness, which in the missionaries' mind turns to stingy accounting, does not seem to be of great concern to the Cuiva: within relatively broad limits, it never seemed to matter much whether individuals produced more or less, according to their inclination, energy and taste, as long as there was plenty for all. This, to the missionaries, is supremely unfair. And behind their position, as well as behind so much of the »American way of life«, lies the notion that human action can always be quantified and moneyfied. Everything has a value which translates into material wealth. This materialistic philosophy is surely one of the more blatant paradoxes of an organization claiming that spiritual salvation is the central focus of life on earth.

The missionaries pay for the construction of a house, pay for its repair, pay for food, pay for all menial services and pay their informants. For the Cuiva, this translates into clothes, cooking pots, knives, machetes, and other foreign goods. But since the missionaries cannot supply the needs of the whole community, they also buy Cuiva handicrafts at whatever prices these may fetch with other missionaries at their base camp of Lomalinda. The problem, of course, is that the Cuiva make little more than hammocks and bows and arrows, which can never hope to occupy a competitive place on a handicraft market dominated by the elaborate artifacts which other missionaries bring back from Amazonia or the Choco. So, this new trade is almost irrelevant for the Cuiva: they can produce many of these items in a few hours and the market created by the missionaries is too small to justify additional efforts. It also means that the missionaries help maintain the need for imported goods and that, when a Cuiva wants something from Colombian society the simplest solution is to work for wages at one of the local ranches. In this indirect way, the missionaries press the Cuiva in to entering the lowest level of the Colombian economy.

The only time the missionaries have interfered, but without their characteristic sense of mercantilism, is when they helped the sick and provided free medical supplies. Their equipment is adequate, they have received professional training in nursing and on the whole their medical assistance has been efficient and of high quality. But this assistance can only last the length of the missionaries' stay with the community. When they proudly said to me, shortly after a woman died, that this was the first death ever to occur while they were present in camp, the claim was, of course, that they had saved all the others. But if one calculates how long they had actually spent with the Cuiva over the last decade, their claim was reduced to saying there had been no death over a period of about six months. I could make the same claim, without any professional training and with only very inadequate medical supplies. It may be very unfair to try diminish the missionaries' valuable medical assistance, but so much is made of their role as medical officers that it seems important to replace it within its proper context and reduce it to its real proportions. The SIL often stresses the glory of its medical assistance, but it must also be stressed that this is only occasional help at best and that never has an ounce of penicillin cost a people so much.

The missionaries also interfere with many other aspects of daily life besides economic and health matters. They are quite outspoken in their opposition to hallucinogenic drugs. They insist on wearing dresses, even during the mosquito season when they wear them over trousers, simply because this is to them the only proper dress for a woman. Of course, anything approaching nudity would offend their great sense of decency and would be met with strong verbal disapproval. The practical problems created by this attitude are well known even to the missionaries. Cuiva traditional clothing had the double advantage of being easily replaceable and of leaving most of the skin exposed so that the frequent rains did not mean one stayed wet for hours risking respiratory diseases. The missionaries insist that clothing is an essential protection against mosquitoes and they want to eliminate the health hazard by providing the Cuiva with more and more clothes and teaching them to change dress more often. Never would they suggest that Western clothing is not really necessary during the dry season, when it never rains and there are no mosquitoes. It is also tempting to add a more subjective, personal note and say that the clothing given to the Cuiva usually consists of old rags which make them look like tramps, which is precisely how they enter Western civilization.

The missionaries also interfere with disputes or quarrels and do not hesitate to walk across camp, in the middle of the night and with flashlight in hand to stop a marital fight. These disputes can certainly be dangerous and sometimes people do get hurt, but again, this is an example of how the missionaries do not hesitate to pass value judgements on Cuiva society, decide what is wrong, show no concern for Cuiva authority structure, while interfering directly to change the culture. Any behaviour is evaluated on the basis of middle-American Christianity which always prevails in the end.

On the whole, the Cuiva's reaction to the missionaries has been dominated by their remarkable sense of polite hospitality. Unlike many settlers, the missionaries have behaved in a rather civilized manner and the Cuiva have responded in kind. We must also understand that Cuiva culture and social organization, like that perhaps of many other hunting and gathering societies, are characterized by flexibility and the ability to incorporate foreigners smoothly and, to a large extent, also their ideas. For example, new Western medicine is not seen as a threat to traditional Cuvia curing techniques, but as an added and welcomed contribution; in fact, it would be just as impolite to refuse this help as it would be impolite not to give away most of one's personal belongings. So, by helping cure the sick, the missionaries are behaving correctly and this is much appreciated. The same holds true to some extent for the introduction of new ideas, may these be tales of distant lands or new concepts on cosmology or theology. Cuiva adults, during their long hours of leisure, seem to enjoy nothing better than intelligent discussions of abstract concepts. The missionaries' doctrine of a single God, creator of all things and father of us all, is not necessarily very intelligent, but it does provide an interesting topic for discussion.

The Cuiva's sense of politeness often presses them into appearing as if they gladly accept the authority of the missionaries. It is never proper to disagree openly with someone or to appear to be blatantly refusing what has been requested. The customary and polite way to show disagreement is for a person to remain calm, keep smiling, say nothing openly, but go and live in another part of the territory. After a few weeks, the disagreement will most often be forgotten and all can live together again. Since the missionaries never stay in camp very long, the Cuiva relate to them with somewhat of a double standard. Their informants, those individuals most closely associated with the missionaries, know perfectly well how they disapprove of drugs, certain modes of clothing, etc., and will normally refrain from these whenever the missionaries are in camp. As soon as they leave, these informants quickly return to a more normal life style; so much so, in fact, that one is at times left with the impression they are celebrating the missionaries' departure.

But all politeness aside, the overwhelming reason why the Cuiva react the way they do to missionaries, anthropologists, or any other friendly outsider is simply that given their tragic history of contact with White society, they are very much aware of needing all the help they can get and that any future is better than genocide.

The two SIL missionaries certainly do appear strange to them, but probably no more than any other non-Cuiva. The sight of two adult unmarried women living together connotes lesbianism, a source of amusement among some Cuiva males. Their habit of taking people away for a few months at their base camp of Lomalinda causes grief among their close relatives (who can be heard crying for days after their departure), but it is now well-established knowledge that these informants will on the whole be treated nicely and that there is little to fear for them.

The missionaries' relations to the anthropologist were often far more delicate. During the two months we spent in the same community our relations were of correct avoidance and neither side interfered with the other's work. However, I did get the clear impression I was an intruder on a territory with scarce resources. I was also clearly seen as a very bad influence on the Cuiva. To give only one example, I was told that by being the first non-Indian to take drugs I was encouraging the Cuiva to use them. It had never before crossed my mind that the Cuiva needed a foreigner's approval to take drugs! The more aggressive side of the SIL was never shown by the two missionaries themselves but came from more indirect sources. Friends who at the time were doing fieldwork in the Vaupés area of Colombia reported to me how SIL pilots had told them that I was importing guns from Venezuela in preparation for a Cuiva revolt and that I was sharing my hammock with at least five or six young Cuiva girls. I immediately wrote a letter to Mr. Clarence Church, then head of SIL operations in Colombia, pointing out that nothing was gained by his organization spreading such rumours. He never bothered to reply.

The missionaries' relations to Colombians, and to Colombia in general, seemed characterized by a mixture of fear and contempt. They had practically very little to do with Colombians, since they flew almost directly from the U.S. to their base camp at Lomalinda and then to the Cuiva. It seems that only the highest officials of the SIL have relations with Colombia and then only with higher government authorities from whom they must obtain the necessary permits and protection for the whole operation. Individual missionaries are cared for and transported by fellow Americans, often without any Colombian intervention, and some do not even speak much Spanish. The missionaries I knew tried as much as possible to avoid contact with Colombians and appeared definitely ill at ease whenever settlers came to visit them or when they had to travel to a nearby Colombian village. What is worse, they seemed to suffer from some acute form of revolutionary paranoia. In 1970, when it was reported that a group of Guahibo Indians in the Planas area had begun a guerilla uprising, the two missionaries became extremely nervous and made hasty preparations to return to Lomalinda. The Planas area is at least 300 kilometers from Cuiva territory, but they were convinced the rebels would soon arrive and execute them. This kind of paranoia may be in part the result of the ancient persecution of Protestants in Colombia and of American anti-communist indoctrination, but it also clearly indicates an extraordinary ignorance of Colombian society and politics. It further explains why the SIL, through its missionaries in the Planas area, is said to have been eager to provide scouts and interpreters for the army during its repression of the Guahibo. If true, that incident alone should be enough to undermine forever the myth that the SIL works to protect Indians from massacre at the hands of Colombians.

The distance which they carefully maintain between themselves and Colombian society can only constitute an insult to any nationalist. When we say that the SIL tries to integrate the Cuiva into Western society, we really mean that they force upon them the values of white Anglo-Saxon Protestant Americans and certainly not those of rural Colombia. To the SIL missionaries, most Colombians are little more than backward and ignorant peasants for whom they have very little sympathy. Once their entry into the country is sanctioned by the upper echelon of the government, they are quite wary of any form of intervention by Colombian institutions. They do not trust Colombian planes, Colombian food, and even less Colombian linguists or missionaries. To them, Colombia is a third-world country on its slow path to becoming as advanced as the United States and there is thus no point in living like Colombians or in teaching Colombian society to the Cuiva.

Yet, the very presence of Colombian peasants constitutes an essential part of the SIL ideology. Whatever their efforts to transform Indian society, these are always justified *post facto* by the claim that change is inevitable and, if it were not for the SIL the Cuiva would be left in the hands of Colombians. And that, by their own definition, would of course be far worse. The argument makes some sense when one looks at the number of settlers in the area who would gladly rid their neighbourhood of all Indians. But the missionaries are much less convincing when they face friendly settlers, local medical authorities, or the new generation of Colombian linguists and anthropologists who have all shown interest in helping the Cuiva. The SIL does not really want to hear of such people since much of the justification for its presence rests on a simplistic view of the most typical Colombian in the area as an armed cowboy fully intent on genocide. This is how the organization tries to convince the world of the value of its missionary work. Of course, this leaves the SIL open to embarassing questions on the merits of Colombian Catholic missionary activities, not to mention the much wider question of what, in their opinion, would happen to a Cuvia missionary working in, say, Montana. This is not the sort of question SIL missionsaries ask themselves, secure as they are in their belief that Christianity is unique and universal.

It would be surprising if they do not succeed, through repeated bribery or the sheer weight of their propaganda, to convince and »convert« at least a handful of Cuiva. This would be enough to transform profoundly a society which has always depended on consensus and close cooperation. Although Christianity teaches love and tolerance, it has a long history of generating prejudices and social divisions. The new Cuiva converts will begin producing by themselves, living by themselves and the proudness of their faith will turn into contempt for those who do not »recognize Jesus-Christ as their personal savior«. The goal of the SIL will then be achieved, Indian society will be divided and shaped more along the lines of a Western model, and the Cuiva will begin despising one another. Fractured and divided, Cuiva society will be even more vulnerable, even less capable of resisting or even surviving the foreign invasion of its territory and its life. But, the missionaries would say, a handful of Cuiva could then make it to heaven.

Bibliography

Arcand, Bernard
1972 *The Urgent Situation of the Cuiva Indians of Colombia*, Copenhagen: IWGIA, Document No. 7.

Missionaries and frontiersmen as agents of social change among the Rikbakca

by ROBERT A. HAHN

Introduction

Mid-twentieth century saw a resurgence of extractive industry in the Amazon basin; and while the focus of this activity in the region has since shifted, from rubber to minerals and to land clearing for cattle raising, the exploitation of resources in general has intensified and seems likely to sweep the region, thus phasing out another frontier.

Beyond this frontier are autochthonous societies for which this expansion will bring absorption if not extinction. The expansion of the frontiers of industrial society has meant the equivalent reduction of territory of those indigenous groups beyond these frontiers. Indigenous groups have fled physical and cultural devastation since the arrival of Columbus (Crosby 1972); but there will soon be no place to hide from contact with a society whose impact on their own societies has seldom been better than violent and disruptive. In his broad survey, Ribeiro (1957) estimated that during the first half of our century one third of the Brazilian indigenous groups living in isolation were physically extinguished.

In this essay[1] I examine the case of the Rikbakca of the Juruena River, Mato Grosso, who first came into direct and seemingly pacific contact with the Brazilian frontier in 1957. The Rikbakca have in the twenty years since been greatly reduced in number by several epidemics; their territory of residence and usufruct has also been reduced by gradual restriction to a 'reserve' and by the intrusion of the Brazilian frontier into their traditional territories; their economy, social and political organization, and cosmology have similarly, and partly in consequence, undergone substantial change; their self esteem and their respect for their own traditions have in many individuals been eroded and supplanted by an ideology which values 'civilized' goods and traits, and which even denies their Rikbakca identity.

Physically they have done better than many groups under similar circumstances; though severely limited by past disruptions and restrictions, political boundaries today are defined and defended, and cultural integrity is promoted by the Jesuit mission which is the broker between them and the Brazilian government-frontier forces.

In this study I shall concentrate on the changes which have taken place in Rikbakca society and on the possible sources of the changes. I shall begin with a description of Rikbakca social tradition and history as I can reconstruct them for the period from 1900 to 1950. I shall then present a chronology of the events of the 'pacification' and of the reduction to the present Reservation. I shall attempt to ascribe agency in this social transformation to various social groups which have participated directly: the Jesuit Missao Anchieta, the Summer Institute of Linguistics (S.I.L.), a Lutheran mission, and Brazilian frontiersmen (rubber tappers and land clearers) and the firms which employed many of them[2]. I shall discuss the role which Rikbakca themselves have played in their own social transformation, and I shall speculate on the connections of the Juruena frontier with the wider economic system.

It has been argued (Hart 1973) that SIL and other Missions actively and intentionally promote the economic and political interests of the industrial society from which they have come rather than the interests of the indigenous groups with which they work. While the explicit objective of SIL is the translation of the *Bible* into indigenous languages and the fostering of literacy skills to allow reading and

Robert Alfred Hahn, born 1945 in New York. Ph. D. Havard University, 1976. Dissertation: Rikbakca Categories of Social Relations: An Epistemological Analysis. Currently doing research in Comparative Medical Systems.

study of the *Bible,* not only, Hart claims, does this translation and study itself destroy the indigenous cosmology, but undermines social and political organization.

Those missionaries, SIL and others, involved with the Rikbakca have never, to the best of my knowledge, been motivated by a goal of promoting the interests of Industrial society. It seems clear, however, that despite their own interests, their efforts have served the interests of the Industrial society. In effect, the Rikbakca population has been removed as an obstacle to the exploitation of resources in the region. In this work, the Jesuit Missao Anchieta has been the principal agent of change, and the SIL has worked mostly within Missao Anchieta plans, itself responsible for little of the change which has taken place.

While the Rikbakca have survived the transformation, their situation and its development are far from the ideal. I oppose any 'mission' whose object is unilateral conversion of another person or group; I believe that indigenous populations should be treated as are sovereign nations, with rights to be respected. It is my assumption that the members of these societies have a good deal to teach us, as we may have to teach them. My ideal here, contrary to the evangelical missionary ideal, is one of communication and exchange.

Chronology of Rikbakca Transformations

Given a speculative reconstruction of precontact society, a sketchy chronology of subsequent events, and a more comprehensive acquaintance with only contemporary social life, causal and historical account of change in Rikbakca society can be at best hypothetical. Such an account is what Hempel (1965) calls an »explanation sketch«. Comparative information, moreover, is scarce since contact histories are commonly obscured or idealized where recorded at all. An exception is Bonilla's (1972) superb history of the Sibundoy valley in Colombia. My account of the Rikbakca contact will thus be explicitly speculative and at best suggestive.

I present the Rikbakca case in three parts. First I suggest some prominent features of Rikbakca traditional life between 1900 and 1950. I then describe the 'Rikbakca Wars' (Dornstauder 1975) of the 1950's and the 'pacification' of the Rikbakca as it proceeded until 1962. I describe developments since 'pacification', the current state of affairs, and future prospects. I conclude with several propositions concerning agency in this history.

(A) Rikbakca Society: 1900-1950

From the recency of Rikbakca conflicts with Brazilian frontiersmen on the Juruena and Arinos, from Rikbakca familiarity with regions only west of the Juruena, and from the absence of mention of anything possibly Rikbakca in the accounts of the nineteenth century travellers on the Juruena (e.g., Chandless 1962), we may infer that prior to at least the 1860s Rikbakca inhabited regions west of the Juruena, and that they only recently have migrated to the Juruena valley. (See Map 1.).

We may guess that between 1900 and 1950 they occupied a territory whose eastern frontier was marked by the Juruena and the Arinos. The territory reached from north of the confluence of the Juruena and the Papagaio Rivers to south of the Augusto Falls. The Rikbakca inhabited also the triangular region lying between the Arinos and the Juruena, probably also north of the confluence of the Juruena and the Papagaio. Older Rikbakca have knowledge of regions west of the Juruena and almost no knowledge of regions east; they commonly refer to a river called »Pihiknobwica« – »Fishes«, presumably the Aripuana, and they report the fauna and flora of the region in detail. It is possible that Rikbakca have been pushed out of their earlier region by one or more of the 'Cinta Larga' tribes which they fear. In the 1950s they began to encounter new conflicts, this time with the Brazilian frontier.

I estimate that the population during the first half of the century was an average of approximately one thousand.[3] The 1973 population was slightly below three hundred and was increasing.

Rikbakca occupation and use of land varied with the seasons of the year. In the rainy season, from November to May, Rikbakca occupied their semi-permanent settlements, harvesting from their fields, and hunting, fishing, and gathering in a region of two or so days' walk surrounding the settlement; I refer to this form of occupation as 'residence'. Within this region, settlements were somethimes separated by

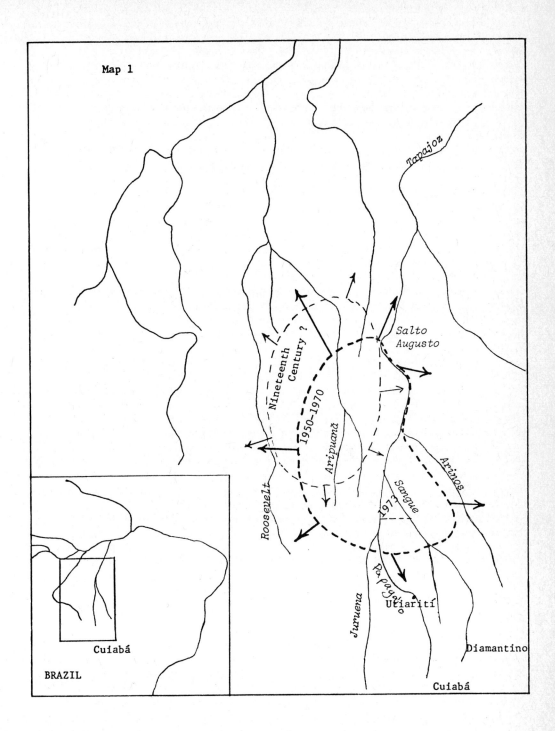

Map 1

Tapajoz

Salto
Augusto

Nineteenth
Century ?

1950-1970

Aripuanã

Arinos

Roosevelt

Sangue

1973

Papagaio

Juruena

Utiarití

Diamantino

Cuiabá

BRAZIL

Cuiabá

87

only a few hours' walk. During the dry season, following the clearing of jungle for later planting, a segment of the settlement's inhabitants would travel for approximately two months, in search of various resources, including cane and feathers for the manufacture of arrows. I describe the total region of occupation as one of 'usufruct'. On Map 1 residence is indicated by dashed lines, usufruct by arrows radiating from regions of residence.

The region of usufruct and dry season occupation was very extensive. Maniha, an older Rikbakca woman, told me of expeditions of two months which her father made to the northwest; he sought a special wood used to make bows. He crossed a river which she called »Buburuduba« – »Only River« (large river), which may have been the Amazon, since the Madeira is at no point very wide. Other Rikbakca know of regions south and north along the Juruena, but principally west. In all of these directions, they name other Indian groups. Some Rikbakca are familiar also with the different terrains, for example, the savannah to the south and west. Only recently, I believe, have a few Rikbakca, particularly those who inhabited the Juruena below its confluence with the Arinos, travelled east.

Rikbakca recall or recount only relations of hostility with foreign tribes. I have been told of parties of men who ambushed other tribes or rubber tappers, or who raided rubber tapper encampments. Occasionally the ambushers failed; Marapa's (an older Rikbakca man) legs are atrophied from wounds from the shotgun of a rubber tapper for whom he and others waited in ambush. I know less about foreign attacks on the Rikbakca. The foreigners were sometimes killed and their artefacts taken. Occasionally children, including some of the rubber tapper families, were abducted to be raised as Rikbakca; they participated fully in Rikbakca social life. Stolen artefacts may have been commonly imitated. Here was one route of diffusion, and an internal source of change.

On returning from the dry season expeditions, Rikbakca burned their fields for planting. When they expected the rains, they planted principally corn and manioc. Other food crops were sweet potatoes, yams, and other tubers, and possibly beans. Nonfood crops were cotton, urucu, and tobacco (used medicinally). Hunted and fished and gathered foods were also important. Men hunted wild pigs and peccary, tapir, monkeys, birds, and turtles, and they shot fish as well. Women, sometimes men also, gathered the plentiful Brazil nuts, honey, wild fruit, wild tubers, fish caught in small pools and certain kinds of caterpillars. These foods were seasonal in availability, some were seasonal in location as well. In the more traditional settlements I have seen, Rikbakca have lived quite well in their environment, with an abundance of food. Field clearing, planting and harvesting were the occasion of dancing, mostly by men and generally in the evening. The cycle of dancing culminated in an elaborate and intense celebration of several days which took place toward the end of the rainy season.

Rikbakca settlements were comprised of family households and a house for unmarried men, mature but unmarried youths, widowers, and men who were not living with their wives. In some of the settlements described by the Jesuits, by the rubber tappers who visited these settlements, and by Schultz (1964), the unmarried men's quarters were a section of a long house separated by a square of logs on the ground. Unmarried men slept here, but all adult men met here daily.

Rikbakca society was divided into two patrilineal exogamous sections. Uxorilocal post marital residence was prescribed and generally practised, so that dwellings consisted of older couples, their immature sons, all of their daughters, and their daughters' husbands. Each couple had a separate hearth, but sharing of food was common between hearths. Polygyny may have complicated this pattern.

Men brought their game to their wives, or to their mothers if they were unmarried. Game of good size was butchered in standard ways, and the women of the household would keep certain parts, while the hunter would take other parts, once cooked, along with other foods to the unmarried men's house. He would offer this food to another man who would divide it among those assembled. Mature men more often ate here than with their wives or parents.

The unmarried men's house was a meeting place at which news was exchanged and decisions made. Other decisions and agreements may have been reached more privately in visits to other's hearths or elsewhere. There is evidence that there was no role of chieftancy, though this role clearly exists today, seemingly instituted by the Jesuit priests. There may previously have been effective leaders, but Rikbakca deny having a word of 'chief', and I have found no word for 'leadership' or 'command'. In cases of collective action or control, decision seems to have been a matter of consensus, and sanction a matter of threat. Homicide and the splitting of settlements were normal means of resolving or avoiding conflict. Cases of conflict and disruption I know of were explained in terms of marriage and adultery, theft, and personal qualities. I know of one instance in which a man and his sons killed off almost an entire

88

settlement; I was unable to ascertain their motive. While homicide was a means of coercion, I have no evidence on its frequency.

Traditional Rikbakca life, as I have been able to reconstruct it and as I have witnessed it away from mission posts, was one of relative abundance. Internecine conflict may have been common, but those settlements I have seen or heard of were relatively peaceful. Moreover, it is not clear how much of this internal violence may have been a response to territorial pressures.

(B) Conflict and 'Pacification': 1950-1962

In the late 1940s and 1950s Brazilian frontiersmen began to settle along the Juruena and Arinos Rivers in significant numbers. Several rubber firms in Cuiabá hired men (and occasionally families) to collect rubber along given stretches of these rivers and the smaller creeks which fed into them. This rubber, pressed into large bars, was then collected by the boats of each firm, trucked to Cuiabá, and then to Sao Paulo. One of these firms, CONOMALI, was owned by Sr. Willi Mayer who in 1957 (the year of first pacific contact with the Rikbakca) founded the first town in the region, Pôrto dos Gauchos. (See Map 2) This town, some 75 km. upriver on the Arinos from its confluence with the Juruena, was the center of frontier development on the Arinos. Twenty years later this region has a population of several thousand engaged principally in agriculture, including the planting of rubber trees. While early settlement was carried out by boat from the headwaters of the Arinos, currently a road connects the town to several other towns nearby and to the Cuiabá – Pôrto Velho highway; west of the Juruena another road leads to the extensive land holdings of AGROSAN which borders the present Rikbakca Reserve on the Sangue ('Blood', for its color) River. More than two other firms operated as well on the Juruena, one with a collection center across the Juruena from the Rikbakca Reserve, the others with centers further upriver on the Juruena and its tributaries.

The conflicts between Rikbakca and the rubber tappers and other settlers may be explained by the conjunction of a number of factors: an occupation and use of overlapping territories, mutual ignorance, uncertainty and fear and the interest of the Rikbakca in some of the settlers' possessions. It is not clear how the conflicts began, or even whether they began at one point of contact or several. In any case, there were characteristic responses on both sides.

The rubber firms sent workers to prepare trails (and sometimes shelters) for rubber tappers. Sometimes a pair of workers lived together or with their families, but dispersion of the trees required disperse settlement. The trees were tapped only during the dry season; a few of the tappers remained through the year, but during the wet season probably the majority returned to the city (e.g., Cuiabá) or later to Pôrto dos Gauchos. The tappers moved into the region and, on regular schedule scored the bark of the rubber trees to collect the rubber on their different trails. During the day their encampments would often be unoccupied. The tappers would return daily and press the collected rubber into large bars. They commonly walked armed with shotgun or revolver, both to shoot game and for protection against Indians. Some shot in warning, others to kill.

Few of these settlers regarded Indians as humans with rights. Most regarded them as less than human and as obstructions and threats to their work. Occasionally, when Rikbakca had upset the collection cups on their trails, stolen their possessions, or killed their fellow settlers, they undertook missions of vengeance, or they killed when the opportunity arose.

I do not know what Rikbakca thought of the increasing activity in their territory, what they saw in the future, or how they conceived of their own responses to the invasion. (It is difficult to assess even contemporary attitudes towards involvement with the outside world). Rikbakca clearly felt threatened by the outsiders. They overturned the rubber tappers' collection cups, sometimes stealing these cups, but sometimes stealing many more than they could use. Dornstauder states that they sometimes placed thorns under leaves in the paths leading to their villages. They also ambushed the rubber tappers, either on the rubber trails or in their encampments. Saake (1962) claims, without specifying sources, that 18 frontiersmen were killed during these years of early contact.

The Rikbakca response was an ambivalent one, comprised not only of fear, but also of an attraction to the settlers' possessions. They had used these artefacts, though only in small numbers for at least 75 years. Older Rikbakca reported that their grandmothers had chopped firewood with steel axes. These artefacts were valued for their efficiency and durability. Other goods sought were pots, beads, and cloth

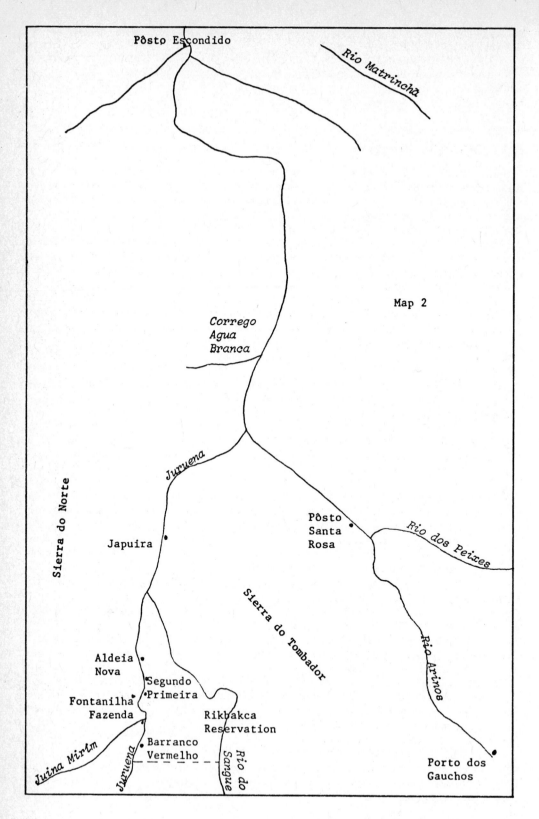

goods. Machetes seem to have become elements of men's attire and ceremonial use; cord loops are attached to the handles and the machetes are acrried on the back, suspended by the loop which crosses the top of the head. In one isolated village in 1972, men visited the unmarried men's house with this artefact. And in the final feast of a ceremonial dancing in 1973, the host ritually invited the participants with a machete; traditionally, I assumed, war clubs were worn instead.

Rikbakca, as I have noted, had a tradition of hostility with foreigners. The settlers on the rivers were particularly resistant. Some were killed, others scared off, deserting their work; but the rubber firms kept sending more workers. Dornstauder (1975:12 ff) refers to the conflicts with the settlers as the »Rikbakca Wars«. I believe this phrase exaggerates the intensity and organization of the conflicts. Saake's figure for a period of several years gives some notion of the intensity of the conflict. Rikbakca offensives were probably organized by several men from single nearby settlements, and on particular occasions rather than long term strategy. Certainly, the greatest percentage of casualties to the Rikbakca came not with the wars, but following their 'peaceful' cessation.

Into this scene of mutual fear and hostility came Padre Joao Dornstauder, Austrian born, a Jesuit, teacher of Natural Science in Novo Friburgo, in the State of Rio de Janeiro, until 1946 when he took up the missionary life in the Prelate of Diamantino, Mato Grosso. Before working with the Rikbakca he had in 1955 set up a reservation for the Kayabi of the Peixes River.

Dornstauder (1975) describes his mission of pacification among the Rikbakca as both religious and humanitarian. He writes:

> To pacify became a task of saving Rikbakca lives (30).
> The pagans have culture, but also a twisted sense of things, an obscured intelligence. By their ignorance, hopelessness, and evil, they are far from God. To evangelize them is to free them. (80).

Dornstauder also claims (1975) that he saw his mission as one of pacifying the settlers as well the Rikbakca. But he seems to have foreseen some consequences of his work of both sides:

> It is not a program subject to discussion, seeking improvements. It is a matter of saving whatever possible.... It would not satisfy the rubber firms or the colonizers, because pacification imposes, between them and the contested frontier, neolithic human groups, surpassed and anachronistic. It would not satisfy the Rikbakca, because it would impose a restriction on vital space and the forced presence of ill-willed individuals. But it is the only viable option.

Here he seems to take the presence of the frontiersmen as given, but compromised by the presence of Rikbakca; peace, then, is to be established through the restriction of Rikbakca territory.

His wishes here were ambivalent. In a letter to Benedito Bruno, requesting support, he wrote: »This expedition has as objective neither the repression of the Indians nor the violent affirmation of our rights to occupy the territory which they occupy; rather it is an organized attempt to enter in pacific contact with the Indians of the region, and then to arrive at a mutual agreement with respect to the rights of each party, as a basis for good relations (1975:45)«.

Having decided to undertake this mission, Dornstauder sought, both directly and through intermediaries, the approval and support of the SPI (Indian Protection Service). He received little response, and was then told that the SPI had a shortage of funds, personnel, and information. He did receive financial assistance from Sr. Willi Mayer and from Sr. Benedito Bruno, the owner of another firm; both of these also aided by donating supplies and personnel, and in requiring their employees to follow Dornstauder's principles on relations with the Rikbakca.

Dornstauder was initially confronted with establishing peaceful relations with the Rikbakca whose first response to a non Rikbakca was either to run or to shoot. His method was a standard one, one used also by Castro and Franca in 1812 on their trip on the Juruena and Arinos; this metod is currently used by FUNAI's (National Indian Foundation) teams of 'attraction'. Presents such as knives, machettes, pots, beads, and combs were left at a site which the Indians seem to frequent. Dornstauder also left the expedition's flag. His principle of operation was to show no violence and to disturb nothing which he encountered.

In October, 1956, Dornstauder and three Indian (Kayabi) guides began their first exploration of Rikbakca territory, between the Juruena and the Arinos, just above their confluence. During the next several months, Dornstauder and a team which varied in membership, mapped out Rikbakca trails and settlements, deserted and occupied. It was the rainy season, and travel was slow and unpleasant; they were often hungry and uncomfortable, and sometimes ill and feverish with malaria or bronchitis. They left gifts but never directly encountered the Rikbakca until July 30, 1957.

Their first encounter was with a group of Rikbakca who were stripping the bark from a tree to twill fibre or cord. After several moments of looking at each other, the Rikbakca ran off and the team followed after to find a shelter (of nine hammocks), in a clearing just deserted. The members of the team tied up their hammocks nearby and waited. After ten hours, one Rikbakca returned, and Dornstauder attempted to communicate with him. Dornstauder was doubtful of his success, yet he seemed to believe that some understanding had been achieved. He believed, for example, that the man indicated himself to be shaman when he raised his arm and pointed first to the sky and then to himself. Dornstauder also came to believe that this man is a chief. He imitated the Rikbakca gesture and repeated a Kayabi word for shaman, and the Portuguese word for priest. It seems more likely here that, as Rikbakca commonly do, this man was indicating a time when some event had happened or would happen, by indicating the position of either the sun or the moon.

Such early attempts and presumptions of communication are common in Dornstauders' account. Early in his visits to Rikbakca settlements he reported the Rikbakca using a word 'ko ko' for 'eating'; I believe that in this instance the Rikbakca were using the Portuguese phrase 'come, come' – 'eat, eat' which the Missionary team had used in offering food to their hosts. During this first encounter, one of Dornstauder's assistants gave the Rikbakca man a knife, and Dornstauder himself gave a comb and some beads, others of which the man was already wearing. When Dornstauder sent to find an axe to give, the man turned and left.

Dornstauder decided to allow the news of this peaceful exchange to spread to other Rikbakca settlements. He returned only in November. This time he and his companions entered fearfully and inspected a Rikbakca household (with sixteen hammocks). Following some exchanges, he invited some of the Rikbakca to meet him at the river for more goods; he believed they invited him to attend »the corn celebration« in two months time.

During the next few years visits continued. Dornstauder explored different regions. He was well received. He gave gifts, but began to worry about these exchanges and those which began with the rubber tappers. It was some time before Rikbakca thefts stopped and Rikbakca came to trade manufactured goods for their own artefacts and agricultural or gathered products.

By far of greater consequence was the exchange of disease. Dornstatuder declared (1975:126) »Since the first contact, we have avoided contagion as much as possible«. Yet he mentions also the disease which he and his companions contracted while on their expeditions. Some contemporary Rikbakca attribute the early disease, principally influenza and measles, to him. An alternate source may have been the rubber tapper camps which Rikbakca visited, and the contaminated artefacts which they stole. In some of the villages which Dornstauder visited many were sick and dying. He brought medicine, but did not always have enough. At one point he notes (1975:148) »The Rikbakca show a strange reserve … I am bewildered and don't discover the reason for the withdrawal of confidence.« It is difficult to estimate the extensiveness of these epidemics. Clearly they resulted in violent social disruption, and in the regrouping of survivors. Here, perhaps, was the beginning of territorial consolidation. Survivors or those afflicted by the epidemics may have come to the river to gain the priests's assistance. Several posts were set up to take care of the problems of the Indian contact: one, Santa Rosa, on the Arinos, was closed for its excess of blood sucking gnats; another at Japoira operated until 1972, when it was taken over by an agricultural firm, with very little compensation for its worth. The priests eventually gathered children who they assumed orphaned, and they took these children to the Mission school at Utiariti.

In 1962 a rubber tapper shot a Rikbakca who with others was visiting his camp. The Rikbakca is reported to have said »Rice no good. Rubber tapper no good« which infuriated the tapper. Dornstauder arrived on this scene and attempted to convince the Rikbakca not to steal or kill and the tappers not to kill. He declared the recently killed Rikbakca »The last victim of the great equivocation«. Having done so, and having seen the opening of the post, Japoira, he considered completed his work of pacifying the upriver Rikbakca. The remaining work was left to Padre Edgar Schmidt.

Rikbakca woman and daughter in field, gathering manioc. Traditional dress and carrying band. Copyright: Robert Hahn 1974.

(C) Consolidation and Transformation: 1962-1973

The Jesuit Missao Anchieta

Schmidt was of German descent, but born in the south of Brazil. He was stern, though friendly, and devoted to his task. Unfortunately he saw Rikbakca custom at best as curiosity and at worst as hindrance to progress. He expressed his task as one of helping Indians to make the transition from the Stone Age to the Atomic Age. (In 1972, after having lived for twenty years in the hazardous jungle, he was killed in an automobile accident.)

One of his earliest efforts was the setting up of a central Rikbakca post, Barranco Vermelho (»Red Embankment«, for the color of the soil); this post has become the administrative center of the Reservation. It was believed that this spot had been an earlier settlement of the Rikbakca, called »Eremicahkihi« (possibly, »The spider monkies' lover« for unclear reasons). I believe that Rikbakca were attracted to this mission post by the availability of manufactured goods and medical treatment.

Barranco Vermelho as it is presently laid out (1973) took a number of years to complete; for some of the construction, Schmidt employed Rikbakca labor for which he paid. While the plan of this settlement made use of a few features of traditional Rikbakca settlements, it was otherwise quite untraditional. Several of its features disrupted Rikbakca social life, left the Rikbakca more subject to Mission domination, and otherwise also disadvantaged the Rikbakca.

In 1973 the settlement was laid out as shown on p. 95.

At Barranco Vermelho the embankment rose some 20 to 30 feet above the Juruena so that it was not easy to carry water. The Mission dwellings and buildings were built in a line parallel to the edge of the embankment, with the unmarried men's house at the end of this row near the Jesuit's sleeping quarters. At the opposite end were the nun's quarters, a chapel, a kitchen, an infirmary, and a chicken coop. Eventually, a building was constructed approximately in the middle of the row, which now houses the school room and the Rikbakca cooperative.

Some two hundred feet further back from the river and parallel to the Mission shelter were the Rikbakca houses set out in a straight line; this row has come to be known as »A Rua« (Portuguese, »The Street«). Between the Rua and the Mission houses, an airstrip was built in 1970. The houses of the Rua are now occupied principally by nuclear families. Their distance from the river makes getting water difficult, and some Rikbakca prefer to use a creek which flows into the Juruena below the settlement. Fruit trees – citrus, guava, and cashews, have been planted around both rows of houses. About a quarter mile further back are fields cleared for corn, manioc, sugar cane, and other products; other fields are now used for planting rice which has been introduced and which produces well.

The simple physical layout of this settlement has been socially disruptive. The bipartite division has emphasized the separation which Schmidt believed existed; it is not clear what purposes he thought this plan would serve. Family dwellings are much further apart than they were traditionally, and visiting has diminished. The unmarried men's house, where formerly men spent most of their time in the village, is now a bachelor's dormitory, and has recently been divided into apartments, some with locking doors. Men sometimes meet casually with each other on the street, but all the men meet together only when meetings are called on matters of business, often by the suggestion of the missionaries.

Schmidt also attempted, generally successfully, to regulate Rikbakca life in other ways. He instituted a weekly calendar, encouraged agricultural work five days a week, hunting and fishing on Saturday, and rest and recreation on Sunday. Church attendance was not required, but many Rikbakca have attended, particularly the yong Rikbakca raised at Utiarití. The cooperative, organized several years ago, is open for trade on Sunday morning following the mass. It is run by a young Rikbakca couple, raised at Utiarití who speak none of the Rikbakca language. Traditional Rikbakca have difficulty trading here, and are treated with slight contempt. Rikbakca exchange artefacts and Brazil nuts, corn, rice, or rubber for manufactured goods. Some of these goods fit in well with Rikbakca tradition – pots, knives, etc. Others are clearly luxury items, and can only seduce Rikbakca to further involvement with the civilized world, e.g. clothes irons and shiny purses.

The introduction of rice, hybrid corn, sugar, fruit trees, and domestic animals, the encouragement of greater agricultural activity and the production of marketable goods, has made Rikbakca much more sedentary and much less dependent on a large territory of usufruct. Annual treks are rare, though groups of men sometimes go on hunting expeditions of several days. Game and fish are much scarcer as the

Map 3

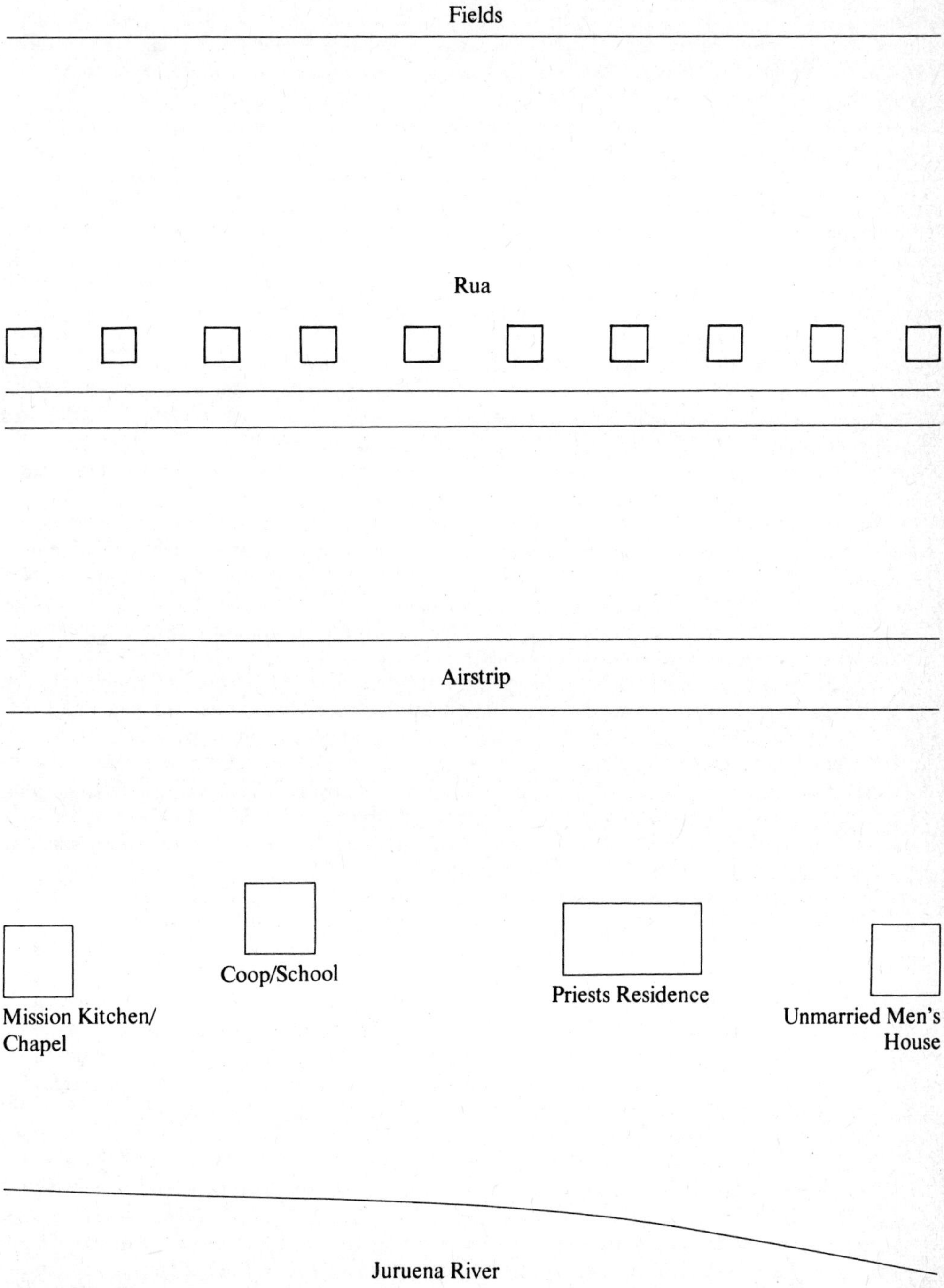

Fields

Rua

▢ ▢ ▢ ▢ ▢ ▢ ▢ ▢ ▢ ▢

Airstrip

Coop/School

Priests Residence

Mission Kitchen/
Chapel

Unmarried Men's
House

Juruena River

increase of population in the area has frightened animal populations away, and has overhunted and overfished what remained.

Rikbakca political organization has also changed in response to mission activities. The use by all Rikbakca of only a Portuguese word, *»capitao«* – »chief«, the denial that there is a similar word in their language (and no evidence that there is such a word), and their denial that they had *capitoes* traditionally, suggest that there were no chiefs. The institution of chieftancy may have arisen in response to the conflicts of the 1950s. It seems likely that Dornstauder fostered its institutionalization as he believed certain Rikbakca to be *caciques* and as he dealt through these men and treated them with particular respect. This system of brokerage still functions today. Each settlement has a *»capitao«* whose office seems to be granted by local consensus, though perhaps not without the influence of the missionaries.

The Jesuits were early concerned with the decrease in population, and attempted to promote marriages between Rikbakca in order to restore the population. They voiced their concern often during my stay, by noting the great disproportion of young males per young females in the population. In arranging marriages, however, they did not consider, or at least they did not follow Rikbakca principles of section exogamy. A sizeable proportion of the marriages which they promoted violated Rikbakca principles. Rikbakca, sometimes the parties concerned, found these marriages difficult to accept. Others refused to attend the Church ceremonies which celebrated them. Current practice of the priests is to allow Rikbakca to arrange their own marriages. The nuns with some medical training, have attempted to assist births and to prevent (rare) infanticide. They have promoted the adoption of orphaned newborns.

The mission has also taught sewing to those women who have sought to learn. All Rikbakca today wear clothes, although those who lived until recently beyond mission contact wore only traditional necklaces, cotton bindings, bark fiber pubic aprons (for men), and ear pendants (also for men). They have all come to wear Western dress, even sandals or shoes at times, subtly mocked by other Rikbakca as »Indian« – *»Indio«* (Portuguese) or »naked Indian« – *»Indio pelado«* when they dress traditionally. Western dress may serve to defuse contact with the Brazilian frontiersmen by making the Rikbakca seem less strange.

The priests have also trained selected Rikbakca boys in carpentry and mechanics, and some of these regularly assist in the maintenance of mission equipment; they are paid for their work. The nuns have likewise trained several Rikbakca girls in the administration of medicine; these girls seem to bear prejudices against those Rikbakca who live more traditionally, which discourages the latter from seeking medical assistance. The mission contracts Rikbakca men to work on projects such as construction and road clearing (see Map 3), and it pays them for this work.

In addition to these practical skills, the mission also maintains a one room school at Barranco Vermelho. The school at Utiarití which many present day Rikbakca youths attended, had a complete primary school, and included as well technical training in agriculture, cooking, sewing, and the production of sugar. I have not carefully observed classes in the Barranco Vermelho school, but am of the impression that classes here are strongly authoritarian, and that they treat Rikbakca traditions by ignoring them, or by denigrating them, or at best by noting them as curious. This, I believe, reflects the attitude of the nuns who run the school, the infirmary, and the in-mission kitchen. Some Rikbakca commonly complain about the sister-nurse as unpleasant.[4]

Many, but not all, of the children raised at the mission school of Utiarití are now more interested in being Brazilian *'civilizados'* – 'civilized ones' than Rikbakca. Some of them deny being *'Indios'* and speak none of the Rikbakca language. Some avoid contact with more traditional Rikbakca and work to acquire emblems of Brazilians whom they see – dress, wrist watches, revolvers, radios, habits of conversation, and sometimes liquor. In 1970 some of these, principally young men but also one couple, built a settlement across the river from the frontier road building headquarters, a settlement they called »Indianópolis«. A year later most of the inhabitants of Indianópolis had moved away, either to a nearby village on the Reservation or, at least part time to the road workers' settlement or to the nearby Fazenda. It is my impression that these youths are accepted across the river as *'Indios'*, and that they are uncomfortable in this role.

A few of the mission-raised youth have returned to reservation village life. Some have learned or relearned their own language and participate along with others in more traditional daily life and ceremony. They also make visits to the road workers' settlement and to the Fazenda, to play soccer, to trade artefacts for food, or just to visit. They also sometimes are host to the workers who call on the villages, most often to trade. Rikbakca interests in dealing with the settlers across the river have less to do with the acquisition of material goods than with matters of identity and status, for they almost always acquire more for their trade items at the reservation cooperative.

Table I. The Rikbakca Population

Settlement	Married Males	Married Females	Children		Single Male	Single Female
			Male	Female		
Reservation:						
Barranco Vermelho (60)	12	12	12	13	10	1
Primeira (65)	15	15	14	10	7	1
Segunda (30)	7	7	8	7	1	0
Aldeia Nova (43)	9	11	8	9	6	0
Small Settlements						
1. (6)	2	2	2	0	0	0
2. deserted several weeks						
3. (6)	2	2	1	1	0	0
4. (5)	1	1	1	2	0	0
5. (4)	1	1	2	0	0	0
6. in construction						
7. deserted several months						
8. (8)	2	2	1	3	0	0
9. (5)	1	1	1	1	1	0
Total (232)	52	54	52	46	25	2
Non Reservation						
Pôsto Escondido (14)	3	5	3	2	1	0
Isolated (23)	5	6	6	3	2	1
Isolated (8)	1	2	2	2	1	0
Fontanilha –						
Fazenda (8)	0	0	0	0	8	0
Total (53)	9	13	11	7	12	1
Grand Total (285)	61	67	63	53	37	3

A majority of older Rikbakca have played in a middle ground, maintaining basic patterns of Rikbakca traditions, modifying others, and using the mission and other resources to somewhat traditonal ends. Some change has been unavoidable: settlement is becoming more sedentary and food production is changing following a depletion of game – this due to changing patterns of occupation in the region. Exchange and authority have also changed as I describe below. But these more traditional Rikbakca have resisted many of the changes, criticising them, avoiding them, and following tradition where possible.

The various groups of the population in 1973 were distributed in settlements as in Tables I. The direct Mission influence has been greatest in the Reservation settlements of Barranco Vermelho, less in that of the Aldeia Nova, described below, and less still in those not supervised by a mission emissary. Most of these settlements have functioning unmarried men's houses, but the larger ones have *capitoes* also. Most of these settlements follow a weekly schedule, have a greater orientation to agriculture than was traditional, and engage in the production of trade goods. Some individuals visit Barranco Vermelho on Sundays to trade. But some of those nearer to the road building settlement at Fontanilha or to the Fazenda trade there.

Other Posts

In 1960 a German missionary, Friedrich Richter, sponsored by a Lutheran mission in the south of Brazil, opened up a post much farther north on the left bank of the Juruena; it was the northermost post, and became known as Pôsto Escondido – 'Hidden Post', named after the creek at the mouth of which it was built. This post was maintained by the Lutheran mission and its various pastors and representatives until 1969, when, after brief attendance by an employee of F.U.N.A.I., it was ceded to the care of the Jesuit mission. The Jesuits made various efforts to persuade the Rikbakca residents of this post to move upriver, because of the expense and difficulty of maintaining this distant post. What finally convinced them in 1973 was the invasion of the post by mineral prospectors demanding women and food. The Rikbakca response was to burn their houses, cut down their fruit trees, and retreat to the jungle (Joan Boswood, SIL, personal communication). This was the last group of Rikbakca to move onto the Reservation.

In approximately 1962, the Summer Institute of Linguistics sent its first team of linguists to the same Pôsto Escondido. There was eventual conflict between these missionaries and the Lutherans of the post, so that the SIL linguists persuaded some of the Rikbakca to move upriver, still below the mouth of the Arinos, to build a new post. Eventually this post was adandoned and its Rikbakca and SIL residents moved back to Pôsto Escondido.

There were also, I am told, hostilities and rivalry between the Lutherans and the Jesuit Missao Anchieta (and later between the Missao Anchieta and the Servico de Protecao aos Indios, and then the F.U.N.A.I. and its employees). Each mission tried to persuade various Rikbakca to join and remain at its posts, and there may have been considerable movement between posts, back and forth.

Japoira was a large post which, at the time of its sale, was very productive and well located in terms of game and fish. It was 'attended' by a series of frontiersmen employed by the Jesuit mission to supervise Rikbakca production and medicine, and contacts with outsiders. Like most of the mission settlements other than Barranco Vermelho, it still had an active unmarried men's house. In 1971 an agricultural firm, claiming title to this land, persuaded Padre Edgar to give over the land for clearing. The Rikbakca were paid little for their shelters and for cleared and planted land. It is doubtful that the firm had any legal right to this land since it was occupied by an Indian population. (According to land maps, publicly available in Cuiabá, all of the land along the Juruena and Arinos, including the Rikbakca Reserve, is privately owned.)

The move from Japoira to 'Aldeia Nova' – 'New Village' has been extremely costly. Both Japoira and this new settlement are supervised by a mission appointed frontiersman who is illiterate and insensitive to the subleties of Rikbakca life. Until recently he was also responsible for medical assistance about which he knew little. Supervision and medical assistance are now provided by a Rikbakca couple, the female of which denies being Rikbakca. Neither speaks the Rikbakca language, as both were raised at Utiarití.

One of the two isolated groups lived a half day's walk up a creek, Agua Branca, feeding into the Juruena from the left. This group consisted of approximately twenty people, one man having recently been killed by the others. Another group was persuaded by a team of Rikbakca from Posto Escondido and an attendant of this post to join the mission. I am told that this group had planned to kill a nearby rubber tapper for his machette, on the day following the arrival of the mission post team. This group was resistant to Mission post life, and moved to the post and then back to a clearing a few days' walk away. There were illnesses, some attributed to Padre Edgar, and there were conflicts with the other Rikbakca of this post. In 1973, following some preliminary visits, this group too was persuaded to live on the Reserve.

In 1970 the Jesuits decided to close the mission school at Utiarití, and to keep Utiarití solely as a sanatorium for the treatment of (rare) cases of tuberculosis. I have not examined the Utiarití registration lists, but I estimate that more than one third of the Rikbakca population has spent some time at Utiarití; most of the population younger than their early twenties and older than a few years were raised there with little or only seasonal visits to Rikbakca settlements. At Utiarití children were taught the catechism in addition to a standard elementary school curriculum. Some Rikbakca youth who completed and excelled at the Utiarití program were sent to Cuiabá for further education, perhaps in a trade. In addition, boys were taught agriculture, sugar production, and some mechanics; girls were taught sewing and cooking. All care was in the hands of the Mission. As far as I am aware, no attempt was made to learn or maintain any facet of Rikbakca tradition; these Rikbakca were to be made good Brazilian Catholics. I am told that at one period in their efforts to control their Rikbakca foster children, use of the Rikbakca language was forbidden at Utiariti.

The gradual move of all inhabitants of Utiariti back to the Reserve was done by discovering links of kinship at various distances between the children and youth and the adults of the mission posts. In some cases, children were given to be raised or adopted by families when no ties could be discovered.

Many of these youths have not adapted (or readapted) well to more traditional life on the posts, and have either worked with the missionaries or have associated themselves with the frontier communities across the river.

Concomitant with the consolidation and sedentarization of the Rikbakca population has been the expansion into the region of extractive and agricultural fronts of various sorts. Land clearing for eventual cattle raising has increased greatly. Prospecting for minerals has also increased; there was a large gold panning camp not far from Posto Escondido which interfered with post life. More recently large firms have begun to prospect in that region. Possibly only rubber tapping and fur trapping have declined, because of changes in the market (illegal in the case of feline fur trade) and increased occupation of the territory. Recently a road construction crew has begun work on a road to connect Fontanilha, a planned community built across the river from the Reserve, to the town of Salto which will be the center for the study of Amazonia. The prefecture of Aripuana hopes to connect this road to that which goes west to Porto dos Gauchos and then to the Cuiabá – Porto Velho highway; it hopes to make this connection by crossing a corner of the Rikbakca Reserve. The outcome of this issue was uncertain when I left in 1973. The road desired by the prefecture would run through the Reserve between Barranco Vermelho and other Rikbakca settlements.

SIL Among the Rikbakca

It was only in 1962, at the beginning to the phase of consolidation and then the Jesuits (and the Lutherans) had already set up or planned a number of posts, that the SIL first entered the Juruena to work with the Rikbakca. There these linguists have always played a role of influence subordinate and secondary to that of the Missao Anchieta; though perhaps not always in agreement with Missao Anchieta policy, they always operated within its bounds.

SIL has worked in Brazil with permission granted by the Ministry of the Interior; I believe that it is not allowed, as I was not allowed, to interfere in the political or social life of the indigenous societies with which it works. The Missao Anchieta, on the other hand, is the delegate to the Rikbakca of the FUNAÎ (itself a branch of the Ministry of the Interior); this mission is legally responsible for the Rikbakca within the strictures of Federal Indian Policy. The Missao Anchieta has thus been required to accept the work of SIL, and the SIL has been required to work within the dictates of Missao Anchieta plans. The Rikbakca, of course, not considered an autonomous population, have had almost nothing to say about the presence or activities of either institution; they seem to accept both.

Since 1962 there have been three principal SIL linguists among the Rikbakca, assisted on occasions by approximately four others. I am personally acquainted with the three, and have observed two at work. SIL linguists generally work in teams of two, though at present one is at work alone. They generally spend periods of several months in the field, then returning to their base in Cuiabá to analyze their findings, to discuss their material in conferences, and to buy supplies. Every few years, they return to their homes; the three linguists among the Ribbakca have been English. They have individually gained support from churches at home.

The SIL team first worked at Pôsto Escondido alongside the Lutheran Mission. They had built there both a house and a landing strip for small aircraft. While in the field, they maintained frequent radio contact with the SIL base in Cuiabá. Following an initial period at Pôsto Escondido they have worked at different settlements, including the Anchieta posts, Barranco Vermelho, Japoira, and Segunda. The remaining linguist has her own house at Segunda.

In Rikbakca communities they have, as far as I know, always kept quarters separate from Rikbakca dwellings, though within the community; they have generally eaten separately as well, though sharing food somewhat in Rikbakca fashion. They have worked several hours a day with linguistic informants, and sometimes with classes of them. They have assisted women (as I did also) in the making of clothing. They have made significant contributions in the administration of medicines for various illnesses. And in

99

a more casual vein, they have interacted with the Rikbakca and participated in Rikbakca life, receiving and making home visits, and observing Rikbakca life; at least one linguist kept a journal of events and practices in the settlements, and of her reactions to them.

In contrast to the Jesuits, the SIL activities and influence has so far been concentrated principally in the settlements in which their missionaries lived. While the Jesuits have been oriented toward the whole tribe and to its relations with the outside world, the SIL linguists have at least until recently lived in Rikbakca settlements in order to learn the language. Only in the last few years have they attempted to organize classes to teach literacy, but still in an exploratory fashion, and still restricted to single settlements. Their influence has been felt principally by means of face to face personal relations rather than through policy formulation and implementation.

Missionaries commonly recommend their way not as an alternative to indigenous ways, but as the only way; and there is more concern with the accordance of native custom with Christian teachings than with the integrity of indigenous life; for these missionaries, of course, there is here no inconsistency of principle. In contrast, SIL linguists among the Rikbakca, with some differences among them, have generally respected Rikbakca practices, though they have been disturbed by such practices as 'adultery' and violence. Even here, however, I do not think they have attempted to impose their beliefs. Here also I do not think the SIL has been as forceful or influential as the Missao Anchieta.

Moreover, SIL, in seeking to learn indigenous languages (and the indigenous customs requisite for this task), has been less ethnocentric and self-righteous than other mission groups which take their mission as teaching without any prerequistite learning from the indigenous group. The interest of missionaries in learning the indigenous language may assist indigenous groups in maintaining their integrity while it is undermined in other ways.

Among the Rikbakca, SIL linguists have also been opposed to the reduction of territory, though they have not actively resisted this reduction. They have also mediated relations with frontiersmen in order to protect the Rikbakca from exploitation at those settlements where they worked.

SIL has been accused (Hart 1973:16) of being »a manifestation of U.S. cultural and economic imperialism«. In the Rikbakca case this claim distorts the facts. While SIL may effect some changes in Rikbakca life with consequences beneficial to imperialistic interests, these are not its only effects. Nor are they part of the linguists' intentions. (It is not only U.S., but Western cultural and economic interests that are promoted.)

In the first ten years of their presence, SIL linguists have had little effect in comparison with the Jesuit Mission. This may change as they teach literacy and the Biblical texts. Such work would generally complement that of the Jesuits; or rather, it would revitalize, though with quite different methods and emphases, an activity now set aside by the Jesuits.

Rikbakca young man, playing goalie on a frontier settlement. Copyright: Robert A. Hahn 1975.

(D) Agency in Social Change Among the Rikbakca

The Jesuit efforts with the Rikbakca of the last twenty years may be divided into three phases. SIL has thus far played only a minor role in the last two phases. (The phases overlapped in time, and the interests at each phase did not exclude those of the other phases; nevertheless, there was a shift in emphasis.)

During the first years of conflict, the Jesuits were interested in reducing conflict between Rikbakca and frontiersmen. They did this quite successfully: there were few incidents of violence following 1962; the atmosphere of relations changed so that Rikbakca and frontiersmen were not longer terrified of working and living in a common territory; and such disturbances as occasional thefts consequently diminished in importance. At the same time, other sources of the desired industrial goods were established.

As the conflicts were reduced, the Jesuits began to concentrate their efforts on the consolidation of the Rikbakca population; their objective in this effort, successfully culminating in 1973 when the last Rikbakca came to live on the Rikbakca Reserve, was to be able to give their services and administration, limited in personnel and financial support, in a more efficient and comprehensive way. Until 1973, while there were still Rikbakca at Pôsto Escondido, the Mission made several expeditions of 700 kilometers each (from Barranco Vermelho) in order to bring medical care, to trade manufactured goods for artefacts, and to protect against the ominous violation of Rikbakca land rights by frontiersmen in the region. The Jesuits considered these visits very costly, and for a number of years they attempted to persuade the Rikbakca of that post to move upriver.

During the third phase, the last few years, as the Rikbakca have been territorially consolidated and as economic and political relations with outsiders have been regularized, the interest of the Jesuits have turned to the development of an autonomy in Reservation affairs and a revitalization of traditional life. This last interest may be coincidental with the end of consolidation, and it may accord also with a current general interest of the Church in a somewhat anthropological perspective rather than in a catechistic one. The director of a Brazilian Jesuit Mission Council, Don Tomás Balduino, has recently asserted in an interview (Martins e Tintin 1977:3), »Today, missionary activity discovers evangelical values in the indian culture... It is in deepening this condition as Indian that he will be able to affirm himself as a disciple of Christ.«

Padre Balduino Loebens, now delegate of the FUNAI within the Mission, encourages Rikbakca solution of internal conflicts. He has encouraged also the practice of traditional ceremony, and he has himself made significant efforts to learn the Rikbakca language and customs. It is ironic that this interest appears when it is least likely to succeed in more than a token way, and when the complementary interests of the expanding frontier have been assured.

Even so, the boundaries of the Reservation are threatened by road projects. Rikbakca knowledgeable of traditional life are dying off; some young Rikbakca raised by the Mission reject even Indian identity, and are rarely concerned with restoring tradition; and the economic base and social organization have been so altered that revivals can at best serve to maintain a sense of identity and integrity which has also been threatened.

It may be that no Rikbakca wish to restore pre-contact life or even parts of it. Yet it is clear that whether or not those who once knew now wish such restoration or not, no one was originally given a significant choice. It is Rikbakca options which have been severely compromised, and not those of the frontiersmen and their society.

I conclude here by reviewing the changes which have taken place in Rikbakca society, by attempting to evaluate these, and by attempting, but only in a suggestive way, to determine the causes of these.

The transformation effected in Rikbakca life during the last 25 years has been profound; the process is not yet complete, and Rikbakca relations with the frontier have not yet stabilized. Rikbakca territories of occupation have been reduced to at most 1/40; the Rikbakca population has suffered great loss in numbers, only now being restored. Traditional sources and means of livelihood have been altered and have been replaced by others. Social and political organization have changed radically also, more in some settlements than in others. Even the Rikbakca cosmology has been changed.

What persists are traditional values and rules; but these remain principally with those older, perhaps, than 35 years. Since the basis of these values and rules in traditional social, economic, and political life have themselves been radically altered, and since both the carriers of these values and rules and the traditional means of their communication between generations are also disappearing, it is reasonable to predict that the values and rules will themselves be shortlived. Among youth, moreover, particularly, I believe, among those raised by the Mission during the phase of reduction, there is a profound ambivalence in identity – a conflict between the world of their parents and that of their foster parents, the transformers of their parents' world. They were born into a period of extensive uprooting, unsettlement, of disease and death, and of social disruption. In some of these youth, the traditions of the Mission school world have come to dominate; these youth identify themselves as *civilizado;* conflict remains insofar as they are forced to resent both more traditional consociates with whom they deal and themselves as well because of a shared Indian tradition.

Others of these youth have returned to participate in the little of traditional life that persists; yet for these also there may exist a conflict between the traditional values and those of the Mission world in which they have been socialized.

How should we evaluate these changes? Certainly the initial disruption and its consequences in lost lives and disturbances in the lives of those who remained are to be deplored. As Appell has argued convincingly, »Every act of development involves, of necessity, an act of destruction. This destruction – social, ecological, or both – is seldom accounted for in development projects, despite the fact that it may entail costs that far outweigh the benefits arising from the development« (1975:31). The Missao Anchieta had neither the knowledge, nor was it given the means to adequately carry out the task of contact. Nor was the Mission assisted by the agencies whose responsibility was precisely this.

How can we evaluate the society which has resulted from this transformation in comparison with traditional Rikbakca society? Here I wish to take neither the relativistic position that both societies (or versions of one society) are equally valid systems; nor shall I take the romantic position that traditional societies and those living in more direct contact with nature are superior and should be maintained. I support a criterion which stresses people's control over the events of their own lives, thus their knowledge of the various dimensions of their environment and their ability to choose among alternative courses of action. Personal and social health and creativity are concommitants of control.

If we begin with and take as given the state of conflict between the Brazilian frontiersmen and the Rikbakca, then it is clear that the Jesuit Missao Anchieta is principally responsible for the changes which have affected Rikbakca society. That is to say, the appearance and specific activities of this Mission in the social environment of the Rikbakca were the most significant ones of this environment; Rikbakca interaction with this environment has produced today's results.

From the response which Dornstauder received from the SPI it seems unlikely that this governmental body was prepared to resolve the Rikbakca – frontiersmen conflicts. I believe that had the SPI intervened, it would have done so with generally similar means and results, except perhaps for the internment at Utiariti. Without the intervention of either of these bodies, I speculate that the conflicts would have continued much longer and on increasing numbers of fronts. Perhaps more of the frontiersmen would have been driven out; and they, in return, might have more often staged revenge raids. (It is widely believed on the Juruena that the rubber tappers working on the upper Juruena were extensively armed against the 'Cintas Largas' – 'Broad Belts' in the late 1950s and 1960s, with machine guns and caches of ammunition.) Eventually, it seems quite clear, the Brazilian frontier would have established itself, properly protected. Perhaps 'peace' would have been established at various pionts of contact, yet it seems that, under these conditions, the Rikbakca population would have been fragmented and quickly absorbed into the local extractive activities. It is unlikely that anyone would have been concerned with the well being of the Rikbakca in this frontier system to whose diseases and individualistic practices their own society (and physiology) would not adapt. Diseases contracted through the Rikbakca raids on frontiersmen would have spread unchecked.

What, then, were the options open to Dornstauder and the Missao Anchieta? We might distinguish real possibilities from the possibilites that were recognized. I maintain that in an ideal situation, Dornstauder (or whoever directed these first contacts) should have been able to call a halt to all frontier activity on the river, at least temporarily removing all frontiersmen. He should then have made contacts, insuring the health of his team, and prepared to immunize and deal with diseases which were communicated despite precautions. He should have learned the Rikbakca language and social organization and values, and then have communicated with the Rikbakca the nature of the society which had been moving into their region. Only on these foundations might a mutually compatible compromise with the frontier have been established, perhaps with Dornstauder as arbitrator. I do not believe that any contact between a powerless native society and industrial society has ever come about in this way. Yet such an ideal does not seem remote from the principles of democracy on which some governments claim to act and from the Christian ideals which are the basis of the missionary activity.

Yet the government did not respond, and the Mission, which assumed responsibility, took the expanding extractive frontier as already and inevitably established. Reduction of the autochthonous society thus also became an invevitability.

It is unlikely that, even if it had wanted to, the Missao Anchieta would have succeeded in the ideal program described above. Firms involved in the frontier economy cooperated with the pacification, but seemingly believing that their activities would be at most temporarily interrupted, and then even facilitated by removing the danger in access to the various resources; pacification would more than likely be to their benefit. It is doubtful whether they would have supported a pacification which involved the cessation of their own activities. Here the government would probably have responded with ambivalence as it has responded elsewhere more recently. It has given economic incentives to expanding fronts, while at the same time proclaiming inviolatable the lands occupied by indigenous groups. In some instances the incentives have been more forcefully pursued than the proclamations, and occupied land has been taken over for exploitation. I believe that had Dornstauder attempted to halt expansion while establishing a true compromise, he would have been met by resistance on the part of the interested firms. It is likely that these firms would have gained more support from government firms than did Dornstauder himself. Given government practice, Dornstauder's pacification and the drive toward reduction were expected and tolerable moves. Even as the reduction progressed, it encountered pressures from the economic interests in the region, pressures effectively supported rather than reduced by government activity. And even as Rikbakca have been contained in a legally established reserve, such pressures continue.

Nor need we ascribe final agency to these local firms and to the government which supports them to the detriment of the well-being of indigenous populations. For there have been suggestive demonstrations (Davis and Mathews 1976) of links between firms locally involved in extractive industry in the Amazon and multinational corporations. And we may go beyond these to the societies which foster them, to their directors, to their employees, and to the consumers of their products. In these economic systems, aboriginal societies are often waste products.

I have argued so far as if the Rikbakca had no responsibility for their own fate, that is, as if they had been entirely passive in these events. Clearly this is not true, for a society and its members are not mechanisms which react automatically to their environments. Rikbakca as well as the frontier society have made at least some choices in reacting. It was, of course, their reactions and the routinization of these which constituted the change. The Rikbakca were interested in procuring the products of the Industrial society with whose frontiers they met, and their interest grew; they were presumably interested also in establishing peaceful relations.

Yet Rikbakca options were restricted in several dimensions. They were, to begin, forced to choose, for their territory was increasingly circumscribed. Their first choice was not whether to maintain their tradition or to adopt foreign ways, but how to react to forceful encroachment – by attempting to defend their territory or by establishing peaceful relations. Resistance has commonly meant great losses if not annihilation; acceptance has often had similar consequences. Secondly, they had little knowledge on which to base their choice. They did not know how improbable were their chances of defense; nor did they know the consequences of peace. Ignorance is a normal component of human decision making, yet here was a case in which ignorance was great and the consequences catastrophic. Certainly the industrial society knew more of their fate than they of its. In an ideal situation, both this ignorance and the possible catastrophic results would have been mitigated.

Rikbakca have chosen a path of little resistance, one acceptable to the industrial society which surrounds it. One motive for the acceptance has been the interest in the products of the Industrial society. Their lack of resistance accords also with their general tolerance and their curiosity about the foreign world. I have seen Rikbakca imitate for their own use the arrows which they had found. Indeed the distribution of facial ornamentation and decoration in the Amazon suggest frequent borrowing and imitation. This openness, which has played a significant part in the transformation of Rikbakca society in the last twenty years, contrasts greatly with some other Amazonian societies which have fiercely resisted encroachment.

In this study, I have made some claims which are only speculative. Clearly, methodological strictures make more detailed and comparative information necessary for firmer conclusions. Nevertheless some hypotheses are given evidence in the Rikbakca case. It seems likely that the principal agent of change of Rikbakca society was the Missao Anchieta. To this mission, the SIL (and the Lutherans) have been only assistants. And if we ask for whom these missions are agents, we may look further to national governments and the economies of Brazil and foreign societies.

In this work of pacification, the missionaries claim to be the servants of God; I have argued they are the servants of industrial society. In seeking to save the souls of Rikbakca and to promote Rikbakca well being, they have led the reduction of the Rikbakca population and the restriction of its life space; Rikbakca have become orphans of their past and foster children of a society which wanted not them, but resources of the land they lived from. It is as Dornstauder himself recognized (1975:41): »On the value and danger of pacification, it is necessary to declare, once and for all, that for the events of the Rikbakca war the controlling society and its directors are much more responsible than the common rubber tappers.« Yet by himself taking these events as inevitable, he also served to promote them. Bonilla's rhetorical title, *Servants of God or Masters of Men?*, might be rephrased for the Rikbakca case, for men, both within and beyond the frontier, have become servants of Industry.

Unless there is a radical change in the regnant world political economy, the twentieth century will see the end of a process of exploration and expansion which began in the fifteenth century. In their quest for further resources, the members of the the Industrial society which now dominates most of the earth's occupied territory, will conquer the last of earthly frontiers, its cultures and its humanity.

Notes

1. My analysis here is based on observations made while conducting research on the Rikbakca language and social organization for a doctoral disseration, *Rikbakca Categories of Social Relations; An Epistemological Analysis,* presented to the Department of Anthropology Harvard University, in August 1976.

2. I must note the significance of my activities among the Rikbakca as a source of change. I believe that my stay with the Rikbakca had relatively little effect; and I believe that my activities promoted rather than detracted from Rikbakca integrity and well-being. The Brazilian government authorization of my work legally prohibited my interference in Rikbakca life. I believe that the anthropologist, simply by showing interest in the depths of native thought and custom, may promote self-respect in an environment which directly and indirectly undermines it. I also administered medicine, gave informants gifts which they requested, and traded other goods for their artefacts. I attempted to explain some of the difficulties of the industrial society which produced these goods, and of the goods themselves.

3. Dornstauder estimates (1975:28) a total population of four hundred to five hundred in the period prior to the pacification. His map 2 (p. 90) for 1962 shows fifteen functioning settlements and forty nine settlements no longer occupied. (Dornstauder has expressed dissatisfaction with these maps (Shiela Tremaine, SIL, personal communication); I do not know the reason for this dissatisfaction.)

There are several indices of this greater pre-contact population size, some indices from comparable situations of other tribes, others from the Rikbakca case itself. The reduction of 70 % is smaller than the general rate of reduction in the Americans following Columbus' arrival. Dobyns (1966) has estimated that on the average, aboriginal populations were reduced by 95 % from the fifteenth century to their periods of lowest population. Ribeiro (1957/1967) estimated that 32 % of the tribal groups which were isolated in 1900 had been extinguished by 1957; 32 % remained in isolation, while the remainder had established some form of contact, principally 'intermittent' and 'permanent', rarely 'integrated' contact. He found also that the proportion of tribes extinguished in this period was greater in regions of extractive economies (rubber and Brazil nuts) than in regions of pastoral economies, but not as great as that in regions of agricultural economy. He claimed that this proportion reflected both the violence with which the groups of tappers and gatherers of forest products have come into conflict with the Indians, and the conditions of life that the former have inspired upon tribes with whom they have established pacific relations.« (97). He estimaterd also (109-10) that »the average population per group tends to fall as the group passes from the condition of isolation to that of intermittent and permanent contacts, in the proportion of 1,000 to about 300 persons per group, and to rise thereafter, in integrated groups, to 600.« Thus my estimate for the Rikbakca corresponds to observations which have been made elsewhere in the continent.

There is evidence also from the Rikbakca case itself. During the first few years of direct contact there were several epidemics of influenza and measles. Padre Edgar Schmidt, one of the priests of the Jeusit Missao Anchieta, estimated (personal communication) that several hundred died during this period. These estimates seem low. They were based I believe, on direct observations rather than on projections to the Rikbakca groups not directly observed. Many villages, particularly those west of the Juruena, were not visited. Padre Joao Dornstauder, who established the first pacific contact in 1957, observed (1975) the rapid transmission of influenza during his visits. The disease sometimes reached villages before he did, carried by the Rikbakca themselves. It is uncertain whether these diseases were brought by the pacification team itself or by the frontiersmen whose possessions the Rikbakca were stealing during this period. In either case it is likely that the epidemics spread through all of the villages which maintained contact.

Padre Edgar also claimed (personal communication, 1970) that Padre Joao has passed through forty two villages. It was not clear whether these were all occupied or whether deserted villages were also included in the count. If we allow that some of these were deserted, but that many other villages were not visited, and if we propose a mean figure of twenty five occupants per village, the population must then have exceeded one thousand. Some of the settlements on which Dornstauder reports numbers, had fewer than twenty five residents; seasonal variation may have accounted for his figures.

Rubber tappers in the region who visited several Rikbakca villages during the early contact period also report 'large' and active villages. One of these frontiersmen reports a settlement inhabited by many Rikbakca who were dancing, ornately decorated; it may well have been that one settlement invited others, so this village may not represent normal size.

Rikbakca accounts are no more precise, but also suggest a much larger population. This corresponds with the genealogies which I attempted to collect. Older Rikbakca claimed that there had been »many« – »sidubainca« (literally, 'them only') and that many had died during the pacification. Deaths were caused also by internecine conflicts; these may have been influenced by external pressures as has recently been suggested concerning Yanomamo violence (Davis 1976). One of the oldest Rikbakca told me that there were formerly many more old people, »caikbaca«, and that there were now none left; he denied being old. The age pyramid within the population thus seems to have been affected also.

4. I note that medical treatment is generally excellent. I exchanged medicines and medical information with this nurse, and left myself to her good care for one of many attacks of malaria which I had and was unable to treat myself.

Bibliography

Appell, George N.,
1975 »The Pernicious Effects of Development«, Fields Within Fields, 14.

Bonilla, Victor Daniel,
1972 *Servants of God or Masters of Men?,* Hammondsworth, England, Penguin Books.

Buckley, Walter,
1968 *Sociology and Modern Systems Theory,* Englewood Cliffs, New Jersey, Prentice Hall.

Chandless, William,
1862 »Notes of the Rivers Arinos, Juruena, and Tapajós«, Journal of the Royal Geographical Society, 32: 268-280.

Crosby, Alfred,
1072 *The Columbian Connection,* Westport, Connecticut, Greenwood Press.

Davis, Shelton and R.O. Mathews,
1976 *The Geological Imperative,* Cambridge, Massachusetts, Anthropology Resource Center.

Dobyns, Henry,
1966 »Estimating Aboriginal American Population«, Current Anthropology, 7;4: 395-416.

Dornstauder, Joao,
1975 *Como Pacifiquei os Rikbakca,* Sao Leopoldo, Brazil, Instituto Anchietano de Pequisas.

Hahn, Robert,
1976 *Rikbakca Categories of Social Relations; An Epistemological Analysis,* unpublished Ph.D. dissertation, Department of Anthropology, Harvard University.

Hart, Laurie,
1973 »Pacifying the Last Frontiers«, North American Congress on Latin America, VII; 10: 15-31.

Hempel, Carl,
1965 »The function of general laws in history«, in Hempel, C., ed., *Aspects of Scientific Explanation and Other Essays in the Philosophy of Science,* New York, The Free Press.

Martins e Tintin, Luis R.,
1977 »Entrevista com Com Tomás Balduino«, Opiniao, 223.

Ribeiro, Darcy,
1967 »Indigenous Cultures and Languages of Brazil«, in Hopper, Janice, ed., *Indians of Brazil in the Twentieth Century,* Washington, Institute for Cross-Cultural Research.

Saak, W.,
1962 »Dringinde Forschungsaufgaben in Nordwestern Mato Grosso«, Bulletin of the International Committee on Urgent Anthropological and Ethnological Research, 5: 132-139.

Schultz, Harald,
1964 »Informacoes Etnograficas sobre os Erigpagtsa (Canoeiros) do alto Juruena«, Revista do Museu Paulista, 15: 393-414.

Ayoréode woman, Santa Cruz, Bolivia. Copyright: René Böll.

Go Forth to every Part of the World and Make All Nations My Disciples
The Bolivian Instance

by LUIS A. PEREIRA F.

In the propaganda brochure of the Summer Institute of Linguistics (hereafter referred to as the SIL) published under the auspicies of the Ministry of Education and Culture in La Paz under the title »*Forjando una Manana Mejor*« (Forging a Better Tomorrow) it is stated:

> »*Obey your legal superiors, because God has given them command, There is no government on earth that God had not permitted to come to power*« *(Romans 13:1)*[1]

The quotation has been translated into eight different Indian languages: Guaraní, Cavinana, Chipaye, Ese Ejja, Chácobo, Chiquitano, Sirionó and Ignaciano.

These words selectively chosen from the Bible by the SIL belong – as authorized experts have confirmed – to a subject matter that is touched upon only sporadically elsewhere in the Bible. Indeed, statements of a much more far-reaching nature which are contradictory to this admonition are greatly in the majority. The Bible, however, has been constantly used to prop up well-defined political interests – but naturally only for simplists impervious to any form of dialectics. However, distinctions must be made, because God's adjutant, the USA, wields a weighty judgement as to the legitimacy of governments. Otherwise the Devil might easily rear his ugly head. For instance, shortly before the change of government, Torres-Banzer, SIL misionaries preached to a group of Ayoréode »If the agents of Torres come you must kill them, for they are evil spirits. If they come in large numbers, you must take to the forest, go to Brazil... there we (the missionaries) will receive you.« (Verbatim from the missionary in Poza Verde, the Chiquitos province, Depto. Sta. Cruz de la Sierra), and in the Chiriguano – Izozeno area we are told that »the communist Torres makes soap of all childless women and burns old men and women...«.[2]

Protestant sects deliberately spread such atrocity tales among the Indians in the struggle against any social revolution.

The Many Offshoots of North American Ideology

Before analysing the methods and aims of the mission bases in detail, we must first establish in our minds the real interests of the North American sects in South America, which means that we must strip them of their humanitarian guise. First we should note the sects' form of organization: in Bolivia, as in Peru, the SIL collaborates closely with the SIM (South American Indian Mission) and the SAM (South American Mission) and other Protestant sects. This method is characteristic of the Protestant sects' work in the whole of Latin America: a large number of small organizations which apparently operate independently – and which diligently maintain this appearance – but which are really under the close surveillance of an umbrella organization. In Bolivia the headquarters are in Cochabamba, where the SIL, the SAM and the NTM (New Tribes Mission) live in a complex of buildings situated in a block to facilitate internal communication. The dissolution of the SIL-center near Riberalta, Tumi Chucua (Depto. Beni), for instance, is in keeping with this policy. A SIL deputy manager had this to say in a confidential conver-

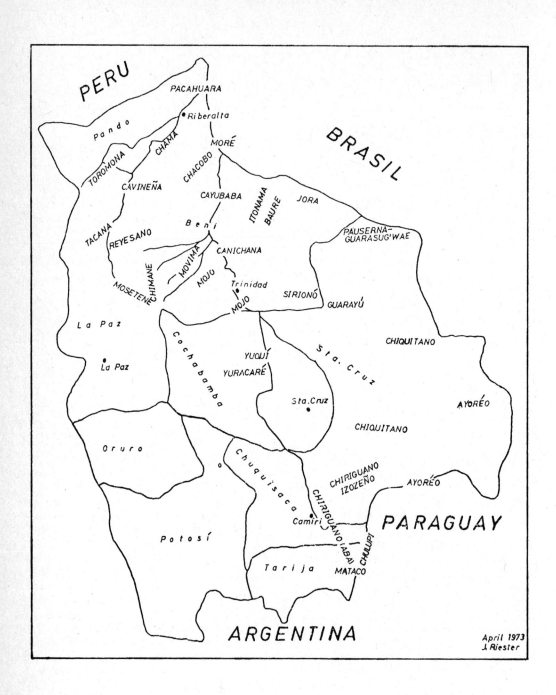

PERU

PACAHUARA

Pando

• Riberalta

TOROMONA

CHAMA

MORÉ

BRASIL

CAVINEÑA

CHACOBO

CAYUBABA

ITONAMA

BAURE

JORA

TACANA

Beni

REYESANO

CANICHANA

PAUSERNA-
GUARASUG'WAE

MOVIMA

MOJO

MOSETENE

CHIMANE

Trinidad

SIRIONÓ

GUARAYÚ

La Paz

MOJO

• La Paz

Cochabamba

YUQUÍ

YURACARÉ

Sta. Cruz

CHIQUITANO

Sta.Cruz

AYORÉO

Oruro

CHIQUITANO

Chuquisaca

CHIRIGUANO
IZOZEÑO

AYORÉO

PARAGUAY

Camiri

CHIRIGUANO

Potosí

CHIRIGUANO ABA

CHULUPI

Tarija

MATACO

ARGENTINA

April 1973
J. Riester

110

sation: »The SIL and the other North American churches must change their procedure. Experience from Colombia and Peru confirms this. The mission basis in South American countries provoke the envy of the states, stoked by communist students and intellectuals. You see, for quite some time the U.S. army has not established any bases in Latin America, but that does not mean that the army is any less present. The same applies to us«.[3]

When in the following mention is made of the military interests – and in a broader sense, the economic interests of these organizations, one thing must be made clear at the outset: in most cases the missionaries themselves are naive – and thus ready tools; they are unable to discern the ideological foundations and political interests of the policy that manipulates them. However, the efficiency and virulence of such »tools« has been proven all too often by history. This naiveté, nonetheless, does not prevent the missionary from backing up his humanitarian efforts financially, as shown by the following report: In 1952 a missionary from the SIL was arrested by the Bolivian border police in the frontier village of Puerto Suarez, the Chiquitos province, Depto. Sta. Cruz de la Sierra, because his pocket flashlight contained gold dust instead of batteries. In 1970 an Ayoreo Indian from the mission station of Torbité told an officer from the Instituto Geográfico Militar the following: »At night the missionaries go to a mountain near the mission station. The mountain is surrounded with barbed wire and we must not enter it. They carry torches on their heads and shots are heard from inside the mountain. There is a big runway near the mountain. Now and then big airplanes come...«.[4] In short, the Indian unwittingly gave the Bolivian officer a description of a goldmine. We heard similar stories from neighbouring farm owners.

However, such enterprises can hardly contribute to the rescue of the American economy, and do not justify organizational expenditure which is counted in millions. There can be no question of reimbursing it with gold dust brought home in pocket flashlights. South America holds incredible riches whose exploitation »justifies« by monetary gain every effort to subjugate it.

So let us first examine the overlapping objectives of the sects – or, to be more accurate, of North American politics, whose legions follow the word of the Bible: »Go forth to every part of the world« ... but go primarily to where it pays. In the earth of South America lie treasures that have been exploited since the conquest, and that still fill the coffers of the Western world: ore, oil and natural gas. The forests are rich in fine wood, valuable animals, medicinal herbs and, of course, cheap labour. On this rich continent more than 90 % of the population live on the brink of the subsistence minimum, exploited by a small propertied stratum. The profits of this exploitation are almost exclusively exported abroad; very few of them are invested in lucrative domestic industries or in agriculture. As a Bolivian peasant leader put it, »The vampire of the North is clinging to our veins«.

Local revolts by those living at subsistence level are crushed. A human life is not highly valued on this continent. The discontent and hatred of the masses of the oppressors is growing constantly. But a population that is increasingly aware of its situation and begins to rebel against it is a threat; it may one day put a stop to the exploitation of this convenient store of the mineral resources that are running out in the rest of the world.

So the northern oppressor – sometimes in the guise of the Good Shepherd – goes about among the people and tries to turn the hatred into fatalistic adjustment, adjustment to regimes which in their turn exist only at the mercy of, and for the benefit of, Big Brother from the north, who has learned a lot from his experiences in Vietnam. Che Guavara's guerillas in Bolivia were located by Chiriguano Indians who were under the care of the Methodists, and subsequently the guerillas were liquidated by government troops aided by these Indians. We can mention another example of SIL interference in the internal affairs of a South American state: the participation of the Protestants in the struggle against Teoponte's guerillas in Boliva. A former high ranking officer in the Bolivian army, who now lives in exile, told us of his previous experience. »At the time I was a member of the Bolivian military apparatus and was in a leading position in the anti-guerilla movement against Teoponte. We established contact with the SIL missionaries, who supplied us with maps of the guerillas' area of operation. We were surprised at the precision of these maps. In addition they supplied us with data concerning the ethnic composition of the population and the location of the productive fields. Furthermore they could tell us with great correctness which population groups supported the guerillas...«

These examples, together with the constant presence of North American ministers in the Latin American jungles, with their exact knowledge of local population and geography, create the suggestion of a well-calculated campaign on the part of the North Americans to establish an anti-guerilla corridor from Colombia to Tierra del Fuego.

Length of SIL's work with Indian tribes of Eastern and Highland Bolivia*

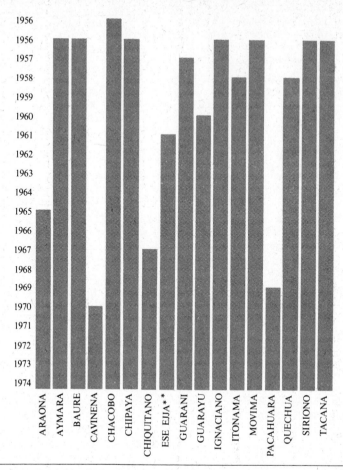

from »Forjando un manana mejor«, SIL 1975.
** Ese Ejja mentioned in another SIL publication: »Chama«.

The incident just cited again involved economic interests, as did the case of Bolivian Gran Chaco, whose interior was of no economic interest until a few decades ago. The expansion of the agricultural sector and the discovery of oil and natural gas there quickly altered the situation. Since time immemorial the Ayoréode Indians had ruled this area. They were a nomadic people numbering 4500 at most. They were famed for their fearlessness in battle, which since their first encounter with the white man had mainly meant defensive warfare. After the Chaco War between Paraguay and Bolivia, white cattle farmers tried to penetrate the Ayoréode tribal territory and seize the land, but they encountered strong resistance. In order to pacify the Ayoréode North American missionaries were called in. By the end of the 1940's W. Pencille was able to establish the first friendly contact with the Ayoréode. This missionary led the Indians to a mission station close to the railway line Sta. Cruz – Corumbá. During the first weeks approximately 300 Indians died of influenza (Fischermann 1976:68-69). There can be no doubt that it would have been possible for the missionary, who had a jeep. an airplane and funds at his disposal, to save the lives of these people. But the missionary, Pencille, was convinced that »It's better they should die. Then I baptise them, and they go straight to heaven.« (Extract from a conversation between William Pencille and Father Elmar Klingler O.F.M.).

Another example is the attempted annihilation of the Peruvian Mayorunas. In 1965 a SIL missionary placed his local geographical knowledge at the disposal of the North American marines stationed in

Iquitos. While the Marines made reconnaissance flights from Iquitos, Peruvian units guided by the aerial observations attacked the Mayoruna. Not even the most fearless Indian warrior can prevail against napalm bombs. Shortly after, drilling units occupied the area and struck it rich (Moscoso 1977).*

Two further examples created a stir in the Bolivian press in September and October 1977 – instances which all too clearly reflect the economic interests cited above, interests which obviously disregard any respect for human lives, let alone human dignity. On Oct. 4, 1977, the Yuqui (a sub-group of the Sirionó) killed a worker from the Estancia Santa Martha (Provincia de Nuflo de Chávez).[5] The measure taken will probably lead to the extermination of this group of Yuqui. Their desperate struggle to survive against the white cattle owners created two new overwhelming enemies: the Protestants and the Rangers, an anti-guerilla group. If the first enemy cannot contrive their peaceful transfer to captivity, then the order to the Rangers is »Exterminate the Yuqui«. So far six messages of success have been received. Six Yuqui have been shot for the benefit of Bolivian cattle-breeding.

In the second case Ayoréode killed a worker of the Western Geophysical Company.[6] The few Ayoréode who still lived freely in the forest found themselves surrounded by the above mentioned company. Every five kilometers cleared aisles traversed their area. The animals fled – but where could the Ayoréode flee? Everywhere they turned they encountered boundaries set up by the drilling crews. They became so harassed that they feared to fell a tree lest the noise give them away. In their extremity they chose three warriors to take up the hopeless defensive struggle. These warriors killed a worker. This prompted the Protestants to appear on the scene. They were assigned the task of taming these Indians, all but the last of the free Ayoréodes.

»They were taken to the mission station of the New Tribes Mission, Puesto Paz, by the North American missionaries Pablo Wyma, Juan Wins and Lorenzo Golder« (Presencia, La Paz, 14.9.1977). As a token of gratitude the manager of the Western Geophysical Company, Donald Phillips, engineer, arranged for a water well to be drilled, a project which was completed in September 1977.

Today no Ayoréode Indian lives as a free person in Bolivian Gran Chaco, but there are certainly many white cattle owners and oil companies. Instead the Ayoréode live in settlements unfit for human habitation in the »care« of North American missionaries. Now and again they are viewed by tourists or visited by anthropologists who for the most part only want to collect scientific material, and afterward leave the Indians to their misery. One may also »view« the Ayoréode at the market in Sta. Cruz de la Sierra, when the North American missionary Ramses[7] brings Indians in by air from the mission station Zapocó and exhibits them among tractors and pure-bred cattle. Postcards showing this can be bought in Sta. Cruz. The Ayoréode who live at other mission stations are no better of. They live in miserable cabins, mostly surrounded by barbed wire. The visitor cannot rid himself of the depressing feeling that he is in a concentration camp. The Ayoréode are conscious of their situation, but they are also aware that they

---

* The account of the Mayoruna incident and of SIL's complicity therein has been questioned. There has not been time, without unduly delaying publication, to receive a response from Dr. Pereira on the alternative interpretation or to check the references. We have, therefore, chosen to quote an alternative account of the incident by Stephen Corry of Survival International from his forthcoming book »Towards Indian Self-Determination in Peruvian Amazonia«:

»In 1964 the Matses, or Mayoruna as they are commonly known in the region, were attacked and bombed. As with all major attacks on Indian settlements in Amazonia over the last 20 years or so, what actually happened is difficult to establish accurately because of conflicting stories. The following sketchy account is drawn from an article by Emilio Mendizábal Losack 1967. The author has pieced the story together from various newspaper accounts of the time and subsequent journalistic investigations. Many other sources refer to this incident but none give as many details.

It appears, then, as if the mayor of Requena's rubber working interests in the area, had been brought to a halt because of harassment by »hostile« Indians at the beginning of 1964. The mayor, Gumercino Flores, organised a punitive expedition into the Matses area using the cover that it was to »conduct preliminary investigations for the construction of a road from Requena to the Yavarí«. The expedition, consisting of 30 civilians (many of them *comerciantes*), 2 Civil Guards and 9 soldiers, left Requena on 12 Febuary 1964. On 10 March, ten expedition members returned to Requena, the following day the expedition was attacked by Indians as it was, again, on 14 March. Press reports mentioned that 2 expedition members were killed and that 4 were wounded in these attacks, although it was subsequently found that only one, and not 4, men were wounded. The attackers were variously described as »smugglers, opium dealers, political agitators, outlaws, communist elements…« and/or Indians in the pay of these miscreants! They were, of course, Matses trying to defend themselves against the expedition…

On 16 March, two B-26 war planes were called in from Chiclayo to machine-gun the Indian area. A bomber was also called and used to drop fragmentation bombs on the Indians. On 17 March, 41 soldiers and 8 civilians arrived to reinforce the expedition. On 22 March, 3 soldiers and 7 civilian *comerciantes* were evacuated from the zone in U.S. helicopters which had been flown in from Panama to assist. On 24 March the expedition arrived at the Yavarí. Here a naval gun-boat was waiting to take them to Iquitos, where they arrived om 30 March.

Accounts of the number of Indians killed vary from about 30 to 60 and more »although the Matses told Romanoff that no Indians had been killed.« Editors' note.

113

cannot return to the forest, as it no longer belongs to them. This so-called »integration« of the Indians into national society, which is being carried out by the SIL in agreement with the national government and the United States of America will, in the case of Eastern Bolivia, lead to the elimination of the Indian population in economically interesting areas. Instead of the Indians, »capable« whites, well-schooled in ideology in their countries of origin, will be admitted. The removal of 150.000 white South Africans to Eastern Bolivia (Beni and Izozog) has become a world-farmous »secret«. Not much imagination is required to picture the future of the remaining Indian groups in these areas.

The Holy Experiment: Many Roads Lead to the Goal

What picture can we form of the contact established by the missionaries with the Indians? The missionary appears as an interested and charitable helper of the Indians, accompanied by his wife and family. The family aspect is of special importance in this connection, for cohabitation with spouse and children is the normal situation for the Indians, who consider the celibacy of Catholic priests absurd. Furthermore, what manner of man is it who undertakes »the jungle life, full of deprivations and dangers«! – Although, admittedly, the civilized world in the form of bungalows, refrigerators, radios, telephones, airplanes and tinned delicacies are standard equipment for any missionary.[8]

Starting work always meant first learning the local language, familiarizing onself with the habits and creeds. The ulterior aim of this will be explained below.

However, the intitial contact is not always friendly. In that event a whole gamut of »means of persuasion« is available to the missionary, from which we have chosen a few examples.

During their efforts to convert the Ayoréode Indians of the Serrania de Sunsas (between Santiago de Chiquitos and Sta. Corazón, Depto. Sta. Cruz de la Sierra) several missionaries were killed (Fischermann 1976:68). Their widows continued their missionary work, and two of them married Ayoréode men in order to make the testimony of suffering even more »immense«, even more »divine«, for surely they must have hated their husbands, must have found them dirty and repulsive, at least if one accepts the cynical statements in the book *God Planted Five Seeds* by D.J. Johnson (Grand Rapids, 1968). The incident is the leitmotif of his book. One could be prompted to ask oneself to what lengths religious perversion can go.

»Living proof of faith« is one means. Kidnapping is another. The case of the Peruvian Mayoruna achieved local fame through the press, and the same happened in the case of the Araonas. By the missionaries' own account, a Mayoruna boy ran away to the SIL. In fact the boy had been kidnapped so that the missionaries could learn the Mayoruna language from him. Later the missionaries (Mrs. Fields and Mrs. Kneeland) were flown over the Indians' territory and spoke to them in their own language through powerful loudspeakers. In the last phase of the »Sky Mission« cassette tape-recorders were dropped, from which the Mayoruna could hear the following speech in their own language: »We are good people who want to help you. We bring everything good.« The result: in 1976-77 the Mayorunas were killing their newborn babies so that they would not have to live in the missionaries' »good world«.

The width of the persuasional gamut can be extended indefinitely. Also, it frequently exposes an excellent cooperation between the Protestant missionaries and the military, as can be seen in the examples cited above. The use of napalm bombs against the Mayoruna and of the Rangers against the Yuquis thoroughly prepared the ground for the Holy Experiment. Unfortunately, the preparation was so thorough that the objects of the crusade will be dispatched »straight to heaven«, this time not by influenza and other diseases of civilization, but by bombs and machine-guns.

A Better Tomorrow or the New Man

Why do the Indians not accept the »charitable« aid from the white missionaries? Or to phrase the question differently, what is the aim of the missionaries? Either question leads to the same answer: The total destruction of the Indian Culture. In the propaganda brochure »Forjando una manana mejor« (Forging a Better Tomorrow) this aim is paraphrased thus: »The process of cultural transfer includes the introductioǹ of Christianity without sectarianism by translating the Holy Scriptures into local languages«. Transfer', 'integration' and 'cultural change' are fine-sounding ideas, and the Protestant elite know how to make use of them. However, there is a reality hidden behind them that cannot be seen by a scholar alienated by the European discussion of theory versus practice: a reality which calls for more than analysis, – which calls for an indictment against the so-called civilized world who daily permit the physical and mental annihilation of people in South America. Paraguay is no extreme or isolated case (Arens 1976; Münzel 1973).

»Cultural transfer« is effected systematically from Colombia to Tierra del Fuego. After the phase described above, the establishment of contact, follows the phase of isolation and indoctrination, which has the purpose of breaking down the cultural identy of the Indians. In phase three the sub-human has developed into a human being and is considered capable of becoming a member of society. Of which society is a matter that remains to be discussed.

First, as to phase two: Bernd Fischermann (1976:114-118), probably the greatest expert on Ayoréo culture, and a man who for years was in a position to closely observe the missionaries' work, demonstrates how systematically the aforementioned policy of isolation is pursued. A prerequisite of effectivity is geographical isolation. The mission stations, with very few exceptions, are situated in areas very difficult of access, so that it is almost impossible for mission pupils to establish contact with the national society. Similarly only very few mission bases have schools, although the establishment of schools is incumbent upon the state. In the schools which do exist, and which visitors are allowed to view, the missionaries teach reading and writing to hand-picked pupils and neophytes on the basis of religious texts translated into the local Indian language. The chosen few, who are later sent to continue their studies at the mission centers or even in the U.S.A., are the future ministers who will be active during phase three. Practically none of the mission pupils know Spanish; only a few young people, who have acquired their Spanish *outside* the mission stations, break through this »linguistic isolation«. These tactics are facilitated by the creation of prejudices against non-protestant groups, which necessarily means the entire national society, which consists partly of non-Christian Indians, partly of Catholics. Withholding practical skills includes both withholding training in any practical activity such as a trade or craft, and also rejecting aid from government resources or from other organizations for this purpose. This policy of isolation reaches its apex in isolation of the philosphy of life, which still prevents Bolivian citizens from inquiring into their rights and duties, not to mention obtaining information about the Bolivian government, economy, geography and history.

One question remains: What does the »new man of tomorrow« created by the missionaries look like? How will he present himself in phase three? For one thing, his cultural identity, preserved and defended for centuries, will be destroyed. Concerning this the »Forjando una manana mejor« has this to say: »However, the New Testament has recently been translated into their languages, and Jesus Christ has liberated many of them from this *slavery*« (author's italics), i.e. the autochthonous religious concept of the Indians. »Those liberated are prepared to face the social and economic changes...«

All specialists in the field of Indian research testify that such statement by the SIL are *not* true, that they are merely clumsy self justification on the part of the missionaries, who were never invited by the Indians to live in their villages, much less to destroy their culture. No Indians on the South American continent asked for the Christian God. He was foisted upon them. What do the representatives of the Christian God bring to the Indians? Destruction of their social organization, disease, death and despair. They are hostages of civilization without any benefits – a true enslavement. At the railway station at Sta. Cruz de la Sierra one can see women from the Ayoréode tribe, working as prostitutes of the lowest order, without even the benefit of medical control; one asks oneself »Why did this have to happen?«

It happened partly because the way back to the forest has been blocked to the Ayoréode, and partly because life in the mission stations is unbearable. The daily humiliation stokes the hatred against the missionaries (Riester 1977). Only one example need be mentioned: In October 1977, at the mission station of Poza Verde in the Chiquitos province, Depto. Sta. Cruz de la Sierra two youngsters of the New Tribes Mission were found »sniffing« gasoline – the reasons for their behaviour seem obvious. In punishment the water for the entire village was turned off for several days during the dry season. At this time the village (of approx. 190 inhabitants) was ravaged by a serious measles and whooping-cough epidemic – an epidemic, incidentally, which might have been alleviated with the help of drugs and vaccine. As a result, an increasing number of Ayoréode are leaving the camp, unprepared for Bolivian society. The only thing they have learned from the missionaries is that everything has a fixed price, just as in the mission shop where the missionary sells his merchandise to the Indians. The price is paid by the Ayoréode, and paid twice over. Traditionally, Ayoréode girls are permitted to have sexual intercourse, subject of course, to certain norms of their own culture. Now, therefore, if it proved possible to earn some money by prostitution in the neighbourhood of the railway station before marriage, this did not seem so reprehensible. However, they knew nothing of the dangers of venereal disease. The Ayoréode, who know nothing of a world beyond their own, cannot be blamed for the fact that today the tribe is infected with venereal disease and that the child mortality rate is consequently high. The blame rests on the missionaries, because of their policy of isolation as described by B. Fischermann.[9]

One might almost think that it is a question of tactics, the goal being the decimation or extermination of the Indians. At least, instances of the methods employed by the American Peace Corps in Bolivia do not indicate the reverse.

In the above we cited the break-down of cultural identity through implanting Protestant Christian concepts. A much more far-reaching operation is indicated in the latter example. There it is not only creeds, habits and customs that are ruined but also entire autochthonous social structure. Indian communities are characterized by an economic and social structure based on common ownership and the distribution of all goods produced. Only in this way was it possible for them to survive for centuries in an inimical environment. The ideological foundation of the Christianity preached by the North American missionaries is based on the individual chosen by God.[10] The goods produced by this individual, even when they are produced in conflict with others, are signs of having pleased God. This is a basic feature in any puritan religion, which Max Weber sees as the origin of capitalist economy. Looking at the missionaries' teachings, this thought does not seem too remote. In one mission, for instance, limited agricultural activities were introduced. The missionaries sold the Indians manual sowers. One such machine can sow over 50 hectares of land in one season. In the whole of the Indian village there were only 20 hectares of land. The missionaries sold 15 sowers.

We meet these tactics again in the SIL schoolbooks, written in the Indian languages:

> *»Juan and Pedro are sitting by the river fishing.*
> *Juan catches two fish. Pedro catches no fish.*
> *Juan is lucky. Pedro is unlucky.*
> *Juan sells Pedro a fish.*
> *Juan was lucky, he fished and sold Pedro a fish.«*

Why didn't Juan give Pedro a fish? Because Juan leads a life pleasing to God, because he was chosen by God.

A song[11] we heard from the Mojos in Beni, from the Chácobos in Pando and from the Chiriguanos in Dept. Sta. Cruz goes as follows:

> *»And here, who comes? and here, who comes?*
> *It is Jesus, it is Jesus,*
> *He brings us riches, he brings us riches,*
> *For me, for me.*
> *He brings us freedom, he brings us freedom,*
> *To me, to me.*
> *He will bring everything, he will bring everything.*
> *Jesus, Jesus,*
> *I shall go to Heaven, I shall go to Heaven,*
> *To be with Jesus, to be with Jesus.«*

We said that the third phase was to introduce the being who had become a human into the society. Into which society? B. Fischermann says: »It can be said that the practices of the missionaries do not further the integration of the Ayoréode into the Bolivian society« (1976:117). It is true that the policy of isolation described – involving his very language, alienating the Indians from society instead of preparing them for it – permits no other conclusion. On the contrary, the overturning of the economic and social structure which have been cited here through the presentation of examples spur us to the realization that a policy is being pursued which has nothing to do with Bolivia or her inhabitants, as the missionaries pretend, but which has a great deal indeed to do with their own country, the United States of America. No stone is left unturned, as these examples from the Protestant missions show.

In order not to leave phase three as a mere matter of conjecture, we would like to describe briefly the result of the protestant teaching, using the example of a tribe in which the missionary work was brought to a »successful« conclusion. In the opinion of the Protestants the members of this tribe are Christians, i.e. their souls have been saved for eternal life. The functions of the missionaries have been vested in a member of the tribe. A registration of the report of success can be summarized as follows:

1. The traditional economy has been destroyed. It doesn't exist anymore.
2. Among other elements introduced: Permanent settlement with a center containing church/school/ sanitary station.
3. Installation of a sawmill (owned by eight Indians).
4. Wage labor.
5. Prohibition of the celebration of traditional and national holidays.
6. The creation of an elite minority among the Indians.

During the years of Christianization the world view of the SIL missionaries was implanted in the elite, the central values being concentrated on physical cleanliness and puritan life-style. The Indians were exposed to a curious mixture of Christian ideas on »the value of life and the true man« combined with the ideas of the SIL missionaries that profit-making is ethically valuable.[12]

The SIL selected some young Indians, removing them from their tribe and sending them to the SIL head-base, in order to educate them systematically in the SIL's values. These Indians, who today form the elite, and who wield the political and economic as well as the ideological power, were inoculated with a tribalism, the development and affirmation of which is extremely interesting. Everything is done in the name of the new identification. Bolivian nationalism is antagonistic to tribalism. According to the Indians, all Bolivians and Catholics are evil and should be rebuffed. All other groups belonging to the same faith are not enemies of ones own tribalism. The friend/enemy dichotomy is now prevalent in a new situation, that of religious conviction. This categorization is rigidly applied and allows for no flexibility. To the elite, the Bolivian Catholic and the communist are on the same level. Tribalism is converted into an instrument for defining external relations and one's own (new) situation. The Indians have come to the conclusion that only now are they complete human beings, whereas before they lived as wild animals.

By its very nature this new identification does not promote dynamic action: it was implanted by the SIL workers, and not developed by the Indians themselves.

The enemy, logically enough, was relocated to groups who might threaten the status quo. This makes the Indians sceptical of a progressive regime. The tribal identification in a sense restrains internal and external development. The SIL created an elite which was to acquire prestige by assuming new functions. The mastering of new mechanisms distinguished the elite more and more from the rest of the Indians, who in turn were sceptical of the privileges of this elite group. But as the power of the elite grew they could become more and more despotic. The quest of the Indians – as a tribe – for a conciliation between the traditional system and the new order has become very difficult, and the conflicts are constantly growing.

In speaking of the SIL-tribalism we referred to the elite, and characterized only one aspect of the reality of the group. The total group experiences a critical and manifest crisis of identification, making it extremely difficult for the Indians to define their own situation. They vacillate between the old and the new system. While old people define themselves according to their clan system, the young and the elite no longer consider themselves members of a clan. The elite does not in any way present itself as a closed group, which ought not suprise us if we consider its origin. According to the education implanted by the SIL, every person should procure individual benefits, and in this system the only road to success, economic as well as ideological, is at the expense of others: that is, by individual exploitation. In this sense it is impossible to speak of an elite consciousness, let alone of a homogenous consciousness of the rank and file.

Of course, the elite acts as an interest-group if their privileges are threatened. If expedient, any member is dropped and replaced by another person.

The conviction that »finally they have found their own culture« is based on the fact that they now possess the Bible and basic texts in their own language. But the content transmitted to them in this form is on the one hand very far from their own situation, and on the other hand alien to the Bolivian reality.

Finally, this emphasis on the importance of the language was employed by the SIL in order to restrict communication with other groups, since – after long years of teaching and evangelization – the Indians apart from the elite have not mastered the national language even rudimentarily (see Kelm 1972:245-246, quoted in Riester 1976:52-54). Without any doubt the Indians have been isolated in order to facilitate their manipulation.

The number of those who seek new ways to escape from this isolation and the forced destruction of their indigenous culture, to establish themselves as peasants and thus identify themselves with a new group is constantly growing.

NOTES

[1] »The Institute's text is at variance both with that of the English Revised Version of the Bible and its Spanish equivalent. »Let every soul be subject unto the higher powers« becomes »Obey your legal superiors, because God has given them command«, while the SIL quite remarkably translate »the powers that are ordained by God« as »There is no government on earth that God has not permitted to come to power« (Lewis 1978:12). Editors' note.

[2] Interview with a Izozeno – Chiriguano which can be substantiated by means of a tape-recording. The Indians retell the opinions of a member of the UCE (Unión Cristiana Evangélica) church. The Protestant sects have operated in the Izozeno-Chiriguano area since 1927.

[3] Personal information to the author from Mr. Krüzi, Cochabamba – Tumi – Chucua. Mr. Ekman Anderson Lambert, former missonary among the Tikuna Indians expressed himself along similar lines at the SIL-base in Yarinacocha, Peru. At the time Lambert was the head of Yarinacocha.

[4] Here and in all other cases where names are omitted, this is done to protect individuals.

[5] 'Presencia', La Paz, 10.10.1977.

[6] 'El Deber', Sta. Cruz 13.9.1977.

[7] Ramses, North American missionary of the New Tribes Mission, is head of the mission station Ayoréode Zapocó, in the Nuflo de Chavéz province, Depto. Sta. Cruz de la Sierra.

[8] This is a description of the mission station set-ups, as e.g. Puesto Paz, Poza Verde, Zapocó, Rincón del Tigre, Tobité.

[9] Two events taking place a short time ago in Sta. Cruz de la Sierra should also be seen in context of the missionaries' policy of isolation. Things of this nature would not have taken place if the SIL made their extensive data available to the public thus contributing to the urgently needed policy of informing the urban population.

In an article in »Presencia« of 16th October, 1977 there is a report of a young Ayoréode who ran to help a girl from Sta. Cruz who was being raped by two young men (white). The outcome of this help: The Ayoréode, who did not know Spanish, was taken to the station as the culprit by the police, he was tortured and shot through the head; all this because his skin had a different colour, because he was a native on whom all the prejudice of society are discharged when he is caught. In the second case a young Ayoréode told us of an action on the part of Sta. Cruz criminals who tried to hire Ayoréodes as assassins ... a reflection of the way the natives are rated.

[10] We remember one Indian who had the book »Asi somos los Norteamericanos«. He was constantly and enthusiastically citing the life-story of H. Ford »How I became rich«, and an article from the same book by E. Monroe »How I became famous«.

[11] Tape-recorded at various places in Protestant cults.

[12] See: »Primera Reunión de los Ayoréode 22-24 de Setiembre de 1978 en Sta. Cruz/Bolivia«. Sta. Cruz 1978.

Bibliography

Arens, T. (ed.)
1976 *Genocide in Paraguay,* Temple University Press, Philadelphia.

Fischermann, B.
1076 Los Ayoréode. in: *En busca de la loma Santa. Indigenas en el Oriente Boliviano.* Análisis de su situación actual p. 67-188, La Paz-Cohabamba.

Kelm, H.
1972 Chácobo 1970. Eine Restgruppe der Suedost-Pano im Oriente Boliviens. in: Tribus No. 21, pp. 129-246, Stuttgart.

Lewis, N.
1978 *Eastern Bolivia: The White Promised Land,* IWGIA Document no. 31, Copenhagen.

Moscoso, R.
1977 *Los Mayoruna (Matsés).* Tesis de bachillerato de la Universidad Católica, Lima, Peru.

Münzel, M.
1973 *The Aché Indians: Genocide in Paraguay,* IWGIA Document No. 11, Copenhagen.

Riester, J.
1975 *Indians of eastern Bolivia: Aspects of their present situation.* IWGIA Document No. 18, Copenhagen.
1976 *En busca de la Loma Santa. Indígenas en el Oriente Boliviano. Análisis de su situactión actual.* La Paz-Cochabamba.
1977 Los Ayoréode de la estación brasilena. in: Debate No. 1, Santa Cruz de la Sierra.

Summer Institute of Linguistics
1975 *Forjando un manana mejor.* Ministerio de Educación y Cultura – Instituto Lingüístico de Verano 1955-1975, Cochabamba-La Paz.

Text from:
1978 Primera Reunión de los Ayoréode 22-24 de Setiembre de 1978 en Sta. Cruz/Bolivia. Sta. Cruz 1978.

Amuesha leader, Oxapampa, Peru. Copyright: Gorm Rasmussen 1978.

The Summer Institute of Linguistics: Ethnocide Disguised as a Blessing

by RICHARD CHASE SMITH

»*The Wycliffe (Bible Translators Inc.) position is that these (primitive) peoples have never heard that any alternative to their own mythology exists, and that therefore by explaining Christianity they are giving them the chance to make an informed choice... is it wrong for the linguists to tell the natives about beliefs held by so large a proportion of world peoples?*« (Maxwell 1974).

The Christian Missionary is a sacred institution, and like other sacred institutions, it is protected by a system of defences which teach us not to question or criticize it. Missionary activity is surrounded by an aura of mystery and divine sanction which fills many of us with awe. The common idealized image of the missionary in action has little to do with the actual people and activities which go by the name of Christian Missionary. The institution is accepted as an act of faith. As a result the Christian Missionary has, intellectually, been put at such a distance from those in the home country who protect it faithfully and support it financially that they no longer have any real idea who the missionary is, nor what he does, nor how he does it. The need to examine critically the reality of the missionary work is evident; the task of demystifying it is before us.

For the past eight years my work with the Amuesha people of the upper Amazon basin of Peru has brought me into contact with many missionaries of different persuasions; I have witnessed the Christian Missionary in action. At the same time, I have maintained close friendships with both Christian and non-Christian Amuesha. I have talked at length with the old Amuesha about the changes they have experienced during their lifetimes. I have shared many struggles with the young and changing Amuesha. I have gotten drunk on native beer during the traditional religious celebrations, and I have sung Christain hymns along with the Amuesha during their Sunday church services. The following are a series of excerpts from the diary I kept for the past several years detailing some of these experiences. Through them I intend to reflect the influence of the Christian Missionary, the native religiousness, and the situation created when the two meet.

The Amuesha are one of many small nations with a distinct language and culture located in the Amazonian part of Peru. There are today roughly 3500 Amuesha living in the forest-covered portions of the Departments of Pasco and Huánuco, divided into 45 small groups ranging in size from a few to almost one hundred families. All Amuesha practise subsistence agriculture, supplementing their garden produce with protein from hunting and fishing and with cash from rudimentary commercial agriculture.

The first Christian missionaries among the Amuesha were Spanish of the Catholic Franciscan Order who have worked in the Peruvian Amazon for the past three hundred years. At one point they had established a chain of eight mission posts linking together several thousand Amuesha. Today there is but one Franciscan Mission among the Amuesha; it is located at Quillazu. My work with the Amuesha there has brought me into direct confrontation with the Franciscan missionaries over the administration of Amuesha lands and resources (see Smith 1974). Today their influence over the Amuesha is almost nil.

North American missionaries of the Seventh Day Adventist Church have worked among the Cam-

Richard Chase Smith (1944-   ) has a Ph.D. from Cornell University, and has since 1966 spent most of his time on research among the Amuesha people in Peru. He has been deeply involved with the political struggle of the Amuesha, and has published several articles on this topic.

pa and Amuesha for over fifty years. Their work has centered principally in the Perené and Pichis River Valleys. Their influence among the Amuesha has been small, though growing. Today they maintain one outpost on the upper Palcazu River.

I first came into contact with the fundamentalist missionaries of the Wycliffe Bible Translators Inc./Summer Institute of Linguistics (WBT/SIL) in 1968 when I visited their offices at the Ministry of Education in Lima to solicit their support for the developing struggle to obtain titles for Amuesha land. Though their hoped for support never materialized beyond encouraging words, I continued to have contact with them for the next several years, working with them on a technical training project for the Amuesha, and visiting their base of operations several times.

The WBT/SIL began working in the upper Amazon basin of Peru in 1945, after negotiating a very favorable contract with the Ministry of Education. Many years later they spread their work to the heavily Catholic, Quechua-speaking peoples of the Andean highlands. Today almost 50 linguistically trained missionaries work individually or in pairs with 42 different language groups, including two dialects of highland Quechua. They, along with several hundred equally motivated North American support personnel, live in a modern compound at Yarinacocha, on the outskirts of Pucallpa, one of the boom towns of the jungle area. The air transport and communications branch of the organization, known as JAARS, maintains a fleet of several air- and hydroplanes, as well as a radio communications set-up to serve the needs of the missionaries.

The WBT/SIL established and continues to oversee a program of bilingual education whose purpose is to offer an elementary education in the mother language of the monolingual native before progressively entering into Spanish. Until 1975, native teacher candidates, hand-picked by the missionaries, were brought together at the Yarinacocha base for three months of primary education, teacher training, and evangelist indoctrination. Then, during the nine month school year, these carefully molded teachers returned to their villages to relay what they had learned, using well prepared school materials in the native tongue produced by WBT/SIL. Today the bilingual teachers have been incorporated into the regular state education organization corresponding to the province where they teach.

I have only the greatest praise for the WBT/SIL's work in bilingual education. They are pioneers in this field in most countries where they are established, and have advocated reading and writing in the native tongue even against the greatest odds. But one cannot fail to recognize that the bilingual schools and the handpicked teachers who operate them are the WBT/SIL's prime Christianizing wedge into the field of the »heathen«. WBT/SIL makes use of both public and bilingual education programs to carry on traditional missionary activities. Miss Maxwell, in defending the missionaries, says that they offer the native people a new alternative, after which they can make an »informed choice«. Nothing could be further from the truth. For the native peoples under the influence of WBT/SIL, primary education and Christian fundamentalism have become synonymous: children who are educated in the system simply become fundamentalist Christians as they become literate. They are offered no choice.

The WBT/SIL has been working with the Amuesha for over 25 years. The original missionary/ linguist who transferred after five years, was followed by two young women, who accomplished the major part of the work with the Amuesha. One of these women continues to be active in the bilingual education program and is presently finishing the translation of the New Testament into the Amuesha language. Today the WBT/SIL exercises a termendous influence and power over many Amuesha. In the past 25 years, more than 25 Amuesha men have been trained at Yarinacocha to teach in the dozen or more schools scattered in different communities. Most members of these communities, who represent at least 60 % of the total population, now claim to be Evangelists, and operate their own churches, organized under the auspices and guidance of the missionaries.

Excerpts from a Diary

After a two year absence, I returned to the Amuesha in late 1972 armed with a grant to do research on Amuesha social and religious ideology as expressed through the ritual celebration with music. By January 1973, my companion and I were settled into a house in the community of Miraflores, located within the shadow of the Franciscan Mission at Quillazu. As it was the rainy season, we had to wait another two months before looking for a suitable site for our research. Native music disappeared from Miraflores about twenty years ago.

During those rainy season months, we accompanied a small group of Amuesha, faithful to their traditional religion, to a holy site not far from the village, a site which used to attract large pilgrimages of Amuesha, but which is now largely abandoned:

»February 17, 1973; Miraflores; Today we woke up to the sound of heavy rain on the tin roof, the steady kind of rain which usually lasts all day. The rainy season is not the time to plan any outdoor activities, but nonetheless today we planned to visit the site of YOMPOR YOMPERE' (Our Father YOMPERE') and YACHOR MAMAS (Our Mother MAMAS). The manioc beer was thick and smelled strongly of fermentation. By eight o'clock the rain passed and the ancient grandfather, Santiago, appeared at our door with his son and several grandchildren. Within fifteen minutes a dozen of us were walking the eight kilometers of dirt road which winds along the river's edge.«

»The first to arrive at the site, several women, embraced Our Father, the larger stone, and then spoke to and touched Our Mother, the smaller stone at his side. Grandfather Santiago stood behind Our Father, chanting a long and beautiful prayer which lasted at least fifteen minutes. The other men brought out jugs of beer, and the women produced pieces of roasted manioc, handing them to the old man. He placed the offerings at the head of Our Father, and recited another prayer, thanking different deities for sharing their food with us. We then retired to the shade of the few trees at the site: the women behind Our Mother and the men behind Our Father.«

»The grandfather began to recite the history of these sacred stones. YOMPERE' is the brother of Our Father ROR, the sun. They once lived together with their other brothers on this earth. As the time approached for them to leave this earth for the newly created heaven, YOMPERE' became very impatient with his brother ROR for being so slow and insulted him. ROR, the more powerful one, changed YOMPERE', his wife MAMAS, and their children into stone, commanding them to sustain this earth for as long as Ror remains in heaven. The site has been a holy center ever since.«

»Then Pedro told how the white colonists violated the site fifteen years ago, overturning the stones, smashing some of them, and dragging others out of the site in their search for buried gold. Afraid of retributions from the local authorities, the Amuesha remained at a distance, helplessly watching the destruction. Now after many years, their faith still strong, a small group has returned for a visit, finding Our Father and Our Mother overgrown with weeds and shrubs, lying on their backs in a large hole. They looked pathetic. Pedro excitedly told us of his dream of getting people together to lift the stones back on their feet, to clean up the area, and to rebuild a religious house there. I secretly shared his dream.«

»The grandfather arose, walked slowly over to the larger stone, poured a cup of the beer, and repeated another prayer, blowing – ooofff, ooofff – over the top of the cup. We were engulfed in silence as he gulped down the cupful, poured another, and passed it to Pedro, who did likewise, shortly we had all taken a drink of the beer. Several women began to sing, a hauntingly beautiful music performed to celebrate Our Fathers and Mothers. The men were more timid, saying they needed more beer. Only the grandfather, squatting beside Our Father, sang quietly by himself.«

»I was deeply moved by the experience as was, I think, everyone else. We had visited the center of the Amuesha universe, communed with a group of stones which had the power to hold this earth together. I could feel the power radiating from them. There was something alive about them. But how very sad they must feel now, abandoned, broken, and forgotten.«

By the end of the second month the rains had abated enough for us to travel in search of a second community to live and work in for the next few years. The choices had already been limited to one or two places where the traditional activities I was interested in continued. We first visited Asreso and stayed with a family with whom I had lived on different occasions in previous years:

»March 9, 1973; Asreso; On Sunday we walked to Asreso, arriving at Santos' house in the late afternoon. The whole family received us openly and warmly; we were all delighted to see each other after so many years. I stayed up quite late that night chewing coca and exchanging news with Santos.«

»Today Santos' son leads us up the steep trail to his uncle Miguel's house. The carefully made house with a palm leaf roof, and palm slats for siding, is perched on the top of a mountain, far away from all the others. We had another spirited reunion there, exchanging news with Miguel and his new wife. Miguel is leaving this week to spend several months in Yarinacocha assisting the WBT/SIL missionary with the translation of the Bible. He has been helping her for four years now. Towards the end of our visit his face lit up with a big smile and he pulled out a small portable tape recorder which the missionary had lent him. He turned it on; a crackling, then out jumped the missionary's voice singing Christian hymns. He played about fifteen of them for us, all of them vaguely familiar American gospel and folk tunes. The WBT/SIL people seem to have an endless supply of these portable playback machines with pre-recorded tapes. Obviously Miguel was delighted to have one.«

»March 12, 1973; Asreso; Earlier this evening, Santos and I got into a discussion about the religious situation here. He confirmed my earlier observation that there is a division in this community based on religious beliefs. In one group, the larger, are the 'believers' who have accepted the religious doctrine introduced by the WBT/SIL. In the other group are those who have remained faithful to the traditional Amuesha life and values, and who refuse to accept Jesus Christ as their only saviour and god. Santos is very solidly in this second group.«

»But there are very few traditional Amuesha left anymore, and the pressure on them from the missionaries and their converts is constant. Santos told me that the other day the WBT/SIL trained village nurse, who is now a staunch and aggressive Fundamentalist, came by his house. Santos, in traditional fashion, offered him some food and manioc beer. The nurse promptly refused the hospitality, saying that he cannot eat the food of a 'son of the devil.' He then gave Santos a blistering sermon about a burning hell awaiting all those who do not accept Jesus Christ and God's word as written in the Bible. Santos told me sadly that he no longer goes visiting the others in his village because they often try to convert him to Evangelism or call him names like 'mundano'.* Then he asked me with great sincerity: 'When I am sitting here chewing my coca and somebody comes to visit me, do you think I would make him chew coca if he dosen't want to?'«

From Asreso, we moved on to Sepeso, a settlement accessible only by foot trail. After some deliberation, we decided to establish ourselves in this community and made arrangements for temporary housing while the men organized themselves to build us a small traditional house. Within a short time I began work on learning the language with a young Amuesha man named Domingo, whose friendship I still highly value:

»April 16, 1973; Sepeso; I am already somewhat disappointed in having chosen this community to work in, though that may be a premature judgement. I have only been here for a few weeks now, but I am already getting some bad feelings. From what I have observed so far, the people here seem much more interested in being Evangelists than in being Amuesha, more so perhaps than in other communities I have known. The influence of the WBT/SIL missionaries, especially through the two community leaders and the bilingual school teachers, is pervasive, immediate, and strong. Everyone seems to be a believer.«

»April 25, 1973; Sepeso; I find myself getting annoyed at times with Domingo, my language teacher, because of his attitude that there is or was nothing of possible value to be learned from the traditional Amuesha culture. He often shows real scorn for the world of the 'old Amuesha'. Whenever he does tell me something of the traditional belief system, he makes the point that it was the 'old Amuesha' who believed it, and that today, 'we know better'.«

»I asked him today why the WBT/SIL missionaries in their belingual school texts changed the name of the sun from *YOMPOR ROR PARTSESHA'* (Our Father *ROR* Powerfull One) to the single word *ATSNE'* (heat) and then use *his* name for the Christian god. He replied that the Amuesha (Evangelists) now know (through the teachings of the WBT/SIL missionaries) that the sun is in no way divine, but was simply created by the Christian God. 'The moon' he said, 'used to be called *YACHOR* (Our Mother). The old Amueshas believed that it too was sacred and powerful. But now, through the word of the Evangelists, we know that the moon is just a simple star which has nothing sacred about it.'«

»The finality of his words left me with a feeling of hopelessness; his total acceptance of the Evangelist doctrine and its implied Western world view has eliminated for him all the possibilities offered by his own culture. Is this the fate of all the Amuesha? Will they all eventually succumb to the missionaries' point of view?«

»May 8, 1973; Sepeso; I am convinced that there is a quiet conspiracy afoot to replace Amuesha music and dance with lifeless hymns and disfigured folk songs. This morning I was awakened early by the sound of singing in the house next to ours. The tunes were uncannily familiar: My Darling Clementine, You are my Sunshine, Battle Hymn of the Republic, and others. The words were Christian adaptations in Amuesha; they are some of the hymns which the WBT/SIL people promote.«

---

* Literally this means mundane, worldly; it is used disparagingly for all non-believers, i.e., non-fundamentalists.

»In the traditional life, Amuesha families awake very early in the morning, and stirring the previous night's fire back to life, they sing traditional songs until the sun rises. In the evening, after the sun goes down, the family moves indoors and chews coca leaf to ward off sleep and harmful forces of the night. This too is a time for singing. Both the early morning and late evening are times when the children can learn the complicated verse structure and intonations of the traditional music. Many people here still sing during those times, but now, without exception, they sing Evangelist hymns. How are the children going to learn their own traditional music?«

»The WBT/SIL missionaries have translated hundreds of Christian hymns into Amuesha, and adapted Christian lyrics to many North American and European folk tunes; they have printed them in all sizes, shapes, and colors, and distributed them very generously throughout the areas of their influence. These hymns, following the same order as in the printed hymnals, have also been recorded on cassettes which, along with portable cassette recorders (with only playback capacity) are then distributed to the bilingual teachers, community leaders, and other faithful converts to promote Christian hymn singing in the villages. Needless to say, the Amuesha are delighted to listen to these machines.«

»The bilingual teachers are a very important part of this conspiracy. While attending the yearly training courses at Yarinacocha, the teachers learn to sing hymns as well as to teach reading and writing. Back in their schools, the teachers pass on the hymns to their students and to other village members. And they are usually the song leaders at the weekly hymn sings. Damn, the traditional Amuesha don't have a chance against all these tactics.«

»May 27, 1973; (Sunday), Sepeso; The community looks deserted this morning; everyone is attending church services held in the bilingual school. I can hear the hymns, many of them in Spanish. This week I have been thinking a lot about the work of the WBT/SIL and its effects on the Amuesha. I am feeling rather angry at them right now. The Amuesha are very religious people: one old man told me that in the past no one knew better than the Amuesha how to talk to Our Father. They had been known as the holy people of the central Peruvian jungle. Their religiousness cemented them together socially, politically, ethnically, and spiritually. It gave their existence a wonderful richness, and meaning. It was their reason for being here on this earth. They had achieved a very particular and profound understanding of what Our Fathers and Our Mothers are: of the multiplicity, the plurality, and the variety of the sacred.«

»Taking advantage of the openness in religious matters which the Amuesha assumption of plurality allows, the missionaries began introducing concepts of sin, culpability, Jesus Christ the one and only saviour, damnation, and in the final analysis, oneness and sameness. The Amuesha continue to be just as religious as before, but their experience and understanding of Our Fathers and Mothers are being supplanted by the fundamentalists' frantic search for the one and only god and the one and only truth. I wonder if the impoverishment of the Amuesha experience of the multiplicity of the sacred will not soon leave him emptyhanded; that is, if he will not begin to feel the narrowness and intolerance of the experience of the Christian god which the Evangelists have brought them.«

At the end of June, I left Sepeso by foot on a trip which lasted more than three weeks, during which I visited seven Amuesha communities. For the first two days we followed the Sepeso River, through a very rugged and uninhabited area. On the third day we reached the larger Palcazu River, cut inland, crossing a series of mountains, and arrived at Mueneso by late afternoon. I had been to Mueneso almost four years earlier and I include a diary entry from that trip to set the stage for what I found at this time.

»April 26, 1969; Mueneso; I am here for a short visit to check out the land tenancy situation of these people. The trip took two days, coming upriver in a small dugout canoe against a pretty swift current. This is a large and very isolated community which was organized by the Seventh Day Adventist mission perhaps 30 years ago. The village is layed out along a narrow landing strip used by the mission plane. At the center of the strip there is a large church where people gather every morning, evening, and all day Saturday, obeying the call of a large bell. There is a private school run by the mission with one Amuesha teacher whose salary is paid by the villagers. Though the fee is nominal by our standards, it is enough to force these people to sell their labor cheaply to the local white land owner in order to keep their children in school.«

»It seems that many people here now want a WBT/SIL bilingual school to replace the Adventist school. The decision seems to be in the hands of the long time chief, Francisco, and his brothers. He told me that he will first consult with the Adventist missionary before he makes a decision as he does not want to make them angry. He realizes that in theory they are free to do as they please, but nevertheless he is frightened at the idea of confronting the Adventist missionary.«

»The main reason to change schools is economic: the fee charged by the Adventist school is too high. The bilingual schools through in all ways run by the WBT/SIL, are state-supported and therefore free. The problem is religious: the bilingual schools come wrapped in a package which includes Evangelism and a different interpretation of the Bible. I'm sure the Adventist missionaries will not sit back while an Evangelist school is installed in one of 'their' communities'.«

That was in 1969; the following is from my most recent trip:

»June 28, 1973; Mueneso; It must be four years since I last visited this community; it is still as beautiful as I remember it, perched on a high bluff above the blue-green waters of the Palcazu River. But its peacefulness has been shattered by the establishment of a WBT/SIL bilingual school three years ago. About half the community, together with the Adventist missionary, protested the decision on religious grounds. Within a year a bitter struggle erupted, and the protestors moved across the river to form a new community called Poneso. The two groups continue to co-exist, but I sense a tremendous tension between them. The split has been demoralizing for everybody involved; members of both groups have expressed to me their sadness.«

»This situation is very common among the Amuesha where similar divisions, though not always as antagonistic and open, plague many of the communities I know. These divisions reflect the rivalry between the different Christian missions which are engaged in a struggle with each other to attract the greatest number of 'heathen souls' to their particular flock. The Amuesha have been subjected to the activities of the Catholic mission, the Evangelist (WBT/SIL) mission, and the Adventist mission. Each has staked out its 'claim' among the Amuesha villages, and has preached intolerance towards the other religious doctrines. In the end, it is the Amuesha who lose: they become the confused victims of the missionaries' rivalry. Their national unity and their collective spirit are broken in the process.«

From Mueneso, the Palcazu River is navigable by raft or dugout canoe. I embarked on a small balsa wood raft with a half dozen other Amuesha who were heading in the same direction. After spending the night in a small settlement along the river, we cut across the forest from the mouth of the Izcosacin River heading west towards the village of Porrayo. We arrived after a two day trek across a thickly forested flat basin, broken only by an occasional meandering stream. Porrayo is still a very isolated group of Amuesha. It is not really a village as everyone lives dispersed along the streams and in the lower hills. All of the adults here are refugees from the higher elevations of Oxapampa, having fled from the abuses of the white settlers. There has been a WBT/SIL school and church here for about a dozen years.

During one of my previous visits to Porrayo, I was 'adopted' into a family there who took pity on my aloneness. They were delighted to fit me into their world of kinship and to treat me with the accord and respect due my position as son in the family. I experienced a reciprocal delight learning to fit myself into their family structure. I was now returning with a large number of small gifts for my extended family, a small exchange for their past hospitality.

»July 9, 1973; Porrayo; Sebastian, the teacher here, was one of the first WBT/SIL trained bilingual teachers, and he is regarded by the missionaries as one of their most faithful converts. I was told by many Amuesha that he was likely to be very interested in my project of recording Amuesha music and oral tradition to leave here for the future generations. I was hopeful of soliciting his opinions and ideas on the project, but I was baffled by his lack of response. He evaded my questions, changed the subject, or was silent.«

»Later that afternoon, my father Juan, shed some light on that situation. He said that the older people like himself don't tell their oral history any more because so many others make fun of it, or accuse them of lying or of making up stories. Many of the younger Amuesha now attribute their 'poverty, backwardness, and lack of civilization' to their once having believed this oral tradition. This same group usually insist that the Amuesha should be learning the 'true' history written in the Bible and in books. His own son, Sebastian, the school teacher, is particularly adamant in condemning the oral history and often angrily reprimands his father for telling it. That certainly explains his response to me this morning.«

»July 15, 1973; (Sunday;) Porrayo; This morning I sat beside my father at the church service held in the school. Sebastian, the school teacher, was preaching and leading the hymn singing, using materials prepared and distributed by the WBT/SIL. I couldn't understand what he was saying so I asked my

126

father to translate. I couldn't believe what I was hearing as he translated. The teacher was telling the gathering that they were 'Jews' because they don't believe in anything, and for that reason, they are killing the Christian god, just like the Jews persecuted and killed Jesus. My heart sank, how could Sebastian be saying such a thing. I couldn't get his words out of my head for the rest of the day.«

»I thought of his words in terms of alienation and how vulnerable a people like the Amuesha are to this kind of alienation. As I have observed it, the process looks like this. First the Amuesha are convinced that their traditional existence constitutes a problem; that is, that they do not belive in anything, and that therefore are making things difficult for the Christian god (the one and only). Once convinced of this, they are alienated from their native sense of self. Then they are convinced that the white man's world possesses the solution to their problem; now they are doubly alienated. Finally, they are convinced to reject their own interpretations of reality, since by definition that is the problem, and to accept white man's interpretation as the solution to their problem... at that point they are triply alienated from themselves. The perpetrators of this kind of violence act with such kindness, such benevolence, and such conviction that the Amuesha are defenseless against it... they do not refuse it.«

»This seems to be the same kind of mystification which Laing talks about. Mystification: making things seem to be what they are not... the creation of a mist between a person and his sense of self... the obfuscation of one's own reality. It can be stated in different ways. Before he is subjected to this kind of alienation, the Amuesha is a very profound believer in his traditional interpretation of his world, a world which for him is rich, full, and charged with meaning. Then representatives of white man's world tell him that he doesn't believe in anything, that his interpretation is false, that his world is nothing. He is told that if he will believe in white man's world, he will then be believing in something. Isn't this a kind of mystification? Isn't the missionary turning something into nothing, and nothing into something? Isn't he telling the Amuesha that he doesn't believe in anything, when in fact he does? Is it this same mystification in reverse to say that by believing in white man's impoverished materialist world, one is believing in something?«

»There is no way I can avoid the conclusion that the WBT/SIL is an agent of this process of alienation and mystification. They prepare the Sebastians, Domingos, and Miguels to preach alienation to their own communities, in their own language, manipulating their own concepts. And the WBT/SIL missionary keeps his hands very clean; he can still smile.«

After spending several more days with my adopted family in Porrayo, I returned home to Miraflores in a small plane from a landing strip a half day's walk downriver. There was excitement in Miraflores: many people talked hopefully of reconstructing the holy site of Our Father *YOMPERE'*. As the month of August passed the excitement mounted; plans were made; invitations were sent to other groups; and finally the manioc beer was prepared.

»September 5, 1973; Miraflores; It has happened! It has actually happened! For years I've been dreaming of raising Our Father *YOMPERE'* back on his feet. And yesterday we did it. We worked half a day among 40 men, women, and children. What an incredible day and night... we are all very happy.«

»It dawned a beautiful day, clear and sunny. Only the jagged peaks of the Chemellen mountain range were lost in clouds. I walked behind the main group, talking with some visitors from other communities. We entered the site just as the grandfather was finishing a long prayer. He had placed the jugs of manioc beer at the stone's head. I awkwardly walked in among the gathering and embraced *YOMPERE'*. By the end of the hour, all the prayers completed, a handful of coca and a cupful of beer had been passed out to everyone, even the smallest children. The older men were sitting together, consulting their coca for a sign that the time was right for attempting to lift the huge stone. At the grandfather's word, we all gathered around, trying to get a grip on him. We lifted, but he would not move. We rested and tried again... no result. Discouragement, a feeling that the task was impossible. We retired back to the shade.«

»It was an effort to get the people moving again. A tree was cut down and several poles were installed to act as levers. A rope was tied around the top of the stone. With the men and women lifting on the poles, and the children pulling on the rope, we tried again. The stone lifted a bare inch off the ground. A surge of excitement swept through the entire group. There was shouting and laughter. I felt a big lump in my throat. Again we lifted him, having just enough time to wedge a few rocks under him before the rope snapped, spilling the long line of children to the ground. *YOMPERE'* settled down slowly onto the rocks.«

»New poles were cut and placed under him; a new rope was tied around him. Charged with excitement and confidence, we made another attempt to lift him. Each new effort produced better results: the pile of rocks wedged underneath him grew steadily. By noon Our Father *YOMPERE'* was standing back on his feet. The excitement was tremendous: the grandfather chanted a lengthy prayer, the women sang their songs of praise and happiness, and the grandmother cried.«

»On returning to the village, we began drinking the manioc beer. It was delicious: smooth, sweet, and nicely fermented. By the early evening, the house was filled with people, laughing, singing, and joking, all feeling the combined effects of the beer and the coca. Traditional music filled the noisy spaces of the night; thoughts of Our Father *YOMPERE'* filled the silent spaces in peoples' hearts. Last night I gained a much more profound understanding of the concept and meaning of the traditional music and the celebrations with manioc beer. I actually experienced it. I felt what it means to be happy for Our Fathers and Mothers, to sing for them, to drink beer for them, and to get drunk for them. As one of the songs proclaimed: 'We are drinking Our Mother Manioc; we are getting drunk for Our Father.' Through the celebration, the world becomes one, the fragments are united, and a wholeness is experienced.«

The following week I returned to Sepeso where I stayed until the end of December. In mid-October I was invited to a traditional celebration, held on the night of the full moon.

»October 16, 1973; Sepeso; It seems that everytime I attend a traditional celebration, I am overcome with a feeling of sadness and frustration. Inevitably, the changes and new values which the Amuesha are subjected to influence these sacred occasions and paralyze the performance of the music and dance. Last night's feast was no exception. Very few people wanted to perform their songs, and when they did, they were fortunate if one other person accompanied them. Around nine o'clock someone brought out a portable record player and all of the young people jumped into the monotonous rhythm of the popular *cumbia*. When each record began, there was a flurry of activity as the boys rushed over to grab a girl to dance. Many of the older people quietly complained about the record player, but went on with their traditional music, despite the competition. By midnight, the traditional music ran out of energy; the older men and women retired to the warmth of the fire. The record player and the *cumbia* had won. I went to sleep.«

»I try to understand what is happening in an effort to keep the sadness of it from engulfing me. The traditional feast, the gathering to drink manioc beer and to perform music, is being secularized; its transcendental fullness is being lost. It is no longer held to make Our Fathers and Mothers happy, no longer a celebration of cosmic relations, of social relations, and of ecological relations, all of them sacred relations. It is losing its *raison d'etre*. It is becoming just another form of entertainment, folklore for the whiteman. Why is this happening? There are many reasons: missionaries, schools, the overwhelming pressure from white man's culture. The missionaries, especially the Evangelists and the Adventists, inculcate a moral code which condemns such celebrations as sin; the fermented beer, the coca, the music, and of course the ritual prayers and offerings are labeled 'works of the devil.' The missionaries, especially those of the WBT/SIL, manipulate the Amuesha religious symbols to rid them of their traditional meaning. They tear out the heart of these sacred celebrations, and simultaneously tear out the soul of the Amuesha being. The vacuum they thus create is easily filled by other aspects of white man's world: the radio and record player, alcohol, consumerism, and even Evangelism. And true to form, the Amuesha slowly become passive instruments of these forces; their relations with their external world are no longer based on creation and re-creation.«

I felt a mounting tension within myself as I continued on in Sepeso. The Amuesha's unquestioning acceptance of the WBT/SIL religious doctrine bothered me and I wanted to be open about it. But would they interpret that openness as a negation of whom they had become? It became a dilemma for me. To both disagree with their point of view, and to negate their being in that point of view is to play at the same destructive relations as the missionaries. But to disagree with their point of view, while affirming their existence, allowing room for the difference, is to establish a relation based on a creative dialectic. But for us Western people, children of a long imperialist and supremacist tradition, it is a relation very difficult to achieve.

»December 7, 1973; Sepeso; Last night I broke the silence I've built up with Domingo about the religious issue. I've been wanting to talk with him for a long time about it, but it seemed so difficult. He has been a very convinced WBT/SIL convert ever since he recovered from a back operation at the WBT/SIL headquarters in Lima. His prolonged contact with the missionaries gave rise to his conversion. He now feels that he is in possession of the truth; other non-Evangelists are, in his words, 'in error'.«

»He told me the story of their conversion to Evangelism in Sepeso. The new religion was brought to them by the WBT/SIL missionaries, both directly through personal contacts, and indirectly through the bilingual teachers and preachers they trained. Fifteen years ago, the first bilingual teacher/preacher visited Sepeso. He talked of God's word (the Bible), the new laws of the new order, and bilingual schools. The new laws included a ban on drinking manioc beer, on chewing coca and using it for divination, and on maintaining their faith in the curative powers of tobacco and its master, the shaman. Furthermore the new religion required them to discard their traditional music and oral tradition, accepting in their place the Evangelist hymns and the written word of God. That first visit was followed by many more; the missionaries promised them a school teacher for the following year. It was the first time they had ever been offered a school teacher. They accepted the new order blindly, said Domingo, despite the inconveniences it caused and the doubts they had. But by the following year they became convinced that the missionaries spoke the truth. The missionaries kept their word and sent a school teacher for the community. The Amuesha too kept their word and became Evangelists. Was Domingo implying that the WBT/SIL had offered a school teacher in exchange for the Amuesha's acceptance of their religious doctrine?«

»Later while discussing the problem of the WBT/SIL school in Muneso, he implied again that a similar exchange had been made there. He justified that community's decision to accept the WBT/SIL school and to open themselves to Evangelism on the grounds that the Adventists had never really helped them. Sure, he said, the Adventists had installed a school there, but the Amuesha had to pay for the teacher's salary. On the other hand, the WBT/SIL school was free. Then he paused... a reflective silence. No, he said, that would only be accepting Evangelism in exchange for material gain. He became confused. The WBT/SIL indeed offered a trade-off, and the Amuesha accepted.«

»I asked Domingo what he thought of the religion of the traditional Amuesha. While he agreed that they had a religion, he throught they were basically 'in error' because they, unfortunately, did not have the Bible to teach them the right way to live. I responded that they always showed consideration for Our Fathers and Mothers, and respected their laws of sharing whatever they have and of not being an angry person. He agreed, but insisted that they were 'in error'. They went astray in one respect, he said, they did not know about the all powerful god Jesus Christ, the one and only saviour.«

»A wave of exasperation struck me. I asked myself outloud why the god of the white men, the Europeans, must always be one and only, and all powerful. Domingo looked puzzled; why had I said the god of the Europeans? I explained my point of view, but he couldn't or wouldn't understand. We had reached an impasse.«

»After he left, Victoriano, an old blind man staying at my house, and I consoled each other, naming the few Amuesha, like himself, who hadn't accepted the WBT/SIL tradeoff. At that moment I was feeling the collective heaviness which saddens this community; everyone here has to supress his own cultural self for fear of trespassing the new laws of the all Powerful God.«

»December 9, 1973; Sepeso; Today I went to Shequecho, about a half hour's walk from here, to visit Gaspar, Domingo's brother-in-law. Victoriano came along with me, hopeful of finding some manioc beer. Gaspar is a self-imposed outcast from Sepeso; he rarely visits the village and does not allow his children to attend the WBT/SIL school. It became clear to me today why he maintains a distance from the village. He does not accept the Evangelist religion, and prefers to continue living in the traditional way. And he wants to raise his children in that way, too.«

»As soon as we were seated, Gasper's wife began to strain a large potful of manioc beer. Almost immediately, Victoriano and Gasper launched into the ritual greeting in which they exchanged news while invoking Our Father's blessing for each other. It lasted for about twenty minutes. I was thrilled to witness the greeting as it is no longer used in the Evangelist communities. When they finished, Maria set a potful of beer in front of us; Gaspar served each of us, and then himself. He then brought out a large bag of freshly dried coca leaves, offering a large handful to each of us.We chewed coca together for the rest of the day.«

»Gaspar and Victoriano talked about the community of Sepeso and about the gathering of the Evangelist Presbytery taking place there that day. They both complained about the presence of the white preachers in attendance. The Amuesha, they said, had never before needed white men in order to talk to Our Father; why should they need them now? Victoriano said that he had gone to the presbyterial kitchen around noon yesterday to ask for some food. Those in charge asked him if he had made his offering to the church yet. He asked us angrily: »Do you think Our Father put food on this earth for us to sell? No, he gave us food to eat and to invite our family and neighbors to eat. And what is worse,' he continued, 'they say that this meeting is for God, but still they want money for their food.' He allowed his anger to pass before he continued again: 'So after a while they gave me a little burned rice from the bottom of the pot.' He laughed as he asked us: 'Do you suppose that is what God eats?!?' We all laughed and passed around more beer.«

»Gaspar seems very down on the Evangelist community, and perhaps rightfully so. He lives with an abundance characteristic of the traditional Amuesha families, and in contrast to the food scarcity which pervades Sepeso. He always has an abundant supply of manioc and bananas in his garden and gives away large quantities of both to his relatives from Sepeso who come to ask for food. He is a skilled hunter and rarely lacks meat in his kitchen. He always has on hand a supply of coca and manioc beer, and shares both of these with all who drop in for a visit. Gaspar's generosity is unreproachable and it reaches every family in Sepeso. But none-the-less he is still subjected to pressures and slanderous gossip for not conforming to the Evangelist doctrine.«

At the end of December, I returned to my house in Miraflores to spend the long months of the rainy season away from the mud of Sepeso. During the month of February, I began to work with three young Amuesha on the transcription of a large body of oral tradition which I had previously recorded. We hope to eventually publish in the Amuesha language, as complete a collection of histories as possible to make it available in writing to the Amuesha. The recorded versions will remain for those who prefer the spoken word.

»February 15, 1974; Miraflores; Today the four of us had a long enthusiastic conversation about our project of writing down the Amuesha history. We began by discussing the confusion we are in about the general structure of the history and the identities and roles of the many different divine beings. We had a long list of names and a lot of conflicting information. There was general agreement that most of the confusion is the result of the work of missionaries, both Catholic and Protestant.«

»For the Amuesha there are three groups of divine beings, the members of each group are distinguished by a different title of respect. There are those we call YATO, Our Grandfather; those we call YOMPOR, Our Father, and YACHOR, Our Mother; and those we call YEMONASHEN, Our Brother, and YOCH, Our Sister. The three groups correspond to three different generations of kin. It was a member of the first group, YATO YOS, who created the world and everything in it; he later sent his sons and daughters, Our Fathers and Mothers to take care of his creation. The most important of his sons is YOMPOR ROR, the sun who allows our food to grow, who warms us, and who gives us good health. It is said that he will return to this earth one day to relieve the suffering of the Amuesha. Most of the traditional religious ritual and thought center around YOMPOR ROR: he is invoked in prayers at his rising and setting, he is served beer every morning, and he is celebrated with music, dance, and beer during the all night feast. His children, Our Brothers and Sisters, serve us directly as food plants, medicines, useful materials, animals, birds, etc.«

»The WBT/SIL has introduced a great confusion in this system of thought. When they translated Evangelism into the Amuesha language, they used the sun's name, YOMPOR, for the Christian creator god, changing the sun's name to ATSNE', or heat. Now in the Bible translations, in the hymns, and in the church service, the Christian creator god is called YOMPOR, Our Father. They are now taught that it was YOMPOR who created the world, when in fact for the Amuesha it was not Our Father, but Our Grandfather who played that role. They are also taught that Jesus Christ is both god and the son of God (YOMPOR). Jesus too is given the translation of YOMPOR, compounding even more the confusion. How can Our Father be the son of Our Father? In an effort, I suppose, to make the transition easier for the Amuesha from their traditional religion to Evangelism, the WBT/SIL attempted to reduce the three Amuesha categories of sacred beings to a single concept of a universal Christian god. The result? Terrible confusion.«

»The WBT/SIL missionaries have used their linguistic skills to dress up Christian Evangelism with native terminology and with bilingual education, in what looks to me as an attempt to make it more palatable to the unsuspecting native person's taste; seasoned with his own language, the native person has a much easier time swallowing Christianity. By manipulating the native language and concepts in this way, the missionary puts an unbearable strain on the native categories of thought, and they slowly collapse, causing a trible theological confusion. As his cultural system is based on an integrated socio-religious world view, it inevitably puts his whole world in turmoil.«

»This is not an insignificant nor even inevitable by-product of the meeting of two cultures, as the missionaries and their defenders would have us believe. It is a deliberate and necessary first step in the process of imposed cultural change. Only by weakening the native people's system of thought, can the missionary or other westernizer replace them with his own Western and Christian categories and values.«

The final two diary entries describe visits I made during March, 1974, to two very different and contrasting worlds. The first visit took me into the depths of the traditional Amuesha world at Asreso, where I was confronted by the sense of tragedy that pervades that world, facing as it does its impending extinction. A week later I flew by jet plane to Yarinacocha, the heart of the WBT/SIL operations in Peru. There I was confronted by the world of contradictions of some of those responsible for the extinction of the traditional Amuesha.

»March 4, 1974; Asreso; Yesterday Samuel invited me to accompany him up the mountain to Cruz's house where he had been summoned to drink maize beer. We arrived shortly before dark. Andres was there, his face painted a bright red forming a contrast with the brown tones of his native tunic. Cruz, our host, was painted more subtly, and had a stick passed through the hole pierced in his nose septum. He had a strikingly handsome apperance. In the usual manner, he brought out a large pot of maize beer, serving each of us our fill. The beer was delicious, and after several bowlfulls, we all loosened up, talked more freely, and began to laugh. He offered each of us a handful of dried coca leaves to chew in order to keep us awake through the night...«

»As the night went on, with the beer's happiness filling his body, Cruz began to brag about the large number of songs he knew... no other Amuesha was his equal, he claimed. He alone had taught songs in three different communities; he alone was maintaining the traditional music. He began to reminisce about how the Amuesha used to perform the music in his home community, before the area had been settled by white people. He was just a boy then but he remembered it as vividly as if it had been yesterday. He described how a hundred or more people would gather, all elegantly dressed in new tunics, bright seeds, and feathers. The headmen, who led the men's music, were especially elegantly dressed with white tunics, and wide bands of colored seeds criss-crossing their chests. In their crown-like hats, two white rooster tail feathers shimmered with their movements, like the leaves of a poplar tree in a light breeze. The beer had been fermenting for several days in huge waist-high earthen vessels, and was at its peak. Then came the dances, the music, and the celebration. Cruz began to cry while telling me; 'But now,' he said, 'it's all gone, and we'll never see it again.' How terribly sad it must have been for him to watch his world fall to pieces. And now only his memory holds those pieces together.«

»We were sitting outside, in the cold, clear night. I kept looking up at the stars... how brilliantly vivid they were. Cruz began to sing the song of the Bat. He wanted Samuel to learn it. Several times I walked away from the group so that I could hear the singing from a distance, and get a greater sense of the harmony of the whole. It had a profound effect on me; it enticed me. Soon I too was singing; I had become a part of that harmony.«

»After several hours of singing and several potfulls of beer, Cruz began to cry again. He was remembering his father and his uncle whom he had heard sing that same song as a boy. 'Who', he asked, 'will remember me someday by singing this song? Who will raise us up after we are dead by singing these songs, and cry, remembering us as their ancestors, as those who sang before them?' That night's experience filled me with both joy and sadness. Joy for the insights I had been given into the traditional world of the Amuesha, and for having been able to share with those gathered an experience of that world. Sadness because I had no answer to Cruz's question, nor much hope that someone will continue to sing his song after he is dead.«

»March 12, 1974; Yarinacocha, the central base of the Wycliffe Bible Translators, Inc./Summer Institute of Linguistics; I can't sleep tonight; the heat here is oppressive. Besides that, there is the constant roar of the huge electric generator keeping me awake while it turns out the electricity to keep this little piece of suburban USA, with all its shiny appliances and gadgets, running... street upon street of neat bungalows and ranch homes, half-hidden in their park-like surroundings, meticulously maintained by local Indians... the coolnes of the missionaries' air-conditioned offices... the PX stocked with directly imported American foods and goods, unavailable elsewhere in Peru... and the endless comings and goings of the missionaries and their children, zooming around on their sleek new Hondas. It makes my head spin, A year and a half with the Amuesha has left me defenseless and vulnerable in this world... the world of the North American missionary and its monstrous contradictions. This vast organization, this 'scientific' institute dedicated to Christianizing the heathen and to civilizing the savage, while wrapped in the security and comfort of suburban living. Here in the Peruvian jungle.«

»The contradictions oppress me; what I see and hear among the missionaries, and what I see and know is happening among the Amuesha. I have the knowledge and understanding of the profound cultural destruction which results from the WBT/SIL missionary activity, the spiritual impoverishment which they produce in the name of their God, the alienation they create among unsuspecting peoples, and the sophistication of their methods for 'civilizing' and evangelizing: the damned deviousness of their imperialism. But I also hear them talk of defending the cultural integrity of the native peoples, their sincere wish to bring a 'better life' to the tribal peoples, their apparent goodness and innocence, and their round-the-clock smiles. When I am here at their nerve center, all their work looks so wonderful, so harmless, if not even helpful and ideal. Their organization is so well polished that even I can't see a spot of tarnish. That is how it must look in the heartland of North America where the dollars and cents come from to run this operation. Well-polished goodness. But no one wants to look at the confused and broken remains of a people that result from their work. After all, why should there be any doubts? Don't they have God on their side!

Bibliography

Maxwell, Nicole, F.R.G.S.
1974 An Answer to NACLA, unpublished manuscript, October 21, 1974.

Smith, Richard Chase
1974 *The Amuesha People of Central Peru: Their Struggle to Survive,* IWGIA Doc. no. 16, Copenhagen.

SIL and a »New-Found Tribe«:
The Amarakaeri Experience[1]

by THOMAS R. MOORE

The most serious charge that has been made against the Wycliffe Bible Translators/Summer Institute of Linguistics (SIL) is that they are responsible for ethnocide in the native communities with which they work. If these accusations are to be substantiated or refuted, we must have evidence of just what it is that SIL does in as many concrete situations as possible and what the consequences of these activities are and have been for the peoples in question.

Since 1957 SIL has had missionary-linguists working with a community of Amarakaeri on the upper Karene (Colorado) River in the tropical forests of Madre de Dios, southeastern Peru. The Amarakaeri are a subgroup of an ethno-linguistic population usually referred to by the pejorative term »Mashco«; I prefer to call this larger group Harakmbut,[2] their word for »people«.

A SIL publication (Slocum and Holmes, eds. 1963:59-69) describes the Amarakaeri as »a new-found tribe.« There is often great excitement when an isolated ethnic population is »discovered«. Thus, the Amarakaeri received extensive publicity at the time of peaceable contacts by Dominican priests in the early 1950's. They were invariably described as »fierce unknown savages still living in the stone age.« (e.g. Bello 1956).

Indeed, prior to the appearance of the Dominicans in the area, the Amarakaeri not only lacked such elements of Western technology as metal cutting tools, but even by traditional tropical forest standards they had an unusually simple material culture, without watercraft or hunting and fishing traps, and with only rather crude pottery (cf. Carneiro 1962:61). However, they had an efficient and harmonious adaptation to their natural environment, a communalistic and egalitarian form of social organization, and a rich ideological tradition which integrated all dimensions of the Amarakaeri world and allowed ritual expression of its transitions and resolution of its contradictions. Moreover, primitive Amarakaeri individuals found fulfillment and delineation as human persons within this natural, social, and supernatural setting to an extent which has not been equalled by the Western invaders of their world.

The vulnerability of such an ethnic group to ethnocidal pressures is readily apparent. Indeed, the breakdown of traditional Amarakaeri culture since the earliest contacts has been dramatic and progressive, and SIL's presence for most of the post-contact period provides us with excellent circumstances for the examination of its role in this process. In the two years, 1973-75, that I conducted ethnological research with the Amarakaeri, I was able to observe some aspects of the ethnocide process as it occurred, as well as some of SIL's activities and their effects on the development of Amarakaeri culture.

Let us first define what we mean by ethnocide and describe how it works generally. Then we may consider to what degree SIL activities are a part of it with respect to the Amarakaeri.

The Ethnocide Process

The concept of ethnocide gained currency in South America, especially, as a result of the writings of Robert Jaulin (1970, and Jaulin, ed. 1972) among others, and of the »Declaration of Barbados« (IWGIA

Thomas R. Moore is a doctoral candidate in anthropology at the New School for Social Research in New York. He has done field research among the Amarakaeri in Peru in 1971, 1973-75, and 1978. Born October 29, 1940, at Martinsburg, West Virginia, USA, he studied at the University of Arizona and at the Universidad de las Américas in Mexico prior to entering the anthropology program at the New School.

1971). Briefly stated, it refers to the destruction of traditional cultures, that is, the denial of their possibilities for survival as viable ethnic units having integrated structures and historical traditions.

It is not necessary for genocide – the physical destruction of a people – to occur in relation to ethnocide, although that has often been the case. A people may survive physically after having their traditional culture replaced by a new one. This has been the recent experience of many South American peoples who have survived earlier genocidal policies of domestic and foreign states.

Ethnocide must also be distinguished from culture change. All cultures change historically, both from internal innovation and from interaction with other cultures. When interaction with other cultures involves exchanges of a relatively equal nature, both cultures ultimately benefit and are strengthened in their ethnic possibilities. Thus, if one ethnic group adopts a weaving technique from a neighboring group with which it shares a previously unfamiliar vegetable dye, both groups have experienced innovations and the ethnic foundations of neither have been undermined.

In order for ethnocide to occur, there must be a series of unequal exchanges, associated with economic imperialism. A politically stronger economy exacts raw materials and labour from a politically weaker native economy and gives something of lesser value in return. But for the process to be complete, it must go beyond economic exploitation. The victims of ethnocide must sacrifice not only their natural resources and their labour, but also the technological, sociological, and ideological foundations of their cultures. This happenes when the exchanges are so unequal that what the natives receive in return for their land and labour is not enough to permit the simple reproduction of their ethnic tradition.

The unequal exchanges which occur take the form of patron-client relationships, with the patron determining the conditions of the exchanges. New needs are created for the client which can only be satisfied by the latter's submission to the conditions established by the patron.

If, for example, a group of natives, in order to obtain trade goods for which new needs have been created, enters into a debt peonage relationship with mestizo logger-traders, which requires that they work full-time seasonally or all year on an individual basis in a new location nearer an urban center, the natives cannot maintain either their traditional patterns of food production and sharing or their customary social organization and beliefs. Their culture breaks down, and new techniques, social relationships, and values, are adopted, following regional or state-wide patterns. The group is thus incorporated into the region or state as part of a rural proletariat or peasantry, marginal yet dependent and subject to the vagaries of a market economy. As a result, these natives lose their separate ethnic identity.

But ethnocide is not usually perpetrated exclusively by any individual or even any organization such as SIL. It is an historical process which most often involves several levels of unequal exchanges with a number of mutually supportive representatives of politically dominant societies. These include the extractive industries, traders, government and international agencies, competing missionary organizations, and to some extent explorers, travellers, and anthropologists. Thus, the role of an organization such as SIL in the ethnocide process must be considered in the context of the whole network of ethnocidal pressures.

On one level Christian missionaries have a relationship with members of native communities, the purpose of which is indisputably ethnocidal, inasmuch as the ultimate goal is conversion to Christianity, that is, the negation of a traditional ideology and its replacement with the Word of God. If successful, this development assumes the negation of traditional forms of economic life and social organization as well. One cannot replace an ideology without also replacing its socio-economic foundations. The question here is not whether but to what degree the missionary activities are ethnocidal.

On another level, however, missionaries act as intermediaries between the native communities and the other potential agents of ethnocide.

Their presence may facilitate or impede the expansion of logging or prospecting for minerals, or they may promote or inhibit the development of labour and trade relations with outsiders. Here the question is how the missionary activities affect the development of the ethnocide process generally.

The SIL approach to mission work is to translate the Bible into the native languages, teach some of the natives how to read their language and hence the translated scripture, and create a nucleus of believers who will propagate the faith with the aid of the translated scripture. Thus, while it is potentially ethnocidal in what it seeks to do, the means chosen, through the native language, is an attempt to minimize one ethnocidal aspect of this work. That is to say, the natives need not give up their own language and replace it with another in order to receive the Christian ideology, but they *are* encouraged to replace their own ideology with the teachings of Christ.

However, for the natives to be able to understand the translated scripture, they must learn to read it, and for that to happen, schools must be established. The schools must be built, teachers trained and installed according to Ministry of Education specifications, and salaries must be paid. Moreover, the teachers must be sent out of their communities for training at a central location, and they must be brought back, along with blackboards, chalk, primers, pencils, paper, and other supplies.

The missionary-linguists too must come and go, as well as maintain themselves while in the native communities. To do this they require the support system of their organization, which wields substantial economic and political power. Thus, a series of new economic exchanges and political interactions between missionary-linguist and native must occur, which inevitably involve some degree of patron-client relationship, but which may or may not be ultimately ethnocidal, depending upon whether or not the conditions of the exchanges permit the simple reproduction of the basic features of the culture.

Bearing these thoughts in mind, let us now turn to the Amarakaeri experience with SIL. I shall consider first the impact of SIL's own direct interactions with Amarakaeri natives, then its role as intermediary with the other representatives of the dominant culture. We must recognize, of course, that the Amarakaeri experience with SIL cannot be generalized to all or even many of the ethnic groups with which SIL works. Each ethnic group has a unique history and culture and each missionary-linguist leaves the imprint of his or her own style on the nature of the relationship with the native communities.

Direct SIL-Amarakaeri Relations

The SIL presence with the Amarakaeri has been a modest one, with only one or two missionary-linguists working »in the tribe« from two to six months each year. Raymond Hart and Charles Peck began the work, but Peck soon left for doctoral studies, and Hart died in the United States in 1960. Hart was replaced by Robert Tripp, who has continued the work with the Amarakaeri alone, except for a time in 1967-68, when he was joined by Dick Hyde. Sometimes Tripp is accompanied for part of a school vacation by one of the teen-age youths from the mission base at Yarinacocha, but otherwise the only SIL personnel who enter the community are pilots, who usually depart immediately.

Tripp lived very simply when in the Amarakaeri community on the upper Karene, which was known as Puerto Alegre. His house was of the same basic type as those the natives have been using in recent years, although slightly larger. He imported some food from the mission base but acquired most of his meat, fish, and garden produce from the natives.

Although the Amarakaeri are enthusiastic about any new or unfamiliar material objects, they found relatively little to covet among Tripp's possessions. He had no outboard motor or other vehicle in Puerto Alegre; he travelled locally with Amarakaeri in their dugout canoes or by raft. (The Amarakaeri have been using watercraft since the 1950's.) Even at Yarinacocha he shunned the ubiquitous motorcycles and got about on foot or bicycle.

SIL gained acceptance among the Amarakaeri initially when Hart and Peck successfully treated a common eye infection. Since then the SIL missionary-linguists have provided lay medical attention to the community and have vaccinated against the major infectious diseases common to the region. Western medication is dispensed sparingly, according to need, when a missionary-linguist is present and is usually non-existent when he is absent.

Most Amarakaeri who become ill while the missionary-linguist is present seek pills or injections from him but also hedge their bets by enlisting the services of a traditional curing shaman. Thus, the medical care that has been provided has been an addition to, not a replacement of traditional medicine.

Moreover, it has probably been responsible for checking the spread of the many diseases brought in from the outside that had reduced the Amarakaeri population from several thousand around 1940 to fewer than 400 by the 1950's. Serious epidemics of measles and yellow fever have claimed many Amarakaeri lives since the arrival of SIL, and intestinal parasites and tuberculosis are still widespread. Dysentery, pneumonia, malaria, and numerous other infections have also been problems, but now the population has stabilized and is beginning to increase.

To pay for the medicines and vaccines they administer to the Amarakaeri, the SIL missionary-linguists set up what they call the »Amarakaeri Fund.« They began buying gold and pelts, as well as bows and arrows and other traditional artifacts, from the natives and took these products back with them to sell in Pucallpa, near the Yarinacocha base. They then bought trade good – machetes, axes, adzes, shotguns, shells, Western clothing, blankets, flashlights, etc. – which they sold to the Amarakaeri upon their return. A profit was made both ways which would then be applied to medical supplies and other SIL projects in the community.

This system effectively instituted a money economy within the community. A careful accounting is maintained and the Amarakaeri receive or pay in Peruvian soles the difference between the price of the commodities they produce and the price of the trade goods they obtain in exchange. Even the occasional trading with highland gold prospectors in the area has taken the form of cash transactions. Most Amarakaeri have some money on hand with which they can buy trade goods that are increasingly available.

Money is used almost exclusively for luxury items. For the most part, the Amarakaeri continue to derive their subsistence from the forest, the river, and their gardens, as they have done traditionally. The techniques of subsistence changed as shotguns replaced bows and arrows in hunting, hooks and lines supplemented bows and arrows in fishing, and machetes and steel awes replaced stone axes to modify garden clearing and cultivation practices. SIL has introduced grafted citrus fruit trees and new varieties of several traditional crops. Some traditional crops are disappearing, and the Amarakaeri have come to depend more on plantains as their staple – plantains require less horticultural labour than other tropical vegetable staples – and they are hunting and gathering less than they used to. But within Puerto Alegre they maintained an essentially traditional diet; traditional patterns of cooperation in clearing gardens, planting, and fishing with barbasco; and traditional forms of meat distribution.

Tripp used relatively little Amarakaeri labour for personal services such as domestic work, gardening, etc., in the community. When his teen-age assistant was present, that young man assumed responsibility for such tasks as cooking; otherwise Tripp did them himself. A wage labour relationship did exist, however, with the language informants who worked on a regular basis and were paid by the day or hour. And when informants were taken to the Yarinacocha mission base they did gardening and domestic work there for wages, as well as their service as language informants.

The bilingual teachers earned modest salaries which were paid by the Ministry of Education via SIL. These payments were usually offset by debts for trade goods before they became available for cash.

The first bilingual school was established in Puerto Alegre in 1973. After a year the first native teacher left and was not replaced until April 1975, when a new native teacher had been trained and officially designated. Both bilingual teachers had studied in Dominican mission schools and spoke Spanish fluently. Because of their greater degree of acculturation to mestizo ways they were somewhat unpopular with the more traditional families.

They held classes each weekday morning during the Peruvian school year and began teaching the fundamentals of reading, writing and arithmetic to Puerto Alegre children in the Amarakaeri language. These children were not with their families learning traditional skills during school hours, but by mid-1975 they had not been in school for long enough for that pattern to have had much effect.

The school has served only the existing community at Puerto Alegre. No attempts were made to recruit pupils from other Amarakaeri communities, since these already had schools set up by the Dominican missionaries. Thus, the school did not adversely modify the demographic configuration, ecology, or social organization of Puerto Alegre, as has been the case with the neighboring Machiguenga community of Tayakome on the upper Manu River (d'Ans 1975, see this volume).

Conscious efforts have been made by the SIL missionary-linguists to preserve the traditional Amarakaeri forms of social organization. The Amarakaeri maintain the traditional kin designations and only marry outside their patrilineal clans. Tripp has tried to reinforce clan awareness among the children by giving them Spanish surnames according to clan affiliation.

Unfortunately, this practice conflicts with the Dominican system of applying the father's and mother's names as Spanish surnames. Thus, when Amarakaeri children move from the SIL bilingual school to a Dominican school, or vice versa, as often happens, they have two separate sets of names and two sets of school records. So far, surnames have not been given much importance by the Amarakaeri themselves. Spanish given names received in childhood are now kept past puberty, instead of being replaced by adult names as was the custom.

In their dealings with the Amarakaeri, however, SIL members, like the other representatives of Western culture, have emphasized individualism. Wage labour and trade are always dyadic relationships between one native and one SIL person. There is never a request that »you and your brothers help me with God's work,« or that »you and your clansmen sell me some manioc or plantains,« but always »you«

136

individually. The Amarakaeri have learned to respond to this, and competition has developed among members of the same clan, in a manner previously unknown to them.

Traditional Amarakaeri society was essentially egalitarian. There were no chiefs and no social classes; social and economic obligations and expectations followed kinship lines, as did political allegiance. Community decisions were made by consensus.

Some Amarakaeri men have more prestige than others and are called *wairi*. Such men were traditionally members of demographically strong clans, had two wives and many sons, cleared numerous large gardens, brought in more wild game than most hunters, were known for their generosity, and spoke well and persuasively. But they exercised no coercive authority, however, and their social status was equal to that of the others.

Social distictions between missionary-linguist and native, however, are glaring. The impact of SIL technology – airplanes, two-way radios, recording and photographic equipment, etc. – places the missionary-linguist in a position of awesome superiority in the minds of the Amarakaeri, whose traditional technology is so simple by comparison.

Moreover, the SIL missionary-linguists have access to a seemingly endless supply of exciting new goods and services, and to some extent they can satisfy the new needs created among the natives. Thus, the SIL missionary-linguists have the power to facilitate or impede access to desired trade goods according to the degree of cooperation the natives give them in their projects. Tripp has consciously tried to avoid favouritism, but some manipulation, however unconscious, is bound to occur, as is some degree of paternalism.

And when Amarakaeri bilingual teachers, language informants, and others, are taken to the SIL mission base in Yarinacocha they are immediately confronted with a rigidly class-structured society with tremendous wealth differences. At Yarinacocha, the opulent middle-class life style of the missionary-linguists contrasts markedly with the modest and segregated facilities that are available to these natives, as well as with the squalor and misery that are the lot of the deculturated natives who perform menial labour on the mission base and elsewhere in the Pucallpa area. Thus, the Amarakaeri who go to Yarinacocha are implanted with a new concept of social order in which their personal self respect is deflated and aspirations for an alien lifestyle are stimulated.

Perhaps the most significant role of SIL in the ethnocide process has been in ideological change. Although few Amarakaeri can read them, many of the books of the New Testament and the first three chapters of Genesis are now available in their language. To facilitate the teaching of scripture, SIL left small cassette players in Puerto Alegre with recorded portions of translated scripture as well as hymns in both Spanish and Amarakaeri. The Amarakaeri listened attentively to these recorded sounds until the batteries were spent.

Some of the Christian doctrines have been confusing to Amarakaeri, who have tried to superimpose these concepts on their native religious beliefs. For example, the notion of salvation is described in terms of souls going to heaven, which term is translated *kurud,* the Amarakaeri word for the sky. The traditional belief holds that when an Amarakaeri dies, his water soul and his forest soul leave his body and take refuge in the animals of those domains. Then, after a long period of wandering, they eventually reach the *serowe,* an underground river that is a universally good and happy place. There is no alternative destination for a soul.

So, most Amarakaeri are rather confused by the notion of their souls going to the sky rather than to the underground river which is their choice and expectation. Moreover, the idea that they should feel guilt for their behaviour is completely alien to them, as is the possibility of damnation if they do not accept Christ. It is easier to be a traditional Amarakaeri than a Christian, but some fear they might not be right and are concerned about running the risk of not getting to some desirable place in the end.

To refer to the Devil or »unclean spirits,« Tripp and SIL translations use the term *toto?,* which is the name the Amarakaeri apply to the soul of the boa, the most potentially harmful spirit in their cosmology. *Toto?* has at times also been associated with Communism in SIL conversations with the Amarakaeri, and some Amarakaeri speak of the *komunista* with much apprehension.

When US troops were withdrawn form Vietnam in 1975, a SIL couple, the Millers, remained behind and were arrested by the Revolutionary Vietnamese. This was a subject of concern to all SIL members, who received daily radio accounts of developments in the matter. One Sunday, Tripp asked the Amarakaeri to pray for the Millers who had been captured by the Communists. The Communists, he explained, were thwarting God's work and aiding that of the Devil. The Amarakaeri envisioned boas slithering around and causing harm to the Millers and anyone else who got in their way.

When Tripp was present in Puerto Alegre, he held prayer and hymn-singing sessions each Sunday morning. These were usually attended by 30-50 Amarakaeri, particularly women and children, from a total population of just over 100 in the community.

One of the bilingual Amarakaeri expressed more enthusiasm than most for Christian teachings, and he was sent for Bible study at a Swiss Protestant mission school outside Pucallpa. When he returned to Puerto Alegre he assumed an unofficial role as the community pastor and attempted to continue the Sunday prayer and hymn-singing sessions in Tripp's absence, but with less success.

This young man, whom I shall call Moisés, was experiencing an acute »identity crisis«, while I was in Puerto Alegre, which was complicated by an unsatisfactory marriage that eventually dissolved. Moisés's adherence to fundamentalist Christian doctrine was at times in conflict with the lifestyle of the rest of the community, and he was torn between the two.

Among other things, he had been taught that drinking alcoholic beverages was contrary to God's will. The Amarakaeri had not traditionally had alcoholic beverages, but prior to the arrival of the SIL missionary-linguists they had learned to make manioc beer from a neighboring ethnic group, and they have been increasingly able to obtain commercial liquors and beer from riverine traders and gold workers. So, drinking and singing bouts had become a sort of »ritual« which occurred every three or four weeks in Puerto Alegre.

At times when most of the other Amarakaeri men were drinking and singing, Moisés would be lying on his bed singing Christian hymns to himself. Sometimes, however, he would relent and join in the drinking and singing. On one such occasion, Moisés got very drunk and began singing Christian hymns interspersed with traditional Amarakaeri animal songs and bawdy Peruvian songs which he had learned in Pucallpa, to the delight of those Amarakaeri who understood the lyrics.

In addition to their religious faith, SIL missionary-linguists, like most other representatives of middle-class Western culture, bring with them a vast complex of »scientific« explanations for many day-to-day experiences that native peoples traditionally attribute to supernatural causes. Thus, the Amarakaeri, like most native peoples who have received Westerners, have been given repeated explanations that, for example, germs and not witches cause illnesses, and medicine, not a shaman's rites, may cure them. Such explanations abound in the interpretation of newly introduced techniques and experiences with which the Amarakaeri are becoming familiar in trade relations and in school, as well as in medical care. When empirical demonstration seems to support the missionary-linguist's claims, the natives begin to place credence in them. The result is an increasing secularization, which erodes traditional Amarakaeri ideology. Elmer Miller (1970) has examined this process for the Toba in Argentina.

The most dramatic changes in Amarakaeri ideology and behaviour have occurred among those Amarakaeri who have spent extended periods of time outside their native communities in intensive contact with Peruvian mestizos. Amarakaeri language informants and others who accompany the SIL missionary-linguists to Yarinacocha have often had few if any such experiences previously. They learn Spanish more proficiently and quickly acquire tastes for mestizo styles of dress, popular music, especially *cumbias,* and jokes and conversation with sexual overtones. They also become dazzled by the world of hitherto unknown material goods.

Commonly, these young men return to their community with portable record players and a few discs fo jungle *cumbias* and highland *huaynos* which now dominate the drinking and singing bouts. The record players became more numerous in 1973-75 and could be heard most evenings after the main meal of the day, when often they replaced the traditional conversation and story-telling that occurred at that time among members of the community outside their homes.

Concern with material things has conspicuously replaced the traditional basis for prestige among the Amarakaeri. Most young Amarakaeri now describe as *wairi* those Amarakaeri who have the most material possessions and express contempt for those valurs and behaviour patterns which traditionally brought prestige.

Overall, we must recognize that SIL has been responsible for the introduction of some useful innovations and some unpleasant and at times disruptive changes in Amarakaeri culture. However, no major community deveopment projects have been carried out, and the Amarakaeri have not been coerced to make changes they did not seek. For the most part, trade and labour relations with SIL have supplemented rather than replaced traditional productive activities. The social integration of the Puerto Alegre community has not been substantially weakened from the relationship with SIL, although ideological confusion has made the world less comprehensible to these natives. So, SIL's direct relations with the Amarakaeri cannot fairly be said to have produced a general breakdown in the foundations of the culture, in and of themselves.

Yet ethnic disintegration continues to occur at a progressively faster and more intense rate. Let us now examine that process historically, along with SIL's role as intermediary with the other external forces that have brought about some basic restructuring of Amarakaeri culture.

SIL as Intermediary

The roots of the ethnocide process were present in the depopulation, ethnic group dislocation, and internal conflicts generated by the diseases and other results of direct and indirect contact between the Amarakaeri and rubber tappers, followed by Dominican missionaries, gold prospectors, traders, and loggers. These developments were already well underway or in the past by the time SIL missionary-linguists appeared on the scene and found a fragile ethnic population with which to begin their work.

The SIL installations in the remote upper Karene area, butressed with medicines and trade goods, offered an alternative to continual seiges of illness, death, and deprivation, which had become the price of remaining in isolation. It was also an alternative to the Dominican missions on the upper and lower Madre de Dios, where most of the other Amarakaeri communities were consequently established. While many of the Dominican policies have undoubtedly been disruptive to Amarakaeri culture, the most important factor has been the location of their missions at sites which are much more easily accessible to outsiders by river or overland.

Thus, more intense contact with highland agriculturists who have settled in these areas, loggers, traders, tourists, and others, as well as with the Peruvian Army, the Guardia Civil, local magistrates, Agrarian Reform officials, and other government agents, has brought greater pressure on the Amarakaeri at these missions to adapt to mestizo ways at the expense of their own. By contrast, the Amarakaeri at Puerto Alegrte remained in relative isolation and with relatively greater ethnic stability, at least until 1973.

Moreover, by providing an outlet for Amarakeri gold and pelts, a precise system of money accounting, a pay-as-you-go policy, and a modest mark-up on the trade goods they made available, the SIL missionary-linguists were able to undercut the prices of riverine traders and gold *patrones* and thereby inhibit the development of potentially disastrous debt-peonage relationships. Most of the trade goods which the Amarakaeri could obtain from these other sources were also readily obtainable from SIL at a lower cost and without long-term labour commitments.

We can identify two historical periods, 1962-64 and 1973-75, when the most dramatic changes in Amarakeri culture occurred – changes that seriously threatened the ethnic viability of the Amarakaeri.

The first of these periods corresponds to a furlough taken by Tripp in the United States, 1962-63, and a delay, until 1964, in returning to the Amarakaeri community from the Yarinacocha base. Soon after Tripp's departure a yellow fever epidemic broke out and claimed the lives of approximately 20 Amarakaeri.

In the absence of any SIL missionary-linguists or other immediate source of Western medicines, and in the fear that they would all die if they remained on the Karene, the community moved to the Dominican mission at Shintuya on the upper Madre de Dios, where they reluctantly installed themselves among their traditional enemies from other Amarakaeri communities and fragments of other ethnic groups (Wachipaeri and Machiguenga). The other Amarakaeri groups had been living at the mission for several years in relatively intense contact with colonists and other outsiders at a time when the Peruvian Army was building a road toward Shintuya from the highlands.

This was a very conflictive time at Shintuya, and the other Amarakaeri groups assumed an air of superiority toward their »backward« cousins from the Karene. They made fun of their traditional oval-shaped communal house, the elaborate puberty rites, and other ritual observances, all of which had been abandoned earlier by these »progressive« Amarakaeri.

Moreover, at Shintuya there were now more than 300 natives in a single location, and the influx of non-natives into the area markedly reduced the availability of traditional food resources. Traditional economic and social organization patterns were no longer ecologically viable. Major dietary deficiencies resulted as yields decreased in more intensely cultivated gardens and as wild meat and vegetable resources became increasingly scarce and remote.[3]

Under these circumstances new quarrels arose among the newly arrived Amarakaeri as well as between them and the others at the mission. Clan and community solidarity quickly eroded. At this time, the Amarakaeri from the Karene began building individual nuclear family houses and adopting Spanish given names. They also stopped marking the major transitions in the life cycle with community ritual.

Moreover, the diseases which had driven them from the Karene continued to spread and there were more deaths. Accusations of witchcraft were made against other natives at the mission and fights broke out frequently. So, after a year af Shintuya, the Amarakaeri from the Karene returned to their homeland and re-established themselves at a new location on the upper Karene. When Tripp returned, he found them there but significantly factionalized and transformed by their Shintuya experience.

The second period of dramatic change for these Amarakaeri occurred between 1973 and 1975 and coincided in time with my own field research. It was also a time when the SIL contract with the Peruvian Ministry of Education was approaching expiration, and in hopes of favourable renewal conditions, many SIL missionary-linguists, including Tripp, were working more intensively on the publication of educational materials and scripture translations at the mission base at Yarinacocha, in order to have more concrete results to show for their work. This meant spending less time in the native communities, and during the two-year interval from September 1973 through August 1975, Tripp was present in Puerto Alegre for only five months.

The limited SIL presence during this time was not as important in the developments with Amarakaeri culture, however, as was a series of external factors, particularly Peruvian Government efforts to increase gold productivity in the region, along with intensive oil explorations, and certain new Decree Laws affecting the jungle and native populations.

Between 1972 and 1974, the price of gold in Madre de Dios tripled, following the international gold market prices. The Peruvian Government made its Banco Minero the only legal purchaser of gold and enabled it to provide tools and food supplies, as well as other provisions, at Banco Minero cost to miners, including Amarakaeri, from a new post set up on the Madre de Dios River at the mount of the Karene.

Now the Amarakaeri need not wait for the arrival of the SIL plane to obtain trade goods. Moreover, SIL could no longer buy their gold. So, the Amarakaeri began making trips with gold to the Banco Minero post where they bought supplies, tools, and other trade goods, at the moment they sold their gold for the official price. Thus, the goldworking labour of the Amarakaeri now bought more goods and more immediately.

There was not only a significant increase in the inventories of such items as aluminum pots – the Amarakaeri no longer make pottery – but they also began acquiring Briggs and Stratton motors with longtailed propellers on credit. By mid-1975, two pairs of brothers or classificatory brothers had motors of this sort attached to large dugout canoes which they made, and two more such motors were on order.

Also in 1973, the Peruvian Government banned the trade of pelts of animals in danger of extinction, including jaguar, ocelot, and otter, which had previously been a significant source of income for Amarakaeri hunters. Some such trade continued illegally, but SIL was no longer in a position to participate.

The other major development during this period was oil exploration. In a joint effort, Peru-Cities Service and Andes Petroleum Co., Ltd., a Japanese consortium, contracted seismic exploration for oil in an area of Madre de Dios which included most of the traditional Amarakaeri homeland.

The seismic work contractor, Geophysical Services Intercontinental, installed a supply depot within the village of Puerto Alegre, in order to make use of the airstrip the Amarakaeri had made there to receive SIL planes. No permission was sought from either the Amarakaeri or SIL. The oil companies simply sent in their workers, put up a large tent, and began their operations. The supply depot remained in Puerto Alegre for a year, June 1974 – June 1975.

Three employees were assigned to the supply depot, but workers en route to or from seismic lines in the area were often left there to wait for transportation. At times there were 30 – 40 oil workers in the village of 105 Amarakaeri, waiting three or four days for a plane or helicopter without adequate provisions. Air traffic was very intense. At times there would be four or five flights of a Pilatus Porter plane and 13 or 14 helicopter flights into and out of Puerto Alegre in a single day.

Urban prostitutes were flown into Puerto Alegre by the oil companies on several occasions to service the workers there – and incidentally some of the Amarakaeri men.

Large quantities of food provisions, tools, helicopter fuel, and other supplies were maintained there. For many Amarakaeri this collection of material goods exceeded their most elaborate fantasies.

The supply depot was constantly surrounded by Amarakaeri men, women, and children – begging, buying, or stealing when possible, the supplies they desired. They began using helicopter fuel as kerosene in homemade lamps, modifying empty fuel drums to sluice gold, fishing with explosive charges, and eating the range of tinned food preserves that had suddenly become available.

Often depot workers gave away supplies which were in excess of immediate needs or otherwise tried to placate the ever present natives. At times, however, supplies were inadequate and the depot workers had to fight off both natives and other oil workers who had not been fed or provided with tools, mosquito netting, and other necessary supplies. The result was tremendous confusion and frequently conflictive relations.

Hungry oil workers stole chickens from Amarakaeri who refused to sell them as many as they wanted. Drunkenness was common. Native women were harassed. Fights broke out, and social chaos prevailed.

The oil company administrators took an unusually callous approach to the situation. They once even had some Amarakaeri men arrested for »stealing« explosive charges and empty fuel drums which the natives had bought from oil company employees. There was also an attempt to cut down Amarakaeri fruit trees and make other changes in the village in order to facilitate the air traffic, without discussing these plans with anyone in the community in advance. This particular project was thwarted when the oil workers refused to carry it out against native resistance.

SIL has been accused of cooperating in oil exploration operations elsewhere to the detriment of the native peoples in the areas in question. There was no SIL collaboration with the oil companies in their work in the area around Puerto Alegre.

SIL members, not including Tripp, did cooperate with Cities Service, however, in a survey mission to the Río de los Mashcos, about 80 kilometers north of Puerto Alergre, in December 1973-January 1974. The purpose of the mission was to locate and contact »wild Indians« which had been reported in that area where oil exploration was being conducted. The »wild Indians« were found to exist only in the imagination of some of the workers who were experiencing shortages of food and other supplies, as well as abusive and illegal treatment by their supervisors (Varese 1974:8).

Tripp's approach to the situation at Puerto Alegre was to do whatever possible to prevent conflicts between oil workers and natives by mediating disputes. There was no protest by SIL either to the oil companies themselves or to the appropriate agencies of the Peruvian Government, even though the former had effectively taken over an airstrip which had previously been used only by SIL.

Under these difficult circumstances, the Puerto Alegre community became increasingly factionalized and internally conflictive. Individual Amarakaeri began quarreling over who should produce food for the others to eat and who had fewer material goods and was therefore worthless.

Trade goods were jealously guarded by their individual owners. Most of the houses acquired padlocks. Traditional patterns of sharing food and tools became increasingly restrictive, often limited to families of biological brothers. Fights broke out within clans.

One young man was accused of witchcraft and banished from the village, and several groups of Puerto Alegre families moved downriver to other locations. They were now working gold more intensively than ever before, especially during the rainy season months, and they found it easier to live away from the conflicts of the village, returning for garden produce when necessary.

Some families, now having greater mobility as a result of the outboard motors, began making the long trip down the Madre de Dios to the Department capital, Puerto Maldonado, where a greater variety of trade goods was available and relatives at the El Pilar Mission (Dominican) were nearby.

Soon eight of the children from SIL's bilingual school were taken to El Pilar, where they boarded during the school year and could be visited occasionally by their now mobile families. Parents of the children stated that they wanted their children to learn Spanish and »Peruvian« ways more quickly there than would be possible in the SIL bilingual school.

In August 1975, the entire community of Puerto Alegre moved to a new location midway between the old site and the Banco Minero post. Here, they had greater access to the better gold beaches on the Karene and its tributaries, as well as to the Banco Minero post and Puerto Maldonado.

Thus, the relative isolation of the upper Karene Amarakaeri was broken, and much more intensive contact with the riverine peasant and urban populations of Madre de Dios began. By mid-1975 some families of Amarakaeri were buying food provisions from the Banco Minero, since they had neglected their gardens and found little time for hunting and gathering. It is doubtful whether this once isolated primitive culture will be distinguishable from that of non-native riverine peasants in another generation.

Significantly, most of these destructive developments went on without much involvement by SIL. The mission was ignored by the various industries and government agencies responsible, and it made no effort to confront them.

During the earlier period SIL had, in fact, inhibited the destructive potential of smaller, less powerful ethnocidal pressures. Part of the credit for that relative success must be attributed to the style and personality of Robert Tripp, who tried to live simply and do his work gradually, in harmony with the natives. He provided the most critical needs, like medical attention, and assuaged appetites for trade goods with a relatively modest flow of them. Thus, gradual changes occurred which allowed for a degree of ethnic stability.

Ironically, one could argue that SIL has contributed most to the ethnocide process by not being present at critical times. However, in the 1973-75 period, agents of national and international expansion used SIL, and the Puerto Alegre airstrip, for their own purposes. The scale of these pressures was such that the presence or absence of SIL may not have been decisive, but some defensive political involvement by SIL might have diminished their impact.

* * *

The fullest possible record of missionary-native relations would help us understand their nature and fill important gaps in the recent culture history of the native peoples concerned. It would also provide provocative new perspectives on the more fundamental problem of the articulation of the primitive world and the national-international polity of which missionaries are only forerunners. And an understanding of the ethnocide process vis-a-vis primitive cultures generally may provide new insight into the nature of power in ways that would not be possible wholly within the state structure, where the absence of unequal exchanges and coercive political relationships is not conceivable.

All non-natives, including anthropologists, who have contact with native peoples are potential agents of ethnocide, and their work should be subject to comparable scrutiny.

Notes

[1] The field research from which this account was drawn, was funded in part by a United States Department of Health, Education, and Welfare Fulbright-Hays Doctoral Dissertation Research Fellowship and a Wenner-Gren Foundation for Anthropological Research Grant-in-Aid. Members of the Summer Institute of Linguistics, especially Robert Tripp, served as important sources of data, as did, of course, the Amarakaeri community at Puerto Alegre. I alone am responsible for any errors.

[2] Lyon (1975) has established the boundaries of the Harakmbut language, which she calls Háte. Mason (1950) classifies »Masco« as a Pre-Andine Arawakan language, but more recent studies (Lyon, 1975; d'Ans et al., 1973; Wise, 1975) have questioned this affiliation and have set Harakmbut aside as an independentlanguage.

[3] The pattern of concentrating small dispersed native local communities into one large mission community with major ecological disruptions has been common in eastern Peru and includes some of the SIL mission sites. Some aspects of this problem are documented for the Matsés (Romanoff, 1977), and discussed generally by d'Ans (1972).

Bibliography

Ans, André-Marcel d'
1972 La alfabetización y la educación de los pueblos de la selva peruana en la perspectiva de su porvenir económico. In Alberto Escobar, ed. *El reto del multilingüismo en el Perú.* Lima: Instituto de Estudios Peruanos.
1975 Influencia de la escuela sobre las migraciones (un caso Machiguenga). Educación 6(13):15-25. Lima.

Ans, André-Marcel d', María C. Chavarría M., Nilda Guillén A., and Gustavo Solis F.
1973 Problemas de clasificación de lenguas no-andinas en el sureste peruano. Universidad Nacional Mayor de San Marcos, Centro de Investigación de Lingüística Aplicada. Documento de Trabajo No. 18. Lima.

Bello, Al
1956 Con los feroces Amarakaires en plena edad de piedra. Caretas (Julio-Agosto): 32-34b. Lima.

Carneiro, Robert L.
1962 Little known tribes of the Peruvian Montana. International Congress of Americanists, *Proceedings* (1960) 34:58-63. Vienna.

IWGIA
1971 *Declaration of Barbados.* International Work Group for Indigenous Affairs, Documentation No. 1. Copenhagen.

Jaulin, Robert
1970 *La paix blanche: introduction a l'ethnocide.* Paris: Editions du Seuil.

Lyon, Patricia J.
1975 Dislocación tribal y clasificaciones lingüísticas en la zona del Río Madre de Dios. International Congress of Americanists, *Proceedings* (1970) 39(5):185-207. Lima.

Mason, J. Alden
1950 The languages of South American Indians. In Julian H. Steward, ed. *Handbook of South American Indians* 6:157-317. Smithsonian Institution, Bulletin of American Ethnology No. 143 Washington.

Miller, Elmer S.
1970 The Christian missionary, agent of secularization. Anthropological Quarterly 43(1):14-22. Washington.

Romanoff, Steven
1977 Informe sobre el uso de la tierra por los Matsés en la selva baja peruana. Amazonía Peruana 1(1):97-130. Lima.

Slocum, Marianna, and Sam Holmes, eds.
1963 *Who Brought the Word.* Santa Ana, California: Wycliffe Bible Translators/Summer Institute of Linguistics.

Varese, Stefano
1974 La conquista continúa. Postdata 1(2):7-8. Lima.

Wise, Mary Ruth
1975 *Datos supplementarios sobre »Grupos Idiomáticos del Perú«.* Yarinacocha: Instituto Lingüístico de Verano.

Jaulin, Robert, ed.
1972 *Le livre blanc de l'ethnocide en Amérique.* Paris: Librairie Artheme Fayard.

Aerial view of the Machiguenga village of Tayakome, beside the River Manu. In the centre is the school; to the right at the end of the airstrip is the house of Martin with those of his allies in rows behind it. On the other side of the airstrip is the house of Italiano (the biggest) and his allies. Copyright: Gerhard Baer.

144

Encounter in Peru

by ANDRE-MARCEL d'ANS

Introduction[1]

When I arrived in Peru in 1969, I was not familiar with the Summer Institute of Linguistics which did not operate in any of the areas where I had previously worked. But as the organization by virtue of an agreement signed with the Ministry of Education had an effective monopoly on all scientific research in linguistics and ethnology throughout the Amazonian region of Peru and had moreover published an impressive number of bibliographies, I immediately contacted the senior staff of the Institute. I was coldly if courteously received and my request for exchange of research information was ignored.

Meanwhile thanks to my official capacity I had been able to start field work without having to rely on any help from the Institute which for an independent researcher would have been nearly impossible. I was thus able to gather very accurate information concerning:
1. the generally nefarious impact of the SIL's field activities;
2. the fraud perpetrated by the SIL which conceals its real action behind so-called »scientific« motives.

In 1971-72, while I was working with the Ministry of Education, I drew its attention to these two conclusions and in January 1972, when my task was completed, a number of my Peruvian colleagues and I signed a petition in which we demanded that the authorities immediately begin monitoring the activities of the Institute and at the earliest opportunity call a halt to its operations in Peru.

When I returned to Peru in 1975, the Government was finally about to follow the advice of progressive intellectuals and terminate the contract between the SIL and the Ministry of Education. But a few »moderate« voices were being raised demanding the postponement of the decision and suggesting that Peru was not yet able to carry out on its own the research which until then had been monopolised by the SIL. In the end, unfortunately, the rise of the Right on the Peruvian political scene, which began in August 1975 and was suddenly precipitated in July 1976, put a stop among other things to the idea of doing without the assistance of the SIL. To understand fully how well implanted and how nefarious the SIL can be in Third World countries, it is useful not only to recall the nature of its field activities among the natives, but also to shed light on the tacit approbation which the Institute has cleverly elicited from officials and civil servants fascinated, as is the established intelligentsia, by the glitter of the technical and pseudo-scientific support system displayed by this Holy Scriptures multinational concern!

It was, I suppose, because the Institute's senior staff immediately perceived that their quackery would in no way dazzle me that they from the start mistrusted me. Although our formal relations remained polite the Institute's initial coolness and refusal to cooperate quickly developed into definite hostility. Yet none of the criticisms which some of my Peruvian colleagues or I had raised were ever officially contradicted. This was in keeping with the Institute's own rule of never publicly answering any criticisms addressed to it since it preferred to act behind the scenes and cautiously but efficiently bring its influence to bear on certain officials. Thus it was only in the very special political circumstances of Velasquist and revolutionary Peru that a domestic campaign against the SIL had any hope of gathering support and achieving results.

The following three papers illustrate three phases of my duel with the SIL:

André-Marcel d'Ans, born in Belgium (1938-   ), has been teaching linguistics and anthropology at various universities in Europe, as well as in Zaïre, Chile and Peru. He worked as a UN-expert in Peru 1975-76, and is now Professor at Departement de l'Ethnologie de l'Université Paris 7. He has published several articles and two major books.

1. The first is an extract of the appendix to the report which was submitted in January 1972 to the Ministry of Education. It concerns the campaign for literacy and education of the people of the Amazonian forest. Using the SIL's own references, I attempted in this paper to show the weakness of its so-called »scientific« research in Peru to date. Though published in French in 1972 (in Robert Jaulin, *De l'Ethnocide,* Paris, UGE, 10/18/pp. 412-417), the document has never been officially divulged in Peru.

2. The second paper is an article drafted in December 1973 where I describe in detail how the SIL tried to oppose the measures undertaken by the Ministry of Agriculture within the Manu National Park and what consequences its own activities had on the lives of the Machiguenga Indians in the village of Tayakome. The paper was published in the first months of 1975 in the Ministry of Education's periodical *Educación* (no. 13, pp. 15-25). I have included here a postscript drafted in 1976 which gives more up to date information on the matters discussed.

3. The third paper was published on 26 November 1975 in *»El Comercio«,* Lima's leading daily paper. I described the procedures by which at the time I felt that the SIL's activities could be terminated and suggested ways in which the infrastructure and facilities until then monopolised by the Institute could be put to use.

1) Evaluation of SIL's scientific work during 25 years in Peru

One of the most unattractive features of the SIL is that it has acquired its vested position under cover of its »scientific« research. Far, be it from me to hold that linguistics or ethnology are always practised by honest men and women. But I am somewhat upset that in Latin America the public image of a linguist or of an ethnologist is to a large extent coloured by the behaviour of the SIL staff. Even when disregarding the ideological slant of their research, one must admit that it is quantitatively and qualitatively negligible; a fact which their orchestrated, flashy public relations campaigns, designed to awe and impress the »underdeveloped Latins«, can not always conceal. To illustrate the already well known point, that the SIL is the laughing stock of linguistic departments even in the United States, I shall draw from my Peruvian experience.

In 1964, when the Institute was preparing to celebrate its XXth Anniversary in Peru, it published a bibliography of its work which was financed by the Ministry of Education. It is a noteworthy document. It was prefaced by the Dean of the Faculty of Letters of the University of San Marcos. It is by the way worth observing that no news-sheet from the Institute is ever published without being praised by the established Peruvian intellectual in office. The Dean for instance wrote:

»We have already said how happy we were with the work done by the Summer Institute of Linguistics. Today our happiness is strengthened and justified by a list of *actual books* (my italics) which are the result of this work and appear in the bibliography that we readily make available to the public«. The preface was followed by a prologue in which Eugene Loos, the present director of the SIL in Peru, gave impressive statistics on the vast output of the Institute. Of the items mentioned in the sole category »scientific publications«:

    175 are in the field of linguistics

     86 are in the field of ethnography.

But in a more thorough examination of the bibliography initial surprise gives way to absolute amazement at the number of items followed by the words »ready for publishing« or »in press«. And it is interesting to supplement Loos' statistics with figures giving the number of actual publications:

    in lingustics: 61 published items

    in ethnography: 13 published items

In other words, 75 % of the 1964 bibliography related to *»unpublished« material.* Since this 1964 bibliography was the result of 19 years of »work« accomplished in Peru by the Institute and considering that between 1945 and 1964 the Institute's staff amounted to 45 research workers (as it claimed in its Xth Anniversary brochure published in 1955; but there were fewer in the first years and more in the latter, so that the figure of 45 can be said to be an average), we too can play the statistics game and work out that:

The Institute's average output was:
in linguistics: 3,2 items per year
in ethnography: 0,7 items per year

The average output per research worker over 19 years was:
in linguistics: 1,4 items
in ethnography: 0,3 items

The average time required per research worker at the Institute to produce a paper was:
in linguistics: 14 years
in ethnography: 63 years

We are indeed awed as was the astute Peruvian author of the preface by this impressive »list of actual books«! To understand the full extent of the gall displayed by the selfcongratulatory evaluations constantly being published by the Institute, it is useful to know that the sums that we have just done refer not to »books« but more often to short articles in periodicals often with a limited distribution such as *The Bible Translator!*

In fields where I have myself had access to the subject under study, I can state that the Institute's so-called »scientific« articles are based on poorly collected data and a confused and obscure methodology and that in general they present unverifiable or unacceptable conclusions. Before I conclude, I should like to add a few statistics to those previously published. In 1971, to commemorate its XXVth Anniversary, the Institute brought out a new bibliography. Seven years after 1964 one would have expected the »in press« and »unpublished« documents to have seen the light of day. I was intrigued to know what had happened to the 114 unpublished items in linguistics and the 73 in ethnography and here are the results of my investigations.

1971 – status of the items unpublished in 1964:
In linguistics: 7 published (6 %)
                     9 in press (8 %)
                     94 lost without trace (86 %)
In ethnography: 0 published (0 %)
                     1 in press (1,5 %)
                     72 lost and gone forever (98,5 %)

Hence it is obvious that more than 90 % of the items promised in 1964 either had never existed or were such affabulations that even the Institute hesitated to publish them. Yet if the Institute's list of scientific publications is so meager one cannot help but enquire as one weekly magazine recently has: »What does the Summer Institute of Linguistics really do in Peru?« What designs does the Institute conceal behind the scientific facade with which it for so long has impressed Peruvian public opinion awed by the glittering statements and laudatory declarations of a handful of defenceless intellectuals rendered speechless with admiration for the gringoes, their planes and radio-sets, their computers, their language and the opulence of their yankee village installed in the heart of the very forest of which the Peruvian and particularly the Peruvian intellectual has such an odd conception?

These lines on the SIL are not out of place here. The contamination of traditional elites and more specifically that of the Ministry of Education have made it almost impossible in the short term to shake the Institute's position. Criticism from linguists, ethnologists, students and native »teachers« are mere storms in a teacup for this institution solidly entrenched as a state within the State. It is significant that though it was attacked in no uncertain terms at the National Seminar for Bilingual Education and later in the press, the Institute has not only found no one to take its defence but has not even itself bothered to answer publicly.

The Institute rightly believes that it is more important to place its agents – or people it can dominate – in key posts and to control the actual organisation of bilingual education. Hence we need no longer wonder how this programme is to be implemented, even if, as in the past, the Institute shows the same talent for rejuvenating its rhetoric: I would not be surprised if already next year it starts agitating against ethnocide!

The Peruvian authorities, whose liberal-mindedness in consulting independent intellectuals and academics in the field of humanities and educational science I have had the pleasure of pointing out, would be gravely mistaken to separate the two parts of their conclusions: on one hand, to state and have recorded their position against ethnocide, but on the other hand to reject casually the demand to ban all activities of the Summer Institute of Linguistics. That is having one's cake and eating it.

A national government like the present should be aware of the considerable surrender of its sovereignty implied in handing over completely the study and education of its national ethnic minorities to a foreign organisation which proselytizes in a religion which is not even that of the majority of the country, and over which hang such grave suspicions of duplicity.

Lima, January 1972

2) The Influence of Education on Migration Patterns – A Machiguenga Case

Introduction

The documents quoted in this paper were provided by Chief of Station Abel Flores Davila. They are official documents and can be found in their unabridged form in the archives of the Department of Forestry and Hunting of the Ministry of Agriculture. Hence one can verify that they were indeed drafted on the dates claimed. It is worth stating that I did not at the time reside in the National Park of Manu, and thus could not in any way have urged or instigated their drafting. Nevertheless, the facts described have been confirmed by enquiries carried out by myself at a later date. As to the evaluation of the situation which our colleague Abel Flores Davila from time to time voices these are his own personal opinions expressed in the manner he chose to convey them to his superiors.

We wish to state that the census data used in this study are the most accurate available given the circumstances in which the survey was undertaken. We will make available to any other interested research worker the personal data cards which give genealogical information on all members of the Tayakome community. With the villagers' consent, we are still in the process of compiling these cards. Even in their present form they have been indispensable tools not only for our own study of the Machiguenga kinship links,[*] but also for the research on genetics which anthropologists Christiane and Jean Dricot are undertaking.

To protect my sources, I could have, in my study, referred to tribe A, village B, chief C and bilingual teacher D. Yet I chose not to. On the one hand the people mentioned by name in my account are public persons in both social communities, playing a decisive role in the history of their ethnic group, as well as fulfilling an administrative function in the dominant society. Thus the subject of my study is neither private lives nor private relationships.

On the other hand, the interest of the case I describe lies in its uniqueness and in the long continuous period of observation carried out by myself which enables me to produce a mass of documents that can be verified in the field by any research worker. I wished furthermore to avoid the depersonalisation of the situation which would have resulted had I suppressed the real names of people and places and replaced them by conventional symbols.

Finally what in fact is at stake here is not abstract plans or esoteric dissertations but the peace and well-being of flesh and blood Peruvian Indians, and what is necessary is a serious evaluation of their chances of securing for the future decent socio-economic conditions.

Generally speaking, education is the variable most responsible for shaping the lives of the Machiguenga community of Tayakome, situated on the Manu River (Department of Madre de Dios, province of Manu, latitude East 71°, longitude South 11° 38').

In fact, the demographic structure of the village varies considerably from the traditional Machinguenga pattern according to which members of the ethnic group live close to their gardens either scattered in single family units or in clusters of a few small allied families. A number of such small Machiguenga groups continue to live in this way today around the headwaters of the Rivers Manu, Sotileja, Fierro (Yomiba), Cumerjali, Pinguen, Polotoa and Pini-Pini, to mention only those situated within the National Park of Manu.

The history of the village of Tayakome started about ten years ago. At the time, the Summer Institute of Linguistics, a North-American missionary organization that assists the Ministry of Education in its activities relating to bilingual education, decided to build a school in Tayakome and to concentrate there the Michiguenga population scattered around the various rivers of the area that later was to become the Manu National Park.

The site chosen was already inhabited by a small group of Machiguenga Indians led by the elder

---

[*] »Estructura semántica del parentesco machiguenga«, in Revista del Museo Nacional XL, pp. 341-361 (Lima, 1974).

Ahuanari, a native of the higher reaches of the Manu. They had had to abandon the latter area having been decimated by other Indians of Pano dialect, whose territory extended largely towards the middle reaches of the Manu.

The site of Tayakome appeared appropriate to the SIL because of its proximity to a river large enough to allow motor launch transport, its high elevation and its firm and unfloodable ground necessary not only for the building of an air-strip but also for the clearing and cultivation of sufficient gardens to supply the needs of a large population. Near the village, there were also several clean and fresh water holes.

Having found such a suitable site, the sole remaining problem was to convince the Machiguenga population scattered throughout the area to come together and live in Tayakome. Two Machiguenga played a prominent role in this matter. They were the teacher, Martín Vargas, and »Italiano« Cabrera. These two men of profoundly different backgrounds, characters, political beliefs and personal ambitions were thus united in the implementation of a common task.

Martín Vargas made literate, educated and converted to the Protestant faith by the »linguists«, is an earnest, forceful man proud of his conversion and of having risen above his culture. But at heart he is tense and obstinate, hungering after the material goods and social prestige which are the reward of hard work and good morals. On the other hand, Italiano was always a vagabond. Proud of having been born, so he says, in Cuzco, and having walked to Puno and Arequipa, he has seen the many faces of the world and consequently has fashioned for himself an ironic philosophy of life. Italiano is illiterate and does not master the Castillian tongue nearly so well as Vargas. Nevertheless he too is an intelligent and an energetic man. Probably his disillusionment with the outside world coupled with his realization that he would never become an integral part of it prompted his return to the forest. His past experiences, his truculence and great eloquence, often even his clownish playfulness all combine with masculine energy and quickwitted and inflexible decision-making to make him fascinating to his friends, irritating to others and yet called upon to play a considerable social role among his people.

Beside the ascetic and monogamous Martín, Italiano projects his hedonistic exhuberant and extrovert personality. His cooperation with »the linguists« never brought him to renounce polygamy. The tender age of his spouses as well as their low fertility still today deserve attention, particularly when compared with Martín's numerous and well-cared for family.

Indeed there is no area in which the difference of personalities of our two heroes is not apparent. Italiano has never omitted to wear the typical Machiguenga crown of feathers whereas Vargas never sported it; Italiano has never agreed to kick a football, to own any outboard motor, radio, sewing-machine or record-player; his house is not a copy of mestizo architecture; he wears his patched and torn clothing without any embarrassment and on the contrary with gay abandon; he is mischievous and happy where Martín Vargas is self-effacing and gloomy. Thus in a society such as the Machiguengan focused largely around verbal ability, Italiano's boisterous, prolific and amusing talkativeness more than compensate for Martín's »cultural« advantages.

Despite their different temperaments, Italiano and Martín successfully combined their efforts to persuade the Machiguenga to abandon their homes in order to settle and inhabit the village of Tayakome. Indeed there were, despite their different personalities, obvious advantages for Martín and Italiano to cooperate. Both were uprooted from traditional life; both were messengers from the »white« world and though one had the proselytizing faith of the convert and the other displayed the ironic detachment of the sceptic, both had high expectations of power and action. Both to an equal degree needed a village in which their ambitions could be realized. Thus they worked together to create it. Martín, on behalf of the Summer Institute of Linguistics, considered as sole fountainhead of wisdom, power, truth and wealth; and Italiano with no other thought than that of using every opportunity which arose. With the result that soon they were both purposefully and indefatigably visiting river settlements to »herd« their fellow tribesmen to the site chosen for the building of the school and village of which they would respectively become the teacher and the leader.

I have known the village of Tayakome since 1969 when the anthropological programme of the Manu National Park was started under my supervision.

As a settlement the village had a characteristic plan. A considerable expanse of forest had been cleared and the school was built un the centre of this area flanked on one side by a 250-300 m long airstrip for the Institute's small planes. The living quarters had to fit into this basic pattern, a »street« or rather a compact row of single family houses was built near the school. The street culminated at the teacher's house, which was on the edge of the landing strip, exactly where the pilots touched their small planes down during landing. Another street built up into the forest was separated from the first by the width of the airstrip. Withdrawn in the woody hill is the village leader, Italiano's house. It is much bigger and not in line with the others and has a different architectural style. Whether one arrives in the village by plane or by climbing the incline after the river the first house to meet one's eyes is the teacher's and the last is the village leader's. The two men's different personalities are thus reflected in the dichotomy of architectural styles in the village. The plan of the settlement is the opposite of what a well conceived integrated village should look like. It is misshapen and reflects a picture of tension and internal contradiction. The very sight of it leads one to suspect that its people live in a state of both open and latent conflict.

In 1969 the first population census was taken. I computed very approximate figures since I was only able to count the number of houses and get acquainted with the name of the head of the family and guess at the number of wives and children. In fact, the greater shyness of women and children made it almost impossible to come into direct contact with them. Communication with adult males was not that easy either, not only because several did not trust me, but also because the great majority of them spoke nothing but Machiguenga. Nevertheless the result of this first census enabled me to record that there had been no significant change in the population (bar an almost negligible immigration percentage) between 1969 and 1971 when we completed the first individual, systematic and complete census which, wherever possible, specified the identity and sex of each inhabitant as well as his/her age, birthplace, number of parents, siblings and other useful data.

In this census the age of the children entered as »born in Tayakome« enabled us to conclude that 1966 had been the date at which the village had taken on the size and characteristics it had in 1969 and that migration and settlement had basically occured between 1963 and 1966.

As I have already mentioned I made my first surveys of the area in 1969 on behalf of the Department of Forestry and Hunting of the Ministry of Agriculture which had in agreement with the University of San Marcos made me the Director of the Anthropological Programme of the Manu National Park. In 1970 after a training period in which I gave a course in elementary anthropology and how to behave when dealing with groups of native Indians the first park wardens of Manu were sent out to control posts and in particular to one situated at Tayakome itself. The park wardens control post was not situated within the village but a short way down the river. There was furthermore no land communication between it and the village which ensured the mutual peace and independence of both.

Before the installation of park wardens in Tayakome I had lived for a week during the month of February 1970 in the Machiguenga village to explain what was about to happen and to make sure that there were no objections on their side to the arrival of park wardens at a control post which was situated in the immediate vicinity of the village. I gathered that they had no objections although several asked me whether it really was true that the park wardens were going completely to forbid hunting and fishing which would reduce them to famine and force them to migrate to another settlement. I was able to reassure them that their fear was totally groundless.

Indeed the *sine qua non* condition of my participation in the Anthropological Programme of the National Park of Manu had always been that no restrictions of any kind would ever be put onto the park natives' freedom of movement or freedom to hunt, fish, gather and cultivate what they needed to survive; but that on the contrary every available measure would be taken to prevent outside elements from purchasing for commercial purposes the skins, trophies, live animals or other objects from the forest gathered or caught by the Machiguenga.

Thus it was that in full agreement with the plans of the public authorities of the Ministry of Agriculture we implemented as of that date the three first points of the Recommendations drafted by the English group of *The Ecologist* at the United Nations Conference on Human Environment held in Stockholm in June 1972 which reads as follows:

> »(1) Certain wilderness areas of tropical rain forest, tropical scrub forest, and arctic tundra be declared inviolate, these being the least understood and most fragile biomes;
>
> (2) the hunter-gatherers and hunter-farmers within these areas be given title to their lands (i.e. those lands in which traditionally they have gained their living) and be allowed to live there without pressure of any kind;
>
> (3) severe restrictions be placed on entry to these areas by anyone who does not live there permanently (while allowing the indigenes free movement);« (A blueprint for Survival, The Ecologist, vol. 2, no. 1, pp. 11-12, London, 1972).

The teacher Martin in his school of Tayakome. Copyright: Gerhard Baer.

Furthermore to corroborate the statement that the Park authorities have no intentions of imposing restrictions or coercive measures on the Machiguenga one could argue *ex absurdo* that should such measures be taken there would be no way of enforcing them or of preventing or punishing transgressions. No one with a minimum of knowledge of the geographical situation in the area can be in any doubt on this point.

With regard to future potential migrations of the population, the following was planned: should the Machiguenga community of Tayakome or part of it, wish to move into commercial occupations such as animal husbandry or extensive agriculture, the Ministry would not be able to encourage such developments in an area set aside for the conservation of the natural environment. In such cases, however, sufficient and suitable land could be made available to the Machiguenga further down the river but outside the park. In their new settlement the Machiguenga, walking at their own pace down the road towards the competitive society of the outside world, could further benefit from the full support of the Ministry of Agriculture in terms of loans, technical assistance etc.

But at present these prospects are purely hypothetical and will remain so as long as the Machiguenga maintain the traditional types of relationships they have had with their environment and are no threat to the ecological balance. For thousands of years their ancestors have lived and developed their culture without endangering the survival of any species, hence there is no reason why their descendants should do so to-day unless outside agents use them to hoard natural resources for profit-making purposes.

This line of action was repeatedly made clear to the SIL authorities whose officials (arriving by plane) became the sole representatives of the outside world to be allowed to maintain contact with the Machiguenga when the park wardens started forbidding access to the area to lumbermen, hunters, tradesmen and other interested visitors who had previously been able to come and go freely in Tayakome.

Nevertheless despite the fact that the initial contact between park wardens and Machiguenga had been very friendly, their relationship gradually worsened to the extent that it became doubtful whether the goals of the park wardens to preserve the natural environment of the park could be made to coincide with the presence of the Machiguenga in Tayakome.

During my stays in the Tayakome control post in the course of 1970 and 1971 I was personally able to confirm that the Machiguenga, a naturally amicable people, were always friendly with the park wardens on duty at the post. Almost every day a small group of them would come and pay a call on us. But any time a small plane from the Institute of Linguistics landed and one of those missionaries stayed with the villagers for a few hours they disappeared from the post as if by enchantment and did not come back for a week or more. At the end of this time the least shy would begin to approach us again and relations would slowly return to normal until the next plane's visit.

Such a state of affairs could not be explained unless the missionary in charge of the indoctrination of the Machiguenga had misunderstood our real objectives. Let us be frank, he was in fact systematically undermining our position.

Document no. 1

Tayakome 29 May 1970, First report to *The Administrator of the National Park of Manu.*

Object: Visit of the Summer Institute of Linguistics' plane to the village of Tayakome.

I have the honour to bring to your attention that Friday 22 of this month at 5.05 pm the SIL's small plane landed in Tayakome carrying four US passengers, three men and one woman. Mr. Arturo Davis, particularly needs to be mentioned. He told me about the work he was engaged in, namely inoculating all villagers in his care against tuberculosis. I can confirm that the said gentleman spoke perfect Machiguenga and dominated his audience whom he had known from his visits since 1963; he also said that the Machiguenga were hostile towards us, that we would have many problems with them and that we should take care. From unsolicited information given by two natives, Aranzaval and Domingo we gathered the following:

That same Friday the Linguists had called a meeting of the villagers and frightened them by saying that 1) soldiers would be coming to remove their few weapons, 2) the President was evil and would send planes to bomb the settlement, 3) white people are a threat to their women and children, 4) white people carry diseases that will infect their people, 5) we were there to forbid them to hunt, 6) they were forbidden to visit us at the control post, 7) we were forbidden to visit them at the settlement, 8) it would be desirable that we should be removed and the village left in peace, 9) maybe the control post should be attacked. To all this, it should be added that on the following day, Saturday, at 5 pm they sailed past the control post in two canoes fishing with a group of natives. We did not intercept them in order to avoid problems with the villagers and only observed all they did. The said plane left Monday 25 at 1.05 pm. That is all I have to teel you.

Yours respectfully.

Abel Flores Davila,

Chief of Control Post

When it became obvious that such tactics were having on effect and that the park wardens were not going to be removed, the SIL decided to resettle the village outside the limits of the park. It has to be underlined that this move had of course never been discussed, let alone agreed upon, by the Ministry of Agriculture. As we shall see later the SIL had not contacted the Ministry of Education either. It is worth mentioning also that when questioned by me the SIL authorities in Yarinacocha always denied that they had taken any decision in this matter and declared moreover that if the Machiguenga were migrating it was on their own initiative.

We shall furthermore recount how the attitude of the native leaders of Tayakome changed between 1970 and 1971. Originally the teacher, Martín Vargas and the health »adviser« Luis Cabrera, eldest son of Italiano the village chief, culturally more »mixed« and more or less fluent in Spanish, appeared to consider us as a new prospect for the development of their progressive ideas. However, as it became obvious that we did not fulfill their hopes, their enthusiasm for us cooled off although our relations always remained outwardly friendly. By contrast, chief Italiano who originally had been extremely reserved, not to say contemptuous gradually came forward and entered into more and more friendly relations with the park wardens and with me personally.

Meanwhile the transfer of the people of Tayakome to the river Camisea had been decided (probably in Yarinacocha, the SIL headquarters, during the summer of 1970-1971) and was being actively prepared by its staff.

Document no. 2
Report no. 012, 1 May 1971.
I have the honour to inform you that according to information volunteered by Ramon Aranzaval five Machiguenga among them, four families have moved to Camisea led by Luis Cabrera (the son of Chief Italiano) to prepare a new settlement for the Tayakome Indians in a place chosen by the linguists. Their preparations will include: building houses, clearing land for gardens, building a school.

In the first months of next year there will probably be a mass move organized by school teacher Martín Vargas. Not every one agrees to this move but the majority do. During the first trip in which my informant Aranzaval participated, they opened a broad passage through which to take their canoes. The entire village was peaceful but the arrival of the teacher from Yarinacocha with instructions from the Linguists changed the whole atmosphere, thus causing the first move. For this purpose they used his motor launch piloted by Aguilar, an Indian, who came back with a few others when he had dropped the agents.

Document no. 3
Report no. 013, 26 May 1971.
On this trip (note: of the SIL plane) Luis Cabrera's family was moved to Camisea.

Document no. 4
Report no. 017, 15 July 1971
(Referring to the SIL plane). The following Machiguenga were transported from Tayakome to Camisea:
1) Theresa, aged 55, wife of Francisco
2) Fermin, aged 6, son of Lucho

Moreover the plane carried a sewing machine belonging to school teacher Martín Vargas, 3 small empty cylinders, 6 ducks, a folding table.

Aware that the final migration of the village had to be carried out on a grand scale during the summer of 1971-1972 neither Ministry of Agriculture nor I myself made any arrangements to retard the process. Personally I was not very happy with the decision and even less so with the way it was being carried out. But to a certain extent if the Machiguenga wanted to leave the park area why prevent them? Their departure relieved the park authorities of a problem that required close attention over and beyond the other problems arising out of the creation of a natural reserve of the size and remoteness of Manu Park.

Hence our role was limited to that of observers although we did not suspend the support given to the Machiguenga, as for instance, in 1971, when thanks to a grant from the Belgian Government a community store was organized to provide the Machiguenga at cost price with a few necessities of life.

Surprisingly, when the total migration of the people appeared to have become inevitable deep dissensions broke out among the villagers. In the end the village chief categorically refused to move to Camisea whereas the school teacher took the transfer of the health post and the school as a *fait accompli* and argued that somehow the people would have to follow.

In January 1972 I participated in the first National Seminar on bilingual education which was held in Lima and organized by the Ministry of Education. Being familiar with the conflict situation which existed in Tayakome I referred to the case during committee meetings with other participants and during private conversations. I was able to confirm among other things that there had never been any decision in the Ministry of Education authorizing the move of the government school of Tayakome. Faced with the impossibility of denying facts the responsible parties tried rather to argue that the migration was a result of prevailing circumstances: the people were migrating and therefore necessarily the school also had to be moved.

But reports from the chief of the control post of Tayakome showed that in the initial stage the move had been accomplished with the SIL's own planes and it was being completed under the direct leader-ship of the school teacher using his own motorlaunch.

Document no. 5
Report no. 019, 17 December 1971.
I have the honour to bring to your attention that to-day, Friday 17 of this month at 6.05 am the following Machiguenga moved from Tayakome to Camisea:

Luis Toribio and his family, Ernesto and his family, Mantsintsiniari and his family, Francisco and his family, Demetrio and his family, Cristóbal and his family, Juanito, Agustín, Mashico, Balareso, Martín Vargas (school teacher).

This move led by the teacher was made in his boat. We know that on the instructions of the SIL three entire families were transported in the same launch. The village chief was in complete disagree-ment with the SIL over the moves and complained about his family leaving him, since it had been quite expensive for him to bring them out of the forest and settle them in the Tayakome community which had begun to flourish and now was totally disrupted.

Several families had chosen to remain under Italiano's leadership and refused to have anything to do with Camisea. The villagers' morale is low since the inhuman breaking up of the community and the withdrawal by the SIL of its health care centre and its teacher. The organisation has even stopped check-up visits leaving several families without care and several more children with no access to school which means they run a serious risk of remaining illiterate. That is all for now.
Yours respectfully
Abel Flores Davila.

It was easy for an inspector from the Ministry of Education to verify these reports. Nevertheless it was already too late to redress the harm done. My intervention occurred too late to prevent the migration which proceeded as planned. All I achieved with my condemnatory report was that senior officials from the Ministry of Education guaranteed that whatever happened a school would be kept open in Taya-kome to educate the remaining school age children. A young Tayakome Machiguenga was quickly made »teacher« and to symbolise his hierarchical promotion he moved his family from one side of the airstrip to the other and took up residence in the house vacated by Martín, which at present faces a row of empty, disintegrating and crumbling houses soon to be overgrown by the forest. All the inhabitants of »Martín's street« moved with their leader whereas those of Italiano's remained. Crippled at the outset the village lay-out now appears severely amputated.

An examination of census data gives us another angle on the provisions of the migration which occurred in the summer of 1971-1972.

Before the migration the adult population of Tayakome consisted almost equally of men (23 %) and of women (24,9 %). Families in general were monogamous with a very few exceptions. However in the school age group (6-15 years old) which also includes individuals of prenuptial age, significant imbalan-ces existed in male/female distribution. The proportionately very high figure of males in this category (11 % as compared to 6,7 %) portended a serious crisis unless the young men of prenuptial age were able to find wives outside their own community.

In 1971 the classification of the Tayakome inhabitants in 6 year age groups (individual ages being determined by appearance and inferred from family relationships) resulted in the plotting not of a har-monious curve but in a graph with two very clear high points situated in the age brackets 24-30 and 42-48, which leaves a gap corresponding exactly to one generation between the two high points. Before and after the 24 to 30 age group the curve shows downswings which entitle us to conclude that individu-als who in 1971 were between 24 and 30 years old were the mainspring of the original migration which founded the settlement of Tayakome. These young people who were between 17 and 23 (at the time when the majority of the population settled in the village) were those most open to the arguments of Italiano and Martín the village »press gang«. They helped them talk the older generation (42 to 48 years old in 1971) into the scheme. The children of this migrating generation were later born in Tayakome itself 0 to 6 years old in 1971). (See tables 1 and 2).

Table 1

1971 census (before the migration)

A. Absolute figures	Men	Women	Total
Adults	48	52	100
6-15 age group	23	14	37
0-6 age group	39	33	72
Total	110	99	209

B. Percentages	Men	Women	Total
Adults	23%	24,9%	47,9%
6-15 age group	11%	6,7%	17,7%
0-6 age group	18,6%	15,8%	34,4%
Total	52,6%	47,4%	100%

In July 1973 we completed a third population census of Tayakome together with a medical examination of each individual inhabitant and a bio-anthropological survey undertaken by Drs. Jean and Christiane Dricot.

The circumstances in which this census was done were such that the figures quoted are absolutely accurate and that the margin of error over computation of individual ages has been reduced as much as possible.

Table 3

1973 census (after migration)

A. Absolute figures	Men	Women	Total
Adults	22	29	51
6-15 age group	7	3	10
0-6 age group	21	22	43
Total	50	54	104

B. Percentages	Men	Women	Total
Adults	21,1%	27,9%	49%
6-15 age group	6,7%	2,9%	9,6%
0-6 age group	20,2%	21,2%	41,4%
Total	48%	52%	100%

On a basis of these results and assuming that immigration and the mortality rate for 1972-73 compensate each other (both being almost negligible and relating only to two or three individuals) we were able to project a profile of the population which migrated to Camisea. These data appear in table 3.

Table 4 shows the ratios of adults, school age youth and pre-school age youth respectively in 2 communities: that which remained in Tayakome and that which migrated under the leadership of school teacher Martín Vargas to Rio Camisea. For the latter group the ages given in table 4 are those estimated in 1971 plus two.

Table 4

Extrapolation from data on migrant group					Ratio of migrants to non-migrants			
A. Absolute figures	Men	Women	Total		**A. Emigrated to**			
					Rio Camisea	Men	Women	Total
Adults	26	23	49		Adults	54,2%	44,2%	49%
6-15 age group	16	11	27		6-15 age group	65,2%	78,5%	73%
0-6 age group	18	11	29		0-6 age group	48%	33,3%	40,3%
Total	60	45	105		Total	54,5%	45,4%	50,2%
B. Percentages	Men	Women	Total		**B. Remanned in**			
					Tayakome	Men	Women	Total
Adults	24,8%	21,9%	46,7%		Adults	45,8%	55,8%	51%
6-15 age group	15,2%	10,5%	25,7%		6-15 age group	34,8%	21,5%	27%
0-6 age group	17,1%	10,5%	27,6%		0-6 age group	54%	66,7%	59,7%
Total	57,1%	42,9%	100%		Total	45,5%	54,6%	49,8%

These figures reveal that in 1971 the population of Tayakome was almost exactly split into two (50,2 % versus 49,8 %), especially with regard to adults (49 % versus 51 %). By contrast important discrepancies appear in the other age groups: almost 60 % of the pre-school age group remained in Tayakome while almost 75 % of the school age group migrated. Thus this age group (which for reasons previously expounded was already restricted in 1971) was almost unrepresented in Tayakome: 7 males and 3 females!

This leaves no doubt as to the fundamental character of the migration: it was not an independent decision taken by even a part of half the population. This time it was the school age group that was dragged over to Camisea and the parents of children who were displaced with their school had been obliged to follow.

Furthermore, the school age group in a community such as the Machiguengan is not rigidly defined especially in the case of males, since a number of illiterate and monolingual young adults come to school and hence come under the direct influence of the teacher. This becomes apparent in table 5, where the average age of adults is given for 1971 (divided into migrants and non-migrants) and for 1973. The figures for the ages of individuals in each category in Tayakome in 1973 do not correspond exactly to the ages of the non-migrating individuals in 1971 plus two because individual ages have been recomputed as explained above.

Table 5

Average age of adults over 15 years old

	Men	Women	Total
Tayakome 1971 (total)	29,4	29,5	29,4
Migrants 1971	25,7	29,2	27,4
Non-migrants 1971	33,7	29,6	31,5
Tayakome 1973	36,4	31,2	33,2

It is obvious that the adult male population which migrated was mainly young. Older adult males who traditionally have more say in the decisions affecting the community remained in Tayakome.

The enforced character of the migration which occurred in the summer of 1971-1972 under the duress of the removal of the school is further underlined by the fact that a number of school age children are missing in families which remained in Tayakome. Although they lost some of their children these families have refused to follow the movement initiated by school teacher Vargas. Clearly the obverse is not true: there are no school age youth in Tayakome whose parents have migrated to Camisea.

Still to-day within the community remaining in Tayakome there is a dissymmetry owing to the removal of some of the children. Yet parents at the time did not have the tenacity required to oppose the move. This to a great extent is due to the extreme shyness of the Machiguenga unable to deal with conflict between traditional wisdom and authority (which is family based and not capable of speedy and efficient decisions at the community level) and the »Progressive dynamism« of the missionaries and their schools.

Branded as »backwards« in contrast to »forward looking migrants« the inhabitants of Tayakome found in their purely negative attitude of 1971-1972 and in their plaintive discontent of to-day their only means of protecting themselves against the dangers which they in some confusion associated with the *avant-garde* attitude of the migrants yet their ideological position was not sufficiently strong, consistent or explicit to enable them to take a stand against the agents of the SIL and enforce their respect.

In fact, if under evident duress only half the population migrated none can doubt that it was because in 1971 the people generally, and its respected traditional elders even more so, were opposed to migration.

Let us now examine the effect of the 1971-1972 migration on the present population of Tayakome.

As a result of my intervention in the Ministry of Education in January 1972 a school has been maintained in Tayakome led by a young member of the community who was formally and rather too expeditiously designated as school teacher. The decision, however, had no effect on the migration since it was taken after the fact.

After the storm, the village settled down again and to-day lives in excellent physical and unhostile conditions. It has an explosive birthrate encouraged by the change in the male/female ratio (20/32 in 1973 as opposed to 48/52 in 1971) which has contributed to the spread of polygamy that in turn may explain the well-being and good spirits of the villagers. At any rate no one talks of migrating anywhere anymore nor contemplates the return of the »escapees of Camisea«.

It would be interesting to carry out a study of the Machiguenga Indians of Camisea to supplement my own. In Tayakome public rumour maintains – and is confirmed by the accounts of a few travelling Machiguenga – that the settling of Camisea was extremely difficult due to the lack of farm produce. Furthermore if there are many women in Tayakome it follows that there are very few in Camisea. The village leader Italiano once told me about one of the visits of the Institute's small plane when it brought a message requesting the transfer to Camisea of a few women »since there is here a surplus whereas in Camisea there is a lack of them«. Italiano paid no attention and what is more in a spectacular gesture shredded the message slip.

Anyway, since young men exported to Camisea still outnumbered women in the same age group (See table 4) we can only expect that the imbalance will get worse in the next few years.

In the absence of accurate data on the Machiguenga of Camisea, we would rather concentrate our attention on the present settlement of Tayakome. The average age of the adult population (see table 5) has increased as a result of the immigration of almost all the young to Camisea and the addition of extremely few young people to the adult population in Tayakome. Besides this relatively old adult population there is an impressive group of young children: 50 % of the present population of Tayakome is under 12 years old; inevitably between the adults and this surfeit of youth there is a big gap as table 6 clearly shows.

Comparing tables 2 and 6 brings to light the relative aging of the adult population and the increase of the 0-6 age group, which in 1971 represented 34,4% of the total population and in 1973 was 41,4%. In 1973 this discrepancy was further enhanced when the gap between young adults and children widened as a result of the school migration in 1971-1972 and the scarcity particularly of young between 12 and 18 years old.

At present since young people between 12 and 18 do not significantly affect the work and productivity of the community, their reduced numbers have not yet caused inconvenience in the village. But the threat remains for the years to come especially taking account of the fact that the productivity of the present adult population is bound to decline whilst it is likely that the total population will continue to grow. Maybe an immigration »Forest Machiguenga« would partly offset the negative impact of the events just described, but nothing is less certain. Indeed, the immigration has considerably decreased since observation of the community first started.

Turning the clock back and making the »Camisea people« come home is impossible and indeed would not be accepted by the inhabitants of Tayakome to-day who believe that the others »left of their own free will and must now remain where they are«. The only practical and acceptable idea that I could suggest is that school age children who were taken away in 1971-72 should be returned to their parents in Tayakome but only when this would raise no psychological or social problems. Although I have made no inquiries on the subject (so as not to draw the attention of the Tayakome inhabitants to a remote and

Table 2 – 1971 census

	0-6	6-12	12-18	18-24	24-30	30-36	36-42	42-48	48-54	54-60	60-66	66-72	72-78	Total
Men	39	17	11	9	17	7	2	7	0	0	0	0	1	110
Women	33	11	7	11	19	8	2	4	0	1	2	1	0	99
Total	72	28	18	20	36	15	4	11	0	1	2	1	1	209

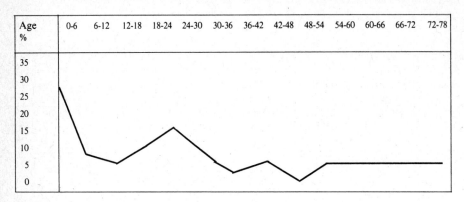

Table 6 – 1973 census

	0-6	6-12	12-18	18-24	24-30	30-36	36-42	42-48	48-54	54-60	60-66	66-72	72-78	Total
Men	21	7	1	4	5	4	2	5	0	0	0	0	1	50
Women	22	1	4	7	9	5	1	3	0	0	1	1	0	54
Total	43	3	5	11	14	9	3	8	0	0	1	1	1	104

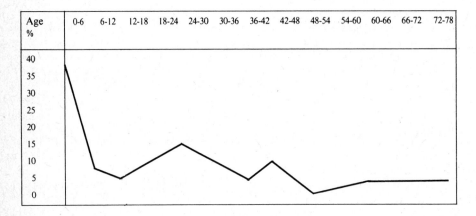

utopian solution) the return of the young people to their community still appears feasible. Their re-integration would in fact give the Tayakome settlement greater balance and better prospects for the future.

But these are not circumstances which can be patched up anyhow *a posteriori*. The situation in Tayakome is characteristic of a whole process which goes far beyond the particular case described and for which there is no single piecemeal solution.

Tayakome could be considered as a model for a new hybrid – the village-post – which would be the first stage of an »integration process« started in »the wild« and culminating in the »peonization« of Amazonian Indians in small villages along the banks of bigger rivers (in this case the Urubamba). In these settlements the Indians would co-exist with Indian-migrants and other mestizos in the same precarious circumstances with regard to food, health and scarce opportunities for decently paid work, all subject to the same employers and unscrupulous traders who organised for their own profit the exchange of goods and work.

In the initial stage of this process (the »wilderness« stage) no one until now has explained why there is resistance to the implementation of the first stage. In Tayakome we observed that the village leader Italiano, originally a progressive element, gradually fought a rear guard battle. Unsuited by birth and by his experience to the traditional lifestyle but equally ill adjusted to white life Italiano was satisfied with the leadership of a community where his knowledge of the outside world and his eloquence on the subject was the basis of his prestige. He carefully avoided any situation where his inabilities successfully to confront concrete problems arising from the white world could damage his prestige.

Martín on the other hand was much more westernized, he knew the value of things and of money. It worked out that as a bilingual teacher he earned a salary that in effect was higher than the aggregate incomes of the whole community. But in Tayakome having a lot of money did not mean enjoying more social prestige, nor was there any point in accumulating the goods that money could buy. In the socio-cultural context of Tayakome, radios, record-players, tape-recorders, sewing machines, outboard engines and so on, were far beyond the means of most inhabitants and thus they were not objects of envy. Far from giving prestige to their owner they rather confirmed the general impression of social and cultural extra-territoriality.

On the shores of the big river, however, money and the goods it could purchase ensured the bilingual teacher's prestige in the eyes of the *cholos* and others of mixed ethnic origin who envied him. There is a general trend among rural teachers (except for those who feel they have deep roots in their community) to try to move closer to bigger centres for economic as well as social reasons. When they succeed it is because they can be transferred to another school. The bilingual teacher in contrast is forever tied to his school and the only way he has of getting closer to larger villages is to tear away with his school, its pupils and the latters' parents!

Unfortunately the progressive attitudes typical of the biligual teacher make him play on a limited level the same role as the oligarchies pledged to a foreign and narcissistic form of development and who sacrifice to this ideal the well-being and peace of their fellow citizens abandoning them to their poverty and their repeatedly broken hopes of real progress.

In Tayakome these historic trends are represented by Martín, »the progressive« and by Italiano, »the nationalist«, and beyond them by approximately 200 people whom I know by name. But this is not a personal problem. At no point in this article have I wanted to argue *ad hominem* against certain institutions, their staff or even Italiano and Martín because I like them and was friendly towards both of them. I appreciated their personalities and their strengths. Yet this very friendship has made it necessary to explain how, for reasons beyond their will or control, they became involved in a deadlock which turned them into agents of the tragic degeneration of their community, once free and proud and peaceful, into a pathetic ethnic minority.

Lima, December 1973.

Postscript.

I had to wait until November 1975 before I could once again visit the new community of Segakiato settled by Martín and his followers on the Upper Camisea, and I found them in a rather absurd situation.

First, considering that one of the reasons given by the SIL for moving the Machiguenga to Camisea was that Tayakome was far from the SIL's base in Yarinacocha and that providing for the community's needs in Camisea would be cheaper, things in fact turned out very expensively since the whole transfer cost the SIL one seaplane. In fact during the autumn of 1974 when the Machiguenga who had migrated to Camisea still had not finished the airstrip in Segakiato so that the SIL was still obliged to land its seaplane on the river, the pilot decided one day to overnight in the village and he moored his plane in a quiet bend of the river. During the night a flash flood washed it away and the wreckage can still be seen at various points down river from Camisea.

Today towards the end of 1975 thanks to strenuous collective efforts the community of Segakiato have finished the building of a beautiful airstrip. Meanwhile unfortunately the SIL has definitely cancelled its plane visits to the village.

Furthermore, another reason given for the migration was that the Machiguenga would be able to »develop« and enter into trade activities prohibited in the National Park (sale of skins, lumbering, and animal husbandry). The facts have turned out differently: the Machiguenga of Segakiato to-day are more isolated and neglected than those of Tayakome. Innumerable prohibitions and the new legislation on forest fauna have been fatal to skin hunting and their geographical isolation has meant that the Machiguenga of Segakiato have until now been unable to sell even one piece of timber.

The only signs of »developments« in Segakiato are the five heads of cattle given by the SIL. Their extreme leanness and dejection is proof that they are not kept for ornamental reasons and yet on the other hand neither can they be of any use to anyone. Another ludicrous development is that teacher Martín Vargas now has a teaching assistant, Victoriano Melchor Marosso, a Machiguenga from Timpia who earns 4000 soles per month despite the fact that according to statistics provided by Martín there are no more than 120 inhabitants in Segakiato of whom 30 are enrolled in the school and of these a full four in the highest class: 3rd grade of Primary school.

In Segakiato where the present population with a few exceptions is the same group which migrated from Tayakome in 1973 there are 20 children between 6 and 10 years old (statistics recently recorded by Martín which I had no time to verify during my short stay but which seemed to be reliable). Martín himself, now longhaired and unkempt, seems to have lost much of his enthusiasm. Just like his fellow villagers he seems to have forgotten why they moved from Manu to Camisea, and does not seem convinced that things are better here than they were there or vice versa. The angriest commments were that after all efforts that had gone into building the airstrip »the gringo no longer came with his planes – but what can we do?«.

Impartiality prompts me to emphasize that concurrently with the foregoing the interest shown by the Department of Forestry and Hunting for the Park Indians started waning slowly in 1973-74 and later reached the depths of serene indifference. This in part was due to the lack of funds which the National Park needs and has until now not been given to recruit sufficient staff to carry out its basic activities. The integrity of the institution itself was rocked when the Department of Forestry was unable to prevent oil companies from carrying out their seismic surveys within the boundaries of the National Park (but not within the area inhabited by the Machiguenga).

I myself have not travelled again to Tayakome since 1973. Under present circumstances it seems unlikely that within a conceivable future I should be given permission to return.

According to reports from confidential sources confirmed by anthropo-biologist Jean Dricot, Italiano and his families continued to live in relative tranquility with one major change: freed from outside intervention of any sort the majority of the Tayakome villagers have scattered to settle again a short distance from Tayakome in small clusters according to their traditional housing patterns. At the moment that is all that one would wish for them.

Nevertheless one can fear that the original intentions of the park promotors – which I opposed vehemently throughout the period of my consultantship – will in time be brought forward once again, namely that the Machiguenga population of the Park should be moved and resettled outside the Park boundaries.

Iquitos, January 1976.

3) Towards the nationalization of bilingual education

When a country decides to become economically independent its first step should be to nationalize foreign firms unfairly exploiting its manpower and natural resources. This would presuppose expropriation of the existing infrastructure. Such expropriations although not in themselves real objectives, nevertheless are the only means for the dominated country to regain access to its own wealth while ensuring uninterrupted employment and production.

In fact, in the basic sector especially (agriculture, mining industry, etc.), the real concern when the revolutionary process has started is to maintain production even if it means relying on the imperialist infrastructure which by design does not make full use of the country's natural resources or provide equitable working conditions. In time, and in so far as the revolution can create new systems of production, it is conceivable that this infrastructure can be replanned so that production targets are in harmony with national development objectives.

In other words what I want to say here is that copper and sugar for instance when produced by imperialist firms are products in the strict sense of the term and are worth no more and no less than the same items produced by nationalized firms. From this I conclude that as a first step in the implementation of revolutionary tactics aimed at achieving economic independence, the government is entirely justified in confiscating and operating the imperialist technical machinery used for the production of copper and sugar.

Well then, what will ensure success when the country wants to become culturally independent? One might for instance consider putting a definite stop to the activites of foreign agencies, such as the Summer Institute of Linguistics, which for more than 30 years – under cover of scientific research and religious teaching – has unbelievably achieved a monopoly on the education of almost all »ethnic minorities« in an independent state such as Peru. Availing itself of numerous privileges granted by former governments, the SIL has systematically indoctrinated the native Indians and sought to teach them a meritocratic model of development based on individualism and personal profit. Thus the SIL upheld in our native communities the harsh and rigid rule of behavior of the most reactionary social group of its own country. And yet this standard is absolutely opposed not only to the traditional life-styles of Peruvian ethnic groups but also to the avowed policy of the revolutionary government.

With regard to the SIL and the termination of the cultural dependence which their very presence in the country has entailed the terms »nationalization« and »utilization of existing infra-structures« have to be used in a fundamentally different praxis from that used in the struggle to liberate the country from economic dependence. In fact if the SIL is considered as an imperialist firm at least we can say that in contrast to copper and sugar its present production – the cultural alienation of our ethnic groups and introduction into their midst of a capitalist mentality – is of absolutely no interest to us.

This is worth noting at a time when apparently cautious, sensible people are calling attention to the »risks« involved in the immediate and complete departure of the SIL. According to them there would be insufficient staff for the moment to take over from the SIL and run the institution without its agents.

For these great minds, the sheer size of the imperialist monster created in Yarinacocha holds a strange fascination similar to that held over the minds of savages by multi-coloured beads. In both cases the outsider exerts domination by dangling in front of the spectator's eyes something fundamentally foreign to the necessities of life. Yet if a clever speech is delivered at the same time one forgets the object's complete uselessness and accepts any compromise in order to own one. In the same way some people believe that what is important now is to ensure the uninterrupted operation of the base in Yarinacocha, and to this end temporarily protect if not the SIL itself at least the greater part of its staff until such a time when they can be replaced by Peruvians.

Let us however pause to think. Is is perchance a question of housing a Peruvian linguist and his family in each of the houses now sheltering a North American missionary »linguist«? Is it a question of putting a Peruvian pilot in each of the SIL's planes and a Peruvian technician to operate the radio and telegraph at the base in Yarinacocha? In brief is it a question of letting the SIL continue exactly as before once North American missionaries have left? Of course not. Revolutionary integrity demands a global condemnation of the SIL's past activities and a questioning of its basic organization since its infrastructure may have been so coloured by the goals and attitudes of the disavowed institution as to be incompatible with the objectives of nationalized education. To persist in wanting to use this structure would thus be equal to giving the policies we rightly condemn to-day a new lease of life for the future.

It is odd that the true problem at hand namely the nationalization of the education of native Peruvian communities has been side-stepped in favour of a debate on the need to nationalize the SIL. To permit its continued operation without any fundamental changes would be an endorsement of all its former activities as if there was no alternative. Yet if we really think about it there is no reason why bilingual education should not be made available to Amazonian Indians without planes, radios, or even without linguists as has been well proved – at least on the latter score – by the SIL itself which for many years has operated without a trained linguist of any repute but with a limited number of mediocre, »summer«, pseudo-linguists.

The resources to be nationalized in this case are educational institutions including teachers and teaching assistants, the latter being the labour force that has been diverted from its original goals by a capitalist enterprise. Yet, I repeat, what this enterprise produced is of no interest to us since it was an alienating education which directly advocated a view of the world, of economic relations and of social organization totally out of step with traditional patterns as well as with modern Peru.

Educational institutes working within the framework of a nationalized educational system will be aiming at very different end-products. If according to the spirit so clearly embodied in our laws we acknowledge that the most essential element in the process is the collective efforts of basic communities, since they – when they are indigenous – have committed to the new civic ethics all their creative power and cultural uniqueness, then it is obvious that it will be their responsibility and later their federation's or association's responsibility to organize the educational system. Conversely the structure set up by the SIL is gigantic, extremely expensive, bureaucratic, paternalistic, technocratic and oriented towards the towns. It is and always will be a factor of disintegration for communities mainly because it founds its educational program on the special status of the teacher in relation to his community.

With these considerations in mind I hope that our national experts in bilingual education will tear themselves away from the dangerous fascination which could be exerted by the Yarinacocha-base and the vast machinery which the SIL will bequeath to Peru when it withdraws. These buildings and this machinery can be put to a hundred other uses by those who truly serve and help local populations. But to convince ourselves of their fundamental unsuitability in a national and bilingual education, why should we mutilate our future educational initiatives and insist on using a counterproductive, expensive machinery when the revolution daily gives us the will to solve our problems through efficient, cheap means based on the collective conscience and efforts of our local communities?

Atalaya, November 1975

Biographical note

During my seven years in Peru approximately half my time was spent on field work in the Amazonian region more especially in the river basis of Madre de Dios, Purus, Urubamba and the upper Ucayali. At first this field work consisted in linguistic and ethnologic research. It later centred on more practical issues relating to community organization.

I worked in Peru from June 1969 to August 1976 except for a 4-month stay in Europe between June and October 1971 and two semesters when I taught in Paris between November 1974 and August 1975. During these yeare I consecutively filled the following posts:

1. From June 1969 to June 1971 I was a Belgian Government expert and my job was to create a teaching and research group on Amazonian linguistics at the Universidad Nacional Mayor de San Marcos (Lima). In accordance with a special agreement with the Ministry of Agriculture I also became the evaluator of the Anthropological Programme of Manu National Park.

2. From October 1971 to October 1974 in my capacity of Senior Professor at the Department of Linguistics of the University of San Marcos I continued the work that I had started two years before as a government expert. In 1971 and 1972 I was also asked by the Ministry of Education to collaborate with the study group working on the Education Reform and the policy paper on Bilingual Education.

3. From August 1975 to August 1976 after a 10 month absence I returned to Peru as a consultant for the United Nations. As an anthropologist I had been asked to circumscribe what was to be done for »ethnic minorities« within the context of project PER/75/012 »Development of the East« on which the UNDP (United Nations Development Programme) and the National Planning Institute cooperated.

Evangelization and Political Control: the SIL in Mexico

by JAN RUS and ROBERT WASSERSTROM

I. Mexico: Proving Ground For the Word

In their official history of the Wycliffe Bible Translators (1959), Ethel Wallis and Mary Bennett describe that fateful day in 1936 when William Cameron Townsend first met President Lázaro Cárdenas of Mexico. The encounter took place in Tetelcingo, a Náhuatl village where, after much prayer and deliberation, Townsend, his wife and niece had a few months earlier established their first Mexican mission. Townsend was already familiar with Cárdenas' hostility toward organized religion; indeed, such hostility had constituted a serious stumbling block for his undertaking. Still, that day in Tetelcingo, he must have felt that the Lord Himself had softened Caesar's heart. In his diary he wrote:

> For nearly an hour we had the undreamed-of privilege of entertaining the chief ruler of the land in our tiny quarters... He assured us that his government was going to put an end to the persecution of religion. When he looked at the garden, he asked pointedly if the young people we wanted to bring to Mexico to translate the Bible would help the Indians in the practical way we were doing...
> »This is just what Mexico needs,« the president (said). »Bring all that you can get to come«
> (Wallis and Bennett 1959:89-90).

What might Cárdenas' thoughts have been that evening as he drove back to Mexico City and the affairs of State that awaited him? Unfortunately, we can only guess what his feelings about Townsend truly were. By 1936, his government had reached a sort of watershed. Only a decade earlier, his predecessor, Plutarco Elías Calles, had fought a bloody civil war of four years' duration in the north-central part of the country. Spurred by the cry of »Long Live Christ the King!« peasant farmers like those in Tetelcingo had taken up arms against the government in an effort of defend both their land and their religion. Behind this uprising, one could clearly discern the seditious influence of Church hierarchs and wealthy landlords. Indeed, peace was finally restored only after the papal nuncio in Mexico City had negotiated a treaty with Calles' government. By the time that Cárdenas was elected, however, conspiratorial rumblings had once again obliged the new president to close the country's churches. Thereafter he embarked upon a program of agrarian reform which not only provided Mexico's peasants with the means of subsistence, but also deprived his principal enemies of their landed estates.

As Cárdenas well knew, however, land reform alone could not transform the nation's economy, much less modify the terms on which Mexico confronted its powerful nothern neighbor. In 1936, this task still lay before him; it was accomplished (at least in part) two years later when he nationalized foreign petroleum interests. Naturally, American investors were quick to represent his actions as treacherously Bolshevik and to demand the intercession of their government. For the next four years, relations between Mexico and the United States were strained almost to the breaking point; even then,

Robert Wasserstrom teaches anthropology at Columbia University in New York. Between 1973 and 1977 he lived in Chiapas, Mexico and worked as a research fellow at the Centro de Investigaciones Ecológicas del Sureste.

Jan Rus is an anthropologist who has worked in Peru and Mexico. In 1975-77, he was coordinator of the anthropology program at the Universidad Autónoma de Chiapas. He now lives near Los Angeles, and works with undocumented laborers in southern California.

four more years were required before these relations returned to normal. Anticipating such difficulties, Cárdenas possessed two reasons to view Townsend and his American missionaries as god-sends. First, they provided an example to the hard work and self-discipline which his newly-formed agrarian communities *(ejidos)* required in order to prosper and grow. And whereas in previous years several of Cárdenas' more zealous officers had ridden around the countryside buring religious effigies and destroying relics, Townsend pursuaded his converts to forsake their saints voluntarily. Second, Townsend maintained close ties with right-wing politicians and businessmen in the United States – men who were not favorably disposed toward Cárdenas' government. By using his influence with these men, he became one of the president's staunchest allies and defenders. Among his numerous published works on religious and linguistic subjects, therefore, one is not surprised to find a loving biography of the man who opened Mexico to the Word of God (*Lázaro Cárdenas: Mexican Democrat,* 1952).

In order to understand this strange marriage of convenience between foreign missionaries and nationalist politicians, we must consider for a moment the origins of Townsend's interest in Latin America. As we might expect, he had begun his activities not in Tetelcingo, but in Guatemala almost twenty years earlier. According to Clarence Hall, a senior editor of the *Readers' Digest,*

> Cam Townsend early developed his urge for spreading the Christian gospel. Back in 1917, when he was 21, he quit Occidental College in Los Angeles, packed a trunk with Spanish-language Bibles and headed for Guatemala. He soon found his Bibles a drug on the market. More than two-thirds of Guatemala's population were Indians: few knew Spanish, fewer still showed any hankering to learn.
>
> One day an Indian to whom Cam had offered a copy of the Bible demanded, »Why, if your God is so smart, hasn't He learned our language?« Then and there, Townsend quit Bible distribution in favor of giving God another tongue.
>
> For the next 15 years he lived with the primitive Cakchiquel tribe in Guatemala, eating their food (one diet item: toasted ants), mastering their difficult tongue, gradually reducing it to written form. Slowly and laboriously, he developed a simplified method for teaching any phonetically written language.
>
> When finally in 1932, racked with tuberculosis, Townsend rode out again to civilization on a mule, he left the Cakchiquel Indians with five schools, a small hospital, a printing plant, scores of small churches and hundreds of literate converts to Christianity. In Cam Townsend's soul was exultation: in his saddlebags was a printed copy, in the hitherto unwritten Cakchiquel language, of the entire New Testament (Hall 1958:4).

Significantly, however, Townsend did not abandon Guatemala before he had made the acquaintance of Moisés Sáenz, a Presbyterian and at that time Mexico's Undersecretary of Public Education. As an anthropologist and political liberal, Sáenz had grappled with the twin problems of bilingualism and native instruction. Unlike many of his colleagues, Sáenz recognized the futility of teaching Indian children to read and write Spanish before they had learned to speak the language. For much the same reasons, he suspected that primary school curricula developed in Mexico City for mestizo children might be inadequate or inappropriate for use in native communities. At this critical point, in 1931, he visited Guatemala, where he is said to have run into Townsend on the streets of Panajachel. Acording to one historian,

> Townsend took Sáenz to his school and told him of the literacy campaigns which he and his associates had been conducting to teach the Indians to read the Bible in their own language... On the spot, Sáenz invited Townsend to go to Mexico and to do the same thing among his country's native people. Sáenz promised the support of his government, and more importantly, he reminded Townsend that Mexico could provide his literacy work the stimulus of a social movement which Guatemala had not yet experienced (Heath 1972:154).

During the next four years, Townsend prepared himself to extend this ministry to other parts of the heathen world. By 1936, he was ready to test his amplified training in linguistics in a much more ambitious undertaking: a major attack on the native languages of Mexico. It was at this point, as he crossed the Mexican border, that he revealed an attitude of political pragmatism which has characterized SIL throughout its lifetime. »As soon as he had trained a few in his linguistic method,« Hall writes,

*Townsend and his students headed for Mexico. They were stopped at the border, bluntly told,
»We don't want translators. The Indian languages must disappear.« Townsend responded, »They
disappear more rapidly if you use the Indians' languages to teach them Spanish« (Hall 1958:5).*

On the surface, this remark suggests that Townsend, like Mexican authorities of the day, believed that
native groups must assimilate in order to progress. In fact, Townsend's reply masked a far subtler political program, a program which he eventually explained in Wycliffe's *Mexican Branch Handbook* (1956).
First and foremost, he declared, translators should concentrate upon spreading the Gospel to unconver-
ted Indians. This ideal he placed far above the narrow and short-sighted goals of Indianist bureaucrats.
After all, he implied, indigenous languages would not disappear in the near future, perhaps never.
Still, he explained, the success or failure of Wycliffe's enterprise, indeed the ability of foreign missionaries to remain in Mexico, depended upon the good will of precisely such bureaucrats. Under these
circumstances, he encouraged his followers to be less than candid in their political relations, to reveal
only so much of their business as non-translators might readily understand. »It is better,« he worte in
1956,

> *to tell just as much of the story as people can absorb and say that we have come to study the
> Indian languages and help the Indians in every way possible including ... winning them away
> from witchcraft. Let the people see our lives before we ... brand ourselves unconditionally as
> »protestants...« (Townsend 1956:12)*

Transparent though they were, such policies proved to be extremely effective in dealing with Mexican
authorities, who continued for many years to view Bible translators as more or less passive instruments
of their official will. To a large extent, SIL's success as a global enterprise may be traced precisely to its
early skill in identifying its purposes with those of the country's political leaders. By emphasizing the
linguistic aspects of their work, for example, Townsend was able to cultivate his relationship not only
with Sáenz, but also with another important anthropologist, Mariano Silva y Aceves. In turn, these men
helped him to set up operations in Tetelcingo and encouraged Cárdenas to pay his celebrated visit in
1936. Looking back on these experiences, one Wycliffe chronicler summarized the process whereby SIL
began its long and close relationship with the Mexican government. »In 1933,«

> *a party of ten entered Mexico, and while on this trip Townsend was invited to attend the seventh
> Inter-American Scientific Congress, in Mexico City. Important contacts were made, and SIL was
> born. Mr. Townsend started work in Tetelcingo--an Aztec village near Mexico City. Word of
> Townsend's work reached President Cárdenas, who soon visited Tetelcingo and was favorably
> impressed with the work of SIL. Such contacts led to friendly relations with people in high places,
> and close cooperation between government and SIL (WBT 1970).*

Once such friendships had been made, SIL took care to broaden and maintain them – a task which was
greatly facilitated after 1948, when Mexico's Instituto Nacional Indigenista (National Indian Institute)
was founded. From the start, INI functionaries – including SIL's academic allies of previous years –
assumed an attitude toward native peoples which did not differ significantly from that of Wycliffe translators. With missionary zeal, they turned their considerable resources against what they perceived to be
the three pillars of Indian backwardness: alcoholism, witchcraft (a sign of pathological ignorance) and
monolingualism. To combat these evils, they intended not simply to provide isolated groups with basic
social services, but rather to civilize them in a much broader sense. Sensitive as always to the prevailing
political winds, Townsend was quick to cast his activities in similar terms. Consider, for example, the
extraordinary interview which *Tiempo,* a popular newsmagazine, published in late 1957 with SIL worker
Marianna Slocum. Describing her experiences among Tzeltal people in the state of Chiapas, Slocum is
reported to have delivered the following *indigenista* homily:

> *19 years, ago, several communities in the Tzeltal tribe led a monotonuos, backward, ancestral
> kind of life, which did not reflect the cultural and spiritual progress of the rest Mexico. From
> his birth without a cradle to his death without a grave, the Tzeltal slid through time without a
> single innovation in his customs. The children were born without medical attention, grew up
> without a school, were limited to speaking Tzeltal, wore the simple clothes of their ancestors, and
> upon reaching adulthood, worshipped the Sun, made sacrifices to the »lords of the mountains,«*

feared witches and terrorized their neighbors with magic and witchcraft... This primitive state of affairs underwent a revolutionary change when, eight years ago, the winds of civilization and humanism swept away the tragic obscurantism in which the majority of Tzeltales' were drowning. Today, more than five thousand inhabitants of Oxchuc, Cancuc, Tenango and many other towns in Chiapas have set out firmly on the road to civilization (Tiempo 1957:3-4).

Despite minor tactical disagreements, then, it is not surprising that SIL offered its services as a source of expert help in the field of native literacy to the Ministry of Education. In 1951, both agencies signed a formal agreement in which they pledged to

> *cooperate in the investigation of native languages throughout the Republic, and to study in a detailed fashion the cultural and biological characteristics of Mexico's native groups, as well as any other factors which might help in their betterment (Tiempo 1957:8).*

Among other things, SIL members agreed to serve as interpreters for government officials in Indian areas, to train rural schoolteachers in linguistics, to »prepare primers in native languages so that those illiterates who speak indigenous tongues may learn to read and write Spanish,« to »develop bilingual primers (Spanish-Indian) with the intention of facilitating the use of the official language,« and to translate »laws, advice on hygiene, agriculture, leather curing and other industries, as well as books of high moral or patriotic value.« In return, the Ministry committed itself to secure residence permits for Wycliffe personnel »as scientific researchers in government service,« to obtain for them exemptions from certain taxes and to allow them to construct their facilities on Federal land. Moreover, many SIL workers now became official consultants within INI's newly-formed system of regional centers, training stations which prepared virtually all of the country's native schoolteachers. Apparently, both sides were highly satisfied with such arrangements: in 1961, President Adolfo López Mateos declared of Bible translators that »Their work has achieved notable success and my government will continue to back such a transcendental task« (quoted in Beekman and Hefley 1968:22).

II. The Word Comes to Chiapas: Missionaries and Medicine men among the Maya, 1938-1977

Up to this point, we have seen how SIL members, under Townsend's direction sought to be all things to all men: burning evangelists to North American supporters, disinterested scientists to Mexican authorities. And yet, neither of these two *personae,* so necessary a part of Wycliffe's public face, explains the tremendous success which Bible translators have enjoyed among the country's native population. How, exactly, did SIL manage to breach the defences of ethnic groups that had resisted cultural and spiritual conquest for centuries? What effects did such conquests have upon these people? In order to answer these questions, so vital to our understanding of missionary activity, it is useful to consider two case studies of successful evangelization in Chiapas, home today of almost half a million Maya people (se map).

Chiapas is a particularly appropriate place to begin such an investigation because, together with the neighboring state of Oaxaca, it has attracted the attention of SIL workers since the days of Tetelcingo. In 1938, for example, SIL member William Bentley had set up headquarters in the town of Yajalón, a marketing center for approximately 50,000 rural Tzeltales. Two years later, he was followed in the region by Marianna Slocum and Evelyn Woodward. Despite the hostility of many local residents, by 1947 Slocum had translated the Gospel of Mark into Tzeltal with the result that, as Wallis and Bennett inform us, »a number of Indians... had turned from their idols and wanted a chapel where they could worship the Lord...« (1959:138). Within two more years, Slocum, now joined by Florence Gerbel, a professional nurse, founded an active Protestant congregation in the hamlet of Corralito. Working from this base, they proceeded to spread their message to indigenous communities elsewhere in the central highlands. »By the end of 1950,« write Wallis and Bennett,

> *the group of believers had grown to more than a thousand, and smaller gatherings... were springing up throughout the mountainous area around Corralito. Still the Tzeltals came over the*

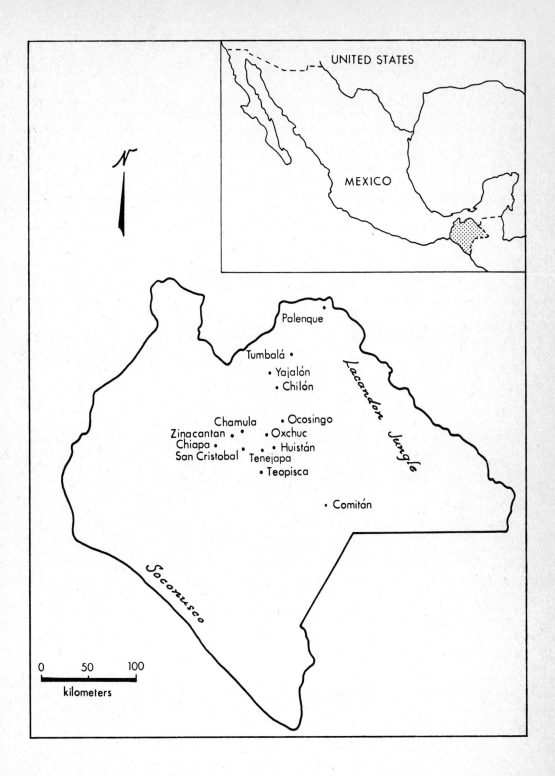

long rugged trails to the clinic... where Florence was doctoring from morning until night, and praying with the patients as well. As many were cured by prayer as by medicine, but Florence used both (1959:139-40).

From this moment onward, missionary activity in central Chiapas increased at a dramatic rate. By 1954, a version of the New Testament in Tzeltal had been completed and 150 native lay preachers had been trained to spread the Word in their *pueblos*. Similar events were occurring a few miles to the north, near the pre-Colombian ruins at Palenque, where SIL translators John and Elaine Beekman had begun work in 1947 among Chol people. In both regions, these missionaries made strategic use of modern medicine to impress upon local residents the superiority of their God over traditional curers. Antibiotics and the Word: these became the twin arms which SIL members wielded in their struggle for indigenous souls. In 1957, for example, according to Wallis and Bennett, Gerbel and another Wycliffe nurse, Avis Crowder, organized their own system of health care in several communities. Under the supervision of John Kempers, a physician and fundamentalist missionary,

> *a spacious new clinic was erected... to replace the rustic building in Corralito. There Tzeltal male nurses are now being trained to do simple medical work and teach hygiene along with the preaching of the Word of God (Wallis and Bennett 1959:142).*

By this time, too, missionaries were reaping the benefits of political and social windfalls not entirely of their own creation. By 1942, agrarian reform in Mexico had essentially come to a halt. In its place, conservative national administrations, anxious to sell raw materials in the American market, permitted large landholdings to be reconstituted and private *hacendados* to dominate agricultural production. In Chiapas, one result of these policies was that many Tzeltal and Chol communities began to feel the renewed pressures of local cattle ranchers and coffee growers. As land in these communities became scarcer, disputes over ownership and power frequently gave rise to bitter factional feuds. In turn, such feuds often led to homicides and house-burnings, events which deeply impressed observers like Slocum and the Beekmans. For their part, American missionaries proved only too willing to accept the idea suggested by local informants – that violence of this sort traced its origins to witchcraft and superstition. After all, such views merely confirmed their suspicions that indigenous culture was hopelessly immoral and depraved. Taking advantage (perhaps unwittingly) of such divisions, then, these missionaries invariably concentrated their attention on members of the weakest faction – men and women who converted to Protestantism as a means of asserting their independence from traditional authorities. Unfortunately, this *dénouement* not unusually led to renewed killings, now under the guise of a religious conflict.

As SIL workers in Chiapas came to understand these events more clearly, they seem to have become genuinely distressed by the economic and political conditions in which native people lived. Almost uniformly, they sought to meliorate this situation by helping Protestant converts to emigrate from their ancestral communities. In the Chol region, for example, Beekman arranged for local believers to purchase lands near their original *pueblos,* in the virgin tropical rainforest south of Palenque. Among Tzeltales, however, no such solution lay close at hand: in order to colonize the jungle, these men and women were forced to abandon their traditional territory altogether. Nonethless, by the mid-1950's, many of them had left their homes entirely to established pioneer settlements in the forest. Thereafter, as land pressure in the highlands decreased, traditional leaders came to terms with those non-conformists who had stayed behind. In this way, a clear pattern was established: rather than fight for land reform and increased political justice in the highlands, many of the region's most active and capable young men in effect changed their religion and moved away. The jungle was virgin territory, and if the missionaries did not mismanage their affairs, it would be Protestant.

Although this movement surely merits a more extensive examination, we shall now turn our attention to the actions of Wycliffe translators in another part of the central highlands, that is, among Tzotzil people to the west. Like their Tzeltal neighbors, Tzotziles drew the attention of Wycliffe missionaries in the early 1940's. And yet, in sharp contrast to the rapid success which SIL workers enjoyed in towns like Yajalón, Palenque and Oxchuc, among Tzotziles they labored largely in vain until the late 1960's and early 1970's. At that time, however, after almost a decade of rising political turmoil, SIL-trained lay preachers began to score impressive victories in community after community. Most significantly, they established a beachhead in Chamula, a conservative *municipio* of 50,000 inhabitants. Significantly, the men of Chamula had for generations earned their livelihoods as migrant laborers on Chiapas' rich coffee plantations. This fact had not been lost upon the men who managed the State's Department of Indian Affairs, men who had attempted deliberately and with considerable calculation to preserve the *status quo* in Chamula. To this end, after 1936 they appointed a series of native *caciques,* political bosses whom they charged with a difficult administrative task: to moderate and direct social change in such a way that the flow of Indians to coffee *fincas* might continue unperturbed. In fact, it was the very repressiveness and illegitimacy of this system which eventually allowed foreign missionaries to undermine traditional practices and introduce their own religious creed.

In order to understand these events, we must examine briefly the behavior of native political bosses in the years which followed 1940, that is, the period which began at the close of Cárdenas' term as president. By that time, many young *caciques* has already gained a measure of political experience as representatives of the *Sindicato de Trabajadores Indígenas* (Native Workers' Union, an organization created in 1936 by the government primarily to contract coffee laborers). Within a short time, however, it had become clear to State officials that these young men – ambitious and bilingual – were ideally suited to perform more complicated political functions. During Cárdenas' administration, then, they had gradually assumed control not only of municipal government in Tzotzil *pueblos,* but also of the region's agrarian reform committees – a position which enabled them (with the complicity of higher authorities) to acquire significant properties of their own. Thereafter, they engaged in a variety economic activities – such as rum-running and money-lending – which enhanced enormously their own personal fortunes. Even so, they did neglect to invest a small part of their profits in religious office, a form of community service through which their forebears had traditionally obtained prestige and recognition. By the early 1950's, in fact, they had displaced village elders both as political leaders and as guardians of religious orthodoxy. And finally, using both their influence and their knowledge of Spanish, they also became bilingual teachers in INI primary schools. From then on, they became *caciques* in every sense: literally no aspect of communal life escaped their control or domination.

As long as this situation persisted, SIL missionaries made little headway in any of the towns where *caciques* had established their unshakable rule (Chamula, Zinacantan, Chenalhó, Huistán, and the Tzeltal community of Tenejapa). For potential converts, the risks of evangelization were too great: by defying local authorities, they exposed themselves to social ostracism, economic ruin, or even a fatal dose of witchcraft (usually administered by machete along isolated mountain trails). For the moment, then, Wycliffe workers became reconciled to the fact that they could expect to win few converts, nor even to work directly on the task of Bible translation. Rather than swim against the tide, they offered their services to local agencies as translators and literacy specialists. In 1951, for example, Ken and Nadine Weathers, who had labored unsuccessfully in Zinacantan and Chamula for more than 15 years, began to train bilingual teachers for INI. In this way, they hoped to overcome resistance to their message – or at least to maintain contact with those communities where they had not established their own base of operations. Ironically, perhaps, among their students they encountered the very same *caciques* who had effectively blocked their work in Tzotzil *municipios.*

By the early 1960's, however, these *caciques* had begun to feel new and unaccustomed pressures, pressures which may be traced to two distinct but interrelated sources. On the one hand, the Native Workers' Union found itself unable to discipline native laborers effectively and allocate them among the coffee *fincas.* On the contrary, for a variety of reasons, plantation owners preferred to recruit their workforce directly – a workforce which now included as many as 8000 Mam Indians from Guatemala. Then, too, many Tzotziles began to rent additional lands from cattle ranchers in the central part of Chiapas, an activity which permitted them to avoid wage labor altogether. On the other hand, by this time a significant number of young men and women had received at least some schooling; quite a few were also employed as teachers in INI schools. Although at first these people had been political supporters of local bosses (to whom they frequently owed their jobs), within a short time they came to resent the degree to which their lives depended upon favoritism and patronage. Rather than risk their fortunes on a palace coup (a coup which would not have succeeded without the support of State officials) they made common cause with Indian sharecroppers, coffee laborers and smallscale traders, that is, with all of those men who no longer depended upon the favor of municipal authorities.

In Chamula, both old resentments and new alliances remained hidden for several years beneath the surface of daily life. Then, in 1968, they suddenly burst into the open, a direct challenge to boss rule and the entire structure of official corruption upon which such rule relied. Led by dissatisfied teachers, many

Chamulas (perhaps one-third of the *municipio's* population) refused to pay a particularly arbitrary and unjustifiable new taw, a tax that had been levied by local *caciques* to finance their own personal projects. As bosses and dissidents jockeyed for political position, confrontation and violence supplanted conspiracy and intrigue as the order to the day. Embarrassed by these events, and worried that the example of dissent might spread to other communities, State authorities eventually moved to restore the *status quo*. In 1973 and 1974, they sent troops to Chamula to disperse the opposition party and imprison its leaders. By the end of that time, therefore, 150 of these unfortunates had been jailed, men who were released only after they had promised to withdraw from politics altogether. And in at least one case, that promise took 10 months to exact.

Until this moment, SIL missionaries in Chamula had made little headway in their efforts to win converts. As disaffection with the *caciques* grew, however, Protestant doctrine seems to have acquired new meaning for at least some local residents. At first, it attracted those men and women who, unwilling to join in the campaign against injustice, nonetheless wished to manifest their dissatisfaction with *caciquismo*. In the hands of SIL lay preachers, this kind of dissatisfaction led many Indians to pray that political bosses, too, might open their hearts to the Word. Consider, for example, the sermon which the first of these preachers delivered to his fledgling congregation at the outset of hostilities:

> ... *If any of you are killed [by the bosses], it is the responsibiliy of those who remain to bury the dead. You are not to retaliate. God is the one who has set the [caciques] in authority over us; therefore we must pray for them. They are part of God's plan... God is in control and He always works for our good. It is impossible for anyone to kill us before God says we can come home. If we are killed by them, let us consider that since God is over all, this is part of His will (quoted in Steven 1976:156).*

And despite the occasional persecution which they suffered for their beliefs, Protestants in Chamula soon found themselves removed from the main arena of struggle. In this way, they created for themselves a kind of third party, an organization of non-combatants that expected fundamental change to occur only in heaven.

Although their followers had renounced direct political activity, SIL missionaries were quick to recognize that such conflicts hastened the dissolution of community ties – a fact which opened the door wide to further evangelization. Commenting upon this phenomenon, for example, Ken Jacobs (another SIL missionary) wrote that

> *Thousands of Chamula people were easily organized under the leadership of a few federal teachers... Not only were the bosses afraid of the strenght of large numbers against them, but of the possibility of the opposition taking armed action...*
>
> *This is just the beginning of a unique tribal conflict whose outcome is still undetermined... We feel... it is part of God's plan to at least begin to crack the tribe for an entrance of His Word... (Jacobs 1968).*

And indeed during the following months, Protestant congregations did grow: from 20 families in 1968 to perhaps as many as 80 in 1972. But it was the events of 1974, in which political dissent was openly repressed, that caused the number of new converts to increase astronomically. By declaring such activity to be against the law, the government in effect encouraged former dissidents to pursue the only avenue of protest still available to them: religious conversion. On this score, their patience was well rewarded: by 1976, more than 800 families had joined SIL ranks; nearly 500 of these included men who had originally participated in the movement for political reform. In the minds of such men, it seems, their recent experiences had merely confirmed what SIL had preached all along: prepare thyself for heaven and let the Lord take care of injustice if it suits His plan.

III. Conclusions

From the preceding discussion, it becomes clear that, at least in Chiapas, SIL workers have pursued with single-minded devotion those very objectives which Townsend set forth more than forty years ago. In their quest for Indian souls, they have exploited political and social tensions within indigenous communities; indeed, their actions have often precipitated a state of crisis within communities where serious divisions had not previously existed. To this end, they have misrepresented both the nature of indigenous poverty and the efficacy of Western medicine – not to mention the sources of their own material prosperity and well-being. Moreover, despite personal misgivings about official policy, they have willingly collaborated with a government that since 1916 has openly proclaimed its intention to destroy native culture and transform indigenous people into mestizos – a policy which has been characterized as ethnocide. Like *indigenista* bureaucrats and economic modernizers, they have not seriously contemplated the notion that Indians have a right both to remain what they are and to make informed decisions about their future. True enough, SIL members have rendered valuable services as linguists, translators and textbook writers. But they have rendered precisely those services which impel indigenous children to identify native life with backwardness and inequitable development with progress.

By lending their support to such a venture, foreign missionaries have participated in a far subtler, far more insidious task: they have used religious conversion as a means of inducing highland Indians to renounce whatever measure of control they may have exercised over their own lives. We have seen, for example, that in the 1940's and '50's they pursuaded Choles and Tzeltales not to fight for larger *ejidos*, that is, not to join the groundswell of opposition which arose throughout rural Mexico in response to conservative agrarian measures and economic policies. Similarly, when teachers and coffee workers in Chamula attempted to protest against boss rule and political corruption, SIL convinced many of them that such initiatives were both futile and hopeless. In all of these cases, Wycliffe workers attached themselves to *municipios* in which social conflict had given rise to a certain degree of political awareness – an incipient political consciousness that was then transmuted into more acceptable attitudes of passivity and submissiveness. Such activity can only be called apolitical – as both SIL and the government have chosen to do – only if we regard politics as the unlawful subversion of legitimate order.

Despite recent criticisms by local social scientists, then, SIL continues to enjoy the support of official patrons at the highest levels of government. Taking Cárdenas at his word, Townsend did indeed populate the remote mountain ranges and jungle settlements of Mexico with eager young pioneers: in 1963, they included 259 missionaries, scattered among 82 different linguistic groups; by 1972, these numbers had increased to 367 and 94 respectively. More significantly, SIL members used their experience in the Chiapas jungle to expand their operations to other areas of the world, notably the Amazon basin and the Philippines (see Table 1). In order to prepare new missionaries for these regions, in 1959 they opened a »School for Pioneers« in the jungle hamlet of Yaxalquintelá, to the southeast of Yajalón. Describing this school, a SIL report explains that

Table I.

Country	1963		1972		
	Number of Members	Number of Linguistic Group	Number of Members	Number of Linguistic Group	% Increase of Members
Bolivia	57	13	96	14	68
Brazil	112	27	206	40	84
Colombia	36	4	217	36	503
Ecuador	52	8	95	6	83
Mexico	259	82	367	94	42
Peru	216	35	260	31	20
New Guinea	182	41	307	90	69
Philippines	109	38	182	35	67

Table 1: Wycliffe Bible Translators, Principal Zones of Operation, 1963-72.

Sources, Wycliffe Bible Translators, Inc., *Who Brought the Word*, Santa Ana, CA., 1963; and *Language and Faith*, Santa Ana, CA., 1972.

> For the first six weeks of the three-month course the recruits train at Main Base, a cluster of palm-thatched buildings at the edge of a jungle river. Here they learn the fundamentals of steering dugout tree-trunk canoes..., endurance swimming, erecting houses of available jungle materials... Included in their schedule are daily classes in Wycliffe field policies and practices; language learning in a tribal location with nearby Tzeltal Indians; and the deepening of their devotional life by personal Bible study...
>
> Closer contacts with the Tzeltal Indians are possible at Advance Base, and this is one of the most important parts of the program. Wycliffe workers go to the jungle to win people. Campers must learn quickly and effectively to identify and communicate with Indians whose language they do not know... (WBT 1963:32-3).

Given these facts, it is obvious that SIL missionaries have earned for themselves a more or less permanent position in Mexican life, a position which will not be altered in response to vague accusations of espionage or cultural imperialism. According to their most recent contract, for example, SIL will continue to serve the Ministry of Public Education until 1990. Confident in their future, therefore, they have recently constructed a new school near Mexico City, the »Centro Lingüístico Manuel Gamio,« on land donated by the federal government. Unlike their »School for Pioneers,« the Centro will prepare both foreigners and Mexican nationals in the techniques of descriptive linguistics. For their part, both the former President of Mexico, Luis Echeverría, and director of INI have agreed to serve on the Centro's board of directors. With friends like these, Wycliffe translators must surely feel that Divine Providence views their work with especial favor. And they will surely bring renewed energy and dedication to the task which lies before them, that is, the task of putting His Word into those »two thousand tongues yet to go.«

Bibliography

Beekman, John and James C. Hefley
1968 *Peril By Choice: The Story of John and Elaine Beekman, Wycliffe Bible Translators in Mexico,* Grand Rapids, Michigan: Zondervan Books.

Hall, Clarence W.
1958 »Two Thousand Tongues to Go,« Reprinted from Reader's Digest, August, 1958, pp. 1-16, distributed by Wycliffe Bible Translators, Inc., Santa Ana, California.

Heath, Shirley Brice
1972 *La política del lenguaje en México: de la colonia a la nación,* México: Instituto Nacional Indigenista.

Jacobs, Kenneth and Elaine
1968 »Letter to supporters,« May, 1968, Huntington Beach, California: SIL Headquarters (ms.).

Steven, Hugh
1976 *They Dared to be Different,* Irvine, California: Harvest Books.

Tiempo
1957 »Perspectiva: una mujer los civilizó,« cover story, 9 December, 1957, pp. 2-9 (México).

Townsend, William C.
1952 *Lázaro Cárdenas: Mexican Democrat,* Ann Arbor: George Wahr.

1956 »Notes of Spiritual Work for WBT Field Workers,« in Mexican Branch Handbook, México: SIL Mexican Branch, pp. 84-8.

Wallis, Ethel F. and Mary A. Bennett
1959 *Two Thousand Tongues to Go,* New York: Harper and Row.

Wycliffe Bible Translators, Inc.
1963 *Who Brought the Word,* Santa Ana, California: WBT.

1970 »Where in the World? Mexico,« pamphlet, Santa Ana: WBT.

1972 *Language and Faith,* Santa Ana: WBT.

»No Tobacco, No Hallelujah«

by SØREN HVALKOF and PETER AABY

> »First of all, let it be made clear that SIL and WBT are deeply concerned for and dedicated to the liberation of indigenous peoples, both in a spiritual sense and in a temporal sense«.
> »The anti-change anthropologists would, at the expense of human life and psychological well-being, preserve reified culture for his children to study« (Merrifield 1976:6-7).

The preceding articles have examined SIL's work at different stages of its development and under diverse social circumstances. We will now try to summarize SIL's effects on the indigenous groups, showing how these reflect the character of SIL's relationship with the dependent capitalist states. As Stoll and many others have described, SIL has constructed an elaborate set of justifications and self-images in order to assuage the conflicting interests of governments, the general public, »folks back home« and fellow linguists and anthropologists. As an apparent reaction to criticisms levelled at the organization by Indian organizations and anthropologists, SIL has recently begun to develop a new aura of legitimacy which accentuates its contribution to the indigenous groups' social and cultural survival. To put this tendency in perspective, we begin by describing WBT's view of the Indian problem and of the solution SIL provides.

WBT's promotional literature conveys the distinct impression that the Bibleless tribes are afflicted with witchcraft, superstitions, sickness, immorality, lack of self-respect, revenge killings and headhunting (see WBT's monthly journal *In Other Words*). How these societies can possibly function under such conditions must remain a puzzle, *unless* one assumes that they are the Devil's paradise; indeed, this notion is not far from the ideas communicated by WBT publicists.

The constantly recurring theme in these descriptions of the tribal societies and their problems is that their causes are to be found in individual shortcomings and cultural inadequacies. The processes of change initiated by the SIL linguists thus focus on transforming individual psyches. Despite their unfailing optimism and devotion to duty, the linguists are often surprised by the resistance they meet and by the delays in finding their first converts. Sometimes, Satan's grip is so strong that all the WBT/SIL members must unite in prayer, or God must perform a special miracle, so that the conversion process can proceed. The missionaries usually find their first converts among their own language informants. If all goes well, the informants manage to convince their family, kin and other members of the group to receive God's Word. The social consequences of this process – »from fear to faith« – have been eloquently summarized by Des Oatridge, a SIL linguist working among the Binumarien (Papua New Guinea):

> »Selfishness began to give way to considerastion for others. Foolishness started to give way to thoughtfulness. Laziness gave way to honest hard labor, pride to humility, drunkenness to soberness, animal-like behavior to self-control. And this was only the beginning« (In Other Words, p. 7, April, 1977).

Regardless of the eventual outcome, this particular kind of analysis is not meant for anyone outside the circles of true believers back home. Instead SIL appeals to other audiences by invoking the scientific importance of its translation project or the political value of having someone who has contact with or control over 'marginal' groups. As Stoll and Rus and Wasserstrom explain, at times Townsend's appeals to the utilitarian interests of state officials were consciously ethnocidal in their intents.

Within the last decade SIL has come under increasing attack, not only because of its debatable scientific character, but also because a decreasing number of people accept SIL's operating premise of a pure and neutral science (The Declaration of Barbados 1971; Hart 1973). As a result, the organization has once more been obliged to reformulate its rationale and its analyses. Since much of the critique comes from anthropologists, many recent anthropological conferences on the Indians have included SIL participants who spoke out in defense of their organization. (cf. Kietzman 1977; Loos *et al.* 1976; Merrifield 1976, 1977, 1978; Yost 1978). We shall discuss two of these attempts to define an anthropological image for the organization.

D'Ans (1972:416-7, and in this volume) once predicted that if SIL's remarkable ability to change its phraseology is any guide, we would soon be hearing the missionaries crying out against ethnocide. D'Ans was not far off; while some SIL spokesmen have refused to admit 'ethnocide' as a category (see Merrifield below), SIL is now in favor of 'indigenous self-determination' and 'liberation'. For example, at the Congress of Americanists in Paris in September 1976, three SIL missionaries from Peru presented a paper entitled »El cambio cultural y el desarollo integral de la persona: Exposición de la filosofia y los metodos del Instituto Lingüístico de Verano en el Peru« (Loos *et al.* 1976) (»Culture change and the integrated development of the person: Exposition of the philosophy and methods of the Summer Institute of Linguistics in Peru«). The basic assumption of their paper is that cultures are always changing and that the Indians themselves want things to change. However, this contact with 'the outside world' has weakened the Indians' economies and has also brought them socio-psychological problems. In this situation, a helping hand is necessary:

> »neither wishing to force the members of a marginal group to adjust to other moulds, nor obliging them to maintain their status quo *(if this was possible), it is necessary to help them retain their identity inside a viable, strong, unified and just culture whose values can survive the cultural contact« (Loos et al.* 1976:7, our translation).

Thus, SIL assists the Indians in Peru by providing them with medical assistance and bilingual education. This enables them to participate in national development projects and to deal with agents of the national society on a more equal footing. Loos and his colleagues also believe that SIL fortifies cultural identity by giving the indigenous groups a written language and an independent literature, and by furnishing them with spiritual values which help them to withstand the traumas of culture contact.

For Loos *et al.*, SIL's intervention – with the goal of creating a viable identity – is based on the 'scientific' notion that all cultures have both »negative and positive traits«. Naturally, only the latter are to be supported (1976:14). Positive traits are defined as those »which are not negative« (1976:9). Negative are those traits

> »which lead to a self-destruction of the culture and/or the physical and psycho-social detriment of its people, or which produce injustices against individuals inside or outside the culture concerned« *(Loos et al.* 1976:9, our translation).

These definitions are hardly a useful guide for determining exactly how to help the Indians. The only cultural trait which they cite as unequivocally negative are physically harmful forms of folk medical treatment. At the same time they conclude that the trait of female infanticide (found among some groups practising wife-stealing) has both negative and positive aspects. It is negative because it constitutes murder, creates conflicts with other groups, perpetuates oppression of women, etc. It is positive because it aids genetic variability, gives outlet for human aggressions, supports social control, helps maintain the ecological adaption, etc. (Loos *et al.* 1976: 11-12). Such attitudes could no doubt be construed as a very liberal form of cultural relativism. We maintain, however, that their categorizations are so nebulous that they are but a camouflage for SIL's real operations. Few missionaries – and few anthropologists – could even tolerate such cultural relativist standards in their analysis, much less make use of them. With cultural relativism as an intellectual »cover«, SIL's actual intervention into Indian life tends to be based on their well-defined Christian principles. No wonder, then, that Loos *et al.* employ the more familiar ideological scheme of fear *vs* faith. In their contact with the outside world

»it would be erroneous not to recognize the necessity felt by the indigenous groups to have help from the spiritual in facing the difficult life of the twentieth century. The teachings of the Gospel are able to replace the basis of fear, common to their religions, with the security of the love of God, which gives hope to man and motivates him to feel and demonstrate this same love toward his neighbor«(Loos et al. 1976:35, our translation).

In spite of such relapses into the WBT rhetoric, the main intention of Loos and his colleagues is to provide scientific justification for SIL's work; specifically that SIL helps Indians to maintain their cultural identity. Considering SIL's problems in establishing a viable identity and image for the organisation, it is hardly surprising that Loos *et al.* have difficulties in determining the cultural identity of the Indians. SIL's identity strategy is to create »integrated personalities« through individual choice. Positive

»qualities, however, do not emerge through imposition; they have to be organized internally as a result of a personal option« (Loos et al. 1976:13, our translation).

Loos *et al.'s* presentation of SIL furnishing help in a nonpaternalistic manner respecting the marginal groups' rights to self–determination, generates several contradictions. The indigenous peoples' cultures are not just characterized by a distance from Christian teachings, as implied by the WBT literature. They have their own intrinsic value, and their maintenance is a prerequisite for meaningful social life. Although it is suggested that fear is the basis of tribal religion, the real causes for the tribes presumed identity crisis lie in the economic pressures and the inability of traditional concepts to deal with changes resulting from encapsulation by the state. According to Loos *et al.,* SIL offers but an alternative; devoid of harmful intentions its work is a meaningful contribution to the maintenance of cultural identity.

Loos *et al.'s* evangelical, humanitarian cultural relativism is certainly a radical reinterpretation of the organization's goals, inasmuch as conversion is not reiterated as the main objective. SIL's Anthropology Coordinator, William Merrifield, has also adopted some of the new terminology.

Like Loos *et al.* (1976:26-9), Merrifield (1978) emphasizes how SIL's linguistic and educational work has acted as a support for the Indian movements. He is in agreement with ideas expressed by many Indian organizations, notably their demands to retain Indian cultures and languages. Thus, he can end one of his articles by writing:

»SIL believes it has played a significant role in some of the programs that now exist, and continues to have a commitment to assist in the liberation *of minority language groups through education where ever such assistance is locally desired« (1978:4,* our italics).

As already indicated by the introductory quote, this is not just a question of the groups' spiritual liberation but of their »temporal liberation«. In another article, Merrifield (1976) attempts to explain »temporal liberation«. His starting point is that »ethnocide is a myth. People die, but cultures do not; they change« (1976:7). The cause of these transformations come from various types of contact associated with migrations and from efforts by national governments to integrate their indigenous peoples in order to improve their situation (1976:7). Merrifield states that Indians themselves should have as much control as possible in determining the kind and amount of changes they will undergo. To enable them to make these decisions, however, it is necessary that the Indians be educated. SIL opposes any use of »coercive force« in directing culture change. Its task is purely educational – to present the alternatives. Merrifield discusses how »the introduction of evangelical alternatives in an anthropologically sensitive way do often result in temporal benefits to those who choose them« (1976:8). As one example of this process, he quotes the following account of change in a Tzeltal community in southern Mexico:

»For this kind of change [from a primitive-historic to an early modern religion] to take place, there had to be a replacement of one set of value orientations with another. The old value orientation can be summarized as follows: (1) man is evil without hope for improvement; (2) man lives in harmony with nature; (3) the past is the time dimension of crucial importance; (4) the personality emphasis is on being; and (5) a collateral emphasis exists in social relations.

»The new value orientations offered a contrasting set of beliefs: (1) man's evil condition is subject to improvement; (2) man can exercise control over nature, especially in the area of health;

(3) the present and the future are the time dimensions of crucial importance; (4) the personality emphasis is on becoming; and (5) a man should work for the enrichment of his own household unit.

»The old value orientations were as anachronistic mal-adaptive as the other features of the primitive historic religion for the Oxchuc Tzeltals. They were being exploited by Ladinos while they were destroying themselves through witchcraft and alchoholism. Their religion at best offered them no earthly hope or relief and at worst contributed to their problems.

»The new value orientations were as superior over the old ones as the other characteristics of the early modern religion were over those of the primitive historic religion for the Tzeltals in their situation. The new religion enables them to take control of their lives and gain power, enlightenment, wealth, well-being, skill, affection, respect, and rectitude« (Turner 1976:17f, as quoted by Merrifield 1976:9).

Merrifield's notion of »temporal liberation« has little to do with a society's self-determination. It is a matter of a »cultural evolution« from evil to good[1]. Although Merrifield attempts to describe SIL's project in »anthropological« terms, his basic model of development differs little from the »cultural uplift« described by WBT's promotional literature: from fear and laziness to faith and honest hard work.

Even though Merrifield has more difficulty than Loos *et al.* in distancing himself from the WBT model for cultural improvement, it is the similarities in their recasting of SIL's role that should be stressed. Both parties talk about liberation, and how SIL's work reinforces the indigenous group's culture and language. They also insist that SIL's work does no more than offer the indigenous groups a possible alternative. Before evaluating the validity of this self-image, it might be instructive to discuss another similarity between Merrifield and Loos *et al.*: namely, the way in which they defend themselves against the recent critiques aimed at SIL by Indian organizations, political groups, and anthropologists. That they have been influenced by this critique is evident in that both papers emphasize SIL's desire to foster ethnic consciousness, cultural self-determination, economic development, a society without exploitation etc.

Some anthropologists have condemned SIL for destroying the traditional culture and social organization of the indigenous groups while others have blamed the missionaries for isolating the Indians and hindering their possibilities for development. To the extent that SIL missionaries have transformed their converts' culture and have been able to restrain groups from pursuing certain forms of development or contact with the state, both critiques would be deemed correct. Nevertheless, the critiques also contain a high degree of ambiguity, since they elevate »tradition« or »development« as values in themselves, using them as ultimate standards with which to evaluate SIL. That one or the other value is chosen probably reflects contradictory theoretical and political assessments of the Indians' social situation and political strategies for the tribal groups. The dilemma over standards of evaluation is not solved by adhering to either traditionalist or developmentalist views, because in their generalized forms they both rest on untenable, or unworkable premises.

A traditionalist critique presupposes tribal cultures to have a built-in tendency to maintain their form; the implication is that *any* kind of intervention is ethnocide. The developmentalist critique implies that tribal societies have a natural tendency to evolve, and that this can be impeded only at the risk of frustrating its members. Neither of these ideologies fits the actual history of indigenous groups. »Traditional« groups have contributed to their own transformation, and sometimes destruction, by intensifying contact with the national society in order to obtain certain tools, weapons, medicine etc. (cf. Murphy and Murphy 1975). In other situations, similarly structured groups have opposed »development« by battling settlers, traders, and others who wanted to exploit their territory and/or their labor (cf. Bodley 1975).

Merrifield's and Loos *et al.'s* articles should be seen not only as terminological attempts to appease the critics, but also as attempts to exploit the inconsistencies in anthropologists' ideas about marginal groups. In justifying SIL's solution, they maintain that these societies have indeed always been changing. In their view, it is unfair to condemn any kind of intervention, as the »anti-change anthropologists« have done. Since indigenous groups have not always had the power to confront the negative consequences of development, it is also legitimate to isolate indigenous groups from certain kinds of contact or defend them against campaigns to »integrate« them with the state.

Recognizing that value dilemmas will arise because certain changes are beneficial while others are harmful, Loos *et al.* attempt to resolve the problem by talking of positive and negative cultural traits. This is hardly a solution, however, since traits in themselves are neither »good« nor »bad«, but dependent on the total system of which they are a part. By focusing on cultural traits instead of the total system of internal social relations and outside pressures, the missionaries manage to individualise both the causes of these problems and their solutions. Although Loos *et al.* recognize that some of the Indians' difficulties stem from the expansion of other cultures, their analysis deals primarily with personal psychological problems resulting from culture clash. It is in relation to these individualized problems that SIL justifies its intervention into Indian life with its offer of »alternatives«. Since SIL's cultural relativist value system is so diffuse, their interventionist »treatment« of culture clash must necessarily end up reflecting Christian rationality and morality.

The missionaries' critique of the traditionalist or developmentalist premises used by some anthropologists, does not entail that we accept SIL's interventionist solution as a better alternative. We need a more viable frame of reference than those offered by the traditionalist or developmentalist paradigms. The Indians' encounters with, or struggles against, the national society represent neither vain attempts at retaining tradition, nor their desire for wholesale, unrestricted development. These encounters are, instead, attempts by the tribes to control their own destiny or to obtain those material goods which could facilitate this control. Thus, it is our suggestion that in evaluating any sort of intervention, we should ask not whether it helps the group to preserve a static system of values, but whether it helps them achieve self-determination as a culturally viable, continuously reproducing social unit. We would call »ethnocide« those social processes destroying their ability to maintain self-determination (see note 1).

Our emphasis on self-determination does not reflect a belief that present-day indigenous societies represent the most perfect social forms, or that they are conflict free, or that their existing social organizations are the most effective defenses against state expansion. On the contrary, it is likely that some problems will arise out of the indigenous group's own value system and social structure. For example, traditional enmity between groups could hinder the formation of a common front of resistance, or internal power/prestige struggles or newly formed material needs could lead the tribe to seek an intensified contact with the national society, thus allowing penetration by the market economy and leading to the eventual disintegration of the society.

Like SIL, we do not suppose that the indigenous groups lead paradisic lives. However, we reject SIL's idea that something better could be achieved for the Indians by replacing their culture with a »new, improved« one. The alternative that capitalism offers is integration at the lowest social ranks: as tourist-objects, petty producers, casual laborers, servants, prostitutes, etc. The best possibilities for the Indians lie in *resisting* this type of integration. This requires that they build upon their own traditions, while simultaneously attempting to restructure those particular features which either push them toward capitalist integration or hinder their struggle against such integration.

In the following paragraphs we discuss how SIL's practices have affected the dynamic between the indigenous groups' internal reproduction processes and the ever present pressures of capitalist expansion. As background, it is necessary to reiterate some of the key factors in this dynamic.

Most of the tribal indigenous peoples originally had economies combining hunting, fishing, gathering and horticulture. While these adaptations are still present, wage labor and market production are coming to play a major role in their economies. The basic social units have been extended households and territorial kin groups. In conjunction with their exploitation of natural resources, Indians have usually had a relatively dispersed settlement pattern. While these societies have varying forms of organization and social control mechanisms, a basic similarity has been the absence of any form of private property rights or private control over nature's resources. Differences in production between different households are equalized via redistributive mechanisms like feasts and gift giving. Increased production can lead to higher social esteem, but has not led to social stratification based on control over wealth or means of production. In these systems, political leadership is based on personal qualities and control over supernatural powers. Religious systems usually express a direct relation between the ideological »organization of nature« and the economic and social organization of society.

Economic expansion threatens the indigenous groups' self-determination in two ways. First of all settlement schemes, cattle ranching, and extraction of oil, minerals, lumber and other natural resources involve the expropriation of lands and resources used by the Indians and thus threaten their traditional livelihoods. Secondly, traders and employers attempt to turn the Indians into producers of cash crops, casual laborers, or plantation workers. The employers and traders are often able to force or cheat the

177

Indians into debt relations and in this way gain greater and greater control over their production or labor-power, leading to social atomization and a breakdown of the traditional system of production and redistribution. In most case, proletarization and expropriation pressures are co-occuring rather than mutually exclusive. We distinguish between the two aspects in order to indicate that a positive intervention must attempt to secure Indian control over crucial natural resources, and must try to impede the creation of exploitative labor and trade relations.

SIL's practice

As evidenced by the articles in this book and by other sources, the precise consequences of SIL's intervention will vary according to the cultural organization of the indigenous groups, their social surroundings, or the quality of the missionaries. We want only to show some general tendencies in the way SIL affects the ideological, social, political and economic aspects of Indian life. Later on we will evaluate SIL's intervention in light of the Indians' potential for self-determination against capitalist expansion.

Although the linguists sometimes function as parish preacher this is not WBT/SIL's intention when they send them off to the Indian communities. The original idea is for the Bible translation to provide a foundation for an indigenous church. Since most of the groups are illiterate the task of building the indigenous church must begin with a literacy program. *In Other Words:* »Translation provides the Book for readers; Literacy provides readers for the Book« (Nov., 1977, p. 1). The linguists begin work with their informants hoping that they will continue the literacy campaign among their own people. The program is most effective where the organization achieves official support to set up schools and teacher training programs.

On the surface, SIL's bilingual education programs appear to be an important contribution to improving the situation of the indigenous groups. The organization itself has reiterated this line, emphasizing how they furnish the indigenous societies with linguistic ability to resist pressure from the national society. Despite the high-sounding rhetoric, most analyses show the school system to be an instrument for fundamentalist indoctrination and social control.

As described in the introduction, the language informant usually undergoes a transformation from heathen to Christian, emerging as a teacher pastor for the community. The linguists expect their informants and the bilingual teachers to spread both the written and the good Word. Control over both teacher training and teaching materials assures that bilingual education in no way becomes a vehicle for the interests of the indigenous group itself.

The literacy campaign is undoubtedly SIL's most important means of »cultural renewal«. The ideological results of these campaigns can best be described as »individualization« and »secularization«. Individualization is the natural consequence of Protestantism's stress on the individual's relation to God, this view appears clearly in both Loos *et al.'s* and Merrifields' exposition of SIL's philosophy. Individualism is more than just a philosophy of personal salvation, however. It is a sharp clash with the duties and the collective ethos of Indian social organization and culture. As Vickers' describes, the missionaries intervene directly into the marriage system. There seems to be a general tendency to advance monogamy and nuclear households. For example, the bilingual Aguaruna teacher brought by SIL to the Congress of Americanists in Paris deemed polygamy a »negative cultural trait.« The new faith of the recently converted Indian shows a remarkable likeness to middle class American mores: honest hard labor, humility, soberness and self-control.

Secularization is just as obvious a consequence of the missionaries' world view as is individualization (cf. Miller 1970). Traditionally beliefs about illness, bad luck, food production, weather and socialization are tied into the religious system. Against this system the missionaries present scientific explanations for these phenomena, usually supported by »empirical proof.« The evil spirits which once were the cause of illness are replaced by bacteria and amoeba. This undermines the original culture's explanatory models and opens a path for the acceptance of the new religion.

While the process of secularization is definitely integrated with the acceptance of Protestantism, it is less obvious that this process results in integrated personalities. Feelings of inadequacy and cultural inferiority arise among those who have not fully identified themselves with the new culture (cf. Ortiz 1976; Kelm 1972, in Riester 1975:51). These people provide fertile soil for SIL's millenarian message.

The conversion process also produces indigenous crusaders who are often completely out of touch with local realities, as Huxley describes in his account of a Campa teacher in his village of 80 Indians:

> »*The product of three Protestant missionary schools, as well as the Government-S.I.L. bilingual teacher-training program, Santos is both educator and missionary. He is also a man with a vision. Santos sees the village of Matoveni as a jungle town like Atalaya, perhaps even like the bustling city of Pucallpa, with an airfield, a hospital, and coffee and cacao plantations; with herds of cattle and lots of people in proper clothes and shoes; a city where every man, women, and child has found God«* (1964:214).

When visions of men like Santos inevitably go unfulfilled, or when the converts realize that they are irrevocably split between two cultures, the results are the identity crises and backsliding described by several of the authors.

SIL's goals and working methods have other implications, too. In order to implement their educational program and accomplish their goal of a society with a native-born church and school, the missionaries and their assistants have tried to induce Indians to move into larger villages (cf. Bradby 1975:158; d'Ans 1972; Riester 1975:55; Siverts 1972:29). Because of traditional animosities between different groups, this consolidation often results in considerable tension. SIL's programs also create completely new types of social conflicts.

The bilingual education gives rise to cultural and ideological differences between young and old. As in numerous other instances of modernization, this process becomes one of de-education in that knowledge of essential occupations necessary for the tribes' traditional livelihood is devalued or ignored. The tribes' dependence on »modern«, i.e. foreign, technologies and commodities is thus reinforced.

The ideological struggle which is SIL's starting point also becomes a political struggle. Since tribal leadership is often linked to control over supernatural powers, SIL's attack on tribal religion undermines the legitimacy of the traditional headmen. The missionaries also manage to instill a belief into their converts that they are destined to assume religious and political leadership over their fellows (cf. Siverts 1965:156). The WBT literature depicts the missionaries and their converts as being in a constant struggle against »witchdoctors« (cf. Hefley and Hefley 1972). Using their salary, and backed by SIL, many of the teachers have established themselves as traders or community leaders, and gained control over development projects, schools, or access to outside resources. What may be called an indigenous pedagogical-pastoral-entrepreneurial elite develops. The new found resources at the disposal of the converts put them in a good position to oppose traditional leaders. The missionary zeal of the new converts leads to tensions between Christians and heathens, and as in cases described by d'Ans, Smith, Rus and Wasserstrom may even result in the actual dissolution of the group.

SIL's ideological and socio-political intervention also restructures the groups' economic situations. The concentration of population and the external pressure reduces access to animal, fish and plant resources, or causes their over-exploitation. The result is often a worsened nutritional situation (cf. Bodley 1975).

While in the field, the SIL missionaries try to help the Indians by assuming the role of trader. Moore indicates that this might be beneficial since the missionaries' convenient terms would limit the inroads of more exploitative traders. Nevertheless, the missionaries also stimulate new needs among the Indians, and impel them to intensify production for the market (cf. Hanbury-Tenison 1973:152-3). As long as the missionaries remain in the field and maintain their »fair« terms of trade, creation of new needs may not be immediately harmful. But considering that they spend a great deal of time at their base, and that their eventual goal ist to leave the group for other Bibleless tribes, they cannot buffer the Indians for long. The end result of the missionaries' economic role leaves the Indians much more dependent on the market and on less benevolent traders. At times SIL's own proselytes take on the trader role to such a degree that they become indistinguishable from the *patrones* the Indians had previously (Huxley 1964:213).

The missionaries have on some occasions formed sale or production cooperatives to support larger population concentrations and increased consumption of foreign goods (Huxley 1964:177, 178, 195). This strategy can be dangerous if the goods produced have an unstable price or are based on resources soon to disappear, e.g. skins, gold. Huxley's description of SIL's showcase cooperative among the Ticuna (Peru) shows yet a more serious consequence:

»Consider, for example, Anderson's [a SIL missionary] recent suggestion, that, in addition to the community rubber plantations, individuals set out their own plots of rubber trees. Inherent in this plan are the seeds of dissension: a man's desire to help himself competes directly with his desire to help his community. This conflict may well erode the present excellent cooperation between the villagers for the welfare of the whole community« (1964:213).

The individualism that emerges under SIL's tutelage is characteristic not just of the organization's formal theology, but of the missionaries' actual intervention into tribal economic life. Each person must learn the value of private property, of goods, and of *his* own labor. These are logical sentiments considering the missionaries' background, for they too operate with certain economic restraints. For example, they must get money for their bungalow at the base, for paying the informants, for the medicine they dispense, and for the flights in and out of the area. Even though the Lord provides, SIL's policy of group concentration and localization also follows practical financial considerations, as Vickers has pointed out.

It is useful for SIL to educate the Indians about the »value« of goods if it helps them to avoid being cheated by the traders. The more serious problem is that the missionaries »commercialize« tribal social relations by forcing on them ideas about private property and the value of money. In Merrifield's scheme, the missionaries' goal is to turn the Indians from »a collateral emphasis on social relations« to »work for the enrichment of his own household« (1976:8). This breaks up the traditional redistributive economy, a mechanism which has served to limit market integration by counteracting economic differentiation and reducing the need to seek wage labor in case of insufficient household production.

Central to SIL's intervention is its effort to transform material goods from »gifts« to »commodities«. By exploiting the traditional ideology of the gift as a sign of peace and solidarity, SIL has created dependence on new products and thus shown the indigenous groups that the »gift« has always been a »good« tied into the market economy. This strategy has been described by Victor Halterman, SIL's director in Bolivia and an official in the Bolivian Ministry of Culture and Education:

> *»When we learn of the presence of an uncontacted group we move into the area, build a strong shelter – say of logs – and cut paths radiating from it into the forest. We leave gifts along the paths – knives, axes, mirrors, the kind of things that Indians can't resist – and sometimes they leave gifts in exchange. After a while the relationship develops. Maybe they are mistrustful at first, but in the end they stop running away when we show, and we all get together and make friends.*
>
> *»We have to break their dependency on us next. Naturally they want to go on receiving all those desirable things we've been giving them, and sometimes it comes as a surprise when we explain that from now on if they want to possess them they must work for money. We don't employ them, but we can usually fix them up with something to do on the local farms. They settle down to it when they realise that there's no going back« (Lewis 1978:13-16).*

The analysis of the Bolivian situation by Norman Lewis shows that, in fact, »»Something to do« on a local farm is only too often indistinguishable from slavery« (1978:16).

Modern Medicine Men

SIL's ability to create groups or entire communities of converts in often explained to the effect that the missionaries protect the Indians and have greater respect for the native language and culture than do other »whites«. While this can explain why linguists are popular or accepted *as individuals*, it does not tell us why they are effective *as missionaries*. As indicated by the contributions to this book, the more likely cause for the missionaries' popularity is that they become resource persons dispensing education, protection, official contacts, medicine and other commodities:

> *»Would they dare stay? When the Ticuna chief was bitten by a bushmaster snake Lambert saved his life with injections of anti-venom. The Indians' suspicion of the foreign couple was erased, and the Andersons were asked to make their home with them«* (Translation, *July-Sept., 1971, p. 2,* italics added).
> *»Yet the fact that he does represent the Amahuaca's only source of material goods must be*

considered as another and very powerful reason for settling at Varadero [the SIL missionary's camp]. Also, his ability to cut them off from this flow of benefits must be ever-present at the back of their minds. No wonder his words carry weight« (Huxley 1964:141).

The actual basis for initial contact is best described by a Kapaukuan headman in New Guinea, responding to a missionary's complaint about why his people no longer attended religious services: »No tobacco, no hallelujah« (Pospisil 1963:94).

Conversion of the Indians by missionaries shows how they can upgrade their relationship beyond the plane where goods are traded or medicine dispensed. The success of the conversion process lies in the missionaries ability to secularize the traditional religion while enforcing acceptance of Protestantism as a replacement. The desire for goods, medicine, or protection are the real motives spurring Indians' contact with the missionaries. As this relationship develops, modern technology can be employed to demonstrate the inferiority of the traditional belief system and the superiority of Protestantism. Because Indian views of illness and health are more intertwined with traditional religion than, say, tools or commodities, strategic use of modern medicine can be one of the most effective ways to confirm the power of Christianity. It is difficult to determine if the missionaries are consciously aware of the strategy they are using. It is worth noting, however, that many of the »rebirths« described in WBT's promotional literature come on the heels of some kind of medical »miracle«. The irony is that this rejection of traditional ideology, and the acceptance of western culture which accompanies conversion, stem not from an understanding of western medicine or pharmacy *per se,* but from the traditional beliefs themselves: The missionaries have shown that they simply have more healing »powers« than do tribal healers. Of course the missionaries then use the other »powers« at their disposal to reinforce their position.

WBT's own descriptions indicate that the conversion process sometimes achieves the momentum of a millenarian revival. Whether this is indeed the case, or just exaggerates the missionaries' own millenarian expectations, is impossible to discern from existing sources.

The impact of SIL's program is greatest where the missionaries – via their informants-teachers– gain control over the bilingual education system. In the schools they can educate the children to Christianity without the crises or resistance characteristic of adult conversion. In the process of ideological and social transformation SIL's indigenous representatives overtake functions as resource persons, emerging as prominent religious and political leaders. With their superior economic positions they become living proof of the connection between material rewards and Protestantism.

To sum up, SIL's material control help it to exploit the indigenous groups' problems and weaknesses and make Protestantism appear much stronger than the traditional ideology. Regardless of SIL's success in obtaining converts, the preceding analysis does not support Loos *et al.'s* and Merrifield's claims that SIL only offers an alternative and supports cultural traditions. On the contrary, it systematically subverts and destroys them.

Considering the importance the organization attaches to Bible translation and its belief in the power of God's own words, it is surprising that SIL's intervention could be depicted as a harmless offering of alternatives. Most missionaries clearly operate from a premise that there is no other correct choice but God's Word. SIL's work is far from a culture-sensitive and value-free effort to educate and present the Indians with alternatives.

The transliteration of the indigenous language and distribution of publications may contribute to the Indians' ethnic pride, but that is about all that can be said of SIL's respect for indigenous cultures. The articles in this book have shown that when the missionaries are dealing with Indian traditions, they tend to work from WBT's view that these societies are characterized by »witchcraft, killings, superstitions, ignorance, fear and sickness« (in the words of Townsend himself; 1963:8). Thus the missionaries try to counteract polygamy, marriage rules, traditional forms of cooperation and ceremony, gift giving, oral tradition, etc. If they simultaneously support other aspects of the indigenous culture, these are either trivial ones (e.g. feathers in the nasal septum) or can be commercialized (e.g. »Indian« tourist articles).

More importantly, there is little in SIL's praxis that can be interpreted as contributing to the indigenous groups' efforts at maintaining self-determination. As we have stated above, SIL's work often results in just the opposite: privatization, political fragmentation and intensified dependence on the market. Indians' control over their pressured resources is not supported by a campaign against state policies which allow or carry out this pressure. Neither does the organization oppose the privatized trade and wage-labor relations which act to break down tribal social structure. Many Indians groups have had trade relations with the national society over long periods of time. As long as they traded in a limited number of commodities and as long as essential resources were available and the internal redistribution system maintained, the destructive effects of these commercial relations were minimized. The individualism and materialism which forms an integral part of SIL's philosophy and day-to-day methods removes these safeguards. Through the resulting individualized integration into the market, the economic basis of the Indian societies will disappear and they will invariably be subdued by forces which they cannot control. With the individualization and political discord brought on by SIL's intervention, the Indians will be unable to defend themselves against encroachment of their land, hunting and fishing resources. Since SIL's work tend to make moral and supernatural premises the foundation for social and political struggle and organization, the Indians will be impeded from creating new organizational forms which could strengthen their political and economic power. Thus, SIL is producing a pacifying effect on the societies in which it works.

What we have emphasized are the long term effects of SIL's work. The missionaries sometimes set up larger villages, or even cooperatives, and they »protect« and »isolate« the Indians from contact with settlers, traders, oil companies, etc. SIL-sponsored isolation can produce short term advantages for the Indians. There are few substantive descriptions of what happens when the missionaries leave for other Bibleless tribes, or for other reasons lose control. For the cases we know of, however, and after examining SIL's goals and methods, there are few grounds for believing that SIL's »consolidation« and »isolation« strategies aid Indians' chances for survival as self-determinant groups. SIL's program might be ineffective and the Indians would go back to their traditional life-style, as d'Ans has described. In other situations the indigenous missionary elite will be able to maintain control for some time, as suggested by Pereira's account. In still other cases the mission station has been but a stage on the way toward a more individualized integration with the market economy, as Moore shows in the case of the Amarakaeri. These results can be explained by the fact that the missionaries use »consolidation« and »isolation« as techniques for obtaining converts, and not to foster tribal self-determination.

SIL is not always as effective as it would have the folks back home believe. Sometimes the Indians are able to exploit the missionaries for their own purposes, using them as a buffer against other unwanted institutions. Some Aguarunas, for instance, have recently fought the expulsion of SIL, not because they have become Christians or accepted the missionaries' »development strategies«, but because they feared that the departure of SIL would lead to the arrival of what they know to be worse – the Peruvian Army (Temple 1977). This case actually indicates that SIL's own program was a failure. Had the missionaries succeeded in carrying out their plans, it would not have been possible for the Aguaruna to build an alternative strategy and use SIL as the lesser devil.

In this summary as well as in the book, there has been a focus on SIL's relationship with tribal groups. As indicated by Rus and Wasserstrom's paper, SIL's methods and consequences do not essentially differ when the organization works among peasant populations (cf. Siverts 1965). SIL's work increases integration into the market economy and reduces the peasants' ability to withstand the pressures and exploitation perpetrated by landlords, traders and officials.

The failure of SIL to strengthen self-determination is a natural reflection of the very essence of the organization's program. It attempts to introduce an alien ideology by preying on the indigenous groups' social and material weaknesses. Despite the fact that SIL's organization, its use of modern technology and its utilization of indigenous languages make it more effective than many other traditional missionary organizations, their methods do not fundamentally differ. Thus, it is categorically false when Loos *et al.* state: »The SIL member does not work with a paternalist attitude which creates dependency and domination« (1976:19, our translation). Considering SIL's institutional commitment to God, to folks back home, and to national governments, there is hardly reason to believe that SIL will divest itself of its paternalism in the future.

SIL and the Dependent Capitalist States

SIL takes pride in its good cooperation with the national governments. In view of the organization's ability to pacify and integrate the tribal groups – both necessities for any national development policy – there is perfect justification for the state to support SIL's work. Whether the government seeks to create development via forces of domestic capitalism or via integration with international capital's hunt for raw materials, what matters is achieving maximum benefits out of the country's internal resources. Depending on the local circumstances, these efforts can take the form of increasing commercialization, expropriation of natural resources found within the areas of tribal settlement, or colonization of so-called »empty« areas. The success of these operations demands the pacification of hostile or partly-integrated groups, and the »modernization« of traditional Indian communities.

Many of the articles in this book have illustrated how SIL tried to ingratiate itself with national governments by playing upon state interests in national integration. SIL's program of working through the tribes' own languages and cultures is seen as an effective alternative to Hispanized educational and cultural programs. For instance, it is hardly accidental that SIL has often been admitted during periods when liberal or populist governments were trying to create national economic development and to undermine conservative forces, e.g. Cardenas' in Mexico, Arbenz' in Guatemala, Paz Estensoro's in Bolivia, and Kubitschek's in Brazil (cf. Grupo de investigación latinoamericano 1977).

In the Latin American context, the critique of SIL has focused on the organization's connection with US imperialism. SIL is viewed here as constantly hunting for military and politically strategic information, or natural resources which could be exploited by multinational corporations. This critique has originated mainly among leftist and nationalist circles, but may also be found in official reports on SIL's work (cf. Matallana 1976). The »imperialist-subversion« critique of SIL has apparently also been used in connection with the Brazilian government's recent termination of SIL's contract.[2]

For understandable reasons, conspiratorial indictments of this kind – CIA connections for example – are difficult to prove. As stressed by Stoll, Robinson and Pereira, the CIA has undoubtedly been interested in collaboration with SIL, but as far as we know, institutional connections between CIA and SIL have never been substantiated. We should remember, however, that US imperialism is much more than the CIA.

There is an unquestionable affinity between SIL and US imperialism with respect to ideology. The basic anti-communism of the missionaries is incontrovertible. As Moore indicates, these beliefs can emerge in strange ways when transplanted onto Indians' belief systems. The identification of Satan with communism and God with America makes political and religious ideologies practically inseparable, as was conspicuously demonstrated during the Vietnam war when SIL intensified its work with various ethnic groups in Vietnam and Cambodia (Hart 1973).

The evident correspondence between the interests of SIL and US imperialism should not lead us to the conclusion that there is an elaborate functional integration between them. We agree with Pereira that SIL's work has probably yielded some valuable intelligence. While it is unknown how much of this data has gone into the CIA or US Army files, it is quite evident that SIL has aided national armies by providing information, maps and air routes over relatively uncharted territories.

There is better documentation of SIL's cooperation with multinational corporations. The best known example comes from Ecuador, where SIL cleared the way for several oil companies into a hitherto inaccessible zone populated by inhospitable and militant Aucas, who had formerly prevented Shell from entering their area (CEDETIM 1976; Hart 1973). SIL succeeded in concentrating the Aucas onto one overpopulated reservation, thus undermining any attempts at resistance. Later on, the organization praised God for having saved the Indians *and* helped the oil companies (Hart 1973). SIL has been used in other situations of potential conflict between foreign companies and indigenous groups (Varese 1974:90).

Although there exists a working relationship between SIL and multinational firms, the extent of this cooperation is impossible to determine because »the way in which (SIL) members are financed – individual support by some Church or benefactor – opens the door to infiltration by anyone with money« (Bonilla 1972:71). SIL views these dangers more benignly: »The Lord has richly blessed our members and branch this year« (SIL Doc. 5:1). It is quite likely that many of the checks which God sends the organization have a more earthly middleman. In the words of an English oil engineer in Ecuador:

> »We send them a check from time to time. They sometimes clear the way for us«. (Personal communication).

While this form of funding undoubtedly influences SIL's work, it would be mistaken to view SIL as purely a cover for foreign economic and political interests. The organization has its own holy mission of bringing God's Word to every man in his own tongue. Since this cannot be accomplished without offering some services to the respective national governments. SIL has joined the official administrative apparatus, especially through its bilingual program. Because of its resources and equipment, SIL has often become the main institution of control over indigenous groups (cf. Bodley 1975:71). In other situations – Brazil, for instance – SIL missionaries have worked in collaboration with existing national institutions »looking after« the Indians. SIL has helped countries with everything from bilingual education to pacification programs, training military pilots, providing air transportation and gathering intelligence (cf. Hart 1973). The organization has always preached to the Indians that God has installed the government, and that man shall render unto Caesar that which is Caesar's. SIL lives by these words and cultivates relations with national elites. Though the missionaries have extensive knowledge of the indigenous groups' miserable situation, SIL has never to our knowledge condemned nor even expressed public concern over the genocidal and ethnocidal policies carried out by many Latin American countries. God may be an American, but the national government is Caesar.

Presumably, there are several reasons to set SIL into functional integration with foreign imperialism rather than with national governments. The most obvious is the dominant role played by the US in the Latin American states. SIL's pretentious efforts at public relations have touched off attempts to find clandestine interests behind the organization. Moreover, disclosures of SIL's attempts to pose as a purely linguistic and cultural institution have furthered speculations that SIL had also cheated the national governments. This was hardly the case. Most governments have certainly been knowledgable of SIL's intentions. For SIL, the spreading of God's Word did not rule out doing valuable services for the national government hosts. In granting this permission, the states acquired efficient agents for administering and controling their indigenous groups. While Stoll and Arcand show that SIL did not always restrict itself to those activities stipulated by its contract with the authorities, it is fruitless to discuss whether SIL or the government got the better part of the bargain. It is unmistakably clear that the Indians were the real losers.

The WBT/SIL's veil over its own intentions has probably been an attempt to deceive the public as well as Catholic interests. When this results in accusations that SIL is a branch of the CIA and US imperialism, it only serves to gloss over those forces which are truly responsible for the Indians plight. Thus, the report from the Colombian commission of inquiry asserts:

> »The indigenous cultures of the primitive people living on Colombian territory constitute the most profound and authentic patrimony of the nationality... The work of the missionary-linguist systematically destroys these cultural values. It is not exaggerated to affirm that it constitutes a true »cultural suicide« for Colombia to accept the presence of the foreign missionaries among the indigenes« (Matallana 1976:70, our translation).

Here we have convergence of the national and Indian interests in opposition to the foreign powers represented by SIL. This unity of interests is further evidenced in the report's criticism of SIL:

> »During their work in the indigenous communities, the missionary-linguists of SIL have not preoccupied themselves with the incorporation of these communities in the Colombian Nation. On the contrary, in most of these communities a social distance to the Indians is observed, because the missionary-linguist has established himself as the only link between the Indians and fellow Colombians and the authorities« (Matallana 1976:67, our translation).

The trouble with this nationalist critque is that it totally ignores the complicity of the national government in the ethnocide (or genocide) of the indigenous groups. It matters little to the Indians whether national rather than internationally owned enterprises are occupying their territory to pump out the oil. Moreover, there are no grounds for believing that the Indians would be better of if it were the national army rather than the foreign missionaries who were administering their affairs.

The struggle against WBT/SIL must contain criticism of their function as cultural and economic imperialists, and of their participation in national development plans which seek to solve national economic problems through capitalist expansion rather than through structural change. It is undeniably true that national development plans can be steered to the benefit of foreign corporations and imperialist powers. Nevertheless, this fact does not absolve the national governments of built in their perpetuation of the Indians' plight, especially since it is they who contract with SIL in the first place.

Without making the double-edged critique, the Indians' periodic alliances with SIL – as the lesser evil – against their very own national institutions will appear as enigmatic examples of Indian foolishness, rather than the rational strategies that they really are.

* * *

Purely apart from their focus on the missionaries, the articles in this book have also given a depressing picture of the various injustices suffered by the Indians at the hands of traders, cattle ranchers, professional hunters, rubber collectors, gold prospectors, oil companies, the army and other state institutions. The underlying force behind these diverse forms of encroachment is capitalism's attempt to resolve its internal contradictions by appropriating the Indians' labor-power, land, and resources.

This pressure, along with the violence and sickness which accompanies the expansion, has greatly weakened the indigenous groups' ability to maintain control over their own fate. In several instances, the end result of this expansion has been the complete extermination of the group, or their dissolution and subsequent »integration« into capitalist society's most underprivileged layers. On other occasions there has developed a partial integration, where the Indians try to remedy some of their immediate problems by interacting with the national society while they retain essential features of their socio-cultural system.

The pressures brought to bear on Indian societies have made political and humanitarian assistance for the indigenous groups ugently necessary. This has been the opening of organizations like SIL. The missionaries have exploited the situation to advance their own goals rather than improve the position of the Indians.

Instead of calling attention be those policies which cause the resource crisis among the Indians, instead of trying to limit the penetration of exploitative trade and wage-labor relations, SIL's Americanized Protestant Evangelicalism has individualized the solution and reduced the question to a matter of God *vs* Satan. In trying to solve »the Indian problem« SIL has become »the Indians' problem«. By implanting into Indian society its individualism and materialism, SIL has deprived them of exactly those social resources and values which could prevent their being totally »integrated« and destroyed.

SIL's program tends to produce tribeless Bibles rather than Bibletribes. If SIL's work does not result in the most disastrous of outcomes it is due only to the indigenous groups' growing resistance, and to the appearance of new Indian movements and organizational forms which build upon the indigenous groups' own prerequisites. Though combatting SIL is not the only task facing these governments, it is nevertheless an essential part of larger anti-imperialist struggle. The campaign against SIL is not against an organization that innocently translates Bibles, provides education or distributes medicine, but against its holy alliance with American ideology, international capitalism and national »development plans».

Notes

[1] Insofar as culture is looked upon as a static and totally intergrated set of customs and beliefs *any* change or interference would constitute a form of destruction (ethnocide), and Merrifield would be correct. Such cultures do not exist, however. Customs, beliefs and their integration are constantly changing. Merrifield raises the following point in his critique of the so-called »anti-change anthropologists«:

> »*Many anthropologists today hold to the premise that the forces of evolution operate upon man as well as upon other animal species... When the environment changes, the resident species must adjust to the changes, seek a more compatible environment, or perish. Is there any reason to believe that culture would be exempt from this same principle?*« *(1976:7)*.

Aside from the fact that it gives a purposely vague image of what constitutes »forces of evolution«, Merrifield's statement is dangerously contradictory with respect to »ethnocide«: if cultures *can* indeed perish, then there *is* something called ethnocide. For Merrifield, however, it is only a *natural* result of the »forces of evolution«.

For us, culture is a way of living together, a means of solving problems. Because cooperation is necessary, social life must entail a degree of social control; this brings with it political boundaries and ethnic identity *vis a vis* other groups. Because of internal tensions generated by this social control, and/or pressures from the social or natural enviroment, any group will constantly be undergoing change. These changes will normally affect only specific customs or beliefs, but on certain occasions they will become fundamental, structural transformations. None of this is especially problematic, nor must structural transformation necessarily result in ethnocide. We speak of ethnocide only when such processes have made it impossible for a group to maintain its existence under its own preconditions. Whether individuals perish or whether they become forced to live at the dictates of another society, these are but two variant outcomes of the ethnocide process. Thus, ethnocide should be defined as the destruction of a group's ability to maintain self-determination.

[2] In connection with the Brazilian government's termination of its contract with SIL, the *Montreal Star* (Dec. 12, 1977) writes:

> »The government is putting an end to the work of 350 U.S. and other foreign missionaries in Brazil, suggesting they are a danger to national security because they operate in remote areas... On Nov. 22, the Rio de Janeiro newspaper O Globo published information, attributed to the Minister of the Interior Mauricio Rangel Reis, accusing the missionaries of doing secret geological surveys in the Amazon area«.

Bibliography

Bodley, J.
1975 *Victims of Progress,* Cummings Publishing Company, Menlo Park.

Bonilla, V.
1972 The Destruction of the Colombian Indian Groups, in Dostal (ed.).

Bradby, B.
1975 The Destruction of Natural Economy, Economy and Society, vol. 4, no. 2, pp. 127-161, London.

CEDETIM
1976 Equateur, CEDETIM, no. 38, Paris.

Corry, S. (ed.)
1976 *Towards Indian Self-determination in Colombia,* Survival International Document II, London.

D'Ans, A.
1972 L'alphabétisation et l'éducation des peuples de la selva péruvienne, dans la perspective de leur avenir socio-économique, in Robert Jaulin (ed.): *De l'ethnocide,* Union Generale D'Editions, Paris.

Dostal, W. (ed.)
1972 *The Situation of the Indian in South America,* World Council of Churches, Geneva.

Grupo de Investigación Latinoamericano
1977 Aproximación a una Institución Misionera. El Instituto Lingüístico de Verano y la Coyuntura Historica, Simposio Barbados II, pp. 181-220, CADAL, Mexico.

Hanbury-Tenison, R.
1973 *A Question of Survival for the Indians of Brazil,* Angus and Robertson, London.

Hart, L.
1973 Pacifying the Last Frontiers, *NACLA,* no. 10, pp. 15-31, New York.

Hefley, J. and Hefley, M.
1972 *Dawn over Amazonia,* Word Books, Waco, Texas.

Huxley, M.
1964 *Farewell to Eden,* Harper & Row, New York.

Kelm, H.
1972 Chácobo 1960. Eine Restgruppe der Südost-Pano im Oriente Boliviens, Tribus, vol. 21, Stuttgart.

Kietzman, D.
1977 Factors Favoring Ethnic Survival, Actes du XLIIe Congrès International des Américanistes, vol. II, 527-36, Paris.

Lewis, N.
1978 *Eastern Bolivia: The White Promised Land,* IWGIA Document no. 31, International Work Group for Indigenous Affairs, Copenhagen.

Loos, E., Davis, P.y Wise, M.
1976 El cambio cultural y el desarollo integral de la persona: Exposición de la filosofia y los metodos del Instituto Lingüístico de Verano en el Peru, CALAP, Pucallpa, Peru.

Matallana Bermúdez, J.
1976 *»El Instituto Lingüistico de Verano«.* Ministerio de Defensa Nacional, Comisión Especial de Reconocimiento y Verificación, Boletin de Antropologia, vol. IV, no 15, pp. 17-95, Universidad de Antioquia, Medellin.

Merrifield, W.
1976 Anthropology, Ethnocide, and Bible Translation, paper read at the Anthropological Symposium of the American Scientific Affiliation, Wheaton, Illinois.
1977 On the Ethics of Christian Mission, paper read at 76th Annual Meeting of The American Anthropological Association, Houston, Texas.
1978 Education for Minority Language Groups, paper read at the symposium »Amazonia: Extinction or Survival? The impact of national development on the native peoples of lowland tropical South America«, University of Wisconsin, Madison, Wisconsin.

Miller, E.
1970 The Christian Missionary, Agent of Secularization, Anthropological Quarterly, vol. 43.

Murphy, Y. and Murphy, R.
1974 *Women of the Forest,* Columbia University Press, New York.

Ortiz, F.
1976 The Present Situation and Future Prospects of Cuiva of Casanare, pp. 21-22, in Corry (ed.).

Pospisil, L.
1963 *The Kapauku Papuans of West New Guinea,* Holt, Rinehart and Winston, New York.

Riester, J.
1975 *Indians of Eastern Bolivia: Aspects of their Present Situation,* IWGIA Document no. 18, International Work Group for Indigenous Affairs, Copenhagen.

SIL Documents
no. 5 Treasurer's Report 1970, Colombian Branch, mimeo.

Siverts, H.
1965 *Oxhujk'. En mayastamme i Mexico,* Universitetsforlaget, Bergen.
1972 *Tribal Survival in the Alto Maranon: The Aguaruna Case,* IWGIA Document no. 10, International Work Group for Indigenous Affairs, Copenhagen.

Slocum, M. and Holmes, S. (eds.)
1963 *Who Brought the Word,* Wycliffe Bible Translators, Santa Ana, California.

Temple, D.
1977 personal communication.

Townsend, W.
1963 Tribes, Tongues and Translators, in Slocum and Holmes (eds.).

Turner, P.
1976 Evaluating Religious Systems, ms.

Varese, S.
1974 *Las Minorías Etnicas y la Comunidad Nacional,* Lima.

Yost, J.
1978 Community Development and Ethnic Survival: The Wao Case, a paper presented to Society for Applied Anthropology in the symposium »Community Development for Minority Language Groups«, Merida, Yucatán, Mexico.

INDEX

Dale, James and Katherine, 25, 26, 27
Dallas, Texas, 24, 35
Daniels, Josephus, 26
Davis, Harold, (»Arturo«), 152
Debs, Eugene, 44
Declaration of Barbados, 133
Department of Indian Affairs, Colombia, 65, 66, 67, 73, Mexico, 169
dependency, 134, 179–80, 181–82
Desano, 70
disease, contact, 12, 13, 53, 55, 60, 85, 92, 98–99, 103, 111, 112, 139, 140
Dominican missionaries, 133, 136, 139–141
Dornstauder, Joao, 91–92, 96, 103, 104
Dricot, Christiane and Jean, 148, 155, 160
drug trade, 63, 64, 66
Dumar Aljure, 66, 73
Duran Dussan, Hernando, 74, 75

Ecuador, SIL in, 42, 44–49, 51, 56–60, 183
Ecuadorian Institute for Agrarian Reform and Colonization (IERAC), 60
El Salvador, 26, 64
Ese Ejja, 109
ethnocide, 13, 133–35, 147, 177, 184
  SIL and 35, 85, 100, 114–15, 121–32, 133, 137, 139, 142, 164, 170, 174, 175

faith mission, 24, 30
  SIL as, 23, 27, 30, 38
Fields, Harriet, 114
Fischermann, Bernd, 114, 116
Flores Davila, Abel, 148, 152, 153, 154
Franciscan missionaries, 51, 121, 122, 126
fundamentalism, 24, 36

Garcia, Roberto, 74
Geisel, Ernesto, 35
genocide, 12–13, 77, 78, 84, 85, 111–14, 134, 184
Geophysical Services Intercontinental, 140
Gerbel, Florence, 166
gold, 111, 123, 135, 136, 139, 140, 141, 142, 179
Golder, Lorenzo, 112
Gonzales, Mario, 78
Graham, Billy, 29
Guahibo, 66–68, 77, 83
Guambiano, 67

Guanano, 69
Guatemala, SIL in 183
Guarani, 109
guerrillas, SIL and, 65, 68, 72, 111
  SIL's fear of, 63, 64, 83
Guevara, Che, 73, 111
Gulf Oil Corporation, 55
Gutierrez, José, 73

Hall, Clarence, 164, 165
hallucinogenes, SIL's opposition to, 82, 83, see *yage*
Halterman, Victor, 180
Hardenburg, W., 12
Hart, Laurie, 24, 68, 73, 85, 100
Hart, Raymond, 135
hide trade, 135, 139, 140, 159, 160, 179
highways, 13, 28, 34, 47, 55, 59–60, 69, 96, 97, 99, 102, 139
Huxley, Matthew, 179, 180
Hyde, Dick, 135

Ignaciano, 109
imperialism, SIL and, 15, 38, 41–49, 73, 85, 100, 109–17, 132, 134, 171, 183–84
Indian Protection Service (SPI), 91, 98, 103
indigenismo, 25, 26, 65, 164, 165–66, 169, 170
indigenous culture,
  traditional 51–52, 116, 133, 136, 137, 176–77,
  SIL's position toward, 12, 29, 30, 35, 36–38, 70, 79–80, 100, 114, 168, 173, 177, 181, see Satan
  SIL claim to respect and promote, 35, 36–38, 80, 117, 118, 132, 173, 174–75, 176
  SIL's impact upon, 58–60, 80, 82, 100, 114–17, 134–39, 165–66, 176, 178–79
indigenous economy,
  traditional, 51, 52, 53, 81, 86–89, 133, 136, 137, 177, 178,
  SIL's impact upon, 56–58, 80–81, 117, 134–37, 138–39, 179–80, 181, 182
indigenous elites,
  Jesuits promote, 94–98, 99, 116–17,
  SIL promotes, 33–34, 56, 58, 84, 159, 179, 182
indigenous identity,
  changes in, 85, 102
  SIL claim to promote, 38, 174–75, 179
  SIL's impact upon, 11, 58, 59, 114, 115, 116, 118, 136, 138, 139, 179,

indigenous ideology,
  SIL's influence upon, 11, 58–59, 82, 128, 130, 131, 137–39, 178–79, 180–81
indigenous movements,
  SIL's position towards, 32, 37, 42, 48, 64, 66, 68, 71, 75, 83, 168, 170–71, 181, 182
  SIL claim to support, 32, 75, 175
  see Consejo Regional Indigena; Muller, Sophia; Maya; self-determination; Ticuna
indigenous music,
  SIL's impact upon in Amuesha case, 122–23, 124–25, 126, 128–29, 131
indigenous religion,
  traditional, 52, 87, 122–25, 127, 128, 129–31, 133, 137, 169, 177
  SIL's impact upon 58, 59, 79, 80, 123–25, 127–31, 137–38, 163, 165–66
indigenous resistance,
  armed, 47, 53, 55, 64, 66–67, 83, 86, 87, 89, 91, 111–14
indigenous response to SIL 45, 58, 66, 68, 69–71, 72, 82, 83, 114, 125, 126, 128–30, 135, 136, 137–38, 149–50, 152, 153, 154, 160, 168, 169, 170, 179, 180–81
indigenous society,
  traditional, 51, 52, 86–89, 136, 137, 177, 178
  SIL's impact upon, 34, 58–59, 70, 71, 72, 75, 80–82, 84, 100, 115, 123–26, 137, 139, 154–60, 165, 166, 176, 178–82
individualism, SIL promotes, 37, 38, 80, 81, 116, 117, 136, 161, 173, 177, 178, 179, 180, 181, 182
Indonesia, 11
Instituto Geografico Militar (Bolivia), 111.
Interdenominational Foreign Mission Association, 29, 30
Internado, 69, 98–99
International Linguistic Center 35, 38
Iriarte, Martin, 53
Izozeno, 109

Jacobs, Ken, 170
Jaramillo, Rafael, 66–67, 68
Jaulin, Robert, 133
Javerianos de Yarumal, 68–71
Jesuit missionaries, 15, 51, 53–55, 60, 85, 87, 89–105,
Jonestown, 63, 74
Jungle Aviation and Radio Service (JAARS), 10, 28, 29, 46, 48, 58, 65, 66, 69, 78, 80, 83, 99, 114,